Sadat and After

STRUGGLES FOR EGYPT'S POLITICAL SOUL

Raymond William Baker

Harvard University Press
Cambridge, Massachusetts
1990

Library of Congress Cataloging-in-Publication Data

Baker, Raymond William, 1942–
   Sadat and after : struggles for Egypt's political soul / Raymond
   William Baker.
      p.   cm.
   Includes bibliographical references.
   ISBN 0-674-78497-9 (alk. paper)
   1. Egypt—Politics and government—1970– I. Title.
DT107.87.B35   1990   89-26692
962.05′4—dc20   CIP

To Kamal Ahmed Muhammad Attiya,
for the love of Egypt

Acknowledgments

The idea for this book originated ten years ago in conversations with Lillian Garbouchian, then my graduate student assistant at the American University in Cairo. A research project about Egypt's possible futures became a central part of my life and the lives of three other Egyptian graduate students, Omar Sa'ad Eddine, Mushira al-Ghazzaly, and Karen Aboul Kheir, who made up the core of the research group whose efforts have yielded this book and their master's theses. I shall always be grateful to these brilliant and caring young people who shared so much of themselves and their country with me.

As our project developed, we were assisted by the following research assistants from the American University in Cairo: Amira Aboulmagd, Manal Badawy, Nahed Dajani, Aly Erfan, Khaled Galal, Iman Hamdy, Maissa Hamed, Khaled Helmy, Iman Kaffas, Iman Kamal, Hesham Khalil, Sawsan Mardini, Nabil Mikhail, Nazli Shafik, Hania Sholkany, and Hady Sobeih; and, from Williams College, Randy Capps, Mark Cullen, Catherine Dissly, Tom Ewing, David Garfield, Jonathan Hay, Joel Hellman, Robert Nicholson, Michael Riley, and Jessica Walker.

Twice we asked Egyptian colleagues to identify the most promising younger Egyptian intellecutals whom we might most usefully draw into our conversations to test ideas. Magdy Hammad and Osama al-Ghazaly Harb, both associated with the Ahram Center for Political and Strategic Studies, were repeatedly recommended; both kindly responded to our need for critical and independent evaluations.

During the actual writing of the book I realized how much I had learned from Galal Amin, Nadia Ramsis Farah, Heba Handoussa, Aly

Eddine Hillal, Barbara and Sa'ad Ibrahim, Nels Johnson, Muhammad Sayyid Sa'id, and Sayyid Yassine. With draft chapters in hand, I turned for preliminary readings to Michael Brown, Wendy Brown, William Darrow, Carlos Egan, Robert Jackall, Michael MacDonald, Mark Taylor, Alan White, and Jim Wood. At various points along the way, Nancy Bellows, Nabila Boulos, Jim and Joan Burns, Nadia Hanna, Ann Lesch, George Marcus, Richard Pedersen, Henry Precht, Matilda Toma, Nesrine Serour, Sonia Victor, and especially Frank Oakley offered various kinds of help and encouragement. Research funding came from the National Science Foundation, the Ford Foundation, Williams College, and the Earhart Foundation. In the final stages, two exceptionally thoughtful readers and Elizabeth Suttell at Harvard University Press immensely improved the manuscript.

Finally, a special thanks to Elaine Baker, Dorothy Baker, Ramadan Abdul Aziz, Richard Bentley, Carlos Egan, Nick and Andrea Fritz, Enid Hill, Kamal and Margaret Aboul Kheir, Marcene Marcoux, Nelda Pedersen, Muhammad Rushdy, Grahame Smith, Nadine and Walter Schrage, and Tim and Jeanie Sullivan—family and friends who have all shared in large and small ways my experience of Egypt. Having received such abundant help along the way, I am only too happy to claim sole credit for any errors of fact and judgment that remain.

Contents

Preface

When I was teaching in Egypt in the late seventies and early eighties, I regularly heard university students and other young intellectuals call into question existing forms of discourse about Egyptian political life. The Sadat government relaxed authoritarian controls in the seventies; yet, these young people still did not know where and how they could live the best possible collective life, given existing political arrangements and their country's place in the world. The new generation decided that available explanations of economic and political failures that blamed the political elite or external enemies did not indicate what ordinary people could do to struggle for a better future. Official "campaigns" for development in the face of external enemies took place on a distant and unreal stage beyond any history students could make and beyond any politics they could experience. Government slogans about economic and military battlefronts said nothing concrete; in fact, these rhetorical battles of official public life blocked constructive social discourse and action. They diverted attention from the repressiveness of existing forms of political life and hindered prospects of changing politics according to values of human community worthy of struggle. Egypt's student youth asked if there was not something in the record of Egyptian public life that might give some sense—however fragmentary—of the kind of community they should try to build.

The students found official Egypt's answers to these questions unsatisfactory. The existing political regime in Egypt originated with a 1952 coup d'état by military conspirators led by Colonel Gamal Abdul Nasser and motivated by nationalism. After 1956, however, the regime carried out a revolution from above. Pan-Arab and socialist aims provided a forward thrust that lasted until the mid-sixties. After the defeat by Israel in the June 1967 war, the Nasserist revolution ground to a halt. Nasser died in 1970, and his successor, Anwar Sadat, promised a revitalization along liberal economic and political lines. By the end of the seventies, Sadat's effort had faltered.

To understand the forces that blocked their society, the new generation of Egyptian intellectuals found little help in modern social theory as applied to the politics of Third World states such as Egypt. For example, neither mainstream functionalist development theory nor the Marxist dependency approach told them much that indicated a way out; instead, political histories written from these theoretical positions reinforced a sense of the powerlessness of people trapped by domestic backwardness or by an exploitative international system.

It is certainly true that Western scholars for the most part write as though the record of the limitations and failures of official political life makes up the whole story of politics in Egypt. Undoubtedly, the power of the Egyptian state expanded after 1952 in ways that restricted the arena for independent political action; it did not, however, eliminate that public space. The official regime has attempted to destroy the power of any group seeking an independent political role or to incorporate such groups into the state system. Yet, my direct observation of politics in Egypt convinced me that alternative political groups did sustain themselves despite efforts to eliminate an independent public sphere. I decided to write an account that affirmed the existence of these domestic groups and explored the ways they used the margin of freedom still left to them; my starting point was the judgment that the political life of Egyptians is more than an endless and essentially meaningless rivalry of powerful individuals, families, and factions within official authoritarian structures, and more than a passive Egyptian response to the foreign pressures that seek to shape their future.

For many Egyptians, the postcolonial state has disappointed the political hopes aroused by the nationalist revolution. Critics charge that the bureaucratic caste formed during the Nasser years and inherited by Anwar Sadat and Husny Mubarak monopolizes state power in Egypt, and that official politics is about little more than the struggle to maintain this power; the liberation of the nation has not been followed by the political liberation of Egypt's people. This book describes the alternative political practices these critical groups have created. A wider view of the possibilities for political life animates the thought and action of the groups examined. Each group strives to remake society according to a new and better pattern. Their preferred alternatives differ, but they share the view that authoritarian rulers and their bureaucratic instruments direct official political society merely to serve their own narrower and lesser ends. The official campaign of democratization begun in the seventies modified this situation, but only slightly. Citizens became safer from arbitrary arrest and physical abuse by the security forces; Egyptians talked more freely about politics. Within dominant arrangements, however, they were still severely hampered from acting politically to limit the arbitrary authority of their rulers.

For each of the political groups considered in the following chapters, collective memory allowed them to survive periods of repression and to reemerge when conditions improved. Because of the importance of shared experience, the particular history of alternative groups frequently does not coincide precisely with the official political history of the regime. Thus, while this book aims primarily to illuminate Egyptian political developments in the turbulent seventies with an eye for the meaning of key events and persons for the present, the historical narratives reach both back and forward in time in a necessarily uneven way. The chapter on the Nasserists, for example, gives a great deal of attention to the meaning of the events of the fifties and sixties, precisely because the Nasserists felt called upon to defend the record of those critical years from the onslaught of official de-Nasserization. Similarly, because it emphasizes the strategic decision made by the Muslim Brothers in the seventies to work through government, the final chapter reminds readers of the vast expansion of legitimate political activity in which the Brothers are today engaged, even though a full treatment of these current developments is not properly a part of the history of the seventies. Thus, this book cannot deal neatly with the "Sadat period." Most of the significant events considered take place during these years, but the experiences and the goals that alternative groups find meaningful are not necessarily those associated with the official histories of the Sadat period. Members of any particular group emphasize different events and phases from those important to the regime or to other circles active in public life; their distinctive histories are part of a collective identity and common practice that express a shared purpose.

A sense of entrapment in unpromising official structures has driven the search for alternatives that unify this book; it also provides an important rationale for a new kind of study that looks at Egyptian politics from the margins rather than from the center. The situation in Egypt, with the government vision losing its hold, finds echoes in other Third World states. Groups throughout the Middle East are calling the developmental vision into question; Iranians are not alone in their efforts to create a new form of collective political life. The conventional paradigms of Third World studies, however, ultimately interpret these alternative visions in terms of the old, that is, as merely different ways (misguided, for the most part) of addressing what are taken to be the general problems of development common to the entire Third World. Yet, unless these visions are grasped first in their own terms, they certainly will be misunderstood.

The much-chronicled failure of official Egypt to create a national arena for meaningful political action is not the only political history Egyptians are creating. Egyptians do feel the pressures of external forces, they are plagued by terrible poverty, and they do not enjoy full freedoms; these unhappy facts, however, do not reduce their political history to victimization by backwardness or dependency. To find how Egyptians have sought political community, it was essential to look to alternative political practices and to do so in new ways. Instead of trying to understand politics in Egypt by looking at dominant state or international structures, using instrumental conceptions of power and politics, I surveyed the broader Egyptian political landscape where politics understood as the projection of possible futures actually goes on.

Out of this effort, I developed a generative notion of political power as the creation of human social worlds; this view draws analysis away from the center, with an all-consuming preoccupation with the state, and toward an angle of vision that brings into view the variety of groups projecting different political possibilities. Instead of a vertical model of politics centered on the state and those internal and external forces that affect or threaten it, I am proposing a horizontal model that directs attention to the lived experiences of politics generated by alternative groups in society.

Why is this shift important? Looking at politics in this way, we are able to understand Egypt today as a civil society in which, despite the apparent domination of a one-dimensional and heavy-handed regime and in the face of the terrible pressures of the world economy, communities are trying to forge different and better futures. To be sure, by the usual calculus of power, the relative importance of these marginal groups varies considerably. Osman Ahmed Osman, once so influential with Sadat, clearly has less influence today with the Mubarak regime, although the Arab Contractors organization remains active and continues to symbolize the new entrepreneurial class in Egypt. Both the Nasserists and the Marxists still have impressive numbers of supporters in Egypt. The Nasserists, especially continue to draw strength from prevailing public dissatisfaction with Egypt's close official ties to the United States. The Muslim Brothers arguably remain the most important of the various groups examined. Islam has long been and remains a powerful social and political force among Egyptians. The Ahram Center for Political and Strategic Studies consists of excellent scholars, but their influence in Egyptian politics has never been commensurate with the quality of their scholarship, and that situation has not changed. The *Economic Ahram* (*al-Ahram al-Iqtisadi*) and its writers generally fit the same description. The Bar Association has been and will continue to be a constant irritant to Egyptian leaders. The lawyers reflect generally liberal attitudes and courageously articulate the need for greater civil and political rights in Egypt. Yet their political influence on the regime is very limited. The Wissa Wassef School, from an instructional point of view, deserves high praise for the model it provides of large achievements possible in small places, but its influence on politics is nil.

Yet, despite their very different weights and roles in public life, the stories of these groups do make a common point. For many Egyptians, the threads that hold together a common life do not run through official institutions and practices; stultifying official politics are not the only politics that mattered in the decade of the seventies. In practices hidden behind the face of official Egypt, groups take advantage of the relative improvement in public freedoms since the early seventies to revive or generate alternative political possibilities. Attention to alternative political worlds enables a fuller delineation of this rich variety of Egyptian political groups—and not just the state and its radical opponents—with which we, as members of a society with particular and diverse political visions of our own, might be able to work in some sort of mutual accord.

In Egypt one meets Americans and other Westerners with a wide range of attitudes toward their hosts. Within this range, two broad types of social scientists predominate: those who want to teach something to their subjects—that is, how to "develop"—and those who have come in order to learn. The model of the first is the expert, in Cairo to advise Egyptians on everything from birth control to the cultivation of mangoes; the prototype of the second is the student who comes to Egypt to learn the language and something of the culture as well. I remain today in the category of student, where I started some twenty years ago. In

Egypt I have been a listener to stories about struggles for political alternatives. It is my hope that these stories, in the retelling, will still be recognizable to the Egyptians involved as well as enlightening to other people who respond, as I do, to the human values that drive these Egyptian struggles. The interactive character of analysis of this kind means that findings evolve from continuous process of mutual clarification. Knowledge derives as much from whatever clarity I have attained about my own situation as from a grasp of the situation of those men and women whose political practice I seek to understand.

Despite my interest in particular histories rather than general theories, my experience with Egyptians has been theoretical in the sense that I take seriously their theories about the meaning of their own political lives. The self-description of every political group includes abstract notions of who they are, the nature of their relationship to other groups and to the government, and the ways in which they hope to achieve a better future. In addition, I scrutinize as self-consciously as I am able to the ideas about politics that I use to make sense of Egyptian self-understandings. Theory, therefore, is an element of both their practice and mine.

Self-consciousness about interpretive processes is standard in contemporary anthropological and sociological work. Regrettably, it is unusual in Third World political studies. Western political scientists generally write as though our theories and ourselves are not a part of Third World social reality. Yet, every scholar who has worked in a country like Egypt knows that such is not the case. My own work in Egypt as a professor and scholar is inescapably tied to a larger Western presence that is motivated by quite practical political, strategic, and economic interests. I am sure that those interest press in subtle ways on my efforts to interpret Egyptian politics. I have tried to be as aware as possible of all of these pressures, including those that already appear in an Egyptianized form. The cultural influence of the West in Egypt, in particular, is not limited to life-styles and the arts. Western social science, including the major competing paradigms of Third World studies, is an active presence. Western theory is part of Egyptian reality because some Egyptian social scientists have adopted it while others, many of them trained in the West, are at least familiar with its formulations. I should add immediately that they also know its limitations and are aware that there is no black bag of ready-made "cures" for Egyptian political ills about which Egyptians are uninformed. For this reason, the image of Third World peoples as passive patients waiting for a scientific diagnosis of their dilemmas is as misleading as it is condescending. In this respect, it should be noted that, as most field workers soon discover in Egypt, intellectuals there generally know a great deal more about our society than we know about theirs. Those social scientists unable to suppress the diagnostic impulse might, therefore, at least have the good sense to reverse the usual assignment of roles.

As with my earlier work on Egypt, the main ideas for this book come from my direct experience of living and working in Egypt in the post-1967 period. I based my first book on field work conducted immediately after the war. Already by that time, a highly charged debate was under way in Egypt over the causes of the defeat. This Egyptian political discussion mirrored the larger theoretical competition between functionalist and Marxist approaches to political life in Third World states. Both paradigms took the position that the essential problem of politics was the failure of development efforts; my own book took off from this assumption. The overwhelming defeat in the 1967 war with Israel was a political event of singular importance for all segments of Egyptian opinion. The "setback" demanded explanation. A developmental view crystallized almost immediately. Egyptian developmentalists stressed the shortcomings of the political institutions created by the Nasser regime. The conflict with Israel was merely a subset of what the prominent political journalist Ahmed Bahaeddine has termed a general "civilization struggle" between a developed and an underdeveloped country. According to this interpretation, the flaws in the internal development effort left Egypt vulnerable to Israeli power. The contending dependency view argued that American imperialism wielding an Israeli sword defeated the Egyptian revolution and with it all prospects of independent development. Through the seventies the dependency perspective influenced the thinking of the brilliant young researchers working at the Ahram Center for Political and Strategic Studies who are discussed in Chapter 6. Such Egyptian dependency theorists judged that Israel struck in June 1967 because Nasser's Arab socialist revolution threatened to remove the most powerful Arab country from political and economic dependency on the world capitalist system, headed by the United States. Israel, according to this view, served as an instrument of the Western global economic and political system. My book *Egypt's Uncertain Revolution* argued the revisionist developmental thesis that Nasser failed to develop the country because his "revolution from above" was flawed in its party institutions and its socialist ideology. The influence of dependency thinking is apparent, however, in the further argument that these inadequacies made Egypt fatefully and unnecessarily vulnerable to hostile external pressures and forces. Those outside powers, I concluded, succeeded in ending the Egyptian development effort.

When I returned to Egypt in 1978 to work as a university professor a decade after my first field work, I made a reluctant discovery. Intellectual and political debate had moved outside the framework of both development and dependency theory. This change came about because growing numbers of Egyptians no longer judged underdevelopment to be the essential problem of Egyptian politics. A whole new set of concerns had surfaced. The 1967 defeat weakened the regime and led to an atmosphere of more open discussion and debate. In the years after 1967 it became clear that many Egyptians were unwilling to reduce their political life to the problem of overcoming underdevelopment. The enforced consensus around official definitions collapsed. Some groups judged Zionism to be the essential threat to Egyptians, not underdevelopment or dependency. Others asserted that overcoming internal repression and winning democratic rights had priority. For still others, neither backwardness nor exploitation nor repression nor even defeat was the real issue of collective life; a powerful Islamic current asserted that the remaking of Egypt in accord with the social ideal of Islam was the only acceptable goal of a life in common.

For all the difficulties of their present condition, groups of Egyptians are enacting stories that tell of their creative struggles to resist oppression and resolve dilemmas as they understand them. Specific communities of Egyptians are generating alternative political visions and forms of association. These groups and the public worlds they create make it possible to struggle together for what they consider to be a better life. Invariably, such enacted stories from the margins of Egyptian public life take a sharply critical turn. Egyptians who admire the achievements of Nasser's successors and Americans who are pleased with the enlarged U.S. presence in Egypt and the character of the Egyptian peace with Israel will be distressed by the view, common among the marginal groups, that U.S. policies toward Egypt, the Camp David agreements, the Egyptian-Israeli peace treaty, U.S. economic and military aid to Egypt, and Sadat's Open Door policy are all part of a larger U.S. exploitative scheme, which the late President of Egypt supinely accepted. Admirers of Anwar Sadat and enthusiasts for the ties that he created with the United States and Israel can reasonably content themselves with the thought that critics who do not bear the responsibilities of exercising power are often prone to idealistic, even utopian formulations on behalf of a nation they do not govern. And it would be a phenomenon common in many countries that when such abstract critics from the outside suddenly have responsibility for policy and policy implementation, they quickly learn that the realities of their new functions require compromise with their previous utopian or theoretical ideals.

Yet, however reasonable and comforting, such arguments cannot justify present ignorance of the actual range of political thinking and acting in Egypt. Egyptian society is more than a single leader and his governing bureaucracy, and there is more than one plausible way to judge Egypt's present global and regional alignments. Alternatives groups active in Egyptian public life have their own power and influence, and they do advance competing views of Egypt's future. In addition, those presently on the margins of the political arena may not remain there forever; even from the outside, they have a larger capacity to shape events than is often realized.

Political lives lived on the margins constitute important experiments that are part of the political resources available to Egyptians to shape their future. Group life releases creative energies that would be stifled by entrapment in official structures. The stories of these groups' beliefs and practices are the subjects of Chapters 1 through 8; they tell of the opportunities particular Egyptians have created for themselves to experience today something of the different political life they are building for tomorrow.

The greatest debt I owe for this book is to the many Egyptians who have shared their life stories with me, sometimes in casual conversations, at other times in formal interviews with this account in mind. What I am recreating here are Egyptian public worlds of common life. All of these political worlds have left their abundant and varied traces in the public realm. The political groups I consider are a presence in public life, and they have consciously made their beliefs and practices known to others. However, I believe that my capacity to interpret these markings has been enhanced by long years of work and residence in Egypt and by conversations with Egyptians who have been either actors in the events I retell or witnesses to them. Yet, I have purposely relied on the public records rather than the private conversations to make my most essential points, so that the non-Egyptian general reader may know the sources for my retelling of Egyptian political stories and the specialist may independently evaluate the ways I have construed the evidence. Above all, it is my hope that Egyptian readers will find useful the careful public documentation on which each of the substantive chapters of Part I is based; in my conversations with the Egyptian subjects of this book and now in my writing about them I have always sought, as T. Cottle once put it, "their words . . . and not material for the generation of something that ultimately transcends their words and hence their lives." I trust they will let me know where I have failed.

One other dimension of my research effort requires special comment. From the most preliminary conceptual stage to the final readings of the manuscripts, this project has engaged the talents and energies of Egyptian graduate students as research assistants; it has done so, however, in what I think is a rather novel way for a cross-cultural study. The work of each of the approximately fifteen students involved in the project over the years was carefully integrated with their own program of graduate studies in Egypt. Discussions of materials for the book initially took the form of a graduate training seminar; later, and especially with Karen Aboul Kheir and Omar Mahmud, that teaching function was supplanted by a process of creative collaboration with young colleagues who, naturally enough, had very strong opinions and feelings about possible futures for their country.

Certain important aspects of the method used in this study evolved out of this unusual arrangement. In my approach to politics I strived to examine not a series of abstracted problems but a series of statements and actions by individuals who are members of identifiable groups. In developing my understanding of these groups, I remained committed to the study of the actual language of these men and women as they tried to give meaning to their experience. In attempting to get hold of conceptions of real persons in their complex and purposeful human relationships, rather than arbitrarily constructed categories such as "elites" and "masses," I kept my eyes focused on specific actions that illuminated the sources and effects of those meanings. My aim was to take seriously the language and perspectives of the Egyptians I sought to know.

The task of allowing others to do their own talking, taking them seriously on their own terms, proved more daunting than I imagined. Ways of speaking and ways of living are so intimately tied that I soon discovered that I needed Egyptian intermediaries who could enter more fully than an obvious stranger into those ways of living. Research assistants drawn to the Egyptians in question for reasons of their own— sometimes because they shared the values and ends around which group members ordered their lives, sometimes because the particular group was the subject of their own graduate research—provided indispensable mediation between Egyptian political actors and an American researcher trying to hear their distinctive voices. My approach required sensitivity to particular language usages and a feel for the significant event that illuminated just what words in fact meant; whatever skill I developed in interpreting language and action along these lines I owe to the indispensable help of my young assistants. Without them, I doubt that I would have discerned how members of different groups used public discourse to signal just who they were as a collective or how certain incidents, given little weight in conventional histories, contained the main elements necessary to tell the group's story. Poring over the texts together, we gradually realized just to whom the essential "we" referred—Arabs, artists, intellectuals, Muslims; together, we figured out why certain incidents, once understood, finally brought the character and purpose of a particular form of group life into view.

Working with the research team, I also discovered important limitations built into my approach and developed ways to deal with them. What were we to make of the things we thought we learned about the groups that remained unknown to them? or of those things that group members obviously knew but distorted for their own self-interest? If group members were going to do their own talking, then obviously "their" chapter could not contain things they did not know or preferred not to recognize.

These dilemmas we decided to remedy in a fairly straightforward way. The depiction of the political worlds of alternative groups would be taken only so far as the language of the group allowed. This guideline applies to supporting text as well as to direct quotations; thus readers should not mistake explanatory paragraphs in a given chapter as indicating either the author's own views on issues or a favorable judgment on the positions that a given group takes. I have always believed it is possible to understand views with which one disagrees; writing this book convinced me of that possibility. Important findings that could not be presented when honoring the rule of respecting the limits of group awareness as reflected in group language and behavior were reserved for other chapters in which other groups, observing the activities of fellow Egyptians, felt called upon to bring these issues into the public realm. The entrepreneur Osman Ahmed Osman, for example, indirectly acknowledges the charges of corruption that have dogged his career. Among other things, he discusses the possibility that among the new millionaires of the Open Door era some might well be corrupt—a small price to pay, in his view, for the benefits of unleashing private enterprise.

Readers interested in a fuller view of Osman's alleged corruption will find it in the treatments of that issue by the left, the Nasserists, and the independent intellectuals in the *Economic Ahram,* all of whom have documented and questioned Osman's controversial activities. While readers are encouraged to enter into the succession of political worlds that are the separate subjects of each chapter, they are also invited to listen as the members of these worlds comment on each other.

While the approach taken in this work means that the marginal groups' views are set forth at great length and with abundant source citation, no corresponding effort can be made to document the origins and the rationale of official policies. The views from the margins reported here inevitably magnify government mistakes and shortcomings. Just as official histories of the Sadat years (and conventional Western scholarship that shares the same focus on the regime) tend to ignore the contributions of marginalized political actors, alternative perspectives frequently downgrade the achievements of the Sadat period.

Fortunately, this distortion can be corrected in part by close attention to the diversity of alternative views. Defenders of the Sadat record rightly insist that his regime represented a significant step forward in opening Egyptian society and sharply reduced the repressiveness of the Nasser era. Readers will discover this official argument echoed by some alternative groups, and not only those closest to the regime, such as the circle around the entrepreneur Osman Ahmed Osman. The Muslim Brothers, for example, flourished in the climate of greater freedom created by the Sadat government. Intellectuals attached to the Brothers do acknowledge the expansion of freedoms in the seventies as they denounce the Nasserist experiment in terms even harsher than those employed by Sadat's followers. Naturally, the new Nasserists of the seventies and eighties put their emphases in different places. In viewing the record of the sixties they are inclined to highlight industrialization and improvements in mass welfare and to suggest that some authoritarian excesses, however regrettable, might not be too high a price to pay for such advances. In response to those like the Brothers who laud Sadat's liberalization, the neo-Nasserists are inclined to see instead the limitations of Sadat's democratization and the foregone opportunities in other more critical areas. Voices from the margins are not monolithic. In the debates mounted by opposition figures the careful listener will even hear an occasional accent on some achievements of those who have wielded official power.

I have expressed my appreciation for the help I have received in the first instance by making sure that all materials collected for the book and any other resources of the project were made available, whenever possible, to all these students for their own work; at last count, five advanced degrees were written based primarily on these resources. Openness and frankness about our purpose have characterized the research process from the outset; my Egyptian research assistants always made it clear to those they interviewed that they were working with an American professor, and we all indicated that the research results would be published. Along the way, all of our important findings have been made available to researchers in Egypt who have had access to the student theses and the several published articles that have resulted from them before publication of this study. The Ford Foundation directly backed this small effort to train and support young Egyptian social scientists, while both the Natural Science Foundation and the Earhart Foundation did so indirectly. In this way, as was my hope, the findings of the larger study reported here for a Western readership have already found their way into Egyptian intellectual life.

Arabic names are rendered according to a consistent and simplified transliteration system that adheres whenever possible to conventional usages, omitting diacritical marks. I have translated the names of journals and newspapers important to the story of particular Egyptian political groups in order to convey more directly both their literal meaning and their meaning to the group. Thus, I have rendered *al-Ahram al-Iqtisadi* as the *Economic Ahram, al-Tali'ah* as *The Vanguard, al-Sha'ab* as *The People, al-Da'wa* as *The Call,* and *al-Ahaly* as *The Masses.* For those who wish to consult the primary sources, both a translation and a transliteration are presented at the title's first occurrence in each chapter.

For in every action what is primarily intended by the doer, whether he acts from natural necessity or out of free will, is the disclosure of his own image. Hence it comes about that every doer, in so far as he does, takes delight in doing; since everything that is desires its own being, and since in action the being of the doer is somehow intensified, delight necessarily follows . . . Thus, nothing acts unless [by acting] it makes patent its latent self.

— Dante

Introduction:
Other Subjects of Politics

We can speak of sense or coherence, and of their different embodiments, in connection with such phenomena as gestalts, or patterns in rock formations, or snow crystals . . . What is lacking here is the notion of a subject for whom these meanings are. Without such a subject, the choice of criteria of sameness and difference, the choice among the different forms of coherence which can be identified in a given pattern, among the different conceptual fields in which it can be seen, is arbitrary.

—*Charles Taylor*

Anwar Sadat was the one Arab leader whom Americans thought they knew and understood. In American eyes, Sadat was the man who repudiated socialism and expelled the Soviets from Egypt; he made peace with Israel, liberalized the Egyptian polity, and returned Egypt to the Western fold. During Sadat's years in power the United States involved itself deeply in Egyptian politics, underwriting everything from the 1979 peace with Israel to the official population control effort. The United States provided Egypt with over $17 billion, making it the second-largest recipient of U.S. aid in the world. Over the years the United States supplied every conceivable technical device, at a cost estimated at $20 to $25 million, to protect the life of the man on whom U.S. Middle East strategies depended.[1] The president of Egypt was *Time* magazine's man of the year, his wife the "first lady" of the Arab world.

Then, in October 1981 Egyptian religious extremists assassinated Sadat. On the outskirts of Cairo, in a suburb called Victory City, Sadat had arranged to review the annual military parade celebrating Egypt's performance in the 1973 October War. At 11:00 A.M. Sadat, attired in a blue-and-white military uniform and high brown leather boots, took his central seat on the bronze platform decorated with the image of Osiris and other gods of ancient Egypt. Two hours later one of the army trucks towing Russian field guns halted abruptly near the reviewing stand. A

1

young officer leaped from the cab and raced toward the stand while his accomplices in the back of the truck threw grenades and provided gun cover. At point-blank range, Lieutenant Khaled al-Islambouli pumped automatic fire into the body of the president.

Americans responded with outrage and sorrow and anticipated an outpouring of mass grief in Egypt. Instead, Egyptians responded with disconcerting quiet to Sadat's assassination. When Sadat's predecessor, Gamal Abdul Nasser, had died a decade earlier, crowds had poured into the streets to grieve at the death of a leader routinely denounced in the United States as either a fascist or a communist. In the days following Sadat's assassination Egyptians went about celebrating a religious holiday as though nothing had happened. Foreign journalists reported that, if anything, the streets were unusually deserted. Interviews by American correspondents revealed that "many people in Cairo expressed less outrage over the assassination than over the week's cancellation of movies, soccer games and regular television programming (including the popular series 'Dallas')." On the day of Sadat's funeral, lines of policemen "stood with arms locked as if to hold back a crowd. But there was no crowd."[2] Later, more than a hint of approbation colored the Egyptian response to the trial of his assassins. The indifference of Egypt's people to Sadat's death made it clear that the United States was once again deeply involved in a key Third World country it did not understand.

In Egypt, Americans mistook their own purposes for Egyptian politics; they "understood" Sadat only to the degree that he reshaped Egypt in the American image. In Sadat, Americans had simply seen their own reflection and heard their own voice. Self-absorbed, they ignored the full range of sights and sounds of Egyptian politics.

Americans will have no trouble discovering a multitude of U.S. national interests in Egypt. On the basis of their own political experience, they will also have observations about the ways Egyptians might attain values and ends such as development or democracy that Americans have come to prize. Knowledge of Egyptian beliefs and practices may well tell us about our national prospects in Egypt, just as it may clarify the relevance of our aims and values to the Egyptian experience. However, these outcomes will result only accidentally from a study with the simpler purpose of knowing more about the kinds of political lives other people live—about how and why they struggle for particular ends and values.[3] A study driven by such a broad humanistic aim seeks primarily to understand the sources of the creativity that allows human beings to realize new and better forms of collective life. Knowledge of this kind will be of interest to Egyptians, Americans, and others who delight in human creativity and hope that human life experiences can be shared in ways that enhance the prospects of all.

Politics deals with the particular struggles people wage to secure ends they set for themselves and not the resolution of some transhistorical set of "crises" that block their participation in a universal process of development or modernization. Therefore, the beginning point for understanding the politics of others should always be set as close as possible to the actual categories of their experience rather than to concepts abstracted from someone else's history. Egyptians and other Third World peoples are, after all, subjects of politics who act in ways that are as complex, varied, and inventive as our own. Egyptians, like the rest of us, have a distinctive political dimension to their lives that they express in the practices of the groups to which they belong. By focusing on these practices, this book assesses politics in ways that will be recognizable to Egyptians and that they will find meaningful.[4] The findings of this research, it is hoped, are expressed in ways that can enter into the debates of Egyptians about the meaning and importance of their rich political experiences.[5]

Human collectivities everywhere create particular relations of power and meaning within which their members can live in the face of common human miseries and, ultimately, death. The fact that human beings share this experience of politics makes an understanding of these relations of power and meaning potentially available to others. An opening to other political experiences, whether it stimulates approval or disapproval, always enlarges our sense of human possibilities. Understanding of this kind has the immediate and practical importance of enabling us to see others as more fully human, living in social and historical situations as complex as our own. We become aware that, faced with what appear to be economic or social necessities, Egyptians too have choices to make. By opening up analysis to the often-unseen range of political possibilities Egyptians create for themselves, we can hope for a better sense of what those choices might be. A grasp of their situation as they perceive it also provides a sounder base from which to speak and act with Egyptians in common projects of all kinds, not just those that advance the interests of one's own state. Such an internal view of other political experiences does run the risk of apology. Yet, resolution of this dilemma is relatively simple if we separate understanding from approval: understanding has to do with the reach from one's own context to the context of others;

approval, on the other hand, can be only in terms of one's own values. It is possible to withhold approval from beliefs and practices that one has come to understand.[6]

The political groups presented in the following chapters seek a future for Egypt different from that envisioned by the regime and by each other. Egypt has always been dominated by the few at the center of power. Whether the rulers are Mamluks, Ottomans, British proconsuls, or Egyptian military autocrats, these personages dictated the direction of Egyptian life. Yet there have been other actors whose influences had to be reckoned with, and this book aims to identify and describe these groups in Egypt of the seventies and eighties. They range in their political stances from the Communists on the left to the Muslim Brothers on the right, and they also include politically quiescent aestheticists, as reflected in the art of the Wissa Wassef School. This book, it is hoped, will make it harder for observers of Egypt to ignore these alternative ways of acting politically.

Each of the eight chapters in Part I delineates the political practice of an alternative group in terms that approximate its own self-understanding. These chapters recreate the political worlds of Egyptians whose collective lives are based in the Osman companies, the Bar Association, various Nasserist groupings, the Marxist circle of *The Vanguard* (*al-Tali'ah*), the Wissa Wassef School at Harrania village, the Ahram Center for Political and Strategic Studies, the *Economic Ahram* (*al-Ahram al-Iqtisadi*), and the circle of Muslim Brothers around the journal *The Call* (*al-Da'wa*).

Why these particular groups? Each of the groups reconstructed sees itself as the carrier of an alternative normative vision; moreover, members of these circles have acted with some measure of success to inform their actions by the norms they have collectively generated. In doing so, they see themselves and are recognized by others as having enlarged the political resources available to all Egyptians. For these Egyptians, the most persuasive visions of a better life and the most promising practices to realize them are articulated as criticisms of the dominant order rather than by routine participation in its structures. Each political group generates a definition of reality adequate to its own experience of the realities of Egypt. Each struggles to create a group practice that empowers members to shape a better future for themselves and, in some cases, for Egyptian society as a whole.[7]

Egyptians can take pride in the resourcefulness and creativity of their fellow citizens who have acted in ways that generated rich political potentialities for a variety of Egyptian futures. American readers, in turn, have an additional need to encounter alternative political groups in Egypt. The participants in Egyptian political and social life who are the subjects of this book are inadequately understood in many sectors of the U.S. government and by the American public at large. For one thing, the view prevails in many official and unofficial circles that Egypt, as the recipient of massive U.S. economic and military aid, is irrevocably bound to and has become a virtual client of the United States. Current Egyptian dependency on the United States is indeed great, but the complacency with which many American officials look at Egypt and tend to take it for granted is unwise. There is a need for public and serious elaboration of those groups in Egyptian society, for now on the margins, who are active in public life, including those who deplore and sharply criticize the nature of the existing U.S.-Egyptian tie.

The Osman circle of Chapter 1 coheres around the powerful figure of Osman Ahmed Osman, Egypt's leading contractor. It coalesced within the Nasserist socialist order as the antisocialist product of the effort by the regime in the fifties and sixties to create "socialism without socialists." In the seventies Osman, along with a host of other covert entrepreneurs, was freed from lip service to socialism. He became a close political ally as Sadat moved the regime to the right after Nasser's death. Osman represented the "new" class elements that thrived in the seventies. The regime adopted the Osman circle's vision of itself as a prototype for socioeconomic transformation based on individual effort, family values, and free enterprise.

Egyptian liberals, with their stronghold in the Egyptian Bar Association, are the subjects of Chapter 2. They speak for the professional strata and traditional middle-class circles who understand themselves to be the authentic heirs of historical liberalism. Claiming a right to speak for the nation and calling for the democratization of public life, they succeeded in making the association a public platform for national debate despite the regime's efforts to curb freedom of expression and assembly.

The various Nasserist groups of Chapter 3 are less visible than the liberals but far more powerful as a political current able to move large numbers of people. Though denied overt political expression, Nasserism is irreversibly embedded in the revolution from above that followed the 1952 coup and continues to represent a potential challenge to the government from the left. It is a submerged Arab nationalist current with particular appeal to the industrial workers and lower middle class, who were the primary beneficiaries of the Nasserist revolution.

The Marxist circle in Chapter 4 formed around the journal *The Vanguard.* The Marxists compensate for the weakness of their popular base by a penetrating social critique that identified them with issues of mass discontent, such as the food riots in 1977. Through class analysis, the Marxist left explains how the limitations of the Nasser regime created social forces and a relatively autonomous state formation that prepared the way for the reversals under Sadat. This group of Marxist intellectuals constitutes an important presence in the officially tolerated left party, the National Progressive Unionist Party. They aim to retrieve the idea of socialism from its dilution by the Nasserist left, while joining with the Nasserists to prevent the Sadat reaction from completely eroding the limited gains of the 1952 revolution.

Very small but important groupings of intellectuals are the subjects of the next three chapters. Chapter 5 explores the Wissa Wassef School at Harrania village in Giza. The school, founded by two artists, is a social experiment designed to prove that the deadening hand of the national educational system, rather than a lack of inherent talent, explained the absence of creativity in the lives of Egypt's children. The artists at Wissa Wassef are a clear and forceful Egyptian expression of the human impulse to remake the world or some small part of it through the free play of the aesthetic sensibility.

Chapters 6 and 7 treat two clusters of intellectuals, associated with the Ahram Center for Strategic and International Studies and the *Economic Ahram,* respectively. The Center is a foreign policy research institution that originally focused on the question of Israel. The *Economic Ahram* provides sophisticated economic and social analyses; in the seventies it constituted itself as a forum for a critical assessment of the regime's controversial economic orientation. Both sets of intellectuals work against the daunting restrictions that an authoritarian society places on independent thought. In the interstices of official structures, they create a critical space that allows the application of analytical reasoning to the major issues of public policy. The experience of groups of this kind establishes important facts about the power of human creativity and intelligence on which all Egyptians can draw; the stories of these intellectuals make the point that underdeveloped societies have their share of creative and imaginative people.

The Muslim Brothers are the subjects of the final historical narrative, in Chapter 8. From 1976 to 1981 they gathered around their journal, *The Call,* in an effort to revitalize their movement. The Muslim Brotherhood movement is probably the most successful mass movement in Egypt's modern history. In the forties they numbered over a million. They survived two decades of repression to renew their efforts to create innovative cultural, social, and political patterns that reflected distinctive Islamic definitions of Egypt's needs. The urban lower middle class, in particular, responds to their call to Islam. The Brothers aim to remake Egypt into a society that more closely approximates what they understand to be the social ideal of Islam.

Each group of Egyptians discussed in this book speaks and acts for a common good not yet realized. The term *group practice* refers to this transformative social activity.[8] Through its group practice each collectivity advances a broad claim about how societies are changed and how the transformation can be advanced. A practical group project specifies the way people can achieve the desired change in Egypt's special circumstances.

The groups that are the subjects of this book are not the only ones in Egyptian political life that conform to the definition of a transformative group. At times the interests of group members themselves required the exclusion of their efforts from this account. An example is the circle of influential women that took shape around Suzanne Mubarak; these women achieve concrete improvements in public education by working in some of the country's most disadvantaged school districts. On several occasions after her husband became Egypt's president, Mrs. Mubarak expressed a strong desire to avoid excessive attention to her own role in the project; unfortunately, it is impossible to tell the group's story without that dimension. In other cases, but for quite different reasons, group efforts would have suffered from public attention. Yet, while the alternatives covered here do not exhaust the category of political groups, they do indicate the kinds of strategies that Egyptians have created to transform themselves and their society. The Osman group looks to the self-interest of individuals; the Nasserists tap what they take to be the special genius of Egyptians as an Arab people; and the Marxists from *The Vanguard* look to the historical role of economically defined classes. The Islamic circle in *The Call* seeks to reaffirm and revitalize the lives of believers of the way prepared for humankind by God. The remaining groups base their hopes for change on some inherent quality of human nature that they judge to be of overriding importance. For the Wissa Wassef community, that quality is the aesthetic sense; for the liberals in the Bar Association, it is the assumed natural desire for freedom; and for the intellectuals at the al-Ahram Center for Political and Strategic Studies and the *Economic Ahram,* is is the critical power of human intelligence.

Questions about human political creativity came from my own experience; specific answers came from Egyptians. By my definition a political experiment that enlarges human possibilities is one that, in a particular setting, serves to reduce such commonly recognized human ills as sickness, loneliness, ignorance, hopelessness, poverty, oppression, and violence.[9] I claim nothing more for this formulation than its designation as a practical humanist point of departure that directs attention to promising political potentialities that presently exist in Egypt.

The Egyptians who are the subjects of this book have acted to form associations, each of which has quite specific notions of change. An interest in change need not be restricted to liberal and radical groups. Conservatives seek to carry the best of the present into the future. Reactionaries seek to regain for tomorrow that lost and better past.[10] In a given society, groups of individuals moved by the transformative impulse may be located at any point within or outside dominant government structures. Wherever they are found, political groups define themselves by cohering around a collective political project that offers to their members and at times to society at large an alternative vision of the collective good.[11] The Egyptian groups covered in the following chapters occupy spaces that range from those internal to the regime, such as the Osman group, who see their projects as a better version of official arrangements, to others such as the Marxists, whose ideas and practices are a barely tolerated opposition. Moreover, some of the Egyptian groups, such as the Osman circle, the Wissa Wassef School, and the Ahram complex, are primarily concerned with the parochial activities of the group and the contribution they might make to the larger society. In contrast, the Nasserists, the Marxists, the liberals, and the Muslim Brothers all harbor larger aspirations to transform society according to their own interests. Despite such differences, all political groups are not to be confused with either narrow interest groups such as unions or power cliques that strive for particular advantage. In other words, political groups do have a general dimension in their thought and practice that transcends narrow group needs even though the conscious commitment to society as a whole takes different forms.

Political groups also have a real social existence. They are neither utopian fantasies nor figments of the ideological imagination. Each of the groups has proven itself as an alternative form of social life than can be lived in Egypt.[12] In addition, political groups are not opposition groups in the usual sense of the term. Relations between the government and political groups can extend from overt opposition to indifference to and even to support of the regime. Analysis of these collectivities aims for knowledge of *experienced* political realities as they are defined within the political group. The narrative chapters are organized around the common theme of political inventiveness in the face of obstacles; they report what possibilities for a better future particular groups of Egyptians are generating. In constructing these narratives I rely primarily on my ability to catch the meaning of the stories specific Egyptians tell each other about their common efforts to forge alternative political possibilities. My objective is to understand particular experiences in their own right and for what they teach on the plane of the human condition about the immense variety of meaningful political lives that people can create.

Because I believe that the meanings of political struggles are embedded in particular-historical narratives, this book explicitly abandons the effort to specify general causes or appropriate goals of political behavior; it seeks instead to interpret the specific meanings of actual political practices. This approach reflects my belief that political realities have no ultimate causes nor deep-structured keys that unlock their secrets. I am convinced that shortcuts to put them in some transhistorical framework that makes it unnecessary to know particular languages and experiences of politics invite a variety of misleading reductionisms. Mainstream scholars generalize by evaluating the record of a particular government in meeting what are taken to be the universal crises of modernization; leftist critics of the mainstream do so by placing the state in question in the world capitalist system. Theoretical reconstructions of both kind suppress the variety of political lives. Invariably, systemic theories emphasize the forces that allegedly determine political outcomes, practically eliminating from view the human agents of politics who might be creating something new and potentially important to us all.

The historical narratives that follow aim neither to explain the causes of group behavior nor to insinuate any prescriptions about the way the Egyptians involved should behave according to some external standard. Rather, the chapters delineate what individuals actually say and do and what those political actions mean in their own terms. In other words, they seek to explain how the speech and actions of particular groups of Egyptians are meaningful in the context of the group's common experience. To the greatest extent possible, therefore, each narrative uses the language and the symbols of the group itself. This approach creates certain difficulties for anyone reconstructing the narrative and wishing to remain faithful to the internal perspective. One of the most difficult issues is the tension between the kind of impressions that readers may formulate because they regard them as implicit in the group's language and practice and the impressions that group members have of themselves. For example, group members might act in ways that have consequences of which they are unaware or that they chose to ignore. In such cases, these conclusions will be made explicit only to the degree that the language and action of the group members themselves are adequate to that task. Although these conclusions may not appear to be fully adequate statements about the group's situation, they are in fact the only kinds of conclusions that can be made without imposing the external values and standards of the author or readers. Conclusions expressed in this way may not satisfy people who seek final judgments, but they will, it is hoped, enhance the reader's understanding of the political group context within which Egyptians are acting.

Each substantive chapter opens with the projection of an event, chosen from the stream of group action. In fact, these particular events are twice selected; group members themselves in their public interactions have already identified the moment in question as somehow central by giving it an important place in the stories they tell about their collective experience. My own recognition of the critical character of these events depends on evidence that group members find the event controversial and worth arguing over in order to clarify their sense of who they are and what they should do. The figures and images that populate the event define the agents and actions most essential to group practice; they serve to remind members of the identity they seek to maintain and the goals they hope to realize in the face of conflicting realities that threaten to absorb or submerge them. The body of each chapter is meant to provide just enough of the group's particular language and history to enable individuals who are not members of the groups to understand the group narratives within which these core events are embedded.

The opening images and scenarios occupy a meaningful place in the political world of the men and women who created them and would be recognizable to them. For this reason, the projections may have an unsettling effect on readers because they assume knowledge of persons and events as well as the group's particular interpretation of their significance. These events carry summations of other people's histories; they have an existence for group members that is independent of my particular statement of them here. The events and my retelling of the narratives that make them understandable report discoveries I have made when Egyptians have shared their experiences of politics with me. I do realize, therefore, that the narratives as I report them have undoubtedly been shaped by my limitations as a listener, and even by the explanatory purposes to which I put them. Still, for group members, the events and the histories out of which they come are a source of appropriate language, symbols, and behavior for themselves and others who would act with them. Group members use these stories to help each other understand their place in the group and the group's place in the larger society.

The sequences chosen to open the chapters are judged central to each group because of the intense reaction of group members that they evoke, the frequency with which group members employ them, and the variety of contexts for which individuals in the group find vocabulary, symbols, and behavior drawn from them appropriate sources of self-description. It follows from this existential standard of selection that the moments chosen and their narrative elaboration are not necessarily important by the standards of conventional history, such as the measurable impact of the event on the national political situation or the judgment that the event contributes in some instrumental way to the group's own prospects. The stories have the meanings members give them. The purpose of the eight narrative chapters is to bring out those meanings.

Part II attempts to articulate the conception of politics underlying the group practice approach, explaining how it provides a different, and for some purposes better, point of entry into the politics of the Third World. These theoretical chapters, drawing on the specific historical narratives that have preceded them, return to a systematic consideration of the issues raised in this introduction of what constitutes politics and how it should be studied. Chapter 9 shows how the political group practice approach aims to make politics intelligible in terms of the logic of the struggles that political actors understand themselves to be waging; it contrasts the aim of interpretative theory to understand the acts of men and women who generate new political choices, with the focus of conventional approaches on structural constraints, material limitations, and social inertia that dampen prospects of transforming the world. The final chapter explains the importance to Third World studies of emphasizing group political creativity through the medium of the material and social structures given in particular circumstances; the focus is on understanding actual political struggles that empower people rather than structural obstacles that discourage human efforts to imagine and create a better world.

Part I

PRESENT NARRATIVES, POSSIBLE FUTURES

1

How to Build a Better Future: Osman Ahmed Osman and the Arab Contractors

What is usually termed "propaganda," especially of a nationalist sort, consists not only of opinions on a variety of topics and issues. It is the promulgation, as Paul Kecskemeti once noted, of official definitions of reality.

—*C. Wright Mills*

"I see politics as work and production," explained Osman Ahmed Osman, the construction magnate whom many identified in the seventies as the second most powerful man in Egypt. According to Osman, "anyone who wants to be a politician must produce, feel the pains and hopes of the citizen, and work to find solutions to his problems of food, housing, and suitable job opportunities."[1] During the seventies Osman argued this authoritative definition of political purpose in scores of interviews in the national media; his construction company, the Arab Contractors, built construction projects that exemplified this conception of politics as a means to create the conditions under which private initiative could meet the needs of the people. Two projects in particular, the October Sixth Bridge and the reclaimed desert farm at Salhia, symbolized the forward movement promised by Osman's approach.

President Anwar Sadat invariably attended the openings of these Osman projects, making the ceremonies a platform from which to celebrate Osman's achievements and to endorse his conception of public purpose. "The Arab Contractors is realizing an absolute miracle for anyone who wants to come and see ... These are not just dreams," announced Sadat. "We saw them today in reality." Front-page pictures in the mass dailies showed President Sadat standing on a new bridge spanning the Nile in central Cairo and driving an American tractor in the newly greened acres of the eastern desert at Salhia. The president welcomed completion of the urban bridge in 1978 and the desert farm in

15

1980 as tangible fulfillments of his promise of a better future for Egypt. Sadat linked these "miracles at home" to the post-Nasserist renewal of national spirit first evident in Egypt's improved performance in the October 1973 War.[2] Together they showed that Egypt had recovered the courage and the capacity to rebuild itself. The bridge brought new movement to congested Cairo. It was the most dramatic phase of a transportation network of four kilometers of elevated highways and fly-overs that would cost an estimated 33.7 million Egyptian pounds (L.E.).[3] Its name commemorates the crossing of the Suez Canal by the Egyptian army into Israeli-held Sinai on October 6, 1973. Farming the new lands at Salhia showed how Egyptians could move out of the crowded confines of the Nile Valley and live in the desert that covered over 95 percent of their country. "Egypt's future is on this new land," Sadat pronounced. He called the Salhia desert settlement "a new October, a heroic achievement that will bring welfare and security to the Egyptian people."[4]

On the world stage, Sadat appeared as a solitary figure. He dramatized himself as the lonely master of diplomatic decisions that shocked the world into new regional and international alignments favoring Egypt. When inaugurating projects such as the October Sixth Bridge and Salhia, Sadat qualified the solitary image by identifying the construction magnate and his company as a special kind of partner in rulership. In the president's view, the Osman "family" of relatives and company employees embodied a political vision, distilled from decades of successful company practice, that held great promise for the nation. Led by Osman, they were the spearhead of new social forces that could transform Egypt. In place of Nasserist images of social revolution and a dominant regional role, the Osman circle offered the possibility of an Egypt remade by individual initiative, private enterprise, and the resources of advanced technology and capital made available through renewed links to the world market.

On assuming power Sadat indicated a new direction for the nation in the Permanent Constitution and National Action Program of 1971. A more important official statement of purpose, however, was the October Working Paper of 1974, which summed up a formula for forward movement: Arab capital + Western technology + abundant Egyptian manpower and other resources = development and progress. Here was the basic idea behind the Open Door economic policy that would set the tone of political and economic life in the seventies. In order to gain access to the most advanced Western technologies and the new Arab oil wealth, Egypt would abandon its ties to the East and reestablish connections to the world market. The most powerful Arab state would turn from confrontation to accommodation with Israel. Nasser's Arab socialism at home would give way to a democratic socialism with a large role for a revived private sector. At home Sadat's reorientation of national policy would open the door to those suppressed social strata with an interest in renewed ties to the West and a private enterprise environment.

Sadat looked to Osman to breathe life into this grand strategy. Osman, like others who held private capital, benefited from Sadat's new policies and provided social support for the new order. Sadat, in turn, used Osman's career to exemplify the developmental formula that he claimed would propel Egypt out of bankrupt Nasserist socialism into a prosperous private enterprise future. In this sense, Osman provided the regime with a ready-make political vision.[5] The ambiguity of Osman's public image made him the ideal figure to guide the transition to the new order. On the one hand, Osman had started out as an engineer and a private contractor and clearly belonged to a new stratum of wealthy and influential Egyptians with contacts to monied interests inside and outside the country. On the other hand, Osman chaired the board of one of the largest public-sector companies. Therefore, reliance on Osman implied simple reform of publicly owned enterprises, although in reality Sadat's strategy moved resources from the public to the private sector and enhanced the wealth and power of those involved in it.

The president encouraged Osman to move out of the shadowy niche the entrepreneur had carved for his construction empire in the public sector. In the seventies Sadat wanted Osman and his hidden model of private enterprise center stage. With official encouragement, Osman Ahmed Osman used the state-controlled media to project the story of his life and his career as a model for the nation.[6] As Osman himself put it, "I aimed to place my life experience and life history, my suffering and my success, before Egypt's youth."[7] The Osman story pointed to the kind of people, institutions, and achievements that would make a new Egypt possible. First, Osman presented his extended "family" of relatives, company employees, and a variety of retainers as people who had mastered modern managerial and technical skills while remaining loyal to traditional religious and moral values. This combination had brought them prosperity and would do the same for the nation. In addition, Osman offered the Arab Contractors and the web of banks and companies spun off from it as the ideal institutional means to move

Egypt forward. The Arab Contractors itself was legally a public-sector firm. However, the construction company helped found a string of private Egyptian firms and joint-venture enterprises that took advantage of Sadat's economic liberalization. Finally, this network of companies registered tangible achievements that, in Osman's view, validated the new strategy. Standing on the October Sixth Bridge or in the fields of the Salhia desert agricultural site, Egyptians glimpsed a better future for themselves and their country.

The contrast between Osman's humble beginnings and his great success and prominence in the seventies made his story an inspirational symbol for those seeking individual prosperity and power. Born in the provincial Suez Canal city of Ismailia in 1917, Osman lost his father at age three. In his autobiography, he recounts how his illiterate mother relied on her strong religious faith and belief in education to raise him, his brothers, and two sisters. Osman was particularly proud that, thanks to his mother's extraordinary efforts, all the children finished their education. He deepened his own religious formation by studying the Koran and a small collection of religious books left to him by his father; later he came under the religious influence of one of his primary-school teachers, Hassan al-Banna, who later became one of the most important Islamic figures in Egypt's modern history.

In Ismailia al-Banna founded the Muslim Brotherhood. In the forties the Brotherhood became the most powerful activist Islamic group in Egypt, claiming over a million members before it was repressed by the revolutionary government. Osman became a Muslim Brother, leaving the group only because of the demands of his work. "I only left the Brotherhood as an organization," Osman explained, "but I remained attached to its principles and values and followed its path from that moment until now.[8]

Osman graduated from the university in 1940 with a degree in engineering. Modeling himself after a successful uncle, he aimed for a career in the construction business rather than government service. In 1942 his fledgling company received its first contract, a garage for a friend. Later, Osman went into partnership with his older brother.

Among the challenges confronting Osman at this stage of his life were the British occupiers of Egypt, who he believed deliberately created difficulties for Egyptian entrepreneurs. Osman also came to resent the British occupation on a more emotional and psychological level. He had particularly painful memories of the large British force that was stationed in Ismailia to secure the canal: "I grew up seeing the British walk the streets . . . I also saw what they used to call the Arab quarter and the European quarter. I saw the discrimination. This was difficult to take. Those who lived in the Arab section were strictly forbidden from entering the European district. We lived with goats and chickens in the Arab section. It was a pity to let the country go that way."[9] Osman noted how a handful of British supervisors merely directed the Egyptians who did the real work. He believed such foreign tutelage blocked the advance of capable Egyptians.

Confronted by a society closed by both British colonialism and a stagnant regime, Osman went to Saudi Arabia in 1950. Taking advantage of the boom in oil drilling and sales, Osman's construction company was very successful. Within a short time, the company was bidding on multimillion dollar projects in Kuwait, Libya, Iraq, and the United Arab Emirates. In spite of his tremendous success, however, Osman's time abroad did not diminish his strong attachment to Egypt; Osman later described this period as a kind of purgatory to be endured until he could make enough money to return to Egypt. Nasser's nationalization of the Suez Canal Company and the subsequent attack on Egypt by Israel, France, and Britain created an urgent demand for Osman's skills; in 1956 he returned temporarily to help rebuild a war-damaged village near Port Said. Osman's commitment to his homeland prompted his return; in his memoirs he wrote: "I was not at that time one of the guerrilla fighters who took up arms to fight the occupying forces, but I carried out my duty in serving my country when I presented myself to rebuild Kafr Abdou."[10] This action by Osman began a long career of seeking to meet the needs of the nation through the activities of his companies.

Osman had returned to an uncertain political climate that might not favor a private company and the profit motivation that was essential to his business. After some initial ambivalence, the 1952 revolution took the form of a regime hostile to private businessmen. By 1956, the political order founded by the Free Officers led by Gamal Abdul Nasser had evolved from a nationalist military coup into a government committed to a revolution from above.[11] The regime declared its commitment to socialist revolution, Arab nationalism, and confrontation with Israel. It was in this unlikely context that Osman's company established itself as the leading construction firm in Egypt by winning a $48 million contract for part of the Aswan Dam project.

The regime's hopes for a strong Egypt rested on successful construction of the dam as a way of generating electricity for the nation. The dam was funded by the Soviet Union, and according to Osman's autobiography the Russians sought to dissuade Nasser from giving his company the High Dam contract; however, the production record of the company so impressed Nasser that he gave Osman the assignment. When Nasser asked him what his needs would be to handle the dam project, Osman made only one request: "I said that nobody interferes in the company's affairs except its sons." Nasser agreed to the condition. "The fulfillment of this request," concluded Osman, "became the reason the Arab Contractors is what it is."[12] Although Osman was never part of the Nasser regime's inner circle, he was able to guarantee his company's reputation and its connection with the regime through the company's part in one of the greatest achievements of the Nasser years. Osman always spoke of the dam as his project, although the Arab Contractors was only one of several companies involved. People in Egypt and throughout the Arab world knew Osman Ahmed Osman as the man who built the High Dam.[13]

Osman continued to operate within a political system that seemed increasingly hostile to any kind of private ownership or management. In 1961, as part of a more extensive shift to the left, the regime nationalized the Arab Contractors. Osman was abroad at the time this decision was made. His advisers argued that there was no reason for him to return; from their perspective "the world has come to an end." They even warned Osman of the risks of placing himself within the reach of the government. Nevertheless, Osman believed that he could still work with the regime, and he decided to return to Egypt: "On my arrival in Cairo . . . the whole company was waiting for me at the airport . . . They were expecting to see a man falling apart. Instead, they found I was smiling."[14]

The situation did not look at all promising; according to Osman, the regime had nationalized every aspect of his company, including the automobiles. Even though he had lost his entire fortune, however, Osman was confident that he could build another. Subsequent events proved him correct. From the Aswan Dam experience Osman concluded that Nasser's drive to industrialize was stronger than any ideological commitment to socialism. Even after the nationalizations in 1961, Nasser allowed Osman to run the Arab Contractors like a private-sector company. In 1964 the government formalized this special arrangement when the minister of housing, charged with supervising the construction sector, prepared a law tailor-made for the Arab Contractors. The law exempted firms that did a substantial part of their business abroad from the socialist-inspired wage and employment provisions of the public sector, thereby allowing Osman to tie wages and job tenure to productivity rather than to government regulation. The minister who secured the government's agreement to these special privileges was a close business associate of Osman's; his private consulting firm relied on the Arab Contractors for a considerable share of its business.[15]

During the Nasser years many public-sector managers found various covert ways to turn their management of public firms into a private resource. Despite socialist rhetoric that attacked the profit motive and the official illegality of the business practices involved, the government turned a blind eye to these practices. Often the strategies of the managers involved subcontracting work from the large public-sector firms they controlled to small private-sector firms in which they had an interest. The managers justified these actions as a way of moving production out of the cumbersome public enterprises and into privately owned, profit-motivated companies that they claimed were simply more efficient. By these arrangements the managers effectively transformed their control of the public resources of their companies into their own private capital.[16] Osman believed that the regime tolerated these maneuvers in the interest of productivity. "Production," he summed up, "is the clever lawyer who can best defend you."[17] The scale of the operations suggests his assumption of official acquiescence was reasonable: hidden subcontracting channeled as much as 40 percent of the state investment funds for the years 1960–1965 into private hands.[18]

Osman was sensitive to charges that he had returned to Egypt primarily out of self-interest and greed. According to Osman, Egyptian nationalism and a strong sense of concern for his employees were far more important than personal ambition or self-interest. After all, he later pointed out, "my business was waiting for me in Saudi Arabia, Libya, and Kuwait without any risks whatsoever." Osman always emphasized that his return was directly connected to the nationalist dimension of the Arab Contractors. He portrayed the company as an instrument to defend and build the country. As a result, Osman argued that "I built the Dam for my country and not for Nasser." In his defense of his cooperation with the Nasser regime, Osman also declared that a decision to leave Egypt permanently would have meant abandoning his employees. "I had 5,000 workers," he explained, "and that means 5,000 families." Osman believed that his departure from the leadership of the Arab Contractors would have meant the dispersal of this core group of workers whom he had "brought up." For their sake, Osman concluded, "I remained, withstood, suffered, and sacrificed."[19]

In his autobiography Osman recalled that Sadat, then an official in

Nasser's government, supported his decision to remain in Egypt after the nationalizations in the early sixties. Osman had asked Sadat why his firm had been taken over by the government. "I am not among the types that such a decree covers," he had argued. "I am not a feudalist, a capitalist, an exploiter, a monopolist nor a stooge of colonialism. I built my company with money I earned from my own sweat and struggle outside Egypt and I brought it here to invest it for the good of the Egyptian people." According to Osman, Sadat told him, "These things will come to an end. You must be patient and not leave Egypt, because she needs all our efforts regardless of what any of her faithful sons may suffer." [20]

Subsequent events fully justified Sadat's counsel of patience. Because the government had allowed Osman exceptional control over the company's internal administration, the Arab Contractors thrived as an essentially private-enterprise company in a system that described itself as socialist. In addition, Osman personally enjoyed a range of special privileges such as freedom to travel and to continue construction work in the Arab states as head of a private-sector company.[21] Nevertheless, Osman and the other hidden entrepreneurs in the public sector felt hemmed in by the restrictions of the socialist society that Nasser was trying to create around them. "We were frozen," explained Osman, "and unable to make our real contribution."[22]

For Osman, the terrible defeat of June 1967 exposed the flaws of the Nasserist regime and eventually led to movement in new directions. Osman acknowledged that the 1952 Revolution "expelled the British, destroyed feudal exploitation, and made fundamental changes in the economic and social system to benefit the people."[23] Nevertheless, the construction entrepreneur believed that Nasser's revolutionary socialism had fettered the economy, embroiled Egypt in a series of unwinnable wars with Israel and in Yemen, and blocked the creative energies of Egyptians by government oppressiveness. In the end, he judged that the socialist experiment had produced a government unable to defend its citizens or its territory. In six days of fighting Israel easily destroyed a substantial part of the armed forces of Egypt, Syria, and Jordan and captured large amounts of territory from each, including the Egyptian Sinai. The Nasser regime never recovered from the 1967 defeat. The effects of the Six Day War were exacerbated in 1969 by the resumption of fighting with Israel over the occupied Sinai. The so-called War of Attrition produced thousands of casualties, devastated towns in the Suez Canal zone, and created over a million Egyptian refugees. The Arab Contractors was directly involved in the Egyptian struggle against Israel.

Osman's company was given the task of building the fortified sites for the defensive missiles received from the Soviet Union to shield Egypt from Israeli penetration bombing. In one day, Osman later claimed, Israeli attacks killed more than 500 laborers on the Arab Contractors project on the west bank of the Suez Canal. Despite these deadly raids, the Arab Contractors completed the defensive missile sites that were necessary to protect Egyptian airspace.[24]

During his involvement with defense construction, Osman had several encounters with the Soviets in Egypt that aroused both his anger and his nationalist instincts. At one point, Osman received a contract to build protective shelters for new planes acquired from the USSR, but Soviet advisers denied him access to the air base where they were temporarily housed. The Soviets also refused to give Osman the exact measurements for the planes. Osman learned that, on another occasion, Soviet personnel refused the Egyptian minister of war permission to land at the airport at Aswan. These and many similar incidents convinced Osman that the 17,000 Soviet advisers "were not experts giving advice, but occupiers enforcing their own opinions."[25] The Soviets, as Osman saw it, were exploiting Egypt's weakness after 1967 to establish an imperial presence in the country.

Nasser's death in 1970 opened the way for new directions in domestic and foreign policy that Osman heartily welcomed. In retrospect, Osman was very critical of the Nasser period. He believed that the Egyptian people had paid a high price for Nasser's combination of domestic repression and foreign adventurism. Osman welcomed Sadat's rule and bemoaned the heavy burden of recovering the occupied Sinai and rebuilding the shattered Egyptian economy. "We are now engaged in clearing the debris left by that era, especially the bleeding of all Egypt's resources, in order to overcome the catastrophe it left us. Instead of aiming our efforts at building our country, we are now aiming them at liberating our land."[26] In Osman's judgment, the "catastrophe" of Nasser's rule cost Egypt its self-respect: "Egypt abandoned hope and embraced despair, until Sadat came and lifted her face from the mud."[27]

Osman enthusiastically backed Sadat's efforts to reorient the nation's foreign policy. Sadat rejected the option kept alive by Nasser of intensifying the "revolution," continuing the confrontation with Israel, and strengthening ties with the Soviet Union. He built instead on Nasser's tentative moves in his last years toward liberalization, conciliation with Israel, and an opening to the West. In 1971 Sadat floated a peace offer, but neither the Israelis nor the Americans showed any interest. The following year he terminated the Soviet presence in Egypt, still without a favorable response from the United States. As a result, Sadat concluded that he would have to alter the power balance, at the time so overwhelmingly in Israel's favor, in order to interest the Israelis in negotiation and to remind the Americans of their own vulnerability in the Middle East. In 1973 Sadat launched the October War as a political war to create the diplomatic conditions necessary to pursue a peace strategy. The Arab Contractors again played a role in war preparations. They built the ferries that carried the Egyptian forces across the Canal and into Israeli-occupied Sinai.[28]

Immediately after the war Sadat acted to swing wide an "Open Door" to Western and Arab investment in Egypt. Foreign investors, still fearful of possible nationalizations and unsure of regional stability, responded with little enthusiasm. Egypt's economy deteriorated. Sadat concluded that American and other Western investment in Egypt would be limited until he liberalized his regime and removed the persistent threat of Egypt's involvement in regional wars. In order to win American support for his country, Sadat concluded that Egypt had to cultivate a liberal image more in keeping with American ideology if the Americans were to underwrite the recovery of the Egyptian economy; moreover, the required U.S. support was highly unlikely unless Egypt reached an accommodation with Israel. In the president's view, the road to American support for Egypt's development ran through Jerusalem.

Two days of food riots in January 1977 drove home the desperation of Egypt's economic position. Osman echoed the government reaction in condemning the rioters as "a jealous minority" stirred up in "an attempt by the communists to seize the benefits achieved by the people under the freedom and democracy of President Muhammad Anwar el-Sadat."[29] Nevertheless, the demonstrators had registered their message that economic conditions were intolerable for the mass of the people. In November 1977 Sadat flew to Jerusalem to begin the peace process that brought the Camp David accords in 1978 and the peace treaty in 1979. Like many others who had felt constrained by Nasser's socialist and adventurist ambitions, Osman welcomed Sadat's attempt to end the impasse with Israel. "Although I could not help him in any way in what he was doing," wrote Osman later, "I wanted to tie my destiny to his. I imagined he was going into the unknown, and I wanted to be with him."[30] Osman made his support for Sadat's dramatic step tangible by accompanying the president to Jerusalem.

On his return, Osman tirelessly argued that the bold new foreign policy orientation would be Egypt's salvation. Since the revolution, Osman charged, "we have spent 26 billion pounds on war." Unless there was stability, there would be no foreign investment or technology, and "stability means first of all peace. Peace opens the road to stability."[31] Climate, manpower, and strategic location provided everything a strong economy needed if investment and especially technology could be secured from abroad. According to Osman, Sadat's peace with Israel was part of a larger American connection that would create new regional and international conditions favorable to Egypt's development.

Osman's public role grew steadily after Nasser's death. Sadat's economic and political objectives were ideal for the kind of private-enterprise initiative displayed by Osman throughout the fifties and sixties. The compatibility between Osman's experience and Sadat's policies allowed Osman to assume an increasingly prominent public role, a role that he had avoided under Nasser's regime. "For years I tried to stay clear of politics," Osman explained, "because I did not like Nasser's socialist policies, which had killed off the private sector." Twice he had declined offers of a ministerial position in governments under Nasser.[32] Under Sadat, however, Osman had a different perspective: "I became convinced that I could serve a useful purpose as a government minister only after I saw that Sadat's goals coincided with mine to end the public sector's stranglehold on our economy."[33] To advance his interest in a liberalized economy, Osman accepted a string of key government, party, and syndicate positions, including minister of reconstruction, supervisor general of the food production program, deputy prime minister of popular development, chairman of Sadat's National Democratic Party (NDP) Committee for Popular Development, chief of the Ismailia parliamentary delegation, and head of the Syndicate of Engineers. The closeness of the Sadat-Osman relationship was underscored when Sadat's daughter married Osman's son on January 2, 1977.

The changes under the Sadat regime encouraged Osman to explain his belief in the advantages of private ownership and initiative. Osman insisted that private ownership should be encouraged whenever possible, "not for the sake of the owners, but for the good of Egypt." Osman argued that "the owner of any private project is interested in expanding it along with his wealth, and expansion of the project can only mean increased production and job opportunities."[34] Nevertheless, Osman wrote, "there are a number of areas in which it is acceptable, even necessary, to have public ownership, such as the iron and steel industry, the military, railroads, public utilities, etc."[34] Osman always carefully balanced criticism of an excessive government role in the economy with a call for selective government support of some public-sector activities.

Osman's supporters, Sadat the most prominent among them, urged that his life experience serve as a "guide and a dictionary" for all Egyptians.[35] The Osman public persona provided an example of how Egyptians could link their private interest to the good of society and the nation. Osman exuded confidence that his practical vision offered promising definitions of individual and national responsibilities that were more appropriate to the seventies and eighties than the socialist ideas of the Nasser era. Drawing on his own experience, Osman explained how de-Nasserization, peace with Israel, and renewal of the American connection created new opportunities for private capital to serve the nation.

In support of the objectives of the official de-Nasserization campaign, Osman argued that freedom in the seventies meant something different from the "bread" of the socialist era or even the political rights of the pre-1952 liberal period. According to Osman, the idea of freedom emphasized the opportunity—whether large or small—open to all citizens to work hard and through individual effort improve their own position. As Osman saw it, individual successes also contributed to the general prosperity of the country. "Patriotism to me has a meaning that is different from other people's . . . I'm not good with words, but I have my own national vision, which I outlined as the national line of my life: it is work. Each citizen must give his nation as much as possible in his sphere of work."[36] Osman argued that by dismantling the oppressive structures of Nasser's system, Sadat was making this opportunity available to all Egyptians.

Osman urged Egyptians of all social classes to follow his lead in establishing private business ventures, whether large or small. Osman made reassertion of the right to private property the heart of the de-Nasserization campaign. No voice in Egypt denounced the seizures more eloquently that Osman. "Nationalization," he wrote, "was a great mistake that victimized all Egypt." Control of the country's resources had allowed the previous regime to "establish itself as another God on earth."[37]

The liberalization that began almost immediately after Sadat consolidated his power in 1971 created a new institutional, legal, and moral climate in which private capital previously sent abroad or hidden in socialist Egypt could now be safely and openly invested in the country. The courts began to return property seized during the fifties and sixties. Many families took advantage of vastly inflated property values to tear down old houses and sell the property at a large profit.[38] Changes in import-export laws also created a myriad of possibilities for profitable projects. Finally, government removal of travel restrictions opened to all Egyptians the chance to work abroad and accumulate private capital as Osman had done earlier in so exemplary a fashion.

Osman's antipathy to nationalization was almost matched by his passionate condemnation of the Nasserist policy of guaranteeing jobs in the public sector to all university graduates. Osman strongly opposed the system of free university education created during the Nasser years. He felt it produced an overall decline in the quality of university education. In his view, the expansion also added little to the country's productive resources because the educational system was not tied to the country's economic needs. Osman wrote that the government had "told the young man, "Come, we'll educate you for free and then wait until we hire you.' They taught him laziness."[39] From Osman's point of view, the moral fiber of Egypt's youth had been weakened by their dependency on the government for both education and a job in the bureaucracy.

Osman used the experience of his own sons as an example of how the young could counter these government influences and learn to become serious and successful entrepreneurs; the combined efforts of Osman's sons led to the founding of twenty-six companies. Originally, Osman employed his boys in the Arab Contractors, where "they made money . . . money over and above their salaries." They disappointed their father, however, by "wasting their money on consumer products." Osman reported that "I suggested to them that they put their extra money in companies. They said they agreed but were not quite sure how to do so. I told them how, and the companies, of which you have all heard, were established."[40]

In his own companies Osman created an alternative to "the myth of office and government jobs" that could work for all young people.[41] Osman warned sons of the possessing classes, like his own, against the perils of idle consumerism. The sons of the poor were cautioned, in turn, against the fatalism and immobility that poverty produces. He urged both groups to make their fortunes in the private sector. As a model for the transformation of "citizens waiting for a government job" into merchants, Osman told this story:

> "Well, come, boys, you're waiting for employment assignments from the labor department, and there are no jobs. Would you come and sell beans and *ta'miyya* [a deep-fried vegetable paste]?" They did and later reported: "We worked and we worked more. We served people until two in the

morning." They were making money and they were content. But I then suggested that they become owners of the stands. Everyone was taking seventy-five pounds a month. I suggested taking only thirty and putting the rest toward the purchase of the stand in installments until it was theirs. Then the stand gets bigger and becomes a grocery store. In this way, I increased production and made new men of them.[42]

Hard work was the ingredient that made the Osman formula available to everyone.

Osman believed that the key to a successful company was the creation of a productive work environment, and that this required freedom from external interference. In particular, he opposed government-regulated wage levels for his workers, although the Arab Contractors was legally a public-sector firm. Although Osman actively sought government contracts, he avoided being placed under the jurisdiction of government regulations. Instead of state guarantees of a minimum wage, Osman made a mutually beneficial deal with his employees that linked self-interest to productivity. A complicated system of bonuses offered workers the opportunity to increase their salaries by as much as 200 or even 300 percent. This system was based on an implicit bargain between the Arab Contractors and its employees: in return for hard work, the company took care of its employees. On the whole, salaries in the Arab Contractors exceeded those of comparable public-sector firms; the company also established and contributed generously to an employees' investment fund. In addition, Osman employees enjoyed a quite remarkable range of company services that shielded them from the harsher edges of daily living in Egypt. Company transportation to work, an extensive network of clubs, summer recreational facilities, medical clinics, and death and disability compensation were just some of the benefits that Osman rightly described as privileges unmatched by any other companies in Egypt.[43]

"We are all one family," Osman commented, "and we all care for each other and benefit from the company production."[44] The Arab Contractors' cultivated image of efficiency and modernity coexisted happily with traditional Egyptian notions of special privileges for the members of the "family" and Islamic ideas of justice and fairness in social relations. Osman explained that these were the values, held by his mother, that had enabled his own family to thrive; as a young man Osman had vowed to himself to make these same ideas the moral basis of his business enterprises.

Osman found a powerful indicator of his successful cultivation of such a "family" environment in the reaction of Arab Contractors employees to the January 1977 riots. When hostile demonstrators approached the company facilities, the workers "stood up to the saboteurs, gathered around the equipment, and did not allow any of them to reach it despite repeated attempts." Osman commented that "this stand resulted from the values that bound the workers to each other and to the company."[45] Even during nationwide disturbances, Osman's bargain with his employees held.

Once created, the linkage between privilege and productivity within the company sustained itself, provided that external intrusions were deflected. Osman aggressively protected his employees from political, administrative, and even legal pressures; all such actions were described as "family" loyalty. For example, in the fifties and sixties the Arab Contractors employed approximately 500 members of the Muslim Brotherhood. The persistent tension between the organization and the regime made the presence of so large a contingent of Brothers in the company risky. Nevertheless, Osman defended the Brothers as hardworking and dependable. "They fear God," he wrote, "and there is no cause to fear those who fear God." Moreover, he entrusted them with important roles in all phases of the company's operations. In a later address to Islamic groups, Osman said: "Osman Ahmed Osman's company rested on the shoulders of the youth of the Muslim Brothers at a time when uttering the phrase 'God is great' invited arrest."[46] Osman explained that any Muslim Brother hired by the Arab Contractors had to agree to stay out of politics for as long as he was an employee. Osman believed the Brothers in the company kept this agreement; he reported that in the 1965 trials of Muslim Brothers accused of conspiracy, 145 employees of the Arab Contractors were tried, but all were exonerated.[47]

Osman's view of the sanctity of the production environment also shaped his hostile attitude toward the Administrative Supervision Bureau, a government watchdog agency charged with monitoring the operations of employees in government agencies and public-sector companies. Osman opposed the agency in his capacities both as head of a company and as a government official. Because of his special "bargain" with them, Osman tended to be all-forgiving provided that his employees produced results.[48] Osman announced that he personally took full responsibility for any wrongdoings by his employees and therefore had no need of a government agency to supervise them. He staunchly resisted the monitoring efforts of the Administrative Bureau. Later, Osman showed the same hostility to the government effort to control corruption when he was minister of housing. Osman made his ministerial domain a sphere with its own rules. He pronounced himself pleased with the results, which he measured in terms of accomplishments rather than adherence to formal rules: "In fact, we accomplished in three years what would have required fifty years to accomplish. I did this because I believe that work requires flexibility. People cannot work with this sword of supervision hanging over their necks. If you give an individual freedom and authority, he will give in return without limits."[49] When Sadat eventually abolished the Administrative Supervision Bureau, Osman made no effort to conceal his delight.

Osman offered new definitions of nationalism that promoted self-interest and productivity in the workplace. The building of private fortunes in the Open Door conditions was not only good for the entrepreneur and good for his employees; it was also good for Egypt. The new entrepreneurs in the Osman mold "owned" Egypt in the same way that they owned their companies. From his youth, this proprietary sense shaped Osman's reaction to the British colonization of Egypt. What angered him most was the way the British had used their supervisory role in the economy to "skim the cream" and "leave only the crumbs" to the Egyptians.[50] Osman similarly resented the Soviets for preempting opportunities and trying to block the role of Egyptians like himself in exploiting Egypt's resources.

Nationalism, from Osman's perspective, meant that if there was cream to be skimmed Egyptians should do the skimming. In the new climate of the economic opening, Osman argued that Egyptian capital must not be pushed aside by "the flood of foreign investors who presented only rapid turnover and high-profit consumer projects such as Wimpy, Kentucky Fried Chicken, Seven-Up, etc." Osman did not condemn the consumerist character of the projects per se, only the fact that foreigners benefited from them: "The Egyptian has first right to his country and its projects."[51] In fact, the private companies created by the Arab Contractors undertook just such consumer-oriented investments, but gave them an Egyptian face.

Osman's anticolonial nationalism thus differed significantly from the radical objectives that had motivated the socialist and pan-Arab nationalism of the Nasserists. Pan-Arabism, in his view, had nothing to do with what he saw as the utopian protest against the artificial divisions of the Arab world by colonialism. Osman also renounced the Nasserist linkage of Arabism with the drive for a socialist and anti-imperial transformation of the Arab states.[52] Osman charged that Nasser's meddling in Arab states had "squandered" Egypt's limited resources in foreign policy adventures such as the protracted involvement in the civil war in Yemen.[53]

In place of what he denounced as Nasser's radical and unsuccessful pan-Arabism, Osman looked to constructive economic projects to strengthen the bonds between the Arab nations. He sought to implement his version of the pan-Arab dream with joint companies that "combined Arab capital with the expertise and experience of the Arab Contractors." He put the matter simply: "My experience in the Arab countries was an embodiment of this idea. I went there with my work, experience and technical capabilities, which they didn't have. They in return gave what they could—money."[54] The best possible bonds to fellow Arabs were several million Egyptian laborers who, thanks to Sadat's liberalization, could travel as temporary workers to enrich those Arab countries with their "human capabilities." In return, Osman asked that "the millions amassed in the hands of our Arab brothers" be invested in capital-starved Egypt rather than handed over to Western banks.[55]

Osman's redefinition of Egypt's Arabism placed him in the forefront of those who consistently sought to downplay the importance of the question of Israel in the seventies. After the 1967 defeat, the focus of concern for many in Egypt shifted from the colonization of Palestine to the return of occupied Egyptian territories. In the seventies attention narrowed further. The central issues became restored access to the oil of Sinai and the revenues of the Suez Canal in order to improve Egypt's balance-of-payments position. Osman consistently opposed efforts to focus on Israel's expulsion of the Arabs of Palestine and its potential threat to Egypt. After the Egyptian-Israeli peace treaty was signed in 1979, Osman hoped to draw Israel and Egypt into even closer cooperation. From his point of view, Israel was simply an economically and technologically superior country that could aid Egypt. By the eighties Osman was openly arguing that an exhausted Egypt could not commit any more of its resources to the struggle with Israel; from now on, the absolute priority had to be national development.[56]

By the late seventies Sadat was creating a new official framework in which the social forces, the institutions, and the values Osman championed were able to operate. After the treaty with Israel was signed, Sadat announced that he would devote his efforts to internal affairs. His flatterers in the national press announced that the man who engineered the miracle of the October 1973 War and then shocked the entire world with his peace with Israel would achieve similar breakthroughs on the domestic front.

Sadat, in turn, looked to Osman, referring to him as a "general" who commanded an army of construction workers, poised to rebuild Egypt. According to Sadat, Osman was "one who has done the work" and who could explain to the people "what has been achieved and how we were able to find the right beginning."[57] Companies modeled on the Arab Contractors, Sadat argued, should be the engines of national progress. This judgment justified all the government did to assist them. Sadat looked to the Arab Contractors to make the development campaign a success. Osman in turn used his party and government appointments to guarantee every advantage for the company.

Sadat made construction of housing and food self-sufficiency his priorities for achieving progress and development. To meet these challenges, Sadat "asked the Arab Contractors, the strongest company in our public sector . . . to try to find the right approach using the latest technology and the latest developments in science." Sadat pointed to the Salhia desert community as an indicator that "we have found the solution for food and housing."[58]

Relying on the Arab Contractors, the government launched a series of construction projects to rejuvenate Egypt, including the October Sixth Bridge, the so-called Tunnel of the Martyr linking Sinai and the Egyptian heartland, and rebuilding the Canal Zone cities. Each project symbolized a particular facet of the transition from Nasser to Sadat. The bridge in downtown Cairo was a sign of the new confidence brought by the peace, made possible by Sadat's successful leadership in the 1973 war (as opposed to Nasser's in 1967); the tunnel to Sinai was a sign of the future possibilities of U.S. aid; and the reopening of the Canal Zone cities constituted an important shift in collective history from the Nasser to the Sadat period and a gesture of reassurance to Israel.

According to Osman, all three projects signaled the changed relationship with Israel that Sadat had achieved. The idea for the bridge, Osman recalled in his autobiography, came one day in 1967, after the defeat, when he found himself caught in the traffic feeding into downtown Cairo from the middle-class suburb of Dokki. A consulting engineer was trapped in the traffic with Osman. On the spot they drew up a plan to alleviate the traffic jams with a new bridge over the Nile. When they submitted the project to the Cairo governor, he hesitated and then sent it to Nasser. Nasser refused to approve the project out of "fear that

Israel might destroy it." Osman made the moral of his story explicit: "It was the will of fate that this bridge, which the former regime refused to construct for fear of Israel, was built during Sadat's era and now carries the name of the day on which Egypt destroyed the myth of the unbeatable army."[59]

Similarly, whereas Nasser had feared to build a bridge in central Cairo, Sadat asked Osman to take charge of the reconstruction of the devastated cities on the very front with Israel. Under the Nasser regime, the bombed and deserted Canal Zone cities were a symbol of Egypt's unbroken national will. With Osman's help, Sadat reinterpreted the past: Nasser's wars with Israel had brought destruction, but his peace with the Jewish state would bring national reconstruction. According to Osman, Sadat told him: "I want to rebuild the cities that fall within the range of Israeli artillery. I want to make it clear to Israel that I don't intend to launch another war against them."[60] In parallel fashion, as the United States flooded Egypt with aid to promote normalization with Israel, a substantial portion was targeted for the Tunnel of the Martyr, effort undergirding the Egyptian-Israeli peace by again creating a target deliberately made vulnerable to Israel.[61]

With this official encouragement, Egypt's construction sector boomed.[62] By 1979 it accounted for 6 percent of value added and 4 percent of the labor force (as much as 6.5 percent in urban areas). Sector growth rates reached an estimated 6 percent at fixed prices for 1970–1976 and 11 percent at fixed prices for 1976–1979.[63] The Arab Contractors took the lion's share of this expansion: in March 1981 it held almost 80 percent of major government construction projects.[64]

During the seventies the Arab Contractors became an economic giant. Net company profits rose steadily from L.E. 1.6 million in 1972 to L.E. 22.4 million in 1981/82. Fixed company assets in land, buildings, and equipment increased in value from L.E. 16.5 million to a stunning L.E. 190 million.[65] In 1981 the Arab Contractors group comprised thirty-three companies and four consortia, involved in construction, food production, banking and insurance, hotel and medical care facilities, and engineering services in addition to construction. Three main foundations supported Osman's economic empire. The parent Arab Contractors functioned as the group holding company. The Arab Contractors Investment Company, in which the parent company controlled 95 percent of the shares, supervised and channeled investments. Finally, the Arab Contractors Employees Fund participated with the parent company and investment company in founding new enterprises with its pension funds.[66] Ismailia, the birthplace of the founder, was the center for these Osman enterprises. The value of the eighteen Arab Contractors projects in Ismailia totaled L.E. 2,221.6 million, an investment surpassed only by the company projects in Cairo itself. Ismailia was known as "Osman's estate."[67]

This expansion and diversification put Osman's "army" of workers and engineers (as Sadat took to calling them) in position to respond to the president's call for achieving food self-sufficiency. "The Arab Contractors have not been contractors in the last few years," wrote a prominent journalist in 1979. "They have become an investment bank, financing operations that range from raising poultry and freezing meats, to transporting crops and making soft drinks. Why shouldn't they try their luck at agriculture as well?"[68] "Popular development," the government code word for construction projects and food self-sufficiency, became the key slogan of Sadat's National Democratic Party; and the president placed Osman in charge of official efforts to expand food production. Osman decided that increasing the food supply was possible only by significantly expanding the amount of land under cultivation. The Arab Contractors therefore launched the Salhia desert reclamation project as part of a government commitment to reclaim 150,000 desert feddans (155,700 acres) a year and up to a total of 3 million feddans by the year 2000.[69]

At Salhia the Arab Contractors adopted a Western approach, the Green Revolution, to Egypt's problems of food shortages and overpopulation. The solution entailed application of new fertilizers, improved crop varieties, and new methods of irrigation. In 1978 Osman announced that the Arab Contractors was setting up a model farm of 4,000 feddans of reclaimed land in the desert thirty kilometers west of Ismailia. Almost immediately newspaper headlines proclaimed the greening of the Egyptian sands. "For the first time," a hopeful *al-Ahram* pronounced in December 1979, "experts are exploiting the desert with modern technology."[70]

A month later an exuberant Sadat visited Salhia. Clad in work clothes and driving sophisticated American-made farm equipment, Sadat embraced the project as "Egypt's future" and identified his regime with it.[71] On the spot he proclaimed that "the 29th of January will be celebrated every year as the anniversary of the 'Green Revolution,' a policy to reclaim and inhabit desert land."[72] According to Sadat, the experimental desert farm created a new social space in which the novel possibilities of his era could be displayed. In addition to being a reclamation site, Salhia also embodied a contractor's dream: a plan to inhabit the desert by building a new city on the reclaimed land. To the Salhia pioneers, Osman took this message: "I told them I would build apartments and houses there for them to bring their children to live."[73] By 1982 the first stage of the new Salhia City, an integrated, agri-industrial complex, was a reality. A total of 2,220 residential units were built, complete with utilities and services including markets, a mosque, schools, a hospital, clinics, a fire brigade, a police station and public gardens. The work, the Arab Contractors announced, took only seven months. Experimental projects in animal husbandry, poultry, greenhouse and nursery cultivation, and bee raising were under way. The new city was designed initially for 60,000 people but could be expanded to 100,000.[74]

Inevitably, the Salhia project invited comparison with Liberation Province, Nasser's own showcase effort to reclaim desert land. Eighteen months after seizing power Nasser announced the creation of a new community in the desert south of Alexandria. The 1.2 million acres were eventually to include twelve districts, each with eleven villages. In all, the project would reclaim 800,000 acres, starting with a 10,000-acre experimental project. For Nasser, Liberation Province offered the opportunity to create an entirely new society that implemented the socialist ideals of restricted private ownership and an emphasis on public welfare. The peasants who lived there owned only their houses and a small garden; government cooperatives controlled the farm land and managed it collectively in large-scale, mechanized units. A large professional staff supervised excellent public medical and educational facilities. Within a decade Liberation Province faltered, however, and eventually faded from public view. High-level corruption, mismanagement, and the very poor quality of the soil contributed to blocking the spectacular advance promised by revolutionary rhetoric. The project neither succeeded greatly nor failed; it simply plodded along.[75]

Sadat eagerly seized on this weakness in the Nasser legacy and charged that Nasser's romance with Soviet-inspired heavy industrialization had led to the neglect of agriculture. In contrast, Sadat argued, Salhia displayed the power of the private-enterprise alternative to revolutionize the agricultural sector by drawing on foreign capital and Western technology. At Salhia, Osman worked out the complex institutional and social arrangements that linked abstractions such as free enterprise and technology to concrete actions and real people. In Osman's hands reclaiming the desert was not only good for the country but profitable as well. The project envisioned the cultivation of 150,000 feddans over a twelve-year period at a total cost of L.E. 292 million. From that investment he anticipated that the completed project would yield 260,000 tons of agricultural products annually, worth approximately L.E. 280 million.[76]

Osman made it clear that to achieve these goals for the nation (and these profits for the company), he required substantial government support. The regime did make capital available to the company at interest rates considerably lower than those prevailing in the market.[77] Osman explained in detail how he acquired the foreign technology and the international market outlets the project also required. He used Salhia to show exactly how Egyptians could structure joint-venture projects with foreign investors—and come out on top. As Osman told it, a representative from the Pepsi-Cola Company invited him to establish a beverage company in Egypt. Osman knew that Pepsi was eager to break into the lucrative Egyptian market for bottled soft drinks and that the company also undertook food and animal husbandry projects. Osman agreed to act as Pepsi's Egyptian partner, provided the company also helped provide the Salhia project with its hard-currency needs. Pepsi agreed to the arrangement, eventually taking 15 percent of the Salhia stock.[78]

Osman looked to American agribusiness for assistance in using the right technology to make land reclamation profitable. For this purpose, he brought a group of Arizona farmers to Egypt and invited them to join the company with 5 percent of the stock. The project also required American agricultural machinery of the kind used in Arizona. Without hesitation Osman drew in the American producer of that equipment with 10 percent of the stock in the project. Since Osman hoped to market the produce of Salhia abroad to earn hard currency, he sought an international firm with European distribution connections. The International Swedish Marketing Company met these requirements and was made a partner with another 10 percent of the stock. In all, Osman's foreign partners controlled 40 percent of the stock. The Arab Contractors covered the remaining 60 percent and thereby secured control over the whole project and gained the major share of the profits.[79]

In his public relations, Osman emphasized the dazzling technology rather than the complex financing that made Salhia a showcase for the Sadat development formula. American technology gave Salhia the necessary hopeful, even magical, appearance. No story in the press was complete without at least one picture of the bizarre-looking machines used to water the desert. The Egyptian face given to American technology at Salhia made the effect particularly powerful. The young Arab

Contractors engineers who directed the project took obvious delight in regaling visitors with demonstrations of the advantages in water economy, soil conservation, and even parasitic disease control that the American methods made possible.[80]

Anwar Sadat declared that Salhia was a "school for the nation" where the Osman version of a technocratic approach to Egypt's national problems could be learned.[81] Sadat singled out the young engineers at Salhia as "miracle workers" who carried the message that technology could solve all the challenges of rebuilding Egypt.[82] Salhia showed that private companies, linked to the world market, with access to such Western technology, and with appropriate government support, could channel the energies and talents of Egypt's educated youth to transform the country. Engineer Medhat Bahr, head of the Agricultural Products Division of the Arab Contractors, spoke for the Osman engineers: "The Salhia experience proves that young people can regain their social and cultural balance when faced with responsibility. [It proves] that they are solid and productive if they have a sense of belonging and that they give all their energies to their work when they feel they are justly treated, and that they are paid appropriately for the effort they put into their work."[83] Well-trained, hard-working, and well-paid employees: such were the Sadat heroes of the drama of national recovery.

Sadat used the example of the Salhia "miracle" as a battering ram against Nasserist socialist institutions in the countryside; stories in the media emphasized the way land reform laws, restrictions on foreign ownership of agricultural land, and the presence of agricultural cooperatives all hampered the progress at Salhia. The regime did succeed in weakening the cooperatives, while the attacks on land reform and foreign land ownership suggested future intentions. American experts involved in the Salhia project argued in the Egyptian press that efficient farming required large-scale holdings, which had been broken up by the land reform laws passed under Nasser.[84] Osman joined the campaign to press for repeal of the laws by arguing that the agribusiness of the future would require large landholdings to achieve optimal economies of scale.[85]

Because so much of the Salhia project depended on foreign investment, the laws against foreign ownership of property appeared as a serious obstacle. As early as May 1978 Osman had argued that, with certain restrictions, foreigners must be drawn into land reclamation efforts. "The goal," Osman announced," is the addition of a green patch even if the devil himself did the work."[86] Osman posed only two conditions, neither of which interfered with the kind of joint venture pioneered at Salhia: first, the foreigner must have an Egyptian partner; and second, use of the land by the foreigner would be restricted to twenty-five years. A spokesman for Osman announced the need to "amend the laws in order to attract the foreign investor. He must benefit in order to become our partner."[87]

The Nasser regime had looked to an expanded network of cooperatives in the Egyptian countryside to bring socialism to the peasants. The Arab Contractors pronounced the cooperatives a failure that led to serious mismanagement of resources. The newly reclaimed land, Osman announced, would not be organized into cooperatives. Instead, the profit-making companies that had reclaimed the land would supply the new owners with machinery, fertilizers, and experience.

According to Osman, the triumph of the Salhia experiment over socialism clarified the preferred relationship of private companies and government agencies in land development. Moreover, Salhia indicated what further dismantling of socialist measures was required if the experiment was to be generalized. Osman urged that land reclamation efforts be centralized in one agency to minimize bureaucracy and that the government's role be restricted to "guidance and instruction, and by that I mean experimentation and the provision of services and utilities."[88] As for the government's role in achieving food self-sufficiency, "the state should provide such facilities as roads and electricity and give loans to people . . . to do the reclaiming."[89]

The investment choices made at Salhia diverted government funds from efforts to improve lands already under cultivation. Some argued that government revenues could be better spent on such measures as drainage improvements. Such critical perspectives surfaced, for example, in the left opposition press over "old Salhia," an administrative and agricultural center close to the desert reclamation site but completely ignored by the Arab Contractors. Critics argued that old Salhia had neither adequate drinking water nor a minimal level of health care; according to one account in 1981, "the original, the real Salhia, the mother, is bitterly suffering and lacks all services."[90] Despite unexploited production possibilities and the needs of its inhabitants, old Salhia offered only very limited incentives to the new large agricultural firms and little scope for large-scale construction efforts. According to the standards established by the Arab Contractors and the regime's policies, old Salhia did not have a chance of competing with the profits available at new Salhia.

Public debate over the Salhia project also focused on the relationship between profit and national development. Virtually everyone conceded that the Arab Contractors' operation at Salhia was profitable at the levels of government support it received and that the technology was producing results; the critics focused on the estimated cost per unit of land and on the sophisticated level of technology necessary for the project. Even the Arab Contractors' official estimates ran to thousands of pounds per feddan, in contrast to the costs of less than 100 pounds per feddan in Nasser's earlier effort in Liberation Province. Independent economists estimated that strict accounting (including estimates for government support) might bring the Salhia figure as high as L.E. 7,000 per feddan. They also doubted the general applicability in Egypt of a land reclamation model that required technology so sophisticated that only large companies could run it.[91]

Osman retorted that such attacks on Salhia served "the interest of Egypt's enemies and aimed at destroying the morale of the country's young people." He argued that official government committees had established that infrastructure and reclaiming costs were L.E. 2,400 per feddan, with an additional L.E. 1,400 per feddan for facilities, buildings, water, seeds, and fertilizers. In spite of the various other cost estimates being made, Osman had no doubt that the project "is a pioneering one and a successful venture that will continue despite these critics."[92]

The Arab Contractors occupied a controversial place in the Egyptian development effort. Egyptians alert to public affairs could not be neutral about Osman Ahmed Osman's economic empire. Critics hinted that Osman was only building an elaborate facade behind which a new class of exploiters had arisen.[93] Many people warned that Osman was taking advantage of his privileged economic and political position and using hidden subcontractors and extravagant public financial support to drain resources from the public sector. Supporters, in contrast, accepted Sadat's view that the Osman works were a promising forecast of Egypt's better future. Neither the supporters nor the critics denied the central role that Osman had created for himself and his companies.

Osman zestfully took on his critics in the media; in the process he made explicit the values and the goals of the new group of Egyptian private-sector entrepreneurs that he had come to symbolize. When economists on the left denounced the Osman family role in the Arab Contractors and its spin-offs as "family capitalism," Osman read the charge as a compliment.[94] Just as Sadat took pride in the title "father of the Egyptian people," Osman delighted in the role of patriarch and provider of the Osman clan. Moreover, Osman considered service to the Arab Contractors as a form of national duty for which his extended family should be rewarded. In his view, what was good for the company was also good for Egypt. Legally, the Arab Contractors was a public-sector firm, but the patriarch made sure that Osman family members held the positions of strategic power in the company; from ten to fifteen close relatives always occupied the highest positions. Moreover, Osman argued that all the employees of the Arab Contractors extended family were true "sons of Egypt" because the diverse works of the Osman employees were all tributes to "Egypt's glory and potential."[95] For these contributions, they deserved rich rewards.

Critics questioned the economic priorities implicit in the Osman construction projects. For example, they argued that decisions to build traffic conduits such as the October Sixth Bridge meant that scarce resources went to those who could afford cars instead of those who needed food subsidies or low-cost housing. Although Salhia showed how government-subsidized companies could make profits in land reclamation, critics argued that the project did little or nothing to help the mass of Egypt's poor farmers.[96] "Prevailing patterns," wrote one economist, "were those of the few and not of society."[97] The private-sector companies that the Arab Contractors or its spin-off companies helped finance, such as Pepsi or Schweppes, were geared toward consumption rather than production. Some critics argued that these investment choices provided more in the way of quick profits for a small and newly privileged social stratum than it contributed to national development.[98]

Osman argued that Egyptian investment in the consumer sector would eventually create the conditions for an expansion of Egypt's productive capacity. Participation in consumer-oriented projects allowed Egyptians, and not just foreign investors, to make high profits; "Egyptians," as he put it, "should have first claim on Egypt and its money." Moreover, Osman argued that the initial emphasis on investment in consumer projects would subside once private entrepreneurs had amassed sufficient capital for investment in more substantial and productive projects.[99]

Osman emphasized that his support for the new consumption patterns did not reflect a desire for the return of the prerevolutionary aristocracy. When one newspaper correspondent addressed Osman by the old aristocratic titles "bey" and "pasha," Osman responded: "Never address me as Osman Bey or Osman Pasha. I'm perfectly content when I'm called *Mu'alim* Osman." In the Egyptian vernacular, the term suggests a tough and popular "boss" figure, somewhat arbitrary, perhaps shady, but able to inspire wary affection.[100] Mu'alim Osman self-consciously spoke for new, rough-and-ready social forces, and those who shared his values and objectives looked to Osman as an example of their achievements and a defender of their potential. As the new millionaires created by the Open Door came under attack, Osman supported them. They in turn invoked the Osman model.

In the spring of 1982 Rashad Osman (not a relative), an Alexandrian who had made a fortune in wood imports, was the accused in a notorious corruption trial.[101] A year earlier, the journal *al-Musawwar* had featured Rashad in an article titled "An Interview with a Successful Student of Osman Ahmed Osman." The celebration of Rashad's career emphasized the parallels with Osman's life. The article stressed his humble beginnings, his intense loyalty to the people of the Alexandria district he represented in parliament, and his devotion to the ideal of popular development. The interviewer reported that "Rashad Osman considers himself a student in the Academy of Life whose Dean is Engineer Osman Ahmed Osman, deputy prime minister for popular development, and he says he owes a lot to Osman Ahmed Osman's direction and guidance and considers him his ideal in everything."[102] At the time of Rashad's arrest, the same journal charged that the newly rich public figure was an example of a "general phenomenon" that was becoming a familiar subject of novels and movies.[103]

Faced with cases such as Rashad's, Osman did not deny that the new permissiveness associated with his name invited abuse. Nevertheless, for the sake of the new energies released and the new wealth created, he was willing to live with the excesses when and if they occurred. "I'm not against any successful person," said Osman. "Let's hope, in the name of God, that everyone in Egypt becomes a millionaire . . . and if one is a swindler, it doesn't matter."[104] Osman argued that the emergence of the new class of wealthy entrepreneurs should be seen as a good sign because these were the men who would rebuild the country.

Osman believed that the new class of entrepreneurs should look to engineers for assistance; the partnership of businessmen and engineers would create the same blend of technology and capital that Osman had experienced in his own career. Osman's campaign to use his own career as an example for all of society led to his efforts to make the Syndicate of Engineers an equal and cooperative partner of the business community and private companies as they attempted to develop Egypt. Osman argued vigorously for redefinition of the collective role of the estimated

100,000 engineers.[105] In his struggle to transform the syndicate, Osman placed in sharpest relief the kind of public values, structures, and processes he thought were necessary to transform Egypt.

Immediately after his election as head of the Syndicate of Engineers in 1978, Osman set out to change both its character and its purpose, shifting its focus from political to economic issues. Traditionally, professional associations played an active part in the political life of Egypt. In particular, the syndicates provided important platforms for the expression of opposition views and programs. Before his election as its head, Osman had remarked that the Syndicate of Engineers was "suffering from unrest," a euphemism for oppositional political activity. Once in office, Osman sought to curtail the political involvements of the engineers, "imposing," as he put it, "a new style in syndicate work."[106] "The syndicate," explained Osman, "would change from an institution demanding privileges from the state and burdening it to one in which sons of a profession become a productive power capable of active participation in solving society's problems by work and not talk."[107] Osman was quite explicit about his vision: "Instead of playing backgammon and discussing politics, the engineer now wonders whether a macaroni or fruit juice company is a better investment."[108]

Osman argued that the main issues facing engineers were material ones, particularly their inadequate pension provisions. Osman collected union dues more systematically and then invested the funds in the new profitable enterprises made possible by the Open Door.[109] The syndicate used these revenues for a variety of consumer services for the engineers themselves and, most importantly, for reinvestment.[110] Osman tied the syndicate into the new network of financial institutions he was creating by founding an Engineers' Bank and an Engineers' Insurance Company. In addition, he tapped the syndicate treasury to underwrite twenty-four new companies. Many of them were among the new "food sufficiency" consumer-oriented companies such as the Engineers' Company for Food Production and the Engineers' National Company for Soft Drinks.[111] Osman judged that his changes in the Syndicate of Engineers made it a "producing institution, founding numerous projects for the good of the profession, for the good of its members, and for the good of Egypt as a whole."[112]

Osman's attempts to remake the syndicate in the Open Door image did not go uncontested. The Engineers' Bank drew the syndicate into the dubious financial arrangements that were the backdrop for the corruption cases of the early eighties; for example, Tewfik Abdul Hay was accused of marketing tainted food products; an opposition paper revealed on December 29, 1982, that the Engineers' Bank had lent Abdul Hay L.E. 2 million without the usual collateral arrangements.[113] Confronted with such complaints, Osman responded that he could not understand all the fuss; the loan was an internal matter for a private bank that had the freedom to use its money as it saw fit. In the private sphere, Osman explained, one took risks for profit, and a few mistakes were inevitable.[114] Osman viewed the Syndicate of Engineers as a kind of collective entrepreneur, taking its chances like any other in its profit-making ventures.

The depoliticization of the syndicate, some alleged, really meant bringing the engineers into line with the official politics of the Sadat era. Although all the other major syndicates opposed normalization with Israel when it became clear that the Jewish state intended to annex the West Bank, Egypt's engineers found themselves endorsing the "warm" peace. This general point was driven home when the Engineers' Insurance Company insured the Israeli embassy in Cairo when all other insurance companies refused to do so.[115]

When the engineers renominated Osman as syndicate head in 1982, the opposition press aired the debate provoked by Osman's restructuring of the syndicate. A measure of Osman's success in transforming the syndicate came as much in the charges leveled against him as in his eventual electoral victory. Osman, his critics within the syndicate charged, was turning the syndicate into an investment agency "with no place for the true associational spirit." His endorsement by the syndicate's governing board should be no cause for surprise, argued one critical engineer, because Osman had made sure that board members profited handsomely from the syndicate's new activities by a generous system of bonuses and payments for attendance at meetings. The sums involved ran into the thousands; "the scent of the dollar pervades the place."[116]

Unfazed by such criticism, Osman pronounced the day of his reelection the proudest day of his life. Moreover, he worked to share with other professional associations the secrets of his success.[117] In this sphere, too, Osman projected himself as the creator of models for a new Egypt that avoided the mistakes of the Nasser era. Osman succeeded in bringing the engineers into line with Sadat's economic definition of national purpose. Sadat, especially sensitive to the political challenges mounted from the Bar Association, reveled in Osman's victory. The president pointed to the Syndicate of Engineers to illustrate the kind of structures that were needed in his "state of institutions."

Osman, the Arab Contractors, and particularly the company's projects all became symbols of the power and the attraction generated by the Sadat regime's vision of Egypt's future. Like the cartouche of a pharoah, Osman's name was stamped on construction sites throughout the country; the Arab Contractors seemed to be everywhere the new Egypt was being built. The impact on Ramses Square in central Cairo, once dominated by a giant statue of the pharoah, is typical of this process of change. In the seventies, the Arab Contractors built an elevated highway and raised a pedestrian walkway that circled the square and overwhelmed the statute. Ramses' gaze became fixed on a massive and apparently permanent billboard announcing that the construction was the triumph of the Arab Contractors.[118]

Osman Ahmed Osman showed no inclination to deny the centrality of the role his economic empire played in the seventies. An apocryphal story circulated in Cairo that a newly discovered tomb of the pharoahs bore the inscription: "Built by the Arab Contractors–Osman Ahmed Osman & Co." When a reporter asked him about the anecdote, Osman commented with a smile that "nobody knows for sure whether we could have built the pyramids. But I think it is fair to say that I have spent the last 40 years building modern versions of big and little pyramids all over this country."[119]

After 1981, Osman's close political association with Sadat made him a target for the opponents of the slain president's policies.[120] The honorary chairman for life of the Arab Contractors responded defiantly: "There is a group of people whose interest is to bring down anyone who is a success . . . But I will never tire and never leave. I will keep on working and building projects and building Egypt. I . . . am happy that God has granted me all the resources I need to help my country." Osman went on to praise Sadat's successor, Husny Mubarak, for continuing the Open Door policy. The construction magnate explained that the contribution of his company transcended ties to a single ruler. "We will always be friends with the people in power," Osman explained, because "we have the experience."[121] While others talked, Osman liked to say, the Arab Contractors worked.

The company projects, once again, helped make the case. On August 16, 1983, a picture occupying half the front page of *al-Ahram* showed President Mubarak waving from the King Faisal elevated traffic bridge to the huge crowd in the street below. The president, along with the prime minister and the governor of Giza, listened to Osman Ahmed Osman's brother Hussein, chairman of the Arab Contractors' board of directors, explain how the company's completion of this latest bridge contributed to the long-range plans for rebuilding Cairo's transportation.[122]

Mubarak used the occasion of the opening of the King Faisal Bridge to praise Egypt's public-sector companies, and the president singled out the Arab Contractors. "I am proud of it," he said, "and of its workers because of its enormous capacities and the great achievements it realizes for this country." Mubarak defended the company from its detractors: "I reject the hostile attitude toward the company assumed by some . . . The Arab Contractors is a national Egyptian company that has done marvelous work on Egypt's soil, in the service of Egypt's children."[123]

In the fifties and sixties Osman began to formulate his definitions of individual and national purpose. The Arab Contractors then occupied a niche hidden within the public sector of Nasser's socialist Egypt. Sadat, with Osman's cooperation, used these formulations to project a free-enterprise alternative for the seventies and beyond. Osman's model was the prototype for an alternative to Nasser's socialism; moreover, the model had already proved itself in Egypt's special circumstances. For all the importance of Osman's personal political role and the weight of the Arab Contractors in political life in the seventies, Osman always emphasized the concrete projects his company completed and the values, systems, and processes that made them possible. "I am an engineer, not a politician," he was fond of saying. His legacy to Egypt would be the practical works of the company he founded rather than the pronouncements of government officials, himself included.[124] In the eighties, the Arab Contractors empire had assets of over $1.5 billion; 60,000 Egyptian families depended on the company for their livelihood. As Osman saw it, the Arab Contractors had become "an academy or university" to lead the way for the nation.[125]

2

Fighting for Freedom and the Rule of Law: The Bar Association

In political history it is by no means the bare facts which interest us. We wish to understand not only the actions but the actors. Our judgment of the course of political events depends upon our conception of the men who were engaged in them.

—*Ernst Cassirer*

Mustafa Marei chose the platform of the Bar Association for his speech. The Friday afternoon seminars sponsored by the association had been consistently used for the articulation of liberal views and grievances. The open criticisms voiced at the seminars presented a marked contrast to much of public life, where, as one historian caustically put it, "flattery of the ruling party . . . [was] a sacred national duty."[1]

In early 1980 the tension between the lawyers of the Bar Association and the Sadat regime had been heightened by the issuance of a strict security measure called the "law of shameful conduct." The character and timing of the law typified the contentious relationship. According to the lawyers, the law represented an attempt to exploit liberal institutions and ideas for essentially authoritarian political ends. The most significant issue, from the point of view of the Bar Association, was the use of courts and the law itself to achieve repressive objectives of the government. Many lawyers were drawn into the debate over the law of shameful conduct; the intensity and significance of the debate were revealed at the Friday seminar held on February 15, 1980.

Mustafa Marei led the attack on the new measure. Known as the dean of Egyptian lawyers, he combined an expertise on constitutional law and a history of political activism during the pre-1952 national movement.[2] On February 15 Marei rose amidst warm applause to address his colleagues and the nation: "I thank you for this warm reception, which I find myself unable to meet with a similar show of affection. Here lies the difference between my will and my ability. So please accept my old age as the excuse. I have come to comment on the draft of what is called the law of shameful conduct."[3]

Marei spoke about a sweeping security law that he believed violated fundamental constitutional provisions.[4] The law originated with a statement by President Sadat that "our crisis is one of morals and for that reason I request that we issue a 'law of shameful conduct.' "[5] The measure subsequently proposed made failure to uphold the regime's view of the values of religion, family, national unity, and social peace a criminal act punishable by exclusion from certain types of employment and limitations on political rights. A special Court of Values, outside regular judicial channels, would prosecute offenses.

The government timed issuance of the law of shameful conduct to coincide with termination of the state of emergency in effect since Sadat had taken power in 1970. The president announced both measures as part of the official liberalization. The Bar Association had consistently called for an end to the state of emergency. The Governing Council of the association pointed out, however, that the regime's action was a ruse. The law of shameful conduct explicitly applied to acts punishable under the most repressive security laws, including one that restricted political participation and another that criminalized criticism of the 1979 peace treaty with Israel. Members of the council argued that the new security measure legalized, in effect, the worst of the emergency decrees. According to the lawyers, instead of ending the state of emergency, Sadat's law of shameful conduct debased the legal system itself to a tool of repression.[6]

The liberal opposition to the law of shameful conduct first crystallized as a debate among lawyers. Although the Bar Association spanned all major political views, its commitment to free speech as the basic requirement of public life transcended partisan allegiances; the majority of the lawyers regarded the new security law as an attack on that right.[7] Liberals occupied a special position in the association because of the status they had acquired from their key role in the struggle against the British before 1952.[8] Fear that the law of shameful conduct would destroy their right to speak for the nation on the issues of democracy and the national interest impelled the liberal lawyers to act. They carried the majority of the lawyers with them in their opposition to the new security law.

In a Bar Association seminar held two weeks before Marei's address, three distinguished lawyers challenged the professional propriety of assisting the regime in drawing up the security laws. One speaker attacked those lawyers who "betrayed their integrity and their conscience" by working with the regime to formulate unconstitutional laws. All joined in urging the association not to limit its role to holding a seminar and then dispersing. Egypt's lawyers and judges should "debate the proposal to death" and bring its violation of human rights to international attention.[9]

Mustafa Marei stepped into this energized environment to deliver an authoritative indictment of the Sadat liberalization. Approximately 2,000 people, including Egypt's foremost lawyers and judges, had packed the Bar Association hall in Cairo to hear him. Not all present were supporters. Fikry Makram Ebeid, lawyer, deputy prime minister, and secretary general of the ruling National Democratic Party (NDP), dissented from Marei's critical views. A group of NDP members who backed Ebeid broke in on the meeting before Marei reached the podium and chanted slogans to prevent the seminar from proceeding. These interruptions subsided when Ebeid urged restraint, and Marei was able to speak.

For Marei, the core idea of the inherited constitutional tradition was the control of arbitrary power, whether domestic or foreign. In his view, the issue of public freedoms was inseparable from national independence, since the free citizen was the basis of a free country.[10] Based on these shared liberal assumptions, Marei's lecture evoked reverence for the constitution and the law, reaffirmed the centrality of institutions to life in society, and exemplified the imperative to challenge arbitrary power and foreign pressure.[11] According to Marei, the official rhetoric of the "rule of law" and "a state of institutions" was not true liberalism. Even the reduction of repression, enlargement of the social role of law, and increased discussion of domestic public policy did not suffice to meet the tests of constitutional governance. In Marei's view a genuine liberal order made the ruler himself subject to the constitution. Only a constitutional system would guarantee freedom and win the mass support needed to shield Egypt from foreign pressure.[12]

To all the key provisions of the law of shameful conduct, Marei replied: "No, you are not calling things by their right names." Defending truthfulness and precision in the use of language, Marei criticized the use of "deceitful" phrases as "shameful conduct" in themselves: "in appearance they aim to protect society from shameful conduct, but in reality they seek to shield the regime from criticism." He drew particular attention to the paragraphs in the proposed legislation that aimed to restrict criticism. Phrases such as "offending public sensibilities" and "publishing biased news" cast so wide a net that they would not allow any criticism, however moderate, to pass through them. Marei charged that the law of shameful conduct aimed to silence critics by depriving them of legal protection. The provision in the law for a special Court of Values weakened the independence of the courts. The decree of the minister of justice establishing the new court made it a quasi-judicial body. Only four of its seven members were professional judges: the remaining three were appointed by the government from the general public. These appointments, Marei argued, violated explicit constitutional guarantees of judicial independence.[13] Only courts formed of trained professionals who enjoyed immunity were "courts in the true sense." Marei concluded that "when the law instead of the whip is used to control pens and tongues, we have committed a mistake more serious than using the whip itself. For law is then the tool used for beating in place of the whip." He noted gravely that the "supremacy of the law will remain an empty slogan if we take away its essence . . . We'll return to the days of sequestration and detention camps."[14]

In response to Marei's mention of detention camps, the secretary general of the NDP announced from the floor that the aged critic had "exceeded all boundaries." The remark signaled the end of restraint. One NDP member shouted that "there are no detention camps under Sadat, but if they did exist, Marei should be the first detained." Fighting broke out. "The environment of democratic debate was destroyed," wrote the correspondent of one opposition paper.[15] A group of young lawyers shielded Marei and led him from the hall. As Marei left, his supporters sang a nationalist anthem identified with the 1919 revolution and the liberal era it inaugurated. The government security forces that had surrounded the building did not intervene to protect Marei or to restore order.

Within hours, reports of the confrontation circulated throughout the capital. The small opposition press printed the text of the speech and accounts of the disruptions. The portrayal of the rough clash of so distinguished a figure with the NDP members had a galvanizing effect. Intellectuals around the country mounted a sustained attack on the law of shameful conduct. The Governing Council of the Bar Association spearheaded the campaign, defying government threats to dissolve the group.[16] Authentic liberalism, Marei demonstrated, remained a force in Egyptian public life.

*   *   *

Marei had reminded the liberals who they were and what they stood for. His criticism of the regime drew on a constitutional tradition with deep roots in Egypt. Liberalism was originally a Western import but adherents in Egypt adapted it to their own needs. Egyptian middle-class liberals, calling for the creation of a constitutional system, formed the heart of a powerful secular wing of nationalists who struggled against the British. As a result of the liberals' connection to the nationalist movement, liberalism in Egypt became an ideology concerned with both the Western intrusion into Egypt and the assertion of political rights and liberties. In the late nineteenth and early twentieth centuries the ideal of a free nation, an end in itself for the liberals, was also a means of mobilizing the people against colonialism.

Liberal nationalists were not alone in challenging foreign power and seeking to recreate an Egyptian political system; both reformist and radical Islamic groups and radical but secular socialist nationalists issued similar appeals. The reformist Islamic trend looked to a revitalized Islam to provide the moral foundations of a community able to protect Egypt. Both the liberals and the reformist Islamic movement acknowledged that the British had certain rights in Egypt; both also accepted the general structure of society as it existed within the colonial systems. The radical counterparts of these groups challenged the strategy of compromise with British power and demanded a restructuring of the social order. During the struggle for national independence and a constitutional order, therefore, the Egyptian liberals were flanked on one side by the autocratic rule of the occupying colonial authorities and on the other side by competing ideologies that called for radical resistance and revolutionary change.

Egyptian constitutionalism, so valued by the liberals, developed in a colonial context.[17] In the late nineteenth century the Egyptian monarchy turned to a diluted form of representational government to bolster the popularity of the throne in the face of foreign pressures. Prosperous Egyptians welcomed the idea of constitutional government because it would enlarge their public role; in addition, constitutionalism was compatible with restrictions on voting, rights to representation, and certain legal codes, all of which could be used to contain anarchic pressures from the lower levels of society. Egypt's first constitutions, in 1872 and 1882, served both purposes: they helped consolidate popular support for the British while restricting political participation in the middle and upper classes.

Two nationalist upheavals eventually broke the link between constitutionalism and the crown. The first was the revolt of the Egyptian army led by Colonel Ahmed Arabi in 1882; the second was the revolution of 1919. The Arabi revolt precipitated the occupation of Egypt by the British, who used outbreaks of mass disorder in Alexandria as an excuse to intervene. The second nationalist wave, in 1919, convinced the crown that its own position was endangered by anarchic forces from below. To save itself, the palace formed an authoritarian and reactionary alliance with the occupying power.

The destructive potential of upheaval from below also alarmed the middle class, although many remained committed to a constitutional form of government. By focusing their attacks on the authoritarianism of the crown and the illegality of the colonial presence, Egyptian constitutionalists hoped to direct mass energy toward constructive nationalist objectives that would at the same time defuse potential threats to the social order from lower-class revolutionaries. Henceforth in Egypt, the struggle for freedom from foreign domination and the rule of law defined the middle-class liberal nationalist movement.

The Wafd Party embodied this liberal platform. During the First World War, economic hardships under the British occupation stimulated the beginnings of organized nationalism, led by secular educated professionals but with strong backing from landowners. With its primary goal of independence from British rule, the movement tried to win recognition of its role in public life by a request to attend the Paris Peace Conference in order to speak for Egypt's national interest. When the British refused to allow the Egyptian delegation, or *wafd,* to present Egypt's case to the conference, popular uprisings convulsed the country. The nationalist party, calling itself the Wafd, demanded independence and a new constitution; it aimed "to seek the freedom and independence of the country from the hold of the British usurper."[18] Faced with mass unrest and an organized nationalist leadership, the British in 1922 unilaterally declared Egypt independent and withdrew from the country.

The independence outlined in the 1922 declaration, however, came with British strings. Britain reserved to itself the right of a military presence in Egypt to secure communications, protect foreign nationals, and guarantee Egyptian defense. The 1923 constitution codified this compromise with British power. The Anglo-Egyptian Treaty of 1936 modified the arrangement slightly by officially ending the British presence in Egypt proper, terminating the special privileges accorded to foreigners, and recognizing Egypt and Britain as equal sovereign states. Nevertheless, Egypt had to accept a British military base in the Suez

Canal zone and pledge to Britain access to strategic resources in the event of war.

Many of the powers of governance that Britain gave up in 1922 moved to the throne rather than to the people or to the educated strata that claimed to speak for them. The constitution stipulated a bicameral parliament, with a lower house elected by limited suffrage and an upper house including some members appointed from a restricted pool of governmental officials or landowners and professionals. Through the appointed members, the crown controlled the passage of laws in the upper house. The palace also had the unconditional right to dissolve the lower house, appoint and remove military officers, and manage the affairs of the religious schools and al-Azhar University.

The extent of the powers reserved to the throne by the 1923 constitution so disturbed the Wafdists that they boycotted the constitutional convention. Later the Wafd accepted the new arrangements, fearing that disputes over the distribution of power might hinder an overall agreement on the basis of which the British would leave the country. Moreover, the constitution did designate the nation, rather than the ruling dynasty, as the source of legitimate authority. Therefore, in 1924 the Wafd participated in elections held under the auspices of the new constitution and subsequently defended it.

According to the constitution, government affairs would be run by the cabinet, and the king's signature on official documents was valid only if cosigned by the cabinet members. The cabinet was appointed by and solely responsible to the lower house; the prime minister and cabinet enjoyed immunity from the arbitrary authority of the crown. In addition to this distribution of power, the constitution provided explicit guarantees of individual civil liberties and political rights. These rights included the sanctity of homes and property, the right to form associations, and the freedoms of belief, opinion, assembly, and the press. Within this constitutional framework the liberals made such important social and political gains as the law of criminal procedure, affirmations of the independence of the judiciary and the universities, the required use of Arabic as the official language, provisions for workmen's compensation and social security, and prohibitions against foreign ownership of agricultural land.[19] From the liberal point of view, the British departure and the codification of these basic constitutional and political rights gave substance to the values and objectives of liberalism and became a source of authority and confidence for future struggles.

The political order established by the 1923 constitution brought a three-way struggle for power among the British, the throne, and the middle-class nationalists of the Wafd. The political debates of the twenties and thirties reflected tensions between nationalism and democracy on the one hand and British power and authoritarianism on the other.[20] Throughout this period the Wafd Party led the liberal movement's campaign for national independence and a democratic constitution. Under the 1923 constitution, however, the liberals were forced to concede a central political role to the authoritarian crown and its supporting parties, thereby enabling the British to assert their power through an alliance with the throne. The 1936 agreement permitting British military rights was a product of that alliance. Thus, the Wafd leaders failed to create the conditions of national independence and democracy that they were seeking, although they were instrumental in establishing a political arena in which the Wafd could legitimately lead the liberal nationalist struggle.

In this context Wafdist leaders adopted a nonviolent, legalistic approach to resistance. Their ultimate aim was to lodge decisive power in parliament, where the educated secular elite and the landed classes could use moderate means to press for eventual British withdrawal. As part of this strategy, the Wafd conceded certain limited rights to both the British and the crown, although they expected eventually to limit these powers severely. They exerted pressure against the British through negotiations, and they hoped to strengthen the constitution's limits on the king's authority.

The actual political battles led by the Wafdists clarified the abstract ideological meaning and practical importance of Egyptian liberalism.[21] On a theoretical level, the liberal nationalists linked the idea of the state as the center of independent authority with a commitment to a form of government responsible to qualified representatives of the people. For the Wafdists, these principles were manifested in the specific struggle to limit the power of the king and to increase Egypt's rights as an independent and sovereign nation vis-à-vis the British. The new elites with modern secular educations joined the sons of the old landowning class in leading these struggles.

The liberals' compromises with the British and the throne were dictated by their belief in the destructive consequences for Egypt of radical political actions. By the liberal reading of history, the violent resistance of Arabi had done little more than precipitate direct British occupation. Given these assumptions, compromise and accommodation seemed the only effective strategy available to the nation. Sa'ad Zaghloul, founder of the Wafd, wrote: "I am the first to follow any course in the interest of my country. As far as I can see, the path open before me to realize the nation's aims is negotiation . . . If you or anyone else can see any other way to retrieve the nation's rights, show me and I will be the first to pursue it."[22] Having ruled out radical alternatives, the political language of liberalism framed the struggle against the British as a "case" to be "defended" by "delegations representing the people" and using "legal" means. Thus, the legalistic style of the liberal struggle had roots more profound than the law school backgrounds of nationalist leaders. Given their stake in the established order and their sense of the lessons of history, the legal style defined the essence of the national struggle the liberal nationalists could wage.[23]

Despite the important national and democratic goals achieved by the liberals, the continued stalemate between the authoritarian crown and the democratic Wafd created conditions that exaggerated the role of various minority aristocratic parties, which by allying themselves with the king could come to power despite their minority position. In 1930 a minority government suspended the 1923 constitution and replaced it with an autocratic document that strengthened the power of the throne. The liberals immediately issued a call to defend the 1923 constitution. This denial of constitutionally guaranteed rights and power reinforced their belief that a powerful constitutional order was essential for the protection of national independence and democracy.

Ironically, the Wafd itself precipitated the final collapse of the constitutional framework. Its legalistic strategy did not move rapidly enough for the growing anti-British sentiment of its mass membership. The intensity of that sentiment pushed the party leaders to abrogate the 1936 treaty, and thereby to undermine two props on which the political order rested. The abrogation denied legality to the British presence in Egypt and weakened the legitimacy of the monarchy that had sanctioned the treaty.[24] At this critical juncture, party leaders rejected the possibility that the Wafd could transform itself and guide a popular struggle for complete national independence and full democratic rights.[25] The way was opened instead for more radical forces with new claims to legitimacy and different political strategies.

In 1952, nationalist conspirators in the military, led by Colonel Gamal Abdul Nasser and calling themselves the Free Officers, seized power. The new regime attempted to eliminate all aspects of liberal action and thought that could be seen as an alternative to Nasserist rule. Toward this end, the military rulers abrogated the 1923 constitution and replaced it on December 10, 1952, with one that granted strong executive authority to the president. The official documents of the 1952 revolution denigrated the historic role of the constitutional nationalists, and thus denied the legitimacy of the liberals' struggles. The regime removed liberal spokesmen from public life and attacked their institutional bases, interfering in the internal affairs of such liberal strongholds as the Bar Association. In 1953 the government banned all existing political parties, including the Wafd, and prohibited the formation of new ones.

According to the liberal historians, the greatest sin of the military rulers was the suppression of the 1923 constitution and the political parties. In their view, ratification of the new constitution by referendum and all subsequent constitutional arrangements devised by the Free Officers were only a screen to conceal the reality of arbitrary military rule.

In 1956 the Nasser regime created the first of a series of one-party organizations to replace the multiparty system. The government announced that these political structures would give the mass of Egyptians an opportunity to participate in the new revolutionary political order. The liberals regarded these government parties (the Liberation Rally, the National Union, and the Arab Socialist Union) as efforts merely to fill the political vacuum created by the dissolution of the Wafd and other historic political parties "with artificial organizations that found no real echo or response from the people." In fact, the regime itself recognized that the successive Nasserist parties never succeeded in winning the political loyalties of the masses. The liberals attributed this failure to the political impotence of the official parties; none of these organizations, they pointed out, exercised any real check on the absolute power of the military rulers. The parties' occasional criticisms of official policies were simply a "form of self-criticism used by dictatorships and totalitarian systems to absorb mass discontent and give the illusion of an opposing opinion." The official party forums ignored all the large abuses of power by the government, notably the consistent violations of the political and civil rights of its critics.[26]

To explain the ease with which the military rulers suppressed constitutionalism, the liberals emphasized the people's failure to remain committed to the values and institutions of democratic government. As a result, the nation was vulnerable to the dynamic leadership of an individual leader. Although the one-party structures never won popular support, the liberals acknowledged that Nasser himself exerted a magnetic hold on the masses. According to one historian, "our people became attached to some of their rulers to a degree approaching mania and worship, as in the case of the late President Gamal Abdul Nasser. The people regarded him as divine."[27] The liberals believed that adoration for Nasser obscured the authoritarian features of Free Officer rule.

In spite of the hostile conditions created by popular support for a repressive regime, liberalism remained a presence in Egyptian political life. Whenever the regime relaxed its grip on political debate, the liberals expanded the scope of their discussions and activities.[28] They never ceased to claim that they spoke for the nation; they consistently used their forums and meetings as platforms for criticism of the regime and its denial of constitutionally guaranteed political and civil rights. Finally, through their own activities and behavior, they preserved the existence of a lived liberal alternative to the Nasserist system; they relentlessly asserted the right to free speech and to protection of individual rights. Throughout the period of Nasserist rule the Bar Association experienced various forms and degrees of political harassment. Nevertheless, it continued to provide the critically needed space that allowed the liberals to pursue their objectives. During the Nasserist period, the story of the Bar Association is in fact the collective history of the struggles of the liberal alternative in Egypt.

Nasserist repression of the liberals began early. In March 1954 General Muhammad Naguib, who had served as the figurehead for the younger Free Officers, called for return of the army officers to the barracks and restoration of a multiparty system.[29] The professionals, including the majority of the lawyers, sided with Naguib. Once his power was secure, Nasser retaliated by dismissing the Governing Council of the Bar Association and banning its general assembly meetings for four years. Undaunted, the lawyers at their first opportunity in 1958 elected an open advocate of syndicate autonomy, Mustafa al-Baradie, as head of the association. Baradie did not disappoint the expectations his reputation aroused. At a time when the Nasser regime was turning with increased frequency to exceptional measures such as confiscation of property and preventive detention, the new association head called for the formation of a supreme constitutional court empowered to rule on the constitutionality of all laws. The project was stillborn, but the idea survived as part of the liberal legacy.

The regime's repression of the Bar Association often reflected changing political conditions at home or abroad. For example, in 1961–1962 the regime was shaken by Syria's secession from the United Arab Republic, which had linked Egypt and Syria since 1958. Nasser blamed the move on reactionary forces in Syria and warned against similar antirevolutionary social forces at home. He singled out the professional syndicates as bourgeois strongholds and dangerous anachronisms in a socialist society. With a heightened sense of the dangers they posed, the president called for a national discussion of a new charter to buttress the revolution.

The liberals interpreted the government reaction to the Syrian secession as an indication of possible weakness; in their view, the call for national debate and a new charter was simply a way to justify a tightening of government control. Instead of succumbing to government intimidation, Baradie used the debate over the new charter as an occasion to articulate a series of demands that represented a liberal view of Egypt's future. In a speech to the official committee charged with drafting the charter, Baradie called for constitutional limits on arbitrary state power. He argued for an Arab notion of democracy based on consultation, which he described as "the Islamic system that limited the rights of the ruler." In his remarks Baradie weighted political freedoms as heavily as social justice, thus implicitly questioning official priorities. He called for freedom of opinion, a political opposition, and an independent press. Baradie countered official charges that syndicates were "factions that split society" with a courageous demand for cessation of government interference in syndicate affairs.[30] Baradie's defiance of regime pressure has become a centerpiece of liberal histories of the Nasser years.

The regime met Baradie's challenge with a campaign under the banner of socialist democracy to transform the "bourgeois" associations into mass mobilization organizations. Regime spokesmen urged the government party to exert more control over all popular organizations, including professional syndicates, labor unions, and student unions.[31] The success of the official campaign was reflected in the growing strength of the government-supported socialist trend within the Bar Association. Socialist arguments advanced during association meetings received greater attention; in 1965 a series of lectures at the association that put forward a socialist agenda was subsequently published in the law journal. In 1966 the term *socialist* was added to the journal's title, a further indication of the political debate within the lawyers' community. Some opposed socialism at all times, others thought it a necessary evil to secure a minimum of welfare in a poor country, and still others believed that the liberal commitment to freedom could survive only if the material conditions of the people were improved through socialist measures. Out of these discussions a consensus took shape that any implementation of socialism in Egypt was unthinkable unless it was paired with democratic institutions and freedoms.[32]

Clearly, the Bar Association shifted with the socialist wind; but liberal historians point out that constitutional forces did not lose every battle. For example, the regime sought to dilute the Bar Association's alleged elitism by pushing for the admission of public-sector employees who had law degrees. These employees, tied directly to the regime, would weaken the corporate sense of the lawyers and position important government officials within the association. The Bar Association fiercely and successfully resisted this move until 1968, when the parliament finally compelled admission of the public-sector lawyers. By then this was not a significant defeat, because the regime had been politically weakened as a result of the defeat by Israel. In addition, the lawyers minimized the effect of the admission of public-sector employees by isolating them within the organization, thus assuring that they had only a minimal effect on the activities and objectives of the association.

Baradie's success in shielding free syndicates meant that after the 1967 defeat the Bar Association could do more than just hold on.[33] The syndicate revived Baradie's earlier demand for a supreme constitutional court. Ahmed al-Khawaga, who succeeded Baradie as association head, condemned rule by exceptional measures and called for legal codification of the revolution.[34] In support of Khawaga, distinguished voices in the association articulated the liberal consensus that "the social freedoms won by socialism are no substitute for political freedoms; they are rather their social base."[35] The lawyers exploited the regime's vulnerability by pressing for legal and constitutional limits to official power, and they sustained these pressures upon Nasser's successor, Anwar Sadat.

Though an original Free Officer and Nasser's designated successor, Sadat had only a hazy public image when he assumed power in the fall of 1970. In May Sadat moved successfully against a coalition of powerful figures from Nasser's entourage who openly opposed him. His hand strengthened by the elimination of his most powerful rivals, Sadat began to distance himself from the Nasserist legacy with announcements of the dawning of a new "era of legality." The new president demonstrated his disapproval of the Nasserist disdain for legalities by a dramatic burning of the files of the secret police. The enthusiastic public response to this gesture confirmed Sadat's belief that de-Nasserization under a liberal banner would be widely popular in Egypt. The regime reinstated suspended judges, released political prisoners, and closed the hated detention camps that symbolized Nasserist repression. Voices from the pre-

1952 liberal age led the nation in celebrating the changed political climate "that enabled people to sleep at night without fear of the knock at dawn [of the secret police] from which Egypt and all honorable Egyptians had suffered for such a long time."[36]

In 1971 Sadat stimulated further liberal hopes when he promulgated a new constitution, which he claimed would give lasting content to his "experiment in democracy." Constitutionalism, in the liberal view, indicated Egypt's political maturity as a nation. "We are not like new nations or developing countries," pronounced an article in the law journal. "We were the fifth country in the world to have a constitution derived from the will of the people."[37] The Sadat constitution marked a considerable step forward from the Nasserist arrangements. In contrast to previous constitutional documents, the 1971 constitution included an article explicitly stating that the regime was based on the rule of law. Other articles guaranteed to Egyptians virtually all the internationally recognized political liberties and human rights.

Despite these advances, the power relations among government institutions specified in the 1971 document aroused liberal misgivings. The president of the republic was the chief of state, head of government, and supreme commander of the armed forces. In broad terms, he formulated and executed the general policy of the government. Article 108 also authorized the president in emergency situations to issue decrees having the force of law. Furthermore, in cases in which national unity or security was threatened, the president could adopt "urgent measures" to be ratified by a referendum within sixty days. The liberals noted that the constitution contained no mechanism for controlling the exercise of these great emergency powers, and thus created the potential to legalize tyranny.

The liberals concluded that Sadat did not share their understanding of the appropriate relationship between president and people in a constitutional order. In their view, the citizens of an independent state enjoyed certain liberties by right and not by the indulgence of government. Sadat, on the other hand, had described the official liberalization as his personal gift to the patiently suffering Egyptian people. The president boasted that as "father of the Egyptian people" he had written the basic document of his new liberal order in one evening and with the help of a single legal specialist. This cavalier attitude disturbed the liberals.[38]

A great deal would depend on whether or not the regime used the extraordinary powers available to it, and for what purposes. Almost immediately, Sadat made it clear that while law would play an enlarged role in regulating public life, his own authority had no legal bounds.[39] Under Sadat, Egypt was governed under a state of emergency for all but seventeen months. The president, under the enabling constitutional provisions, exercised the sweeping executive powers of arrest and detention as a means of defending his regime and its policies from domestic criticism and opposition. Over the decade the government chipped away at independent political activity; only the independence of the courts kept the damage within certain bounds. Legal authority and constitutional government were in effect used as the political weapons of a political system.

The regime used the powers of the presidency to revolutionize domestic and foreign policy with an economic and political liberalization and an international realignment with the West that included an accommodation with Israel. These drastic policy reorientations met resistance. In the streets the Egyptian people questioned the government's response to the threat that the power of Israel posed to Egyptian national interests. They also protested the economic hardships of the poor at a time when there was a conspicuous display of new wealth. The regime responded to the disturbances with tight security laws that were routinely legitimated by manipulated mass referenda. The government repression of the popular protests alienated the lawyers and led them to join the opponents of the regime.

The first wave of protest was provoked by the government's refusal to act against Israel, thus perpetuating the stalemated situation of "neither war nor peace" that was draining Egypt. From 1971 to October 1973, university students and workers demonstrated periodically for the renewal of armed resistance to Israel. To contain the unrest, the government issued three new security laws that criminalized vaguely described activities such as "propagating information likely to impair national unity."[40] The security laws also weakened existing procedures that protected those detained or arrested. Sadat's surprise attack on Israel in October 1973 quieted the voices that had protested his inaction, but the new laws remained as a deterrent to future antigovernment protests.

In January 1977 a government decision to reduce food subsidies set off food riots in cities throughout Egypt. The government responded with Law 2 of 1977, the most restrictive measure yet enacted. This law allowed a sentence of life imprisonment with hard labor for membership in a clandestine and armed organization hostile to the state, for participation in a damaging strike, or for planning or taking part in demonstrations that endangered public security. Although the main participants in the riots were the urban poor, the regime clearly aimed these new security measures at political and social organizations that might provide leadership for the discontented urban dwellers.

The regime used the third cluster of oppressive security measures, culminating in the law of shameful conduct, to preempt opposition to Sadat's peace initiative with Israel. These measures circumscribed the political rights of anyone active in political life before 1952 and outlawed their employment in government or communications. Two of the measures (Law 40 of 1977 on Political Parties and Law 33 of 1978 on the Protection of the Internal Front and Social Peace) explicitly forbade public criticism of the peace treaty with Israel.

The Bar Association reacted to each of the new security measures with a determined defense of the right to peaceful public criticism of government policies. Each of the security provisions was declared to be a violation of the constitutionally guaranteed freedoms. The lawyers backed up their protests by offering legal assistance to those charged with violations of any of the new security laws. They also denounced the referenda conducted by the regime to secure popular endorsement of the repressive measures. The lawyers charged that the official referenda were vaguely worded, combined too many disparate elements, and were conducted in an atmosphere of intimidation. Such questionable procedures, they insisted, could in no way substitute for constitutional processes.[41] In addition to challenging the constitutionality and legality of the government repression, many of the lawyers sympathized with some or all of the objectives and complaints of the demonstrators. For the Bar Association, opposition to the security laws came to represent both defense of the principles of liberal political action and an attempt to support those who shared the liberals' view of Egypt's future.

The Bar Association statement issued in reaction to the food riots in 1977 demonstrated its opposition to the security laws and to the ways they were enforced by the government.[42] Although the lawyers rejected "the destruction that occurred, because it only hurts our national economy," they supported the right of ordinary Egyptians to peaceful demonstration as "a means for the masses to express themselves." The association was clearly sympathetic to the substantive demands of the protesters. In addition, the lawyers criticized the government for following improper procedures in reducing subsidies on basic commodities; in their view, the government should have consulted with mass organizations before the price hikes. The lawyers also suggested that government economic policies helped cause the disturbances by contributing to a growing gap between the mass of the poor and a small group of newly rich Egyptians who derived disproportionate benefit from the economic liberalization: "The Egyptian and Arab people are ready to make sacrifices and carry the necessary burdens as long as this is done to benefit all Egyptians and not small groups of exploiters." The association urged that the government address the maldistribution of income by providing wages for increased productivity, raising minimum wages, lessening wage differentials, curbing the growing signs of conspicuous consumption, and planning the country's economic strategy more efficiently. Above all, the association warned the government that "regardless of the causes of recent events, they should not be used as pretexts to curb freedoms or destroy the sovereignty of law." According to the lawyers, not less but "more freedom is the proper avenue for realizing national liberation and progress."[43] Through their statement in response to the food riots, the lawyers made the argument for their vision of an Egyptian future that combined economic development, social welfare, a political climate that protected free speech, and democratic values.

Before the 1977 food riots and the Bar Association's open support of the demonstrators, Sadat had come to believe that the lawyers would be willing partners in the building of his new social order. This assumption was largely based on official confidence that the Bar Association had been politically tamed by two decades of military rule. Developments in the Syndicate of Engineers reinforced this perception of the Bar Association as a potential ally, under Osman Ahmed Osman's leadership the Syndicate of Engineers had in fact been brought fully into line with government policies. Sadat's perception of the changed character of the syndicates was a critical factor in his attempt to enlist middle-class professionals in his revival of the private sector and to establish a closer relationship with the West.

Sadat appealed for the lawyers' support on several different levels. He promised that in the future Egypt's government would be run by legal rather than administrative means, with a greatly increased role for lawyers. Commenting on the Nasser years, Sadat observed that "during the first twenty years of the revolution, when the rule of law was 'suspended,' fortunes of the lawyers deteriorated. The legal business practically came to a standstill, and many lawyers actually went bankrupt or were on the verge of bankruptcy." All that had changed in the seventies: "The legal business has . . . regained its earlier vitality in every respect." With the expansion of the private sector and the return of foreign companies, there were, Sadat claimed, lucrative new opportunities for lawyers in the role of middlemen for foreign investors.[44]

As part of its strategy to attract their support, the government offered the lawyers possibilities for greater political participation. The regime made a concerted effort to draw lawyers into the government at all levels; the increase in the number of ministers with a legal background drew particular attention. The involvement of prominent members of the legal professional enhanced the aura of political liberalization. The presence of lawyers in the cabinet diluted the military coloration of the regime, without affecting in any substantial way the power position of the military establishment.[45]

The positive response of some individuals to these various appeals, however, did not mean the lawyers ceased to exist as an autonomous collective body, nor did it indicate that the lawyers as a collective group had accepted the roles the government defined for them. Important facts of Egyptian public life in the seventies, notably the autonomy of the judiciary, the continued appeal of the Wafd, and the vitality of the Bar Association as a critical force, are all part of a submerged history of liberal resistance to official harassments and blandishments. The Bar Association's role in this history was to create a public space that protected and encouraged the liberal values and goals shared by many lawyers. This experience of common activities and objectives separate from those of the government helped to strengthen the lawyers' commitment to both liberal ideology and practices.

In the Sadat years, the Egyptian judiciary buttressed the liberal consciousness by demonstrating autonomy in the face of the regime's attempt to use the courts to enforce its will by "legal" rather than administrative means. The judges acted in such a way as to preserve the liberal heritage of legality and constitutionality. In a series of major political trials, judges preserved the essential distinction made by the liberals between legitimate political criticism and violent subversion. In the most controversial cases, such as those stemming from the January 1977 riots, they observed due process for the accused. The percentage of acquittals for those charged with political crimes was consistently high at all levels of the judiciary, including the state security courts appointed by presidential decree.[46] Despite the regime's efforts, the lawyers and judges ensured that the courts remained a sanctuary for liberal values and practices such as free speech, legitimate political discourse, and an independent judicial system.

The establishment of the New Wafd Party in 1978 was seen as one further example of official political liberalization under Sadat.[47] In fact, the rebirth of the Wafd is important primarily for the independent and unanticipated response it evoked from liberals. Fuad Serrag Eddine, former general secretary of the Wafd Party and a member of its conservative, predominantly landowning wing, spearheaded the campaign to recreate the party that had led the liberal movement against the British and the throne. The decision to permit the New Wafd to become a legitimate political opposition reflected Sadat's belief that the prerevolutionary traditions of Egyptian political life could be used to legitimate the new political order. Sadat apparently thought that since the leaders of the New Wafd were too old to be effective and the new party was but a shadow of its namesake, his decision would create an appearance of political openness and debate without posing any real challenge to the secure position of the government party. But the New Wafd quickly demonstrated that it would be more than a harmless token of official liberalization; instead of being stillborn, as Sadat expected, the New Wafd was, as Serrag Eddine put it, "born a giant."[48] Egyptians by the thousands rallied to the party's first public meetings in a quarter-century. Within four months, this popular response caused the regime to repress the New Wafd.[49]

The surprisingly vital tradition of liberal political activity that had survived the ban on liberal politics bolstered the New Wafd. This political past created certain expectations of the roles and purposes of political parties. Mustafa Marei explained that "even if the present political parties in Egypt are limited, we still do not begin from zero. We have a past in which parties took principled stands and rendered services to the nation."[50] Because lawyers were a key component of the pre-1952 political class, the Bar Association in particular clung to this historical consciousness. "We are not strangers to this country," announced one liberal lawyer in a lecture at the association; "we are Egyptians with an old heritage."[51] As the liberals saw it, Egyptians had a political history in which the constitution and not the arbitrary whim of rulers sanctioned parties. They assessed the Sadat reforms according to the standards set during the formative experiences of the twenties, when the concept of a political life based on parties received classic expression. Liberal conceptions of this period were dominated by the idea of the Wafd as a political party that genuinely expressed the will of the people. When the crown challenged the party's legality in 1925, the Egyptian judiciary upheld the constitutional basis of the Wafd's right to function as a political party under Article 21 of the 1923 constitution. Liberal historians emphasized that the Wafd owed its existence to "constitutional guarantees affirmed by the judiciary and not to the government."[52]

To the liberals, the history of the Wafd highlighted the essential components of democratic political activity: a constitutional order, an independent judiciary, and a legal opposition. The potential effectiveness of these political principles was demonstrated during the twenties, when competition between the Wafd and the minority parties placed real limits on the exercise of arbitrary power. In the light of these positive results, liberal historians felt justified in de-emphasizing the corruption of some Wafd members: "These are faults to be found in parties and their cadres all over the world, even in the most democratic of states." As the liberals saw it, the existence of authentic opposition parties that could legally challenge the ruling party overshadowed all other shortcomings of the Wafd before 1952.[53]

The liberal lawyers applied this heritage in the way they evaluated and responded to Sadat's experiment in democracy. The liberals welcomed Sadat's announced intention to return to a multiparty system, but they could not accept his limitations on the scope of party activity or his judgment that a long period of tutelage in democratic party life would be necessary; Egyptians already had a rich democratic tradition and experience with party politics. The liberals also criticized the party law of 1977 (as amended in 1979 and 1980) because of its extensive restrictions on the right to form parties, participate in them, discuss a full range of public issues, and publish and distribute party papers.[54] According to the liberals, these restrictions contradicted the historic values of liberal government and compromised the political rights guaranteed by the constitution.

Fuad Serrag Eddine announced the formation of the New Wafd Party at the Bar Association's celebration of the birth of the nationalist hero and founder of the Wafd, Saad Zaghloul. He chose this occasion in order to underscore the connection between the Bar Association as the guardian of liberal traditions and the Wafd as the major institution enabling Egyptian lawyers to play a role in the national campaign for independence and democracy. In his opening speech on August 23, 1977, association head Mustafa al-Baradie called for restoration of the Wafd after the distortions it had suffered at the hands of the military rulers. As a result of official efforts to malign the liberal age, Baradie lamented, "a new generation of lawyers do not know their country's past."[55] "The Bar Association," Baradie announced, "is pleased that the leaders of the Egyptian revolution, Mustafa Kamel, Muhammad Farid, and Sa'ad Zaghloul, were all members of this association." Their training as lawyers, Baradie continued, "enabled them to reach such a level of struggle for the sake of the nation, Arabism, right, and justice," and the Wafd enabled lawyers to play this nationalist role. In contrast to the positive role exerted by nationalist lawyers and the struggle against the throne, Baradie argued that the coup of 1952 and the regime it brought to power were marked by "wars, defeats, loss of values, and the destruction of free citizens."[56]

In his address Serrag Eddine used this harsh assessment to reassert the Wafdist claim to Egypt's future. The Free Officers' regime had tried to deny the legitimacy of the liberals' role in the 1919 revolution and to emphasize instead the historical significance of the 1952 seizure of power.[57] "The July Revolution," Serrag Eddine declared, "was not a revolution in the scientific sense of the word . . . It was a coup that was supported and blessed by the nation and only subsequently gained legitimacy from mass support." The military rulers squandered that support, according to the Wafdist leaders; their abolition of political parties marked the beginning of an age of tyranny, ignorance, and impoverishment. "From this place, the house of law, I challenge any of my colleagues the lawyers to point to any crime in the penal code that was not committed by the 1952 revolution. What else could one expect," Serrag Eddine noted, "from a regime whose leader admitted that 'we have given law a holiday' "?[58]

Serrag Eddine, the grand old man of the Wafd, acknowledged the improvements made in the security and rights of Egyptians after Nasser's death: "We admit and appreciate the role of President Sadat in establishing the political freedoms and democracy we now enjoy."[59] Wafdist praise came with qualifications, however, that contrasted Sadat's brand of party life unfavorably with the pre-1952 political order.[60] Serrag Eddine suggested that on a fundamental level Egyptians refused to believe that the official opposition parties that Sadat authorized were political parties at all. "The formation of the New Wafd Party," he declared, "scared a lot of people because they sensed that a real party was on its way . . . a party that had a mass base, unlike the paper parties that have no existence in people's minds and consciences." Serrag Eddine welcomed Sadat's declaration that he could rule Egypt's new democracy as the "head of the Egyptian people"; however, although "the head of a family always has rights over members of the family, they too have rights." Egyptians in the seventies did not yet enjoy the full freedoms that were their legitimate rights, although the relaxations of control "do allow us to meet, speak, discuss, and criticize." Serrag Eddine concluded that "we want more of these freedoms."

The challenge of liberalism as carried by the Wafd was real, and the Sadat regime was unprepared to meet it in an open political arena. Nevertheless, when the regime blocked the New Wafd Party, it did not thereby close all avenues of expression of constitutional nationalism. Because of the ideological and organizational relationship between the New Wafd and the lawyers' syndicate, the demise of the New Wafd left the Bar Association as the leading defender of liberalism in Egypt. The links between the Wafd and the liberal lawyers extended back to the twenties, but this relationship had been strengthened during the Sadat period. The return of the Wafd was announced in the association, major figures in the New Wafd were lawyers, and once again the Bar Association took up the defense of the Wafd as a political instrument to secure constitutional and legal rights. By the time the New Wafd had been forced out of public life, therefore, the Bar Association had once again asserted its identity as the center of the activities and potential associated with liberalism.

In many ways the Bar Association wrote a far more important chapter in the history of liberalism in the seventies than did the brief experiment of the New Wafd. The Bar Association, less encumbered than the Wafd by the demands of practical political life and its inevitable compromises, expressed more fully the most fundamental liberal ideas of free speech, the right of assembly, and a constitutional definition of national interest. Lawyers consciously sought to create an environment within the Bar Association that protected these rights; at the same time, they also sought to extend these rights to the rest of Egyptian society. In their own self-descriptions, lawyers portrayed themselves as "leading others in defense of the rights of their nation ... and in struggling to maintain personal freedoms of citizens and public freedoms of the people."[61] Within the Bar Association, the right to hold and articulate diverse opinions was fundamentally important; as Mustafa al-Baradie put it, "the legal profession is free speech."[62] Despite its special identification with the Wafd, the association embraced all political trends. Moreover, it acted as a corporate body to safeguard the legitimate rights of all political groups, including communist and Islamic radicals. The Bar Association was able to rally to the Wafd even while it maintained its commitment to protect religious groups and leftist organizations oppressed by the regime.

The lawyers' conception of their syndicate as a national rather than narrowly political or professional institution was deeply rooted in Egypt's history. The Bar Association was founded in 1912, making it the oldest of Egyptian professional associations. From the beginning, lawyers saw the association as more than a closed society to protect group interests; in an important sense it belonged to the entire nation as the repository of the values of tolerant constitutionalism and responsible nationalism; there was to be "no radical, ideological, religious, or even political discrimination among lawyers."[63] The Bar Association was defined as an open forum for lawyers of all opinions; although the liberals gave the group its particular identity, almost every political affiliation was represented there, including both the Islamic groups and the Christian counterparts. Political movements across the spectrum drew on the skills and activities of lawyers from the Bar Association. The policy of tolerance that allowed the association to embrace this diversity also became the source of its strength in resisting official repression, validating its claim to speak for the nation as a whole.[64]

Once Sadat realized that the lawyers would not rally to his new economic and political policies, he attempted to bring them into line by endorsing and advancing progovernment candidates for syndicate offices. However, officers elected with official backing proved susceptible to internal influences. A prominent example of this process was the 1978 election of Ahmed al-Khawaga as head of the Bar Association. The election came in the midst of the Sadat peace initiative; given the lawyers' tradition of taking stands on national issues, the question of Egypt's relations with Israel dominated the campaign. During the campaign Khawaga registered only mild objections to certain of the provisions of the Camp David accords, arguing, for example, that any peacekeeping forces in Egyptian territory should be under Egyptian control. Nevertheless, Khawaga did support peaceful resolution of the conflict with Israel because Egyptians, in his view, were not ready for further war. In sharp contrast, his opponent explicitly attacked the Camp David agreement with Israel and the exceptional security laws that restricted public freedoms to prevent criticism of the new foreign policy.[65] The regime threw its weight behind Khawaga's candidacy, tapping both NDP and public-sector lawyers. Sadat himself in a public speech in Ismailia urged the lawyers to vote for Khawaga.[66]

Standard accounts of the lawyers' syndicate, including those of Western specialists, regularly cite Khawaga's election as evidence that Egypt under Sadat lacked autonomous institutions.[67] But Khawaga's subsequent behavior does not support this conclusion. Khawaga's public identity was more complex than the conventional accounts suggest. Though supported by the regime in 1978, Khawaga was a former Wafdist who had cooperated with the Nasser regime. After Khawaga's election, Sadat supporters within the Bar Association indicated their distrust of the new head by backing for leadership roles lawyers who were identified more fully with Sadat.[68] Khawaga, who had already alienated opponents of the regime by his ambiguous stand on the peace process, risked complete isolation. Faced with the necessity to side either with the regime or with its critics, he turned to the opposition. This realignment was confirmed by his support for a program of Friday seminars, designed to address the most critical issues facing the nation.[69] In the event, the Bar Association seminars strengthened the legacy of syndicate autonomy and contributed decisively to the recovery of the public world of critical political discourse in the seventies.

The Bar Association seminars, and not the official effort to create a multiparty system, constituted an authentic liberal experiment that aimed to create a political and social order based on institutional limits on arbitrary authority. At the seminars Egyptians acted out their commitment to public freedoms as a national right; at the same time, they demonstrated how free speech and assembly could sustain autonomous institutions. The seminars provided a forum in which, as one liberal historian put it, "the cream of the nation could express their thoughts and opinions on national issues ... These men are the pulse of the nation's conscience and a true measure of its feelings."[70] Speakers ranged from Omar Telmesany, head of the Muslim Brothers, to Khaled Muhieddin, leader of the leftist National Progressive Unionist Party (NPUP). By providing the space for the seminars the lawyers effectively asserted their right to speak for the national interest in both domestic and foreign affairs; even critics of the Bar Association's political activism acknowledge that the national impact of the Friday seminars, especially on the key issues of democracy and the peace with Israel, was "serious and substantial."[71]

The regime did not recognize the importance of the seminars immediately; in fact, Sadat supporters in the association initially persuaded the government to ignore them, on the grounds that by harmlessly "talking to themselves" the lawyers would relieve tensions that might otherwise prove dangerous. This view underestimated the power of the lawyers' voice; at the same time, this passive approach failed to recognize the thirst for a genuine national dialogue. Before long, as one opposition paper put it, the regime understood "just how strong the opposition 'word' had become."[72] The weakness of the official opposition parties enhanced the importance of the Bar Association forum as one place where independent critical judgment addressed the common concerns of Egyptians; the seminars became key political events in the life of the nation.[73] From the platform of the Bar Association the lawyers responded to the official Sadat formula of peace and prosperity with the pointed questions: What kind of peace, and at what cost to the nation?[74]

From the outset, most members of the Bar Association dissented from the regime on the question of Israel and Egypt's security. The differences became apparent soon after Nasser's death. The clearest expression of the syndicate's stance came in response to the student movement of January 1972. The lawyers backed the student assessment that the battle with Israel was a prolonged war of liberation rather than a traditional battle between armed forces. The lawyers also seconded the student demand that Egyptians strengthen the internal front by arming civilian volunteer groups as a sign of the national will to resist. Characteristically, the Bar Association statement in the wake of the student disorders asserted that these aims could be achieved only in an environment of expanded democracy. The lawyers argued that complete and voluntary public support would be necessary for the long-term confrontation with Israeli power that offered the only hope of achieving a just peace settlement.

When Sadat flew to Jerusalem in 1977 to sue for peace, the lawyers sharply questioned the kind of treaty Egypt could secure, given that the balance of power overwhelmingly favored the Israelis. The lawyers never shared the president's confidence that a "full partnership" with the United States in the peace process would somehow offset the Israeli advantage and secure an agreement beneficial to Egypt and the Arab world.[75] The dominant liberals in the Bar Association argued that direct negotiation with an occupying power would not bring peace to the Middle East. With its own territory occupied by Israel, Egypt simply would not have sufficient leverage to win a just accord on behalf of the Palestinians. The Bar Association also joined with "the legal and political international community, represented by the United Nations General Assembly and international legal organizations," to contest the legality of agreements reached under conditions that effectively precluded Palestinian participation. In their seminars and official statements the lawyers declared that each stage of the Sadat peace process represented a surrender of the national interest. They rejected all forms of normalization with Israel. They protested the undemocratic measures the regime enacted to isolate foreign policy from criticism. The association's Governing Council called for a complete "boycott of all dealings with Israel until the departure of the last Israeli soldier from Sinai and the occupied Arab territories, including Jerusalem."[76]

Disagreements between the Bar Association and the government sharpened after the treaty with Israel was signed in 1979. In the spring of 1980 the new Israeli ambassador to Cairo submitted his credentials to President Sadat. This official act was the centerpiece of the normalization of relations between Egypt and Israel. At that very moment, members of the Governing Council of the Bar Association raised the Palestinian flag over the association building in Cairo and then burned the Israeli flag. A spokesman stated that "the raising of the Palestinian flag is a symbol to the people that Palestine is a historic fact that will not die." The Bar Association declared "full support of the Palestinian people, its revolution, and its struggle under its legitimate and sole representative, the PLO."[77]

The Bar Association consistently defied regime efforts to pressure the lawyers to endorse the Camp David accords and the peace treaty with Israel. The lawyers also challenged the official statements that there was nationwide support of the agreements. At the 1980 Conference of Arab Lawyers in Rabat, the Egyptian delegation, composed primarily of government lawyers, defended the Sadat peace and claimed it had complete support within Egypt; one government delegate claimed that "not a single Egyptian opposes Camp David and the peace treaty."[78] This general endorsement was especially meaningful, the government lawyers claimed, because of "the supremacy of law in Egypt and the freedom of the Egyptian citizen." A minority Egyptian faction dissented vigorously, challenging both the claim of support for Sadat's peace and the statements that complete freedom of opinion was protected by law in Egypt. "You are a liar," a critical Egyptian lawyer declared to the government delegate. "At this very moment there is a lawyer on trial in Egypt for expressing his free opinion; furthermore, fifteen members of parliament are against the treaty, and I'm one of them."[79]

In Egypt, the government mobilized 300 lawyers who were members of the National Democratic Party to call for application of the law of shameful conduct to the dissenters at Rabat.[80] The official press backed this threat of criminal action against individual lawyers with a suggestion that disciplinary action might be necessary against the Governing Council of the Bar Association for its support of the critical lawyers at the Rabat meeting. These articles directly contrasted the Bar

Association's activities with the nonpolitical stances of other professional associations, notably the Syndicate of Engineers, which "have comprehended the concept of associational activity and have established several [commercial] projects for their members."[81] These arguments were a signal that the regime intended to act to bring the lawyers into line.

The Bar Association responded defiantly with an official statement that defended the right of Egyptians at home or abroad to "objective discussion of the peace treaty" and denied that any harm was done to Egypt at Rabat.[82] The statement denounced the government-orchestrated campaign against the Governing Council and sharply criticized the cooperation of some lawyers in these attacks. The association stressed that its responsibility lay with "continuous work for achieving supremacy of the law, establishment of the basic freedoms of the Arab man, and the honest and nonpartisan representation of Egyptian nationalism." The uproar in Egypt caused by the Israeli bombing of the Iraqi nuclear reactor in 1981 overwhelmed discussion of the Rabat incident. Provoked by this display of Israeli power, the Governing Council of the Bar Association openly called for repudiation of the treaty with Israel.[83]

When Sadat called on the nation to celebrate the prospect of the return of the Sinai to Egypt, the association instead bitterly denounced the impotence of a compromised and isolated Egypt faced with a lengthening record of Israeli intransigence. Association resolutions condemned the Israeli annexation of Arab Jerusalem, the accelerated colonization of the West Bank, and Israeli attack on the Iraqi nuclear reactor, and the escalating military strikes against Lebanon.[84] In 1981 an association statement argued that "the results of three years of the Camp David process indicate that direct negotiations and separate settlements with the occupying Israeli forces cannot be the road to just and genuine peace that guarantees security in the area, but rather it offers an appetite for more expansion and aggression."[85] An association spokesman declared that the inability of Egypt and the United States to hold Israel to its commitments under Camp David, particularly on the West Bank, confirmed the correctness of the collective stand taken by the lawyers.

Lawyers using the platform of the Bar Association also warned of the long-term consequences of the Sadat peace with Israel: isolation in the Arab world; religious, cultural, and economic subversion by Israel; and subordination to American strategic aims in the Middle East. Liberal critics predicted that the price of a separate peace that returned the Sinai to Egypt would be complicity with Israel and the United States and thus the denial of the national aspirations of the Palestinians. This betrayal of the core Arab issue would cut Egyptians off from other Arabs, the Islamic world, and the nonaligned countries; an isolated Egypt would subsequently find itself unable to defend the national interest against pressures from Israel and the United States. Normalization of relations with Israel, in the association's view, was a "cover for an overall cultural and economic Zionist invasion that threatens our national and Islamic heritage." The ambitions of the Zionist assault, according to this plan, included both Sinai oil and the water of the Nile; in both cases, the objective was subordination of the Egyptian economy to the technological superiority of Israel. The lawyers also deplored the fact that "under the Camp David agreements, U.S. early warning stations in the Sinai and military bases given the name 'facilities' are being set up in our country"; this militarization of the U.S.–Egyptian relationship risked "drawing Egypt into the arena of international conflicts" without in any substantial way advancing Egyptian national interests.[86]

The domestic dangers of Egypt's subordination were brought home by Sadat's proposal in 1980 to divert Nile water to Israel in return for progress on the West Bank and Jerusalem. In an interview in *October* magazine Sadat revealed this "dream" of economic cooperation between Israel and Egypt, including the prospect of using Nile water to irrigate Israel's Negev desert. When Ariel Sharon, the Israeli minister of agriculture, visited Egypt that year, Sadat reportedly discussed the technical aspects of the water transfer.[87]

In the autumn of 1980 the Bar Association brought this issue to national attention in a series of seminars that focused on the dangers to the Nile. The case against the diversion project, and particularly Sadat's support for it, was stated firmly and explicitly. Ne'mat Fuad, a distinguished archaeologist and general director of the Higher Council for the Promotion of the Fine Arts, declared that it was a "religious duty to work against the project."[88] Fuad asserted that Sadat's unilateral policy initiatives on Nile water exceeded his proper authority in an unprecedented, indeed sacrilegious, way. She argued that the decision-making process should be reviewed and the issue debated in relevant public institutions. She called, in particular, on Egyptian engineers to denounce the project, despite "the difficulties that they association is experiencing" (an oblique reference to Osman Ahmed Osman's progovernment role). With a bold criticism aimed at Sadat's arbitrary decision making, Fuad concluded that "our prophet Muhammad was guided and inspired by God. Yet, he did not make statements by whim. The prophet was surrounded by faithful friends and believes. Yet, he was never said to be an expert in science and art as is happening now."

The legal experts who spoke at the seminars fleshed out this theme of the arbitrary exercise of power. Article 65 of the constitution, they emphasized, made Egypt a state subject to law; and a decision to divert Nile water to Israel would exceed the legal powers of the president. On still broader historical grounds, one prominent lawyer argued that "the Nile did not belong to Egypt, either geographically or historically; we have no right to give one drop to Israel, even by popular referendum." He likened Sadat's promise to Lord Balfour's 1917 pledge to create a Jewish state in Palestine: "Both are promises from one who doesn't possess to one who doesn't deserve."

All speakers at the seminars agreed that only by muzzling the press could the president hope to screen from the people the detrimental implications of his proposal. Kamel Zohairi, president of the Press Association, reported that the national papers had been prohibited from carrying announcements of the Bar Association seminars protesting Sadat's proposal: "In today's papers we read of the secrets and private lives of fourth-rate Hollywood actresses. Not one word is printed about the threat to Nile water." Reminding his audience that he had a law degree, Zohairi expressed his disillusionment with regime censorship of the media by remarking that he might just return to the legal profession "as long as free expression in impossible in the press." Evoking memories of the vibrant nationalist press of the thirties, Zohairi blamed the decline on "today's bourgeoisie, which doesn't know Egypt's history." He argued that the new social forces that had emerged in the Sadat years were so ignorant of the meaning of Egypt's past that they were capable of giving away the waters of the Nile, the very lifeblood of the nation. When the diversion project was quietly dropped, the lawyers concluded that their efforts to arouse the nation had contributed in a major way to the government's decision.

Like the Nile water issue, the announcement of the Pyramids Plateau project in 1975 generated doubts about the policies and authority of the president. On the desert land around the pyramids, developers planned to build a giant tourist park modeled loosely on Disneyland. The project carried the clear marks of Sadat's vision of Egypt's domestic development. The president personally approved the project and publicly signaled his enthusiasm for it. Pictures in the official press showed

Sadat and Osman Ahmed Osman, whose company had received the contract, on their hands and knees surveying maps of the proposed site. The project was a joint venture between the recently formed Egyptian Company for the Development of Tourism and the Southern Pacific Properties Company, based in Hong Kong. The heart of the deal was the leasing at concessionary rates of about 10,000 acres of desert in the area around the pyramids at Giza. Southern Pacific, the foreign partner, put up capital of $500,000; the Egyptian equity was the 10,000 acres of real estate. By 1977 Southern Pacific had sold 500 acres in lots for $1.7 million from foreign purchasers and another L.E. 1.2 million from Egyptians. Thus, the sale of only a fraction of the acreage brought in about $4 million on a half-million-dollar investment.[89] For the government and its associates in the Pyramids Plateau project, this combination of foreign capital and Egyptian planning and organization was a prime example of the developmental objectives that seemed to promise a better future for Egypt.

Making particularly effective use of the platform of the Bar Association, a campaign of public discussion challenged the plan and ultimately forced Sadat to cancel the project in the spring of 1978. The attack was led by Ne'mat Fuad, who focused on the regime's failure to protect the Egyptian heritage from foreign exploitation.[90] Fuad's outspoken criticism led the foreign partners in the project to bring three separate lawsuits against her. Although the national press ceased to cover her case, the legal community strongly supported her position, vigorously defending her right to criticize official policies. In each of the three suits, the judges dismissed the charges against Fuad. In addition to turning to the lawyers for legal advice, Fuad also took advantage of the public platform offered by the Bar Association to further her case against the project. Her campaign culminated in one of the most significant seminars ever held by the lawyers.[91]

The head of the Bar Association opened the symposium by thanking Fuad on behalf of all Egyptians for her courageous efforts to thwart "an attack on Egypt's history, Egypt's constitution, and Egypt's laws."[92] The speakers from the legal community documented the ways in which the project violated the laws and regulations that protected antiquities and governed foreign investment.[93] In her speech Fuad expressed outrage not simply at the project itself, but also at the new circumstances in Egyptian life that made it possible; she argued that Sadat's vision of the future was in fact an attempt to sell Egypt's history in pursuit of a debased view of national development that served only to encourage greedy individual self-interest. According to Fuad, the shift to the Open Door had produced a climate of moral uncertainty and confusion that legitimated self-interested motives and actions. Although Sadat clearly saw nothing extraordinary in a proposal to involve foreign capital in a scheme to commercialize the pyramids, this normalcy alarmed Fuad. For profit, Egyptians were cooperating with foreign interests in the destruction of their own incomparable past. "This is a national disaster for which there is no precedent, not even invasion." To accept the arguments that the project would not damage the pharaonic monuments would mean that "we abolish our minds, science, and the research findings of our Egyptian professors." Fuad branded the project a conspiracy that would leave Egypt violated in its most sacred historical sites and Egyptians diminished by the loss of pride in their ancient civilization. "No people, not even a people whose daily suffering leaves them with little, should knowingly sell their past."[94] The role played by the lawyers in defeating the project despite its endorsement by the president helped earn the Bar Association the title "conscience and tongue of the nation."[95]

At the Bar Association symposia, lawyers spoke and acted as though they were the legitimate democratic and nationalist voice of Egypt. They wove two major strands into their critique of the Sadat era; drawing on the liberal tradition, they charged that the regime had compromised the national interest. Although the regime had claimed to embrace political liberalization, it did not, to use Mustafa Marei's telling phrase, "call things by their right names." For many Egyptians, the pre-1952 experience with liberalism provided an independent measure of both the claims and the actions of the Sadat regime. Exposure to liberal values and practices had given words such as *constitution, judiciary,* and *political party* an experienced meaning that the regime could not arbitrarily alter. Liberals assessed the dominant order by the democratic and nationalist standards of Egyptian liberalism of the pre-1952 period; they judged the official liberalization fraudulent because the official rhetoric of the rule of law had not altered the fact that those at the center who controlled the military and the police could arbitrarily impose a direction on the nation that weakened democracy at home and compromised Egypt's national interest.[96]

In the seventies the official voice of the regime was not the only one to define Egypt's future. At the margins, liberals generated sufficient power to create a social space in which an alternative could be voiced. Denied full political expression, liberalism appeared as a social critique, mounted from institutions, notably the Bar Association, that had survived decades of repression. The lawyers had kept alive a history that the government leaders tried to suppress; from that history they drew on ideas of constitutionalism and moderate nationalism to evaluate official policies. As authentic historical liberalism reasserted itself in the new conditions created by de-Nasserization, both the idea and practice of liberalism acted against the official definitions of reality.

Angered by the Bar Association's effective and sustained criticism, the government packed a session of the association on June 26, 1981, with regime supporters who voted the incumbent leadership of the Governing Council out of office. President Sadat called on the parliament dominated by his party to investigate. The government commission concluded that the leadership was disloyal and called for the prosecution of the association head. A temporary board was appointed, whose new head acknowledged that "the lawyers' mission is to support and protect people's rights and freedoms . . . It is therefore not strange that the Bar Association would discuss any legislation pertaining to freedoms or the cause of the nation." However, he added that the Bar Association must pursue its aims within an "objective framework" that does not allow "contradictions between the association or the state authority." He went on to criticize the previous Governing Council for allowing the inauguration of the New Wafd Party from the association's platform. This action, he charged, "was the beginning of an attempt to polarize the association along party lines." The new head also noted, in reference to to Egyptian lawyers at the Rabat conference who had criticized the peace with Israel, that delegations of Egyptian lawyers abroad must adopt "a unified stand that is in line with state policy."[97] Thus, while theoretically justifying the association's role in political life and its right to express itself on questions of democracy and the national interest, the government-supported head of the association blamed the previous leadership precisely for taking critical stands on these vital questions.

Many lawyers reacted defiantly to the change in leadership and pursued several strategies to resist the imposition of government authority. They immediately challenged in the courts the "the illegal dissolution" of the Governing Council, organized symposia to present their case to the nation, staged demonstrations in the association building in Cairo, and threatened national strikes.[98] When the supreme constitutional court postponed a decision on the case in April 1983, the lawyers marched through Cairo's streets to the Bar Association in protest.[99] In June 1983 the court declared the government-instigated leadership change uncon-stitutional and restored the displaced Governing Council.[100] Once again, the lawyers and the Bar Association had preserved the potential, at least, of a liberal future for Egypt.

3

Restoring Egypt as Engine of the Arab World: The Nasserist Current

> Charisma is not an erratic force, or a superhuman power, but a very human capacity to reach others forcibly and to allow the images and conceptualizations of another to guide one's actions and affect one's feelings. It is the attraction of one individual to another, based on the human ability to go beyond the sphere of idiosyncratic experiences, as well as the ability to fashion dreams that catch hold in another's world.
>
> —*Marcene Marcoux*

President Sadat explicitly defined his political vision of peace and prosperity for the seventies as an alternative to the "nightmares" of Nasserist adventurism abroad and repressive socialism at home; in Nasser's hands "the revolution was reduced to a huge, dark, and terrible pit, inspiring fear and hatred but allowing no escape." Nasser's reckless foreign policy of intervention in the Arab world and ill-prepared confrontation with Israel had weakened and isolated Egypt: "In the sphere of foreign policy I found that we had no relations . . . with any country except the Soviet Union." Not only had Nasserist "complexes . . . of suspicion and hate" precluded peace with Israel; the inefficiency and corruption of the Nasserist "centers of power" had also made it impossible for Egypt to wage war successfully.[1] The president viewed the sixties as "nothing but years of defeat and pain . . . what we called the socialist experiment . . . was a complete failure . . . [that] never resulted in a social revolution."[2] The state mobilized its impressive resources to impose this official reading of history: in the seventies a flood of anti-Nasser publications appeared; standard school textbooks rewrote the record of the recent past to conform with the official line; and the government-controlled media launched damning assessments of the Nasser years. By exposing the alleged failures of the Nasser regime, Sadat hoped to justify his own radical policy departures of economic and political liberalization, realignment with the West, and accommodation with Israel.

The official rhetoric of the de-Nasserization campaign dismissed Nasserism as a spent political force that had lost the support of the people. Government policy contradicted this assessment, however, by treating the Nasserists as the most likely source of effective political opposition. While continuing to claim that Nasserism was absent from Egypt's political life, Sadat behaved as though it was a powerful historical alternative, threatening his regime.[3]

Nasserists saw the truth of their potential reflected in Sadat's fears. Amin Huweidy, Nasser's minister of war after the June 1967 defeat, summed up the enduring meaning of Nasserism: "The Nasser revolution cohered around the ideas and principles of pan-Arabism, positive neutrality, and the social revolution." Nasser "took the side of the poor, just as he took the side of development, democracy, Arab unity, and nonalignment." In the changed conditions of the seventies and eighties, Huweidy noted, "these principles will undoubtedly take new forms; yet, the ideas are still alive, and they still move people.[4]

Kamal Ahmed, a Nasserite parliamentary deputy and a leading figure in persistent attempts to create a legal Nasserist party, insisted that Nasserism's survival rested on the concrete achievements of the fifties and sixties and not just on the ideas and principles that had motivated them. "Nasserism persists not only in the minds of the Nasserists," he argued, "but also in the record of the Nasserist experience." Ahmed pointed to the reminders of the rich Nasserist legacy in Sadat's Egypt: whatever the criticisms for its adverse ecological impact, the Nasserists claimed the High Dam as a lasting monument to an Arab country's defiance of external control over its development; the much-maligned public sector, the Nasserists pointed out, still dominated the economy in the eighties; throughout Egypt, the public schools built in the heyday of Nasserism stood as neglected and dilapidated reproaches to an indifferent government; similarly, understaffed or empty medical clinics in the countryside reminded the rural poor of the abandoned promise of a better life. The experience of the Nasser years meant, as Kamal Ahmed put it, that "in all Egyptian villages and cities there were Nasserists" who could see and respond to the reminders of the Nasserist past.[5]

Periodically, the suppressed potentialities of Nasserism surfaced in public life, further stimulating the apprehensions of the successor regime. Whenever there were disturbances in the streets, such as those in 1972 and 1973 calling for military action on the Israeli front, Nasserist slogans resounded. Prominent among those who protested the reduction in government subsidies for necessities in January 1977 were those who raised Nasser's picture and chanted his name.[6] A Nasserist perspective intruded into every relatively open policy debate in parliament or the media, most pointedly, perhaps, in the parliamentary discussions of the economic liberalization launched by the October Paper of 1974.[7] If the government made the slightest gesture to a more extended political liberalization, Nasserists asserted their right to organize and be heard. When the government announced in the fall of 1977 that diverse platforms would be allowed to emerge within the official party, the Nasserist Socialists took only two weeks to organize. The public responded so enthusiastically to this explicitly Nasserist grouping that a disconcerted president intervened to disband it with the cryptic announcement that it would "not achieve what we want at this stage."[8] The Nasserists charged that reactionary forces, led by the United States, prompted a pattern of "fierce attacks" on all subsequent efforts to organize legally.[9] "We know we face many problems," explained Farid Abdul Karim, an important Nasserist spokesman in the seventies; "we know America will not accept a party like ours because Nasser blocked American hegemony in all Arab lands. Therefore, America cannot accept a Nasserist party that continues to reject an American presence. Reactionaries also fear our party."[10]

With state power based on the police, the military, and U.S. foreign aid, Sadat contained the assertions of those who called themselves Nasserists. Driven underground or thrown into prison, Nasserists disappeared from public view as an organized political force. "We debated whether to announce the establishment of the party from inside the prison, where most symbols of the Egyptian nationalist movement were jailed," reported Kamal Ahmed.[11]

The political surface controlled by the state appeared cleansed of the Nasserist past. Politically aware Egyptians knew, however, that the Nasserist current remained a powerful subterranean force in Egyptian life that sought expression in both legal and illegal ways. In the mid-eighties a spectacular trial, involving Gamal Abdul Nasser's son Khaled, reminded the nation of the enduring commitment to the ideals and emphases of the Nasser years and the profound attachment that many Egyptians felt to the life of this leader and the ideals of "social justice, real democracy, and Arab unity."[12]

The government charged that Khaled Nasser had spearheaded "Egypt's Revolution," a conspiratorial Nasserist formation that engineered a series of anti-Israeli and anti-American actions, including the murder of the security head of the Israeli embassy in August 1984, the assassination of another Israeli official in 1985, attacks on Israeli employees at the International Fair in 1986, and an abortive attack on three American diplomats in 1987. When the government moved against the group, young Nasser fled to Yugoslavia; security forces did capture some thirty of his alleged co-conspirators, many of them military officers, and placed them on trial. The official press characterized group members as thugs motivated more by drugs and money than by principles, while the opposition papers turned the trial into a blanket indictment of Camp David and the resultant Israeli-American presence in Egypt.[13] Public debate over the trial focused on opposition charges that American and Israeli covert security operatives had conducted surveillance of Egypt's Revolution without the knowledge of the Egyptian government. A commentator identified with the Islamic trend wrote that "the Islamic group issued a declaration announcing its support for 'Egypt's Revolution' and denounced the prosecutor's demand that eleven of the accused be executed." The writer concluded that "the Muslim Egyptian people have not accepted and will not accept the execution of those who confronted the Zionists, no matter what their position is concerning the Nasserists' point of view or ideology."[14] On leaving Egypt for exile in Yugoslavia, Khaled Nasser remarked that "the attack on Nasser has only one meaning which is that his principles are still alive."[15]

Indeed, throughout the seventies Nasserist spokesmen argued that despite the apparent success of official repression, the revolutionary legacy of the fifties and sixties survived beneath the surface. The revolution had lowered class barriers just enough to release enormous social energies and to win lasting converts to Nasserist ideals of revolutionary social change. The Nasserists argued that the new possibilities Nasser had awakened were preserved in millions of changed lives; the human reserves of Nasserism as an alternative political practice were found wherever these individual lives intersected.[16] Nasserist intellectuals such as Hatem Sadek, who supervised publication of two volumes of Nasser's speeches from the post-1967 period, called on these diverse social forces of the revolution to struggle to protect the Nasserist legacy from antirevolutionary or reactionary attacks: "Workers have to struggle for their rights, students must struggle for their rights, and intellectuals must struggle for their rights; every individual must know what his rights are and what his gains from the revolution are."[17]

Egyptians of different ages and backgrounds recognized themselves as Nasserists by their commitments to Arabism, industrialization, and social revolution. Denied a legal existence as a political party in the years after Nasser's death, a multiplicity of groups struggled against official repression to speak and act for the Nasserist alternative. This result is consistent with the self-understanding of key Nasserists such as Kamal Ahmed: "Nasserism is a political current that cannot be encompassed by one party." Likewise, Muhammad Hassanein Haikal described Nasserism as a political force "greater than one party." Even Nasserists such as Muhammad Mabdy who elected to join the legal left party, the National Progressive Unionist Party (NPUP), recognized clearly that these strategies reflected the necessities of "political conditions" in the eighties; Mabdy simply urged other Nasserists to enter into dialogue with such progressive forces as the NPUP because the latter contained "an ample representation of Nasserists."[18] Opposition press reports generally referred to Nasserist groupings around key personalities such as Kamal Ahmed, Hatem Sadek, Abdul Meguid Farid, Muhammad Salmawy, Hamdine Sabahy, and Farid Abdul Karim.[19] The Nasserists themselves recognized the plurality of groupings; "no one has the seal of Nasserism," remarked Kamal Ahmed, "as Nasser left no such thing to anyone."[20]

Speaking of Nasserism as a broad political current, the journalist Muhammad Salmawy argued that a rich and widely shared national experience generated the Nasserists' definitions and cemented the loyalties of the Egyptians willing to act for them:

> Official statistics show that 35 percent of the population is under forty years old. This means that they grew up with the revolutionary experience. Therefore, their political consciousness was formed with the carrying out of the revolution, banishing the king, and declaring the republic; with land reform, evacuation of foreign occupation, nationalizing the [Suez] Canal; declaring the first unification in modern Arab history; with the adoption of the nonalignment policy; with the rejection of alliances and support of national liberation movements; with socialism, free education . . . and finally with the growing importance of the role of Egypt in the arena of international politics. This generation believes in the political theory that yielded all those policies, and that is "Nasserism."[21]

Self-identification as a Nasserist came most easily to those who had benefited most from industrialization, full employment, and the redistributive social policies of the fifties and sixties. First were the million-plus public-sector workers, followed by the roughly 2 million middle- and lower-level civil servants. Sadat's Open Door policies hit both of these urban groups hard and reinforced their responsiveness to a Nasserist alternative. In the countryside were those farmers, roughly 25 percent of the population, who were the beneficiaries of land reform, improved tenancy laws, and the extension of welfare services to the countryside. In addition, all those who had passed through the national system of free education were in a sense Nasser's sons and daughters.[22] Leadership for the varied social forces that fed the Nasserist current came from the late president's former top aides and officials, such as the powerful journalist Muhammad Hassanein Haikal or former officials such as Amin Huweidy or Muhammad Fa'iq, whose reputations remained intact, although these were only the most visible Nasserists. Impressive numbers of younger men and women, marked in some special way by their direct experience of the Nasser years, also stepped forward to speak for Nasserism.[23] From these leaders and the broad social groups that responded to them came spontaneous reminders that Sadat's Nasserist "nightmares" were other people's dreams.

In the central business area and the more prosperous neighborhoods of Cairo, Nasser's pictures, once everywhere, almost totally disappeared within a few years of his death. In the cafés and shops of the poorer districts, however, the faded photos remained in place. The strength of these attachments to Nasser was expressed in strange and unexpected public places, including the movie theaters that the government thought it controlled. Through the government-run cinema industry, the regime attempted unsuccessfully to translate the themes of the de-Nasserization campaign into a medium to reach the illiterate and semiliterate masses. The plots of a series of de-Nasserization films made in the early seventies, such as *Karnak* and *The Dawn Visitor,* emphasized the violence of the police and intelligence forces, although these themes were cast in the proven entertainment formulas of the Egyptian cinema. Love stories featuring Egypt's most popular actors and actresses were set against the background of the devastating defeat by Israel in 1967. Threaded into the plot were examples of government inefficiency and corruption, with the criticism culminating in scenes of prison and torture, most often of innocent young people. None too subtly, these films blamed the 1967 defeat on an incompetent and brutal regime.

All appeared to go well for such efforts at de-Nasserization—until the moviemaker introduced either Nasser's voice or image into the script. One film incorporated an actual news clip of a broken and defeated Nasser offering his resignation in the wake of the 1967 defeat. In the theaters the unintended consequences were electrifying. When the late president appeared on the screen, the more expensive loge and balcony sections were quiet; but in the anonymity of the darkened theater, the lower hall erupted in chants and cheers—for Nasser.

Regime attempts to manipulate mass sentiment with songs that supported the policy departures of the seventies suffered a similar backlash. With the one exception of a joyous ballad that hailed "the return of Sinai to us" after the 1979 peace treaty with Israel, none of the songs that praised government policies took hold in the popular imagination. Instead, the seventies witnessed an underground revival of nationalist, pan-Arab, and socialist songs from the Nasser era. Banned from radio and television stations, they blared all the louder from pirated cassette recordings. Forbidden Nasserist lyrics celebrating the building of factories and the High Dam, the struggles for Palestine and for the "garden of socialism," were heard at weddings and private parties in the villages and poor neighborhoods of the cities.[24]

Survivals of old attachments were not the only signs of the durability of Nasserist sentiments. Themes from the fifties and sixties, often handled with complex and subtle ironies, enriched an innovative underground political culture of protest whose most expressive forms were poetry, music, and humor. At the center of this robust tradition stood the unlikely combination of a poet/songwriter and a blind shaikh, Ahmed Nagm and Shaikh Imam. In their hands, poetry, set to music and sung to the accompaniment of the lute, became a protest medium for the masses. Though too iconoclastic to be consistent adherents of any political platform, Nagm and Imam drew heavily on the sensibilities of the subterranean Nasserist current. They hammered away at the gap between the optimistic propaganda of the Sadat regime and the national and personal humiliations that the poor felt in their own lives. In doing so, Nagm and Imam drew on the submerged experiences and values of the Nasser years to conjure up an alternative world in which Egyptians, despite their weakness in the face of Israeli power, refused to endure humiliation after humiliation for the sake of an imposed peace; they evoked an Egypt in which the burdens of a just war and of the struggle for development were shared equally by all.

Before 1973, the underground troubadours emphasized the imperative of reopening the struggle with the Israeli occupier. One of their ballads, heard throughout Egypt, attacked Sadat's delays in reopening the battle with Israel while it still controlled the Egyptian Sinai, despite the endless talk of preparation and the unceasing calls for sacrifices. The song set the sloganeering voice of state *Authority* against the impatient and skeptical chorus of the *People:*

> *Authority:* No voice louder than the Battle,
> Beautiful songs and melodies for the Battle,
> Every effort and every arm for the Battle . . .
> Of paramount importance, this Battle,
> We must mobilize the people for the Battle,
> One million men for the Battle.
>
> *People:* We baked black bread, the color of the Battle,
> And we ate black bread, the color of the Battle,
> The people starved for the sake of the Battle,
> but where *is* the Battle?
>
> *Authority:* Silence, boy, and dance for the Battle.
>
> *People:* Silence O bey, where *is* the Battle?
>
> *All:* No voice louder than the Battle.

After the October War, Nagm and Shaikh Imam shifted their critical commentary to the economic and social deprivations of the masses in the new era of economic liberalization. They focused on the ostentatious display and corruption of the new middle class who thrived under the Open Door policies. Thanks in part to their efforts, the new millionaires who surrounded Sadat became the "fat cats" who symbolized the dominant order in the seventies:

> Sitting in large fast cars . . .
> Thick pasty necks
> Fat bellies
> Gleaming skin
> Obtuse minds
> Soaring incomes and
> Swelling paunches . . . [25]

Originally performed for small and semiclandestine groups of students, workers, and others, these satirical poems told listeners that there were others who saw through official definitions of reality, others who shared the hopes of the Nasser years for national pride and social justice.

On rare occasions, an authentic Nasserist voice was heard in the official media. Early in 1977 President Sadat launched his version of political liberalization by meeting with the representatives of key social groups, including the representatives of the university student unions. On February 2, 1977, *al-Ahram* reported this exchange over the legacy of Nasserism:

> *Sadat:* Can one of the Nasserists stand up and explain to me this Nasserism from which I have deviated?

Student: We judge that in today's Egypt many things are different from the things that Nasser intended. The first point is the existence of a mass media campaign against Nasser and his revolution. I understand Nasserism as the political agenda of the July Revolution that delineates three basic concepts: liberation, socialism, and [Arab] unity.

Sadat: What are [your] differences [with me] in these areas that you mention?

Student: The liberation [of Nasserism] is freedom from outside pressures in all their different forms and freedom from exploitation. The social forces that fight for this freedom are the workers, the peasants, the nonexploitative bourgeoisie, together with the revolutionary intellectuals and soldiers, all of whom Nasser sponsored and commanded. Nasser projected his vision of democracy as a political organization that expressed people's political rights. The Arab Socialist Union has many shortcomings, yet your proposals to reform it, Mr. President, carry the threat of forming political parties.

Sadat: You are against parties.

Student: We are for the principle of the Alliance of Working People. The second point is the Open Door policy. We were not "closed" or isolated in the Nasser years. There were many forms of economic cooperation, especially from those countries who offered us help.

Sadat: You mean the Russians.

Student: I am not defending the USSR alone. I defend any force, American or Russian, provided it helps us . . . Since the Open Door policy we have witnessed the growth of a new class of smugglers, speculators, and importers of foreign goods. The government has not made the poor equal to the best in the land. He made the son of the peasant an officer, an engineer, and a doctor. Now you know why I am a Nasserist, why I love Abdul Nasser, and why I am determined to salute him on his birthday.

Shawky Abou Akina, a worker from Mahalla, ridiculed those who attacked the problems of the public sector or the environmental damage caused by the High Dam. He spoke of what Nasser had accomplished for the workers in the sixties and pledged that workers "would protect national industry, the public sector, and workers' rights."

Abdul Mawla Atteya, a peasant from Beheira, described himself and his family as "raised in Abdul Nasser's school. We lived with him through the battles he fought for us." Atteya concluded by telling the crowd of an estimated 18,000 that "our party, a Nasserist party, exists in reality. You are the evidence of its existence whether some people like it or not."[26]

Pronouncements like these, Nasserist intellectuals argued, attested that the little dreams of poor people were the most enduring component of Nasserism. They pointed out, for example, that the children of workers on the trains that ran from the industrial suburb of Helwan to Cairo still carried the hopes of the poor. On impossibly overcrowded trains and buses, these young people made their way to the universities and institutes of central Cairo, steeled by their ambitions to become engineers or doctors. Not all such changed lives have remained anonymous; Kamal Ahmed, ex-delegate to the parliament and a prominent Nasserist spokesman in the seventies, explained why he saw himself in such young people:

> I didn't profess Nasserism for ideological or political reasons from from a socioeconomic sense of the July Revolution. I'm the son of a working-class family . . . I was born in a popular quarter in Alexandria. Before the revolution it would have been impossible for any one of my generation to get a university degree or a profitable job. How could a man with my background have participated in political decisions at the highest level without the revolution? People of my generation became lawyers, doctors, engineers, and officers. None of this could have happened without a major change in the socioeconomic system. New forces emerged, the sons of the poor.[27]

Prominent Nasserist spokesmen such as Kamal Ahmed explained that when Nasserist groups forged a program they offered it as a practical "plan for execution" rather than as a philosophical discussion; although they drew on the major ideological statements of the Nasserist regime, notably the 1961 Charter of National Action and the 1968 March 30 Statement, the Nasserists of the seventies and eighties understood themselves to be responding to the practical needs of the people. Describing all Nasserists as "the destitute sons of this country," he argued that the essential Nasserist project formulated the solution to Egypt's problems from that perspective. The program of all Nasserists, explained Ahmed, "aims to meet the needs of the poverty-stricken in society: a happy home for every citizen, the right to work, and the right to a hospital bed."[28]

According to the Nasserists, there was nothing mystical about Nasser's charisma. The late president's popularity derived from the limited but real gains he had made in the nationalist struggles he inherited. With Nasser, Egyptians worked for independence from the British, land reform, the High Dam, industrialization, and a measure of social justice. These concrete measures succeeded in shaping the nationalist sentiments of the masses and stimulating their psychological affinity for the more abstract goals of the revolution.[29] All of these shared dreams were already part of the nationalist consciousness by the forties; they were neither the whims of a leader nor the irrational impulses of the mystified masses.[30]

Intellectuals who spoke for Nasserism in the seventies, such as Muhammad Auda, acknowledged that the Nasser experiment had not fully realized all these nationalist and progressive ends. Yet they insisted that the Nasser revolution "gave the Hope, if not the full tangible benefit."[31] Perhaps the most eloquent exponent of Nasserism in the seventies and eighties was Muhammad Hassanein Haikal, former editor of *al-Ahram,* Nasser's confidant, a man once described by the *New York Times* Middle East correspondent as the "most powerful journalist in the world";[32] Haikal argued that the large goals of the Nasserist state were directly connected with the small dreams of its poorer citizens. The durability of Nasserism proved, in Haikal's view, that a link had been forged between the project Nasser set for the nation and the biographies of ordinary people. Haikal reasoned that the Nasserist dreams of Arab revolution and industrialization could take hold in the lives of the common people of Egypt because their own small experiences of hope opened them to large dreams.

"I claim that the Egypt of the fifties and sixties had dreams," Haikal wrote in 1982. "It led a movement of national liberation; it was the leader of the Arab nation; it was establishing an industrialization base; it was building the High Dam, fighting the battle of Suez, leading the nonaligned countries." The popular commitment to those grand battles of the fifties and sixties was sustained by small private victories in everyday life: "Every university graduate entering practical life knew he would find a job and a home at a reasonable price. There were attempts at stabilizing prices." A sense that the national burdens were shared made the young willing "to sacrifice and suffer to some extent . . . as long as there were no millionaires. If there were any millionaires, they hid their fortunes. They did not appear on the Egyptian street in this vulgar manner; at any rate, there were very few millionaires in the sixties." The disillusionment of Egypt's youth in the seventies could be explained by the absence of large purposes that could be reflected in some meaningful way in their own lives: "Young people once so intensely drawn to Nasser are now withdrawing from society; either they retreat through emigration to the Arab world to improve their financial situation or they escape to radical Islamic groups because they have lost the dream."[33] Hatem Sadek justified the collection of Nasser's speeches and interviews with the argument that "Nasser's words have the answers for all the questioning of a young person . . . in the most important causes of his life . . .

[including] the necessity of continuing the revolution and defending it from threats of attack or reversal."[34]

By the Nasserist reading, the hopes of the fifties and sixties that these diverse Egyptians shared drew strength from objective, structural changes that created new social realities. Important figures on the left challenged this view; intellectuals such as Fuad Zakariyya, for example, charged that the limitations of Nasserism marked the very language that Egyptians spoke. Zakariyya observed that the masses continued to employ the old titles of respect, such as "bey" and "pasha," when addressing the middle and upper classes. Zakariyya saw the persistence of these reactionary practices as symbolic evidence of the shallowness of the Nasserist transformations. While recognizing that the regime had not been able to accomplish all it aimed for, Nasserists, including those such as Muhammad Auda who placed themselves on the left of the Nasserist spectrum, saw enough in the record of the fifties and sixties to dismiss with ridicule the contention that the social revolution of the fifties and sixties was bogus. To the charge that a real revolution would have "removed these titles from the people's memory and daily lives," Auda responded that "if after twenty years of the revolution it is only the title 'bey' that remains, if this title is used primarily for courtesy, and if it is gradually dying out except among certain remnants [of the pre-1952 era] that find their reason for living in their titles, is this really the deadly sin from which we deduce the failure of socialism?" In reviewing the record of the Nasser years for the Egyptian left, Auda argued that what counted was the progressive advancement that marked the Nasserist trajectory: "What all Nasserists, Marxists, and enlightened nationalists have supported and should support is the fact that when the revolution had to choose, it chose socialism and consecrated that choice in the National Charter between the regime and the people; and the socialism it chose was the scientific one—not a facade and slogans but a socialism that nationalizes the main resources."[35]

"To see the social revolution," explained one former Nasser official, "go to an Egyptian village and ask how many children go to school, how many butchers there are to prepare meat for the villagers; see what is available to buy in the shops, if there is electricity and clean water. These are the signs of the real revolution."[36] In the countryside the imposition of ceilings on land holdings in 1952, 1961, and 1969 reversed a trend toward concentration and the dispossession of the rural poor. Approximately 11 percent of the rural population benefited from a redistribution of 15 percent of cultivable land. The giant estates were broken up, ending the dominance of the traditional large landowners. Tenancy laws significantly improved the security of the landless, who decreased from 59 percent to 43 percent in the years 1950–1970.[37]

Nationalization of a considerable share of nonagricultural economic assets and the creation of a public sector had a parallel impact on class structure in the urban sphere. Private concentrations of wealth were curbed. Labor legislation regulated job security and wage levels. In industry the wages of workers rose 44 percent in the period 1952–1967, and workers received a range of additional benefits. The Nasserists pointed out that these measures limited the power of the aristocracy and opened new possibilities for workers, peasants, and the lower middle class. The lower middle class, in particular, found new job opportunities in the bureaucracy as managers for companies, cadres in political parties, or as members in local councils. From 1952 to 1967 the wages of lesser officials in the various state organizations rose approximately 85 percent.[38] Military careers opened up particularly promising avenues for the technically trained, whatever their social background.[39] Wide-ranging state interventions on behalf of the less privileged enhanced the impact of these basic structural changes. Government measures that especially served these strata included guaranteed employment for university graduates, progressive tax rates, rent controls, and subsidies of basic commodities.[40]

Yet, of all these accomplishments of the social revolution, the Nasserists gave pride of place to the expansion of free public education through the university level. Expansion of educational opportunities at about 8 percent a year through the fifties and sixties dramatically improved the life chances of substantial numbers of Egyptians. Training at universities and institutes in turn allowed an expansion of the modern sector, including professional, technical, commercial and clerical positions, from 12 percent to almost 20 percent of total employment.[41]

From the Nasserist perspective, the domestic progress achieved in the decade after the 1956 Suez War resulted from Egypt's success in asserting itself both regionally and globally. The Nasserist vision located the determinants of Egyptian political life beyond the country's borders;[42] a successful development effort, therefore, necessarily entailed effective national assertiveness. According to Nasserist spokesman Farid Abdul Karim, Egypt's historical and cultural connection to the Arab world constituted its greatest resource for playing an important international role; in Karim's view, "the problems of the normal Egyptian citizen are linked to those of the Arab nation generally."[43] Nasserism, as the group around Karim argued in the eighties, was "the ideology of the Arab revolution or the ideology of the Arab's civilizational project."[44] Nasser himself was clear that a vulnerable Egypt would be able to develop only behind the shield of its Arabism. In the Nasserist strategic vision, only if Egypt could draw on the support of Arab movements and states could it hope to parry the external forces that aimed to subjugate and exploit the country. Thus, according to the Nasserists, the strong Arabism of their orientation originated with the reaction to external dangers, first from British colonial power and later from aggressive Israeli nationalism. They pronounced the frequently voiced charge of an irresponsible expansionist dynamic in the Nasserist project to be a myth. The Nasserists pointed out that the first impulse of the Nasserist moment in Egypt's history was contraction and consolidation. After the 1952 coup, Nasser gave priority to negotiating the qualified British withdrawal from Egypt and resolving Egypt's future role in the Sudan. With these measures, the regime aimed to trim Egypt's responsibilities and to gain greater control over its own political fate. After the 1952 coup, Nasser argued forcefully that Egypt should not engage its modest resources in confrontation with Israel; Nasser's position encountered strong opposition within the junta and from society at large. Richard Crossman, a pro-Zionist future British Labour minister who interviewed Nasser, reported: "At the time he judged that Israel ought not to distract him from the problems of Egypt, those of the social revolution."[45] As the Nasserists saw the record of the fifties, pragmatic concern for Egypt's national interest always tempered the regime's actions on behalf of the cause of Arab Palestine; only reluctantly and in response to outside pressures that could not be ignored did Nasser depart from his initial emphasis on building a strong Egypt.

The Nasserists believed that the new ruler adopted an active foreign policy of nonalignment and anticolonialism to buttress Egypt's independence and the country's prospects of self-directed development. Nasser's strategy was to resist pressures from London by playing the British off against other great powers. At the same time, Cairo would strengthen its own hand by acquiring influence in the neighboring Arab areas to compensate for its loss of a dominant role in the Sudan.[46] The quest for influence in the Arab sphere lead Nasser to oppose an Iraqi-based pro-Western alliance; the success of that opposition, in turn, attracted positive Soviet interest for the first time.

According to the Nasserists, Britain pressed on Egypt by planning a regional security system that would be based on Iraq, Egypt's key rival for influence in the Arab world; Israel did so by escalating conflict over the border, notably in a February 1955 raid on Gaza that left thirty-eight Egyptians dead. By 1955 Nasser was convinced by the Baghdad Pact initiative and the Israeli raid on Gaza that he would not be able to isolate his revolution either from hostile Western intrusions into the Middle East or from the military reach of Israel. He had to arm Egypt more effectively. On the battle lines, Egyptian forces "felt insecure and poorly equipped; anger spread among the troops, compelling Nasser to go himself to Gaza to calm the situation."[47] In September 1955, Nasser announced an arms deal with the Soviet Union.[48]

Despite the weapons from the Eastern bloc, Nasser kept his lines open to America.[49] Secret Egyptian-Israeli peace talks took place later in 1955, with American promises of support for Egypt's Aswan High Dam if they succeeded. The talks broke down by early 1956, and the United States announced the withdrawal of its offer to finance the dam. Nasser responded defiantly; Egypt, he announced, would build the dam with the revenues from the Suez Canal Company: "We are going to take back the profits which this imperialist company, this state within the state, deprived us of while we were dying of hunger."[50] Nationalization of the Suez Canal Company, the Israeli-British-French invasion, Egyptian resistance, Soviet missile threats against the invaders, and American diplomatic pressure for withdrawal—all ended with the Canal securely in Egyptian hands. The drama of Suez made Nasser a hero in Egypt, the Arab world, and the Third World generally. The Egyptian leader became, in Hatem Sadek's words, "the first leader and thinker of the comprehensive Arab revolution; the figure around whom the Arab people gathered as they had not done since they first responded to the heavenly message of Islam."[51]

The Nasserists point out the Nasser's success in handling the invasion of Egypt by the former colonial powers and Israel, not some foreign adventure of his own, established his position in history and his hold on the Egyptian people. The risks taken over Suez were linked to the keystone of Egypt's development effort, the Aswan High Dam. Haikal explained why the dam project struck so deep a cord among Egyptians:

> For centuries Egyptians had felt encircled and imprisoned by the desert. The dimensions of the High Dam as seen when it was first widely discussed in 1953 meant a great benevolent invasion of the desert, a way to push it back. One and a half million acres could go under cultivation—one quarter of all the land that Egypt had cultivated in 4,000 years. Now, we had the hope of making such a leap in less than a generation. This was a tremen-

dous vision, new land for a people who had always survived by farming. And it was a vision for a country longing to industrialize. It meant the possibility of electrical power on a legendary scale: ten billion kilowatt-hours a year. Egypt would have 50 percent of all the electrical power in the continent of Africa.[52]

In all its active involvements in the Arab world in the wake of Suez, the Nasserists argued, Egypt never sacrificed national interests for pan-Arab ends; on the contrary, circumstances made Egypt's engagement with the Arab world unavoidable, while Nasser's genius made them both principled and profitable. "Egypt profits from her foreign policy rather than being burdened with it," said Haikal. "For Egypt, foreign policy is one of her largest investments, and her principles constitute one of her greatest resources."[53] By this reasoning, if Egypt made itself a leader of the Arabs and a force in the affairs of the Third World, it could trade on its influence to secure foreign aid needed for industrialization.

According to the Nasserists, this defensive strategy worked until the mid-sixties. Egypt's enhanced prestige, derived essentially from its Arab connections, attracted very substantial resources from abroad. At the high point of Nasserism, from 1957 to 1965, the Egyptian nation received an extraordinary $3.43 billion in foreign loans and credits from both East and West.

Cairo in the late fifties and the sixties was a magnet for radical Third World movements such as the Algerian struggle against the French. From these involvements, Kamal Ahmed argued, Egyptians "strengthened our nation and added to our people's ability to defend the rights of the continent and to protect the human rights of the Arabs and Muslims."[54] For Nasserists such as Ahmed, even the protracted and ultimately unsuccessful Egyptian engagement in the Yemeni civil war in the sixties was prompted by the same pragmatic viewpoint. Britain had pledged withdrawal from South Arabia by 1968, and if Nasser's regime had been able to establish a secure Egyptian presence in the Yemen, it would clearly have had diplomatic and perhaps material benefits as well.

Critics of Nasserism from the right, such as Osman Ahmed Osman, were not persuaded that pragmatism drove Nasser's foreign policy; they charged, in particular, that the Nasserist obsession with Israel, expressed in irresponsible rhetoric and provocative, ill-considered foreign involvements, brought Egypt to ruin. Nasserist foreign policy, such opponents charged, exaggerated Israel's role as an expansionist state that threatened the Arab world; instead of seeking accommodation, Egypt was dragged unnecessarily into the devastating wars with Israel.

In response, the Nasserists argued that they had no need to exaggerate the Israeli danger or to whip up anti-Israeli sentiment; both the Israeli threat and the fears it engendered were real enough. Israel's record of using military power to secure its ends, notably at Gaza in 1955 and Suez in 1956, contrasted sharply with Egypt's moderation. The stationing of United Nations forces on the border with Israel from 1956 to 1966, the crucial decade of the Nasser experience, symbolized the Nasserist commitment to domestic development. The UN presence acted as a shield against Israeli power, while restricting infiltration of Palestinian irregulars into Israel.

According to the Nasserists, firsthand experience of Israel's military power made Egyptians fully aware of the Israeli threat to Arab societies, including their own. At the same time, the Nasserists contended that history recorded a strong nationalist impulse to resist. Both dimensions of that Egyptian response were apparent in the War of Attrition that Egyptians began in 1968 to forestall the hardening of the Israeli occupation of the Egyptian Sinai. According to Nasserist analysts, "the forgotten war, the War of Attrition . . . exhausted the enemy and expanded the capabilities of the armed forces by building up its battle experience." Before Nasser left the scene, they point out, the battle plans subsequently implemented in October 1973 "were ready and awaiting the signal."[55]

Nasser reopened the conflict in desperation. Egypt was unable to renew full-scale war and unwilling to accept the terms of settlement proposed by an ascendent Israel. Israel was consolidating its position in the occupied Sinai with the Bar Lev Line, designed to make its position there impregnable. Nasser reasoned that Egypt's only hope was to use its manpower to exhaust the enemy in a long and punishing battle that would culminate in an Egyptian crossing of the Suez Canal from west to east. Nasser opened the conflict with an artillery barrage. There were no illusions about the price Egypt would pay to regain its territory. Nasser warned a people who had already suffered the trauma of 1967 to be ready for devastating losses as Egypt used her human resources to exhaust the enemy in a long battle.[56]

Israel's response was as destructive as anticipated. Heavy air bombardments destroyed Egypt's defensive radar and missile sites. Amphibious and helicopter raids on an antiaircraft missile site and an Egyptian radar installation humiliated Egypt. In fighting along the Canal, the Israelis claimed at least 1,000 Egyptian dead. Intensive Israeli shelling of the canal zone cities added hundreds of civilian casualties. Rather than surrender, Nasser ordered the beleaguered cities evacuated. Refugees by the tens of thousands fled to the Nile Valley. They brought reports of attacks on civilian targets such as industrial sites, a power station, and a school. Subsequent bombings of a Nile dam in the heartland of Egypt indicated, as Haikal put it, that "our whole irrigation system became their target." Nevertheless, Haikal argued that the "the 'War of Attrition' was a great stimulus to Egyptian nationalism. It kept the Egyptian people in a state of psychological mobilization; consolidated the home front, since civilians were as much under fire as soldiers."[57]

The Nasserists believed that Egypt's stand on the Palestinian issue evolved in response to the string of Israeli military attacks on Egypt, notably the Gaza raid, the Suez invasion, and the destruction of the canal zone cities. According to the Nasserists, Egyptians came to see their own fears in the faces of the Palestinians. "Israel," as Nasser framed the issue, "represents for us two things: the expulsion of the Palestinian people from their land, and a permanent threat to the Arab nation."[58] Later, when Sadat questioned Egypt's Arab commitments, he argued that Egyptians had sacrificed too much for the Arab Palestinians. Haikal responded for the Nasserists that the real issue was Egypt's leadership of the Arab world. Haikal readily granted that "no people can sacrifice its own interests for another people." In Haikal's view, however, the Sadat charge missed the essential point that Egypt was the ultimate target of Israeli power. In the Nasserist view, Israel was a Western implant in the Arab world to "prevent its unification and strength." Egypt's role in the Middle East was "the engine" of the Arab states. Therefore, Egyptian-Israeli conflict was inevitable. "Colonial powers," reasoned Haikal, "have been continually occupied in paralyzing this motor to hinder the entire movement for unity." Egypt in its battles with Israel was "defending its own interest and national security."[59]

Critics charged that the price of Arabism and protracted war with Israel was an imperial Soviet presence in Egypt. For a time, the Egyptian aversion to any foreign presence in the country lent weight to the argument. By the mid-seventies, however, the Americans were inadvertently resolving the debate in favor of the Nasserists by the contrast between their role in the seventies with that of the Soviets in the sixties. As American diplomats, aid personnel, and business executives poured into the country American pop culture and consumer products flooded Egypt, the Nasserist version of the politically limited and economically beneficial character of the Russian connection got a fresh hearing. The

Nasserists were especially fond of contrasting the High Dam and the public-sector industries of the Soviet era with the sewer and other infrastructure improvements that symbolized the U.S. aid program.

Dependency on the Russians, Haikal pointed out, was a phenomenon of the post-1967 period. In the decade before the June War, "there was diversity in Arab relations with the superpowers." While Egypt did have "close ties with the Soviet Union, Saudi Arabia had its special relations with the U.S." This arrangement in the larger Arab context allowed maneuverability. The Egyptians gained the same advantage in Egyptian-Soviet relations by keeping lines to the United States open. After the June War that balance could not be preserved. Defeated by the Americans' proxy, the Egyptians looked to the Russians to rebuild. Later, during the War of Attrition, the regime was forced to turn to the Soviet Union to erect a missile shield to protect the country from the Israeli deep penetration raids. The only alternative to an enlarged Soviet presence was capitulation. Yet, from the perspective of the seventies, Haikal could make the point that "when Egypt bought arms from the Soviet Union, it did not depend on it for wheat." He pointed out that until 1966 Egypt's industrialization effort relied on the support of both superpowers. In Haikal's view, the practice of buying both wheat and weapons from the United States creates a "dependency . . . that remains, to my mind, more than is required to maintain the level of security."[60]

For the Nasserists, the limited Egyptian victory in the October 1973 War was the final vindication of their Arab orientation. In a popular novel, the writer Naguib Mahfuz had Nasser claim that "the victory you have accomplished is but the fruit of my long planning for it."[61] The Nasserists argued that the decisive elements of victory, from the rebuilding of the military and the missile wall to the Arab alliance, which was of decisive importance, were all fruits of Nasser's domestic efforts and diplomacy. The sons of Nasserism—that is, those educated in the national schools and universities—provided the manpower that did the fighting. Because of the free education they had received they were able to absorb modern warfare techniques.

The Nasserists questioned the "master of decision" image that Sadat cultivated, claiming that Sadat's role was limited to making the decision when to strike. They reminded Egyptians that Nasserist student and worker groups pressured the regime to act in the difficult years after 1967. According to Abdul Halim Kandil, for example, Sadat's delaying actions were overcome and he was forced to engage the Israelis in 1973 by "remaining revolutionary powers entrenched in the Socialist Youth Organization and the student movement, which led waves of popular anger in 1972 and 1973, demonstrating a mass insistence on fighting the enemy."[62]

The Nasserists argued that Egypt's limited military victory in the October War dispelled the myth of Israeli invincibility. The war made it clear that Israel would have to pay a heavy price for its occupation of Arab land, by demonstrating that the Arabs, despite 1967, did have a military option. "I believe," wrote Haikal, "that after the October War, all that was lost after 1967 was retrieved. In the October War, we had all the elements of power. The Arab world fought with us using the oil weapon. The world waited; America watched. The Soviet Union was with you. We had a chance to retrieve the dream."[63]

The euphoria generated by the Arab performance in 1973 soon subsided. Sadat initiated the well-known series of moves the led from disengagement agreements in the mid-seventies to the separate peace with Israel in 1979. In 1982 Egypt did get back the Sinai, but the Nasserists argued that, while technically the Sinai returned to Egypt, in fact a demilitarized Sinai was a hostage to superior Israeli power. The Nasserist theme of a betrayal of the Arab victory in 1973 took hold. In the Nasserist view, Sadat's diplomacy isolated Egypt from the Arabs and left Egyptians standing helpless as Israel accelerated the colonization of the West Bank, attacked the Iraqi nuclear reactor in 1981, and invaded Lebanon in the summer of 1982. With dismay, Nasserist historians noted that Egypt and the entire Arab world entered a new era, the "Israeli Age."[64]

On the domestic front, the Nasserists directed their charge of betrayal against the exploitative social elements that dominated the Open Door era:

> The policy of the Economic Opening . . . had negative consequences for the Egyptian economy, such as the growth of parasitical activity, a sharp gap in the distribution of income and wealth . . . a decline . . . in the status of the public sector and the exploitation of its resources for the benefit of the local and foreign private sector, continuous increases in prices and a worsening of the balance of payments problem, the failure to provide basic needs for the majority of the population, interference by such international capitalist institutions as the World Bank and the [International Monetary Fund] in determining price and subsidy policy, and the terrible growth of foreign debts, reaching 18,000 million dollars, not including military debts

(as assessed by the Economic conference held on February 1982). Moreover, the Open Door created a rich soil encouraging corruption in society;
current corruption cases . . . are but a trickle in a flood threatening to
drown the whole of Egypt.[65]

Most of the well-to-do had been at least 100 kilometers from the
battlefield during the war, charged one journalist in an echo of the
Nasserist theme. "If you go over the names of those millionaires, you will
discover that the great majority of them have never done their military
service or valued the homeland for anything other than speculation as
contractors . . . no other battle in history ever had this end: those who
fought got nothing, while the gangs profited from all gains and booty."[66]

The critical voice of Nasserism strengthened as disillusionment grew
with the domestic consequences of the link to the West. By 1977 the
economic liberalization had produced many of the negative effects the
Nasserists had predicted: the government gave less attention to industrialization and neglected the social programs that benefited the masses.
The Nasserists charged that Sadat was dismantling Egypt's industrial
and welfare achievements at home even as he was betraying Arabism
abroad. The flaws of the industrialization effort and the inequalities
lingering from the fifties and sixties loomed large immediately after the
1967 defeat; those shortcomings faded in importance, however, before
the disappointments of the Sadat economic liberalization. In this
changed climate, the Nasserists reinvigorated their defense of the socialist achievements of the Nasser regime.

In making their case for socialism, the Nasserists argued that "the
age of socialism in Egypt lasted no more than fourteen years after the
declaration of the nationalization laws [in 1961]. Maybe its true age was
only six years, until the 1967 war."[67] According to the Nasserists, their
indigenous brand of socialism had begun to prove itself in the critical
years from 1961 to 1965, and it was precisely because of this success that
the revolution was subverted from the outside. In the mid-sixties the
United States turned decisively against the Egyptian regime because of
its independent foreign policy; an industrialized and revolutionary Egypt
at the head of the Arab world was too great a threat to American and
Israeli interests. Both economic and military weapons were used against
Egypt's revolution. In 1965 the United States curtailed its critical wheat
aid; this hostile action exacerbated Egypt's balance-of-payments crisis by
forcing it to use scarce hard currency for food. In 1967 Israel dealt a
weakened Egypt its devastating blow. According to the Nasserists, the

Israeli attack in 1967 ended the drive to industrialize. In the wake of the June defeat the regime had to make disabling concessions to hostile outside powers.

The variant of socialism that Nasser created for Egypt before 1967 had industrialization and improvement of mass welfare at its core. Underlying his policies was the fundamental assumption that a better social order required an industrial economy that would raise the general level of prosperity. Aziz Sidky, Nasser's remarkable minister of industry, personified this general strategy of industrialization; for a decade he presided over a remarkable expansion of the public sector that gave real force to Nasser's vision. Initially, the regime relied on an import strategy aimed at substituting for existing consumer demand. The long-range goal was creation of a heavy industry base. The new public-sector factories would concentrate at first on inputs for agriculture. They would also satisfy consumer demands for durables and eventually produce for export. Labor would shift to the industrial sphere. A new, relatively prosperous working class would create an internal market to sustain the development process.

Nasserist socialism would develop most fully in the cities first; then the revolution would be extended to the countryside. In the urban centers socialism would bring guaranteed employment in a state enterprise, public health care, the means to acquire adequate housing with basic appliances and furnishings, free education through the university level, and an expanding range of social services and protections. Eventually, equitable taxation would generate enough revenues to replace the starter funds from foreign loans and aid. Nasser believed that his socialism would be within Egypt's grasp after a decade or so of planned growth, although full extension of its benefits to the countryside might take somewhat longer.[68] Though acknowledging that there were flaws in actual economic performance during the first Nasser years, Nasserist analysts insisted that not even the harshest critics could deny that Egypt made considerable progress toward the industrial future that Nasser had projected.

Nasserist spokesmen such as Kamal Ahmed insisted that the intellectual foundations of the Nasserist variant of socialism that flowered in the sixties were neither Marxist nor liberal: Nasser did not learn his leftism "from foreign sources." He called for an alliance of advanced class forces rather than class warfare, recognized the higher claims of Islam (but not of those Muslims who sought to exploit religion for political ends), and embraced Arab nationalism while infusing it with progressive social content.[69] Above all, Ahmed stressed Nasser's refusal to support the creation of a workers' party and a worker's dictatorship.

The Nasserist experience, its advocates explained, rejected all these standard Marxist positions, without relying on classic liberal values and definitions in social life. In particular, the lower middle class, which advanced so dramatically in the fifties and sixties, supported the Nasserist conception that real freedoms must be grounded in the new economic realities the revolution was creating. Nasser, they pointed out, had given "freedoms" a content that had tangible results for the poor. In a classic formulation, Nasser explained that to the worker, the freedom of the revolution was that "he works and is not unemployed and after that he gets promoted and his children work and he is protected against firing and has social insurance. That is freedom." Freedom for the student was that "he goes to school and learns and that there is equality of opportunity." The peasant's freedom was that "there is no feudalism, no exploitation, and that equal opportunities are his, too."[70] The Nasserists attacked the "false democracy" that existed before the revolution because it had produced aristocratic rule and foreign influence; the revolutionary regime had quite rightly "given law a vacation" because the legal order under the old regime had been used to protect and promote the privileges of the wealthy.

According to the Nasserists, the industrialization drive and the efforts to create a more just social order gave substantial meaning to these ideological pronouncements. The Nasserist state acquired control of industrial resources through nationalization and the elimination of the role of foreign capital and made the most impressive advance in development since Muhammad Aly's effort almost a century earlier. Not since that time had Egypt controlled its own economic destiny so completely. In its drive forward, the regime did not neglect the countryside; the High Dam was built, and land reform was carried out. The engine of Nasser's socialism was industrial growth, however; and the really substantial gains were made in industry. From 1956 to 1965 the industrial share of gross domestic product rose from 16 to 24 percent.[71]

The Nasserists charged that the antisocialist rhetoric of the seventies deliberately obscured both the great accomplishments of the Nasserist revolution and the real reasons for its curtailment. Not the inherent flaws of socialism but rather the external attack in 1967 and the subsequent enforced concessions bankrupted Egypt. The Nasserists did not contest Sadat's characterization of Egypt's dire economic difficulties on the eve of the October War in 1973, but they rejected the official view that socialism had brought the country to economic ruin. In the Nasserist perspective, the period 1967–1973 was one of imposed paralysis. Drained by the 1967 defeat, the Nasser regime no longer had the political strength to continue to expand its role in production and the redistribution of income to the poor. The goal of doubling national income in ten years was quietly abandoned. Concessions to the possessing classes included relaxation of import controls and tax collection. The land reform of 1969, the only income redistribution measure of these years, probably was not implemented. At the same time, Nasserism as an Arab revolution faded. The regime moved closer to the conservative Arab states, ceased its aid to Arab and other Third World liberation movements, and abandoned leadership of the pan-Arab drive.

By 1977, the negative impact of the Open Door policy on Egypt's industrialization lent authority to the Nasserist judgment that enforced liberalization and stagnation, rather than socialism, caused Egypt's economic hardships after 1967. The Open Door policy proved to be an opening to consumption and not to production; the Egyptian market was flooded with imported goods, reinforcing the Nasserist view that enforced liberalization would impede domestic economic development. Egypt in the seventies, the Nasserists reported, underwent deindustrialization. In the public debate over the economy Nasserists joined others in sounding the alarm: steady growth in industry's contribution to economic life, the proudest achievement of Nasser's industrialization drive, had ceased. Instead from 1970 to 1977 industry's overall economic activity had actually shrunk.[72] In the late seventies the macroeconomic picture did improve. The Nasserists pointed out, however, that the economy after 1977 depended on such *rentier* and windfall factors as tourism, Suez Canal revenues, worker remittances, and oil revenues rather than on any expansion of productive capabilities.

Nasserists reasoned that only a national planning board that relied on the responsiveness of publicly owned enterprises could implement a coherent development strategy; long-term national economic policy should aim for an increase in productive capabilities and some recognizable measure of distributive justice. The state, according to the Nasserists, had an essential role in this expansion of productive capacity and in guaranteeing a modicum of security and well-being for the less privileged. Despite the sharp blows the public sector received in the seventies, the Nasserists pointed out that it remained the single most important institution in Egyptian public life. By pointing to capital assets in the billions, a work force of more than 10 percent of the national total, the capacity of the state to generate substantial tax revenues, and profits of about a billion a year, the Nasserists made their case that the approximately 370 public-sector enterprises were a major national resource.[73]

From this Nasserist perspective, criticisms of the public sector in narrowly economic terms carried little weight. The Nasserists vigorously challenged the factual accuracy of charges that the experience of the sixties proved that publicly owned enterprises were inherently unprofitable. Despite the well-known losses of such enterprises as the Iron and Steel Complex at Helwan, the Nasserists insisted that the overall performance record of the public sector had been reasonable by international standards. According to the Nasserists, the misperception, when not deliberately cultivated by the opponents of socialism, derived from faulty measures of economic performance. If profitability was to be taken as an indicator of efficiency, it was necessary to account for price distortions, currency fluctuations, and import costs that reflected political decisions. The industrial public-sector managers had no control over those factors. Specialized assessments of particular sectors indicated that there were "quite a number of fields in manufacturing in which Egypt's public sector is quite efficient." Fertilizers and pharmaceuticals were two examples. One reliable study substantiating Nasserist claims showed that most public-sector companies enjoyed a 9 percent profit rate in 1976–77.[74] Second, an unprofitable enterprise was sometimes subsidized because it provided goods essential to national autonomy. From the Nasserist perspective, industrialization was a nationalist goal that was inherently important whatever its costs. Industrialization permitted self-directed development. The Nasserists judged that every product that Egyptians manufactured for themselves anchored their freedom from external control more securely; similarly, every reasonably well-paid job in industry was an important step out of a backward agricultural past. Finally, the Nasserists argued that many of the measures, such as employment practices, price structure, and import policies, that cut into the profitability of the public enterprises were the consequences of external political considerations. All of these political decisions, they argued, were open to reconsideration; the essential point for Nasserists was that none of the imperfections of the public sector was inherent in the Nasserist variant of socialism. All were subject to reform from within the Nasserist project of Arabism abroad and socialism at home.

Nasserist self-confidence grew as the difficulties created by the Sadat economic and political liberalization were more and more widely felt; a nuanced self-criticism was one important symptom of Nasserist renewal in the seventies. While bound essentially by positive commitments to the achievements of Nasserism as a social and Arab nationalist movement, the self-descriptions of Nasserist groups came to include a shared belief that the incompleteness of the revolution, particularly in the political sphere, helped explain the reversals suffered after Nasser's death.

The Nasserists acknowledged that the Sadat regime's official assault on Nasserism benefited from certain structural weaknesses of the Nasser inheritance. "The counterrevolution," as one Nasserist commentator put it, "has sneaked through the gaps of the July 23 Revolution to the centers of government; the widest of these gaps was the crisis of the political organization." The attack on the public welfare dimension of Egypt's socialism, for example, was made easier by the unfinished character of the Nasser revolution. In many areas of social life the Nasser regime had tolerated the persistence of alternatives to the new social systems. For example, the revolution expanded the system of free public education, but it also allowed private schools a circumscribed existence. The Nasserists of the seventies and eighties argued that the Sadat regime allowed private schools to "grow and prosper in a way that made private education institutions look like investment open-door companies that were free to raise tuition fees and provide teachers with very high salaries through private lessons." They concluded that the tolerated presence of private schools in the fifties and sixties had created precedents for the "neglect" of public education to such a degree that it effectively undercut any commitment to "equal opportunity."[75] Similarly, the Nasser regime had established a network of public health facilities but permitted private clinics and even hospitals to continue to operate. When the national budget's share of expenditures on public services declined in the seventies and the restrictions on the alternative private structures were removed, the quality of the public service systems eroded. Skilled doctors and experienced teachers moved into the private sphere. The Sadat regime defended the expansion of private systems with the argument that they provided services for which wealthy Egyptians had gone abroad in the fifties and sixties; making premium services available in Egypt would eliminate hard currency expenditure on foreign travel.

On the human plane, the inconclusive character of the Nasserist project resulted from the effort to build socialism without socialists. The Nasser regime had employed in projects crucial to the economy middle-class technocrats and managers who were actively hostile to progressive social policies. Osman Ahmed Osman was the prototype. Later, the

Sadat government was able to purge the public sector with the enthusiastic cooperation of these antisocialist elements. Perhaps the most spectacular move came in the 1977 "public-sector massacre." A decree from
the prime minister removed 21 board chairmen and 76 board members.
In all, 347 top administrators were displaced by administrative fiat from
1974 to 1977.[76]

The relative ease with which such blows were delivered shook the
Nasserists. They remained convinced that external forces played the
determinative role in undermining the revolution. Nevertheless, the idea
took hold that domestic shortcomings increased the vulnerability of Nasserism. In particular, the absence of a political party structure that permitted democratic participation was recognized as a central flaw of the
past and a necessary part of any Nasserist revitalization. "Nasser didn't
leave behind him an organization capable of carrying his idea, deepening
it, and struggling for its final victory," wrote Haikal soon after the leader's death.[77] Nasser himself had recognized that new political arrangements were needed because the revolution had moved beyond the circle
of the Free Officers. "The old centers of power are represented by a class
of military politicians, some of whom have made their contribution to
the revolution," explained Nasser in 1968. "But the revolution outpaced
their abilities, their interests, and their ability to develop. They were after
power."[78] The Nasserists acknowledged that neither in 1965–66, when
he contemplated radicalization, nor with the so-called March Program of
1968, when he announced democratization, did Nasser find an appropriate formula to remedy these deficiencies in the political organization
of the revolution.[79]

Despite this internal critique of failures on the organizational plane,
Nasserists insisted on the continuing validity of fundamental values for
which they struggled. Thus, on the one hand the Nasserists acknowledged the serious violations of human rights in the fifties and sixties,
explaining them as a consequence of the weakness of political forms of
the revolution and consequent reliance on heavy-handed administrative
measures. On the other hand, they argued that these flaws did not
diminish the value of the experience of the sixties in redefining the idea
of democracy inherited from the nationalist struggles against the British.
In the Nasserist lexicon, genuine political democracy had a social content, grounded in such achievements of social democracy as free education and public-sector ownership of critical national resources. "Real
democracy," summed up one former official in the Nasser regime, "rests
on a social revolution, such as that achieved in the sixties."

With this argument, the Nasserists rejected charges from both the liberals and leftists that the Nasserist project was inherently anti-democratic. They responded to challenges from the liberals by attacking the liberal understanding of democracy: "Those who criticize," remarked a prominent old-guard Nasserist, "speak only of political democracy," deliberately obscuring the social content that Nasserist policies gave to the democratic idea.[80] To the left's charge that the revolution had simply created a new class of privileged individuals rather than expanding social democracy, the Nasserists responded that the "new class" argument was a standard weapon of reactionaries, who sought the abandonment of revolution rather than measures that would correct its abuses. Nasserists warned their Marxist critics that the real aim of the "new class' argument was to demoralize the masses at a time when the forces of reaction were gathering strength. "This new class argument is the accusation used by the overthrown classes against socialism all over the world," commented Muhammad Auda. "But the new class is not a 'class' but only small sections or slices." The appropriate response to the appearance of exploitative social forces in an incipient socialist order was to press forward with the creation of socialist structures; as Auda put it, "continuous revolution is the antidote of the new class problem, the means to surround it and eliminate it."[81] The forward movement of the revolution would provide an antidote to the "new class" danger by eroding or dissolving class differences.[82]

In the Nasserist view, the traditional Marxist analysis also erred by taking class factors as natural outcomes of the forms of domestic life. Nasserists argued that the formations of groupings hostile to progressive, nationalist institutions and policies were as much a product of external as of internal forces. In the Egyptian case, Haikal pointed out, American aid funds were "allocated to strengthen the private sector, sometimes in a crude manner; there [was] also a complete media system aimed at changing the complex of values prevalent in society."[83]

The shortcomings of the fifties and sixties, the Nasserists insisted, did not dilute the solid achievements of Nasserism as an Arab, industrial, and social revolution; nor did it dilute the widespread support these accomplishments engendered. The American-backed Israeli strike of 1967 did cripple the revolution, and as a result of the war a weakened political authority could no longer contain the domestic opponents of Nasserism. For this reason, de-Nasserization proceeded with impressive speed and thoroughness once Nasser himself passed from the scene. Yet, for all the apparent momentum of the de-Nasserization campaign, when the Sadat decade ended in repression and assassination, it was clear that Nasserism had survived as a submerged but powerful political alternative.

Such key official policies of the seventies as the rehabilitation of the Muslim Brothers, the encouragement of temporary labor migration, and the deliberate official confusion of Nasserism with Marxism were understandable only with an awareness of the pressures that the regime felt from the Nasserist current. The Nasserist perspective linked each of the major policies to the regime's struggle to defeat Nasserism.

Sadat, in this view, aimed to offset the susceptibility to Nasserism of such key urban groups as university students and public-sector workers when he decided to rehabilitate the Muslim Brotherhood—a decision that many characterized as perhaps the most significant domestic political decision he ever made. In Nasserists' eyes, Sadat concluded that only the Islamic groups had the mass appeal to counterbalance the popular support that Nasserism commanded, especially among radical students and workers. Sadat could count on the political right to condemn Nasserist departures from liberal ideas of property rights and legal procedures.[84] These issues, however, carried weight primarily among the middle class. Sadat knew that the denunciation of Nasser by Islamic groups would be as angry and would cut deeper. While the Islamic activists were drawn primarily from the lower middle class, their cultural and religious critique of Nasserism penetrated further in Egyptian society. The Muslim Brothers, who had been key targets of the security apparatus in the fifties and sixties, would bring a white-heat intensity to their denunciations. Arrested by the thousands and consigned to prisons and detention camps, they could be relied on to deepen de-Nasserization by painting Nasserist authoritarianism in the darkest colors.

The Nasserists pointed out that the silent temporary migration to the oil-rich countries aided the regime's attempted depletion of the human reserves of the Nasserist idea. Thanks to the liberalization of restrictions on travel, those dissatisfied with the direction of public policy, often on Nasserist grounds, were leaving rather than resisting. Remittances from the more than 500,000 Egyptians working in the Arab countries passed the $2 billion mark by the end of the seventies.[85] This windfall exceeded the returns on cotton export, Suez Canal revenues, tourism, and the value added of the High Dam combined.[86] Advocates of the Open Door claimed that one liberalization measure allowing travel abroad had brought more hard currency to Egypt that Nasser's much-vaunted success at Suez.

Nasserists were unimpressed by these alleged benefits. For them, the costs to Egypt of the massive migration were devastating. They saw the issues raised by emigration as a debate between the windfall from worker remittances on the one hand and the loss of needed talents on the other. The Nasserists noted ironically that the regime was allowing the "best brains and most skilled hands" to go abroad in unprecedented numbers to develop other countries while Egypt stagnated. They also drew attention to the deterioration of morals that resulted when the money to be made in the oil-rich states rather than some larger common purpose became the only value of society.[87]

To undermine the force of the Nasserist critique of public policy, the regime attempted to identify Nasserism with Marxism. In Egypt, Marxists were hindered by charges of atheism and subservience to a foreign power that weakened their mass appeal. Nasserism, in contrast, was an indigenous political current, explicitly embracing Islam while battling Islamic activists such as the Muslim Brothers who challenged its authority. Whenever they had the opportunity to distance themselves from the Marxists, the Nasserists did so with alacrity. In 1975 the government announced the formation of platforms with the Arab Socialist Union. The executive committee of the ASU narrowed the contending platforms to four, including a Nasserist grouping. There were points in common between the Nasserists and the Marxist left, including protection of the public sector, a concern for mass welfare, and an aversion to too close a relationship with the United States. Nevertheless, these agreements did not overcome the Nasserists' strong reluctance to tie themselves too closely to the Marxists. Despite the Nasserists' misgivings, a government committee approved three political groups of the right, center, and the left, with the left combining the Nasserists and the Marxists in one left platform that eventually became the National Progressive Unionist Party (NPUP).

The Sadat regime consistently sought to obscure the difference between Marxism and Nasserism by deliberately misrepresenting the NPUP as the voice of Nasserism in the seventies. The Nasserists vehemently rejected this characterization and sharply criticized its acceptance at face value by Western journalists and scholars.[88] The Nasserists pointed out that although there were Nasserists in the NPUP, as in all the parties and institutions of public life, Marxists were known to play a particularly prominent role in the amalgam of leftists who led the NPUP. For this reason, the Nasserists resisted the regime's attempt to designate the NPUP as a Nasserist party and strived to achieve recognition for an independent and uncompromised legal Nasserist organization.

The Nasserists insisted on their differences from Marxism on principled as well as pragmatic grounds. "The main trend of the Egyptian left is Nasserist," wrote the Nasserist journalist Muhammad Salmawy. He argued that "the July Revolution, with its progressive socialist inclinations and economic policies, created a new leftist trend, derived from the heritage of this nation and formed by the process of dealing with its day-to-day problems for eighteen years." Those who "copied their leftism from foreign books failed to provide real solutions to our problems either before or after the revolution."[89] Kamal Ahmed summed up the implications of this reasoning. "The NPUP doesn't represent the July Revolution," he argued. "I don't want to get into trouble with the authorities. Yet, I want to ask you whether there are true parties in Egypt. If so, how do you explain this political vacuum in the life of the nation . . . ?" Ahmed stressed, in particular, that an authentic Nasserist party would have no vulnerability because of its stand on religion: "No, every Nasserist adheres to religious values. What happened in 1954 and 1965 [Nasser's clash with the Muslim Brothers] were political movements. Nasserism is not in conflict with religion. If it were, it would be better for Nasserism to cease to exist."[90]

On March 14, 1976, Sadat authorized these three official platforms to contest the parliamentary elections of October 1976; the ensuing election was generally regarded as the freest in Egypt since the forties.[91] Nevertheless, Sadat intervened early and forcefully against the NPUP, declaring that the left could never produce a truly national program and openly backing the center platform.[92]

It was Nasserism and not Marxism that Sadat saw as a threat, and he had hoped to undercut its appeal by branding it Marxist. Sadat revealed the basis of his fears that his regime might be undercut by the left when he informed the leader of the left platform, "I am the true Nasserist." The regime sanctioned an intense preelection press campaign against the left.[93] The Ahram Center for Political and Strategic Studies did a content analysis of the coverage of the elections in the national press. This systematic survey confirmed that, although rhetorically the regime attacked the left in general, the real target was the Nasserists. Of critical articles in the official press coverage of the 1976 elections, 84 percent were directed at the left. Almost 38 percent of the articles attacking the NPUP platform charged that it was Marxist, with roughly the same percentage of articles claiming that society rejected the left orientation as a solution to Egypt's national problems. About a third of the articles also accused the left platform of being antireligious.[94] This concerted verbal attack on the left occurred in the context of extensive violence; 11 deaths and 216 injuries resulted from more than 70 conflicts related to the elections.[95]

The campaign against the NPUP confirmed the Nasserist judgment that this official left party was a government creation so hemmed in by restrictions that it could hardly function as a party at all. According to the Nasserists, its only real function was to discredit the real left alternative to government policies by branding it as Marxist and alien to Egypt. In the seventies, therefore, the Nasserists made repeated attempts to establish a distinctive legal political presence, unencumbered by the imposed link to Marxist political groups. The regime blocked each such purely Nasserist party. In fact, the Nasserists charged that all genuine political forces were so blocked. The journalist Muhammad Salmawy remarked that "a society that declares its belief in the necessity of political pluralism and whose major political forces are forced to resort to secret organizations, is a society that suffers from major defects that have to be treated."[96] The Nasserists responded with court actions. Those involved in these legal efforts to establish a Nasserist party believed that their repression was linked to the American role in Egypt; Haikal, for example, argued explicitly that the United States would not accept a Nasserist party.[97] A former Free Officer with leftist inclinations, Kamal Rifa'at, acted as figurehead for the first attempt to organize a legal political party in 1975, when the regime first announced the formation of platforms in the ASU. In the first few weeks of its formation this Nasserist grouping attracted thousands of members. The regime eliminated the Nasserist platform.[98] Rifa'at joined the NPUP. However, "only a few tens" of Nasserists followed him; most continued their efforts to form an independent party.[99]

Several months later four prominent Nasserists took the lead in a second attempt. They were all of the generation that grew to maturity in the sixties, and they called their proposed party the Alliance Vanguard. The term *alliance* evoked the Nasserist formula of a coalition of working forces in contrast to the Marxist notion of proletarian hegemony. The regime refused the request. Later, the secretary general of the ASU denied that he had even met with the Nasserist representatives. All four figures involved in the effort were subsequently arrested in the fall of 1981.

University students mounted the third major attempt to form a legal Nasserist organization. The effort grew out of Nasserist university study circles. Hamdine Sabahy, the head of the student union of Cairo University and the editor-in-chief of the university student journal, spearheaded the move. He too was arrested in 1981 and the effort collapsed.

In August 1983 Kamal Ahmed submitted an application to form the Coalition of Popular Acting Forces, with a membership spanning seventeen governorates and consisting of approximately 70 percent peasants and workers.[100] Four months later a government committee rejected the application on the grounds that the party program indicated commitment to a revolutionary Marxist and totalitarian system that would foster class conflict and threaten democracy. In court battles to contest the decision, the attorney for the Nasserists charged that the committee had not given the proposed party the detailed hearing required by law and had deliberately distorted the party program to make it appear Marxist, whereas in fact the Nasserists "refuse the dictatorship of the proletariat and the class struggle; they adhere to principles of social democracy."[101]

With these legal efforts at organization consistently blocked, some Nasserists turned to conspiratorial politics. When such clandestine groups were discovered, the regime predictably branded them communist and Marxist. Members were arrested and treated harshly in jail. However, the courts seldom sustained official charges against the Nasserists; typically they ordered their release after several months.

While covert efforts surfaced only in police and court records, other faces of Nasserism in public life gave rough indications of its strength. In all direct mass action in the streets, from the student movement of the early seventies to the eruptions of the early eighties, there were slogans invoking Nasserist goals and aspirations. In quieter times, there were seminars on Nasserist thought at the universities and yearly celebrations of Nasser's birthday. The latter were probably the most important public occasions for a show of popular support for Nasserism.[102] In addition, a Nasserist presence was felt in all institutions that preserved an independent role in public life, however circumscribed. These ranged from university faculty clubs to the Bar Association and the officially approved political parties.[103] From such bases the Nasserists were able to contribute in a circumscribed but important way to policy debates about Egypt's future.

The regime attempted to remove certain critical foreign policy issues, notably the peace process with Israel, from discussion in the public arena. One device for legitimating such restrictions was manipulated popular referenda. A 1979 plebiscite, for example, forbade the formation of a party that stood against the Egyptian-Israeli treaty. Kamal Ahmed, speaking for the Nasserists, argued that "the plebiscite denied the right of parties that stand against peace, not against the treaty; we are for peace based on justice."[104]

Debate over domestic issues was less restricted and therefore revealed more fully the importance of the Nasserist current. The protracted debate over the so-called national university was a case in point. The idea of a private university that charged tuition first surfaced in 1973, before the October War and the advent of the Open Door. Officials explained that thousands of Egyptian students who did not meet the standards for admission to the national universities spent foreign currency to study abroad. At the same time, large number of Arab students studied in Egyptian universities at very little cost to themselves. Advocates of a private university argued that both groups would be attracted by a quality private institution that would operate alongside the existing government-controlled national university system.[105]

The Nasserists charged that the proposal openly challenged the principle of egalitarian education, the very foundation of the social revolution of the fifties and sixties. From the Nasserist perspective, the education question perfectly exemplified the rootedness of the fundamental Nasserist programs in Egyptian nationalist struggles. The advances made by Nasserism in education were tied to a history that could not be reduced to failed socialism and an abortive foreign policy. The Nasserists pointed out that the 1923 constitution had made education a right of citizens, while a law in 1925 had made the primary schools free. A decade later the nationalist party, the Wafd, had abolished tuition payments for secondary schools and opened them to all who passed the admissions tests; Taha Hussein, then minister of education, had declared that education should be "free like air and water." The Wafdist leadership had intended to extend free education through the university level, but the government of 1950 had fallen before the policy could be implemented.[106]

On assuming power in 1952, the Free Officers responded to the momentum of these nationalist demands for an expansion of educational opportunities.[107] In 1963 the regime established the open admissions principle and in 1964 accepted the obligation to guarantee employment to all Egyptians with a university diploma. Each of these steps, the

Nasserists pointed out, represented the achievement of long-standing national demands.

From 1952 to the end of the sixties, 250,000 people graduated from Egypt's universities. The Nasserists had opened the universities with the expectation that the early successes of their industrial revolution would easily absorb, indeed require, these educated citizens. Ironically from the Nasserist perspective, the expansion of university education came just as the industrialization drive began to slow under the impact of hostile external pressures. After 1967 the industrial sector stagnated and declined while the number of university students continued to grow. The Sadat government responded to the overcrowding by upgrading (on paper, at least) existing higher institutes to the university level and creating new universities in the provinces. As a result, in the seventies there were almost twice as many university graduates as Egypt had produced in its entire previous history.[108] The burden of finding employment for these numbers was staggering.

Not surprisingly, in the Open Door climate of the Sadat years, tuition-free education and guaranteed government employment came under sharp attack. In the late seventies and early eighties Osman Ahmed Osman took the lead in reviving and developing the idea of a private university education system, calling the project the "national university." Osman did not envision a traditional university. He proposed that the new institution be tied more directly to national economic needs, as defined by the Osman circle. The food security projects over which Osman presided would require specialists in "eggs, poultry, milk, fish, agriculture, and import/export" to solve the food problem. Solution of the housing crisis, important to Osman as a onetime minister of housing, demanded construction and managerial cadres specialized in building "the kind of housing we need." Should those problems be resolved, the curriculum would change accordingly; there was no question of guaranteeing jobs for the graduates. Osman explained: "Let [them] look for a job; this is the first step in building character." Salaries for those hired by private-sector companies would be "at least three times and probably six or seven times higher than government wages . . . But it all depends on the effort and the sweat."[109]

The revived campaign for a private university collapsed under a wave of opposition. Nasserist voices were prominent in the chorus that warned the regime: "Caution: Don't Mess with [Free Education.]"[110] In the heyday of Nasserism, a school was built every three days, an article in 1980 reminded readers in its title. The article argued that both learning capacity and teaching skills were declining in the nation's schools to such a degree that

> free education is fading as most students tend to take private lessons. Some make use of this opportunity to attack free education and call directly for its abolition. Others attack it indirectly, calling for the state's establishment of new, tuition-charging schools, schools under the name of language schools, superior schools, or the national university. We don't have to stress that the only result would be serving a very small slice of Egyptian students, those who have, for whom the existing private schools are not enough—while the rest of the sons of the taxpayers, workers, employees, and peasants, would remain drowned in the swamp of deteriorating education.[111]

The Nasserists recognized the severity of the problems afflicting Egypt's educational system; they were unwilling, however, to attribute them to Egypt's open admissions policies. From the Nasserist perspective, the commitment to free education made sense in the context of a drive to industrialize that would raise the common people's standard of living; they advocated a renewed commitment to industrialize rather than abandonment of the educational policies that must accompany the creation of an industrial society. In the seventies the problems of education were only a secondary symptom of the disastrous national consequences of the economic strategy that was deindustrializing Egypt. For the Nasserists, the root causes of Egypt's difficulties were the link to the West, the peace with Israel, and the so-called liberalization of the economy that went with them. In the meanwhile, they were not about to tolerate the dismantling of the social gains the revolution had made; in their view, an industrialized Egypt would require university-educated manpower. Moreover, Egypt's claim to leadership of the Arab world rested on the talents and training of educated Egyptians. A cartoon in *Rose al-Yusuf* in June 1980 summed up the Nasserist view of the evils of the dependency, consumerism, and monied privilege that Sadat had wrought while undermining the Nasserist project. The artist showed a woman exhausted by the heat, drinking a 7-Up and slouched before an imported fan. The cartoonist sarcastically invoked Taha Hussein's famous nationalist slogan that education, like air and water, should be free; the caption read: "Education is like air and water—it all costs money."

Vigorous Nasserist participation in the public debate over education showed that the Nasser revolution did not come out of nowhere; in its goals and achievements, it drew deeply on the Egyptian nationalist movement. Nor had the transformation of the fifties and sixties disappeared without a trace, despite claims to the contrary and strenuous pressure by domestic critics and Western analysts.[112] Above all, the changes in class composition and the social mobility stimulated in the fifties and sixties had a restraining effect. For all the rhetorical attacks, the Sadat regime continued such Nasserist policies as educational expansion and subsidies on basic commodities.

The successor regime did question Egypt's Arabness, and the economic strategy of the seventies weakened the industrial public sector. Nevertheless, the social policies Nasser had launched to advance the Arab revolution and Egypt's industrialization could not be reversed. The Nasser revolution did not unify the Arab world or create a full-blown socialism in Egypt. The public policies directed to those ends, however, did vastly accelerate an underlying process of social mobility that had been gathering momentum since the turn of the century. In addition, Nasserism provided a new consciousness that made sense of those amorphous social changes. The small changes in individual lives proved durable enough for large numbers of Egyptians to keep alive the larger Nasserist project of a socialist Egypt as the driving force of the Arab world.

Three years after Sadat's death, without ever mentioning Nasser's name, Ahmed Bahaeddine, a distinguished journalist who believed in Nasserism but had not been a part of Nasser's inner circle, wrote the authoritative rebuttal to a decade of virulent de-Nasserization in the form of three open letters addressed to an unidentified "you."[113] Both form and content made Bahaeddine's defense of Nasser the definitive one. The articles appeared in the most important of the mass dailies, and their sparse style expressed the basic concepts often taken for granted by those who described themselves as Nasserists.

Every Egyptian who read the letters in *al-Ahram* knew they were addressed to Gamal Abdul Nasser and to those Egyptians who continued to identify themselves as Nasserists. The anonymous "you" of Bahaeddine's letters was an affirmation of the powerful Nasserist presence in public life, despite the long repression of any organized expression of Nasserism. The articles subtly parodied official "charges" against the man who brought down the monarchy, ended the British occupation, and launched a pan-Arab, socialist revolution:

"Why did you wake up the tens of millions who had been perfectly satisfied with old cheese, onions, the death of their infants, and toil from dawn to dusk?" Nasser's accusers felt that the arousal of Egypt's poor caused a host of problems for the half million to a million privileged Egyptians. His critics charged that the revolution brought electricity to four thousand villages that had lived happily without it for four thousand years. Now the peasants wanted radio and television; an energy problem resulted. Public-sector factories produced a butane cooking stove for ten L.E.; everyone, including those who used to burn dried dung, could afford it. Before long there was a shortage of gas. Even worse, peasants of the old "productive" villages who once contented themselves with cheese, onions, and dried bread now at the eggs and chickens they used to sell to the "consuming" city; no wonder the tangled problems of supplies and subsidies were worsening.

"You made us bear the burdens and responsibilities of development because you wanted our people to live in the twentieth century." In the seventies, anti-Nasserist forces pointed only to the shortcomings of the Nasserist drive to increase productivity by reclaiming land and creating an industrial public sector. They were angry because, unlike the monuments left by the ancient pharaohs, the thousand factories built in the fifties and sixties required maintenance and renovation. The Aswan High Dam, too, required troublesome replacement of turbines, exploitation of the new lake it created, and attention to changes in the waters of the Nile.

"You are the cause of all our problems. . . . Why didn't you do the safe things and accept Egypt's lot as a small weak country?" In the eyes of his critics, Nasser's assertions of Egypt's national will lacked a sense of realism. Nasser, they charged, failed to learn abject humility from the experiences of his great predecessors. He did not understand that the dominant powers of every age would prevent Egypt from becoming powerful enough to arouse the Arab world. Muhammad Aly founded modern Egypt and launched an industrial drive. He deployed his power abroad to protect his base in Egypt. But the great powers of his day allied against him, forced his withdrawal to a weakened Egypt, and carved up the Middle East. Nasser's call for Arab unity, his assistance to the Algerian and Yemeni nationalist forces, and his slogan "Arab oil for the Arabs" turned the West against Egypt. Nasser should not have kept alive the nationalist dream of a strong and independent Egypt as backbone of the Arab world.

In the seventies official definitions of reality identified Nasserism as

a spent political force. Yet, Nasserist beliefs and practices were so compelling a presence in Egyptian public life that ironic restatement, rather
than explicit rebuttals, transformed the charges against the Nasserists
into the most eloquent defense of the makers of a socialist and Arab
nationalist revolution.

4

Making Revolution Real: The Marxists of *The Vanguard*

> The fact that we give names to things which are in flux implies inevitably a certain stabilization oriented along the lines of collective activity. The derivation of our meanings emphasizes and stabilizes that aspect of things which is relevant to activity and covers up, in the interest of collective action, the perpetually fluid process underlying all things. It excludes other configurational organizations of the data which tend in different directions. Every concept represents a sort of taboo against other possible sources of meaning—simplifying and unifying the manifoldness of life for the sake of action.
>
> —*Karl Mannheim*

On January 18 and 19, 1977, from Alexandria to Aswan, Egyptians by the tens of thousands rose to protest a government decision to reduce subsidies on such basic commodities as rice, sugar, and cooking gas. Angry crowds of students, workers, and the urban poor demonstrated in all the major cities, attacking symbols of state power, conspicuous consumption, and Western influence. The targets reflected the widespread perception that the International Monetary Fund, backed by the United States, had instigated the regime's decision to cut back on government spending in ways that struck hardest at the poor. The police and security forces could not contain the demonstrators; an estimated 160 were killed, hundreds more were wounded, and several thousand were arrested. For two days, Egyptians lived without a system of public authority; only the intervention of the army restored order.

When the demonstrations began, Anwar Sadat was in Aswan, preparing to welcome President Tito of Yugoslavia to that winter resort city. The president first heard of the disturbances in the major cities late in the afternoon from a foreign journalist. The reporter startled an obviously uninformed Sadat with the news that "the troubles" had spread to Aswan. The governor of Aswan confirmed the report only when crowds advancing on the presidential resthouse threatened to block the road to the airport. Sadat left hurriedly for the flight to Cairo in an old taxi cab to avoid recognition. Arriving at the presidential residence in the capital, he found a helicopter already in place for the lift to the airport at Abu Soweir, where a special plane waited to take him and his family to refuge in Teheran if the situation continued to deteriorate.[1]

Meanwhile, Prime Minister Mamduh Salem, a former police official and minister of the interior, asked that the army be called in. Salem doubted that the regular security forces alone could restore order in the face of the worst mass disturbances in Egypt since the forties. However, when Salem broached intervention with Minister of War and Commander-in-Chief Abdul Ghany al-Gamasy, the general demurred, citing a pledge made by the political leadership after the October 1973 War that the army would not be used against the civilian population. When Sadat arrived in the capital from Aswan, he conferred with Gamasy. The general reported that the army could be relied on to contain the uprising only if the government rescinded the subsidy cuts. The army moved against the demonstrators later that day; the official news agencies repeatedly broadcast cancellation of the subsidy cutbacks, thereby fulfilling the condition for intervention that the military had set.[2]

Presiding at a meeting of the country's political leaders in the wake of the riots, Sadat acknowledged that it was natural for "certain sections of the populace" to reject "the new burdens placed upon them"; an official report assured Egyptians that "the people's food and clothing would not be touched." The president explained that he had foreseen vigorous protests against the rise in prices unless the government tied those increases to improvements in the conditions of the poor and greater burdens on the rich; to those ends, he had urged the government to pass "new tax and housing laws, both on an urgent basis." For the future, Sadat promised that he would direct "a merciless strike" against the "so-called parasites" of the Open Door policy who took advantage of his liberalization to thrive on illicit economic activities.[3]

Attentive listeners noted, however, that even in these first conciliatory responses, the president warned that "all this complaining, this talk about the government being for the bourgeoisie, comes from the communists and the spiteful."[4] Security reports, detailing the role of radical workers and students in the demonstrations, fed Sadat's suspicions of the left. On January 19, 1977, the security police gave this account of events in Cairo and Alexandria to the general prosecutor:

Cairo: On January 18, 1977, at 9:45 A.M. disturbances and demonstrations occurred in Cairo by some workers from the industrial area in Helwan and students from the engineering faculty of Ain Shams University, the faculty of arts, and the commercial institute in Zamalek, as well as some high schools. They were joined by other elements on the pretext of protesting the recent decisions to raise the prices of some goods. The wave of demonstrations extended to include a number of the quarters of the city; they resulted in incidents of arson, sabotage, and attacks on the police forces. The demonstrations continued until 3:00 A.M. on January 19, 1977 . . . The minister of the interior reported that incidents recurred on the morning of January 19 in various parts of the city, resulting in incidents of arson, sabotage, and attacks on public and private buildings. The police forces did their duty in protecting these buildings. The incidents continued until 9:00 P.M. . . .

Alexandria: A group of workers from the Alexandria Arsenal Factory were regularly holding meetings in their work sites and in some cafés to study the economic conditions in the country. They agreed among themselves to seize any opportunity to agitate the masses in the city to provoke discontent with the government and the regime. The most obvious manifestation of these activities was the adoption of labor demands aimed at creating disturbances among their fellow workers and at winning their confidence. They were provided the opportunity sought [with the announcement of a reduction on government subsidies on staples] . . . They decided to gather the largest number of workers possible to demonstrate in the streets of Alexandria to protest the rise in prices and turn the masses against the government. The demonstrators arrived at Liberation Square in Mansheya, where they were joined by workers from other factories. The number of this particular demonstration reached almost 10,000. It later combined with demonstrations of university students.[5]

Once the army contained the uprising, Sadat drew on these reports to charge "leftist plotters" with inciting and organizing the worker and student radicals. According to Sadat, the communists exaggerated every small mistake his democratic government made, including the failure in January to explain adequately the "necessity" of the price hikes. "They exploited it to the utmost," Sadat charged. "Why? To seize power. To seize it how? By destruction, sabotage, killing, robbing. That is what the 18 and 19 of January was all about. They say it was a popular uprising. For shame! It was the rumbling of thieves."[6]

Sadat said that democratic scruples prevented him from divulging all the details of the "odious criminal plot"; to do so while "the affair was still under investigation" would be improper. However, the president claimed to have before him all the proof he needed of the left's plan to destroy Egypt by burning police stations, Nile bridges, central telephone installations, factories, agricultural cooperatives, and even bakeries "in order to spread hunger." The plotters had wormed their way into the state structures, particularly the national press and other public organizations, such as the National Progressive Unionist Party (NPUP). The president charged that communist elements used these public positions "to preserve two things: freedom of action and a legal status through the Unionist Party, while preserving their secret underground operations for sabotage and seizing power."[7]

The regime arranged an eleven-point plebiscite to secure popular endorsement of its definition of the January events as a leftist plot. The plebiscite urged Egyptians "to say yes to peace, freedom, and security" and "no to blood and destruction." Two provisions implicitly recognized the social injustices denounced by the demonstrators. The first declared payment of taxes a "duty" and raised the level of exemption from taxes to L.E. 500 in an effort to make the rich take a larger share of the burden. The second conciliatory provision required registration of personal wealth under penalty of loss of all political rights for failure to make a truthful disclosure. However, both measures were largely hortatory and probably unenforceable. In contrast, the repressive proposals in the referendum called for a sentence of twenty-five years' hard labor for participation in demonstrations that aimed to overthrow state institutions or in strikes that damaged the national economy. The referendum also struck the parliamentary left by sanctioning a new law to stiffen the conditions to form political parties, thereby decreasing opposition strength in parliament.[8]

Without waiting for the predictable 99-percent-plus endorsement of these security measures, the government set about rounding up the "criminals." The chief prosecutor announced triumphantly in *al-Ahram* on January 26 that no less than four underground communist groups had conspired to "bring down the regime" by encouraging demonstrations and acts of violence. Three days later Prime Minister Salem extended the offensive to the NPUP, the legal left party, charging that it harbored "many communist elements" who had tried to use the party to "overthrow the government and install a communist regime." The prime minister expressed regret that an official political party had so "shamefully involved itself in this abominable national crime."[9]

The story of the "leftist plot" mobilized support for the Sadat regime from the United States and the conservative Arab states. Two days after the army quieted Egypt's streets, the grand shaikh of al-Azhar broadcast an appeal to the conservative Arab states to come immediately to Egypt's aid; a day later the government received a billion-dollar pledge. On February 1 the United States announced it would speed the transfer of $190 million in allocated aid funds to help Egypt's beleaguered government.[10]

Sadat read the January events as a grave threat to his power. He chose to treat the crisis of authority as the result of a leftist conspiracy rather than deep-seated social and economic problems. As a result, the president ruled out the possibility of a reformist response to meet the demands of the populist forces that challenged his rule. He turned instead to external forces to buttress his position. Sadat acted to win Western backing for his regime and to halt the drain on resources from the protracted conflict with Israel. In order to secure a continuous flow of large-scale U.S. foreign aid for his troubled regime, Sadat moved Egypt unambiguously into the American camp. Understanding full well that the journey to Washington could be made only through Jerusalem, he launched his peace initiative with Israel. For his remaining years in power, the president held to this foreign policy resolution of Egypt's difficulties. At home, he emphasized the suppression of the "conspiratorial" left rather than the political mobilization of new support for a revision of basic social and economic strategies.[11]

Sadat explained his assault on the legal left as a continuation of his May 1971 "Corrective Revolution," when he eliminated the "centers of power." Within months of assuming the presidency, Sadat met a challenge by a left faction of the political elite, informally led by Arab Socialist Union (ASU) head Aly Sabry, by enlisting the support of the armed forces; with military backing, he moved decisively against his rivals, imprisoning Sabry and the powerful figures aligned with him.[12] Six years later, however, the president castigated himself for "neutralizing the heads only" when he should have neutralized "the tails as well, that is, the hiding places of the left in the media, the press, and other machinery for influencing the masses."[13] The official explanation of a criminal conspiracy justified a campaign that swept up students, workers, and intellectuals, especially leftists or members and sympathizers of the NPUP.[14]

Within days of the uprising, the state security apparatus arrested hundreds of left party members and held them in jails throughout Egypt. Prominent journalists and party activists were singled out to show that no one on the left was safe.[15] Over a three-month period the regime arrested some 3,000 Egyptians and charged them with participation in the leftist "subversive conspiracy."[16] On the radio, television, press, and in official conferences government officials accused the NPUP and its leaders of treason and atheism. The names of NPUP party members who resigned under pressure appeared regularly in the official press.[17]

In May 1978 Sadat moved to ban all "communists" and "unbelievers" from political activity and state employment. The president accused the left party of entering into a "shadowy alliance with the New Wafd Party with the aim of overthrowing the government and the whole regime."[18] In a more pointed attack, the president announced: "The NPUP should dissolve itself because it has no place among us."[19] While the left party ignored this invitation to disband, it struggled against a series of measures designed to undermine its influence. The government banned the left paper, *The Masses* (*al-Ahaly*) and denied the party the right to hold large public meetings. In addition, the regime encouraged the formation of the Socialist Labor Party, a new party to the left of Sadat's NDP, in the hope that it would drain support from the NPUP. When new elections were held under these restrictive conditions, the NPUP lost its representation. Sadat's repression succeeded in reducing the party's public presence; it did not, however, succeed in eliminating the critical voice of the left.

"What is this?" demanded Ahmed Lutfy al-Kholy, editor-in-chief of *The Vanguard* (*al-Tali'ah*) and perhaps the best-known voice of Marxism in Egyptian public life. "What are these lies being told about the events of January 18 and 19, 1977?" Kholy's February editorial defiantly contradicted the regime version of events by declaring that "a legitimate mass uprising" had occurred.[20]

Challenges to official definitions of reality had issued from the pages of *The Vanguard* since 1965, when Kholy inaugurated it as an explicitly Marxist journal, with an editorial board of about a dozen veterans of the intellectual wing of the Egyptian Communist Party.[21] The new publication was housed in the *al-Ahram* building, but by contractual agreement *The Vanguard* was to be independent of *al-Ahram,* and the editors under Kholy fought hard to maintain that autonomy in order to preserve the differences in their viewpoint and methodology.[22] The *Vanguard*'s editors focused on overcoming the national and international obstacles to the "Arab/Egyptian road to socialism" and "Arab unity and struggle," with special emphasis on Palestine. Symbolic indicators of the journal's autonomy included omission of *al-Ahram*'s board chairman's name from the masthead and the statement that *The Vanguard* was "located on the premises of *al-Ahram*" rather than the phrase "issued by *al-Ahram*," which appeared on all other periodicals. More than symbols, however, were required to actualize the promise of independence. As a result of critical positions taken over the years, Kholy was exposed more than once to detention, suspension from work, and jail.[23] However, despite official harassment, Kholy presided over the magazine's editorial board.

The Marxists associated with *The Vanguard* defined themselves by the critical decision made in the mid-sixties to dissolve their former political affiliations and enter the Arab Socialist Union, the official party of the Nasserist revolution. Under Nasser, they hoped to play a leading role in the ASU, pushing Nasser's nationalist revolution to the left through actual political engagement rather than through the abstract debate or underground activity favored by more radical Marxists. Later, Sadat's liberalization held out to the *Vanguard* circle and like-minded mainstream Marxists the possibility of continuing practical party work through the official left party, the NPUP.[24] In both periods the Marxists used their journal to speak directly to the public at critical moments. Until the regime suspended its publication in 1977, *The Vanguard* was Egyptian Marxists' most influential platform.

In place of "riots and a criminal plot," Kholy's February 1977 editorial saw a "public and peaceful" protest of specific government economic policies. The *Vanguard* treatment of the January events stressed that the demonstrations had begun spontaneously; the masses "rose on the morning of January 18 from different geographic, social, and political groups throughout the country, all at one time, one wave after another; the organization of this outpouring was beyond the energy of any one power or party in the country, whether secret or not." The editorial pointed out that "the first day of the uprising did not involve any events of destruction or theft worth mentioning." Only when the government switched from the violence of the "bureaucratic rod" on the first day to the violence of the "rod of bullets and tear gas" on the second day did the people move from "peaceful strikes" to "strikes of rocks and stones."

In his "Comments on the January Events" accompanying Kholy's editorial, veteran leftist Abou Seif Yusuf argued that the masses correctly understood the subsidies decision as a political choice favoring the rich rather than as a response to purely economic imperatives, as the regime characterized it. Sadat's Open Door policy represented a return to capitalism on all levels that threatened to cancel all the advances made in the fifties and sixties toward socialism. Yusuf catalogued the depressing economic toll of the Open Door policy on the lower classes: "the rise in the price of fish and meat, difficulty in obtaining cheap textiles because of the control of the market by a few merchants, the removal of subsidies from basic food stuffs, and difficulty in providing milk for their infants. Despite these trials, "the masses were patient and hid their pain." However, "On the morning of January 18, when the people found that the narrow margin on which they were surviving was getting even narrower (the margin of bread, beans, and rice) and that it had been invaded by the economic decisions, people in all parts of the country said no! This is neither possible nor acceptable!" When the masses threw stones on those January days, they aimed them deliberately against the Open Door policy. Al-Kholy believed that the demonstrators protested government "silence in the face of the corrupt profits of the new parasitic elements in the society"; they found a favorite target in "the glass announcements on streetlight poles that advertised imported luxury products and the windows of the shops that sold them at extravagant prices."[25] Not a single fire occurred in any school or university, though students participated in large numbers in the demonstrations; similarly, the workers themselves protected their factories from arson or sabotage.

The *Vanguard* editorial argued that while a privileged new class flourished, Egypt's productive capacity was declining at an alarming rate. The steady rise of the deficit provided a clue to the social roots of the national economic crisis. The deficit had climbed from L.E. 202.5 million in 1972 to 532.7 million in 1974, to 968.6 million in 1975, to approximately 1.5 billion in 1976. Kholy noted that "most of this deficit did not go to the development of the national economy . . . consumption devoured the largest part." The Open Door policy of encouraging consumption "favored parasitic, black-market businessmen while neglecting the interests of the poor and damaging the development of the economy." Sadat's turn to capitalism "had not established a single productive project of importance . . . instead, a country with an average annual income of L.E. 97 was flooded with imported luxury goods for the consumption of a stratum that represents no more than 2.5 percent of the population." In reaching its decision to cut food subsidies, the government had not even considered alternative means of saving, notably tax increases or the restriction of conspicuous consumption, because belt-tightening of this kind contradicted the interests of international capital and its local allies.

According to Abou Seif Yusuf, the January events revealed more than the exploitative character of government economic policies and the hardships to the masses. He extended his examination of the class character of the recent government measures to the international plane, tying the groups that benefited from the Open Door to the international capitalist system, with its center in Washington. In Yusuf's view, Sadat's economic reorientation was a "shock treatment" for the economy, advocated by the American right wing and exemplified by the U.S. role in post-Allende Chile, where economic austerity measures and a welcome mat for the multinationals combined with a growing income gap and brutal government repression to assure stability. Yusuf warned that Sadat's application of this remedy for Egypt would mean "a bloody absolute dictatorship, cancellation of any form of democracy, and delivery of the Egyptian economy to multinational companies, that is, to companies under American control."[26]

In addition to criticizing regime policies, the *Vanguard* response to the January events also assessed the implications of the uprising for the left's long-term political strategy. The *Vanguard* writers were not the only Egyptian Marxists making such an evaluation. The most radical, underground elements of the Egyptian left believed that in January 1977 power lay in the streets. The radicals charged that an emasculated Egyptian left proved unable to exploit this revolutionary situation. Inaction in 1977 proved that the mainstream of the Marxist current, represented by the *Vanguard* circle, had lost its revolutionary drive. Having mistakenly chosen to collaborate with the petty-bourgeois nationalist revolution of Nasser, they were now compounding their error by operating within the increasingly narrow confines of legal activity (represented by the NPUP) allowed by Nasser's reactionary successor.[27]

Kholy challenged this ultraleft view of the revolutionary potential of the January events and reaffirmed the correctness of the strategic decision to take full advantage of the opening for legal political activity represented by participation in the NPUP. Kholy argued that actions on the streets showed that the left, lacking a hardened and conscious vanguard leadership, could not turn mass anger to progressive political ends. He also warned that the anarchic impulses that surfaced in January could be manipulated more easily by reactionary Islamic political movements such as the Muslim Brothers than by the left. For this reason, an attempt by the left to capitalize on the January disturbances to organize a revolutionary strike would probably backfire to the ultimate advantage of an Islamic fascism. Having concluded that the mass actions in January had reflected spontaneous personal despair rather than organized political consciousness, he urged the left to pressure the government on socioeconomic policies rather than challenge the regime itself. In line with this strategy, Kholy recommended that the "present cabinet . . .

step down in favor of a new one with an alternative policy to be executed by a nationalist government, capable and qualified to overcome this social and economic crisis in the interest of the Egyptian people."[28]

Rather than seeing it as a revolutionary breakthrough, the Marxists of *The Vanguard* placed the uprising in a long history of popular suffering and periodic rebelliousness that the regime preferred to forget and the ultraleft exaggerated. The momentary lapse of public authority in 1977 was simply the culmination of a legacy of mass discontent on national and social grounds from Nasser's last years. Serious worker and student demonstrations in 1968, triggered by the lenient sentences given to military officers held responsible for the June 1967 defeat, inaugurated this cycle of rebelliousness. The demonstrators successfully pressed for harsher sentences for the imprisoned officers, while urging reopening of the military front with Israel. In March 1969 Nasser responded with the indecisive War of Attrition. When the stalemated situation of "no war, no peace" continued after Nasser's death, the Sadat regime drew sharp criticism for its inaction in 1971 and again in 1972, especially from student demonstrators. A broad protest movement with a core of seasoned student activists and a substantial following at the national universities took shape around the Palestine question.

Student leaders soon broadened their critical agenda in ways that linked the battle against Israel to political and social struggles at home. The Higher Committee of the Students of Cairo University, for example, issued a statement calling for abandonment of efforts at "peaceful settlements with the American-Zionist enemy." The students proposed "mobilizing the masses in the form of a people's army of students, workers, and peasants to confront the possibility of a long war against the enemy." The Cairo statement connected Sadat's new economic policies, which "favored the wealthy," with defeatism on the front with Israel; the students challenged the regime to "transform the economy into a war economy by concentrating on military production and prohibiting luxurious conspicuous consumption and making those with high incomes carry a larger share of the costs of the battle."[29] The student left was groping for a program to link national and social issues.

The initial euphoria following the October 1973 War temporarily muted popular discontent. But in 1974, economic hardships stimulated over 400 minor strikes and work stoppages. On January 1, 1975, workers smashed stalled commuter trains in central Cairo and stormed through the streets of the capital, jeering at Sadat for runaway prices and corruption. "Oh, Hero of the Crossing," they taunted, "where is our breakfast?" Two months later a massive strike at the country's largest textile mills at Mehalla al-Kubra posed a still greater threat: for three days about 40,000 workers battled first the police and then some 4,500 central security forces. When military aircraft buzzed the town and the mills, breaking the sound barrier and smashing windows, the workers thought the mills were being bombed. Enraged, they attacked the police station and the homes of the mill's managers. Luxury items and expensive foods such as frozen turkeys, chickens, and alcohol were piled high in the streets under banners that read: "Look how these thieves live while we go hungry!"[30] According to the Marxist left, the dissatisfactions that finally erupted on a national scale in 1977 were rooted in this record of localized disturbances.

Reports of leftist participants in the demonstrations implicitly confirmed the *Vanguard* interpretation of the January events by revealing the anarchic impulses of the urban poor and the spontaneity that drove both student and worker participation. An account by a leftist student from Cairo University, for example, richly characterized the motives that energized Egyptians to demonstrate on January 18 and 19; however, it also dramatized the absence of a centralized political leadership able to coordinate and direct the several strands of mass discontent:

> The First Day. A group of students met at Cairo University at 1:30 on January 18 to discuss the government decisions announced that morning to raise prices. One student explained that "international financial institutions, dominated by the United States, were behind the decision as a new step in the long-range policy of subjugating the Egyptian economy and intervening flagrantly in our life and the destiny of our people." Work groups were formed to write and distribute leaflets and to post protests on wall journals in the university and the city. Anticipating a popular response, student leaders began to formulate a broader plan of action. At this point another group of students just back from the center of the city burst in to report that the workers from the Helwan industrial site just outside Cairo "had begun to move by the thousands." The decisive moment we had long awaited had arrived, the moment when the people would awake from their long sleep and act to protect themselves.

The students began to move off the campus, heading for University Bridge over the Nile to the downtown area. Seeing their own swelling numbers in the streets, they realized for the first time just how many small groups had been meeting that morning. The crowds of students walked toward the parliament, located just off Kasr al-Aini Street in the center of the city. The parliament had been the site of protests in recent months.

As we arrived on Kasr al-Aini Street, the workers too were reaching the area on long rows of trucks from Helwan. The workers in their blue and khaki work clothes were waving their fists and shouting with enthusiasm. The traffic on Kasr al-Aini Street was paralyzed.

The spontaneous decision to assemble at the parliament appeared to express the intention of the workers and the students to use their demonstration to protest both the regime's decisions and the parliament's record in legalizing such measures directed against the poor. The meeting drew masses of ordinary people, including large numbers of women dressed in the traditional black of the lower classes, and hundreds of children, who streamed onto Kasr al-Aini Street from the nearby populous neighborhoods of Bab al-Luq and Sayyida Zeinab. Slogans on banners indicated that students from Cairo's numerous universities and institutes had joined the demonstrators.

The sound of light weapons fired in the air announced the arrival of the security police. Reflections in the parliament's dome from the heavy shooting gave the momentary impression that the building was burning. The police closed in on the crowds from all sides at once. They moved on the right from the popular quarter of Sayyida Zeinab and on the left from the middle-class section of Garden City. Those coming from behind the crowds from the direction of Kasr al-Aini were especially heavily armed with rifles, tear gas, and clubs and shields. As they approached the people, the police charged in unison, eventually silencing the crowds with their deafening roar. Tension spread through the silenced crowds. Then, strong voices arose from the workers, shouting: "We will not fear, we will not fear for Citadel Prison." Student leaders in turn called out: "Youth Youth! We are not afraid of terror."

Tear gas bombs poured down like rain over our heads, and stifling smoke filled the area. The police advanced, swinging their clubs. The unarmed people tore out the heavy stone tiles from the sidewalks and hurled them at the attacking security police. Eventually the people were driven back into Cairo's crowded side streets, but not before the confrontations had engulfed the whole area from the parliament to Liberation Square a quarter-mile away.

The next day Egyptians awoke to an official radio that "spreads its lies." In the national press huge headlines spoke of saboteurs and blamed the strikes and demonstrations on the communists. During the night the regime made large-scale arrests of students, workers, and intellectuals in an attempt to intimidate others from joining the demonstrations. But in the crowded buses of Cairo the next morning the people enthusiastically debated the events of the day before. By seven in the morning masses of people crowded into the main city squares in a triangle from Ramses Square to Liberation Square to Bab al-Luq. Loaves of bread were raised on poles, and the people chanted: "Isn't it enough that we are dressed in rags? Now they are coming to take our bread." Over the next two hours the angry crowds renewed their battles with the police. This time the police fired directly into the crowds with live ammunition. In anger, the people surged from Bab al-Luq toward the presidential palace at Abdin Square.

> The shots rang out from nowhere. Blood ran in the streets. The martyred and the wounded fell. It was around nine-thirty. We carried the victims into the entrance of buildings in a desperate attempt to save them . . . The masses of people, now beside themselves with anger after the bloodshed, proceeded in a terrible rage in the direction of Abdin Square. Tens of thousands shook their fists and shouted slogans that almost shook down the houses with their force.
>
> With their slogans, the people denounced President Sadat for the grievances that united them against government policies. "Tell him who is sleeping in Abdin," they chanted in rhythmic language, "that the people go to bed hungry." Others lamented that "the Zionist is on my land and the secret police is at my door." Still others taunted: "You who rule us in the name of right and religion, you who rule us from Abdin, where is the right and where is the religion?"
>
> At Abdin the police were ready. They surrounded the palace with barricades, manned by armed guards who again fired into the demonstrations. When word of bloody new clashes spread, angry crowds besieged police stations and other symbols of the regime and its American allies. A large demonstration of women in the black dresses worn in the popular quarters, carrying and holding children, moved toward the American University in Cairo in Liberation Square. The glass facade of one building shattered under a torrent of bricks. Then the army intervened and the people were dispersed; the crowds broke up at curfew time when the army in its tanks moved to street corners and intersections to take over.[31]

While defending the demonstrators from official charges of criminality, Kholy warned against being swept away by enthusiasms stirred by reports from the streets. Soberly, he noted that these accounts highlighted the organizational weakness of the left: "It was noticed that not one leftist, whether independent, a member of the National Progressive Unionist Party, or a member of the secret organization that the government calls the Communist Labor Party, was arrested while participating in any direct actions on the streets." Undoubtedly, Kholy's argument helped counter the regime's claim of a leftist plot. However, the absence of leftist leadership during the demonstrations also raised the question why prominent leftists were not in the lead when the masses engaged in legitimate protest.

The *Vanguard* analysis also brought out a more threatening dimension of the January events; Kholy's editorial warned the Egyptian left that, despite the sharp limitations of the Sadat regime from a socialist perspective, worse possibilities waited in the wings. He pointed to the regime's earlier attempts to stifle criticism from the left by strengthening both the internal security forces and the Islamic groups as a political counterweight. Kholy feared that certain aspects of the January events, often submerged in the participant's accounts, indicated a deepening of this tacit cooperation of the security forces and the Islamic groups to weaken the left, allowing the military to deal the final blow.

Kholy counseled that "while correct actions began by respecting the will of the people as expressed through their spontaneous uprising, respect did not mean accepting the violent character of the uprising, as initiated by some irresponsible or fascist elements who appeared on January 19." According to Kholy, the spontaneous character of the popular uprising "carried the dangers of chaos" because of the role the Islamic groups played in the violent incidents. While loudly blaming the left for the violence the regime had in fact allowed the initiative on the streets to fall to the Islamic militants in order to create chaotic conditions to justify military intervention: "It was noticed that it was extremely easy to rob the night clubs on the Pyramids Road in record time and with no police interference in spite of the fact that one of the biggest central security forces is very near this road." The Ministry of the Interior before January 18 and 19, 1977, had accused some extremist religious groups of using violence; however, it "did not mention them even once during or after the January events, concentrating instead on blaming the leftist elements." Kholy pointed out that the resultant disorder, officially blamed on the left, justified the government's open reliance on the army. To reclaim the streets, the regime would "destroy and burn those streets" when the "government appeared to be losing control." In these collusive actions of the security forces, religious militants, and the army, Kholy glimpsed the alarming possibility of an Egyptian fascism with an Islamic face acting to destroy the left.[32]

In the wake of the uprising, the Marxists feared that a regime forced to resort to "terror" to restore its authority would move sharply to the right in foreign as well as domestic policies in order to strengthen its position. Ultimately, therefore, Sadat's abandonment of socialism would entail not only repression at home but also the betrayal of Egypt's progressive national and Arab commitments. As the left saw it, precisely this reaction came in the fall of 1977. On November 9 Sadat announced that he was ready "to go to the ends of the earth, and to the Knesset itself," to make peace in the Middle East. The Marxists made a direct connection between the army arrayed against students and workers on the streets of Cairo in January and Sadat's rush to strategic alignment with the United States that eventually brought the separative peace with Israel, an unrestricted opening to foreign capital, and the incorporation of the Egyptian Sinai into the American Middle East security system.[33]

The *Vanguard* writers, seeing themselves as historical agents of progressive transformation, sought to keep the socialist alternative alive in a changing and often hostile situation. They relied on their concrete experience as well as their socialist consciousness to take the measure of Nasser's incomplete revolution and Sadat's outright reaction. The Marxists of the *Vanguard* circle sought historical understanding to instigate and guide action. Theory and practice came together for them in ways they could and did defend, against the state and critics on both the right and the left. In the sixties the Marxists had intruded themselves into Nasser's "revolutionary state" with the aim of establishing a vanguard socialist party that would drive Nasser's nationalist revolution to the left. After the collapse of the vanguard, the 1967 defeat, and Nasser's death three years later, they had played a more modest role, as Kholy put it; within the legal framework of the NPUP, they had combined with other national and progressive forces to protect the Nasserist legacy against the ascendent new class that flourished in the system of parasitic capitalism fostered by the Sadat regime.[34]

For the *Vanguard* circle, the progressive social changes of the fifties and sixties provided the standard by which to evaluate subsequent events. *Vanguard* analysts interpreted the January uprising as part of a revolutionary struggle in which Nasser's 1952 revolution defined a turning point. Concepts abstracted from the history of the Marxists' strategic engagement with Nasserism, notably the theoretical notions of the vanguard, the new class, and parasitic capitalism served to bring out facts about the January events that interested the *Vanguard* writers; those facts defined the prospects of socialism and showed how those prospects might be improved. In the Marxist reading, the January uprising was important for what it told about how best to preserve the advances made in the Nasser years against the powerful reactionary currents threatening them in the Sadat era.

The *Vanguard* writers premised their thinking about the 1952 revolution on the judgment that the Nasserist experiment had been a genuine though flawed socialist project. In their view, the sixties had indeed held the promise of a socialist outcome. The Nasser regime had begun the process of transforming a nationalist and anti-imperialist movement into a social revolution. A charismatic nationalist figure had held the leadership role; Nasser had already overcome the limitations of his lower-middle-class and military background to achieve much more than the original goals and class composition of the Free Officers conspiracy had suggested. Moreover, Egypt had not stood alone in the world; national liberation movements were sweeping three continents, promising continuous revolutions that would move from nationalist to socialist forms. The emergence of the Soviet Union as a global rather than a regional power neutralized or at least diluted the pressures from the Western centers that aimed to contain these revolutionary movements.

Of course, the victory of socialism in Egypt could not come without a bitter and difficult struggle. Like any other socialist revolution, Nasserism had faced conflicts with class enemies; it had also suffered from the mistakes of its leaders and the progressive forces that rallied to it. Of the internal shortcomings of the revolutionary project, the *Vanguard* writers judged the propensity to create "socialism without socialists" most serious.[35] By not developing a cadre of militant socialists and placing them in leadership roles, Nasser had weakened the revolution from within. Reliance on nonsocialist class forces and institutions eventually hollowed out the revolution and facilitated its defeat by a combination of foreign and domestic foes.[36]

The Marxists applauded the revolutionary achievements of the years 1956–1965, notably the nationalizations, the successes of the first five-year plan, the advances in public sector administration, and the extension of the cooperative movement in the countryside.[37] In 1961, for example, Nasser had mounted a frontal assault on the bourgeoisie by nationalizing physical assets and shares of the nonagricultural economy worth an estimated L.E. 700 million.[38] Such bold strokes had convinced the Marxists that "the top levels of the state apparatus were genuinely revolutionary";[39] they celebrated not only the substance of these progressive measures but also Nasser's stunning success in winning popular support for them all. Even later, when Egypt had been forced to make concessions to external economic pressures, the Marxists noted that Nasser had maintained his political commitments. The process of *political* radicalization had ended only with the American-backed Israeli blow in 1967.

Yet, for all the enthusiasm registered in the pages of *The Vanguard* for Egypt's "revolutionary state," the Marxists consistently warned against "excessive optimism."[40] Marxist analysts strongly resisted the temptation to lift Nasser out of history and see him as a charismatic figure who miraculously realized national dreams.[41] Viewed from the left, Nasser's experiment remained an unfinished socialist revolution that had allowed the continuance of old exploitative patterns, especially bureaucratic ones, and even encouraged new ones, notably those linked to what the Marxists called the new class phenomenon.

Nasser had relied on the traditional bureaucracy to realize his revolutionary aims in land reform, nationalizations, industrialization, and mass education and welfare. Adel Ghaneim, a Marxist academic close to the *Vanguard* editors, argued that this strategy had created a "crucial contradiction" between the "inherited state apparatus, with its reactionary class and ideological makeup, on the one hand, and the objective requirements of social and national revolution and economic development, on the other."[42] As a result, Egypt's drive to socialism had suffered from the persistence of a uniquely powerful state bureaucracy that, as Kholy had warned earlier, strongly "resisted any attempt to take it over and direct it."[43] Nasser had attempted to resolve this contradiction between revolutionary aims and reactionary instruments by purging the state apparatus of corrupt and antirevolutionary elements, maneuvering around old administrative agencies by creating new ones, and placing the military cadre of the revolution, which Ghaneim characterized as "enlightened, nationalist, and of small and middle bourgeois class origins," in top positions.[44] While recognizing their short-term use, analysts such as Ghaneim judged these solutions dangerous; in their view, the revolution remained incomplete and vulnerable as long as hostile class forces remained close to the heart of the regime.

The *Vanguard* writers published empirical studies of education, industrialization, and welfare that confirmed their suspicions that the unresolved class contradictions at the heart of Nasserism had created flaws in even the most important achievements of "revolutionary statism." Although the expansion in industrialization and education had made high-paying jobs in the nationalized public sector available to the lower middle class, the lower classes had not gained in social mobility.[45] The lack of similar gains in adult education or the battle against illiteracy indicated the class bias of the changes brought about under Nasser. In the decade after 1951, the number of students enrolled in universities rose from 35,000 to 69,500 while the illiteracy rate in the population remained at over 70 percent. The *Vanguard* analysis concluded that "this contradiction constituted the objective basis of the emergence of a bureaucracy isolated from the masses, a stranger to their interests and ideas."[46] For all its accomplishments, the Nasserist revolution in education was far from complete.

A similar contradictory pattern had emerged in industry in the critical years 1957–1967. On the one hand, there had been great achievements, "such as liquidating capitalist monopolies . . . and expanding the public sector, which came to own 85 percent of the means of production, excluding agriculture." However, the Marxists warned that these gains had not effectively curtailed the power of the Egyptian bourgeoisie in the national economy. Even after the revolutionary transformations of the sixties, "the bourgeoisie still owned 90 percent of agricultural land and controlled 75 percent of domestic trade, in addition to its fundamental role in the construction sphere." Moreover, the undeniable improvements in popular welfare had coexisted with huge disparities in the way the benefits were distributed. Wage differentials, for example, in the government salary scale during the sixties showed a gap of 40 to 1 from the lowest to the highest levels, "an irrational and inexcusable rate that was rarely paralleled in capitalist countries and unparalleled in socialist countries."[47] Clearly, important structural changes in the economy had left oppressive social relations in the production process unchanged.

According to the Marxists, Nasser's reliance on bureaucratic and administrative rather than political and revolutionary means explained these shortcomings of the socioeconomic transformations of the sixties. Without a revolutionary political instrument Nasser could not make more than partial advances toward a socialist revolution; nor could he secure those gains against pressures from hostile foreign and domestic forces. As early as 1966, a *Vanguard* editorial had warned that the regime's "political organization does not reach the desired level to enable it to lead society effectively and . . . to eliminate antisocialist social and ideological 'pockets.' "[48]

This organizational and ideological void at the heart of the regime resulted from the adverse outcome of the political struggle, *in which the Marxists took part,* to create a socialist vanguard within the official Arab

Socialist Union. In general terms, the Marxists saw themselves as offering in the sixties the necessary socialist enrichment for a regime that, despite its revolutionary leadership, suffered from the handicaps of its origins as a military coup. As Adel Ghaneim argued, Nasser had taken power "without the benefit of a political party or adequate socialist cadre or socialist ideology."[49] Ironically, his conspiratorial skills had backfired: the actual seizure of power was so "tight and successful" that the new military leadership cadres never faced the difficulties and obstacles of struggle that in most revolutionary experiences served as a "realistic political test, eliminating opportunists, defeatists, and negative elements from the organization."[50] The Marxist left had seen itself as the repository of precisely the political experience and tested ideological commitment that the new military leadership and the inherited bureaucracy lacked.

In the first years of his rule, however, Nasser had adopted a nationalist stance actively hostile to the left. During discussions of the political forms appropriate to Egypt after the 1961 nationalizations, for example, the president had pressed for inclusive, nationalist arrangements. In the critical debates of the Preparatory Committee, charged with devising a Charter of National Action, Nasser had openly criticized the left for arguing the necessity of socialist cadres and proposed instead a national unity formula that called for "socialism without socialists."[51] These futile attempts to circumvent the class struggle had persisted through the spring of 1963, surfacing again, for example, during the tripartite negotiations to establish a union of Egypt, Syria, and Iraq. During the unity negotiations in Cairo, Nasser had argued for a formula that defined "enemies of the people" as "all who have worked or are working to impose the domination of a single class upon society." To the chagrin of the Marxists, the president explicitly included the communists in that definition because "their principle is the domination of society by the proletariat, that is, the dictatorship of the proletariat."[52]

During the early sixties many of Egypt's leading Marxists continued to languish in the prisons and detention camps to which Nasser had consigned them in a preemptive strike in 1959.[53] A key factor precipitating the arrests was the communists' active role in Iraq in the wake of the 1958 fall of the monarchy. In his nationalist phase, Nasser viewed such conscious and organized activism as a threat to his own movement. Later, after the practical experiences of land reform and the nationalizations, he concluded that these were political advantages that he needed as instruments of social transformation.

The rapprochement of the regime and the Marxists commenced in earnest in 1963 when Nasser realized that he would require more than a paper party of bureaucrats and ex-officers to pull a reluctant country to the left.[54] At the same time, Third World allies, such as Ahmed Ben Bella of Algeria, and the Soviet Union exerted pressure on the regime to release Marxists from detention. Some of the more independent figures, such as Lutfy al-Kholy, had been released in 1961; in 1964 they were joined by a much larger number released in connection with Khrushchev's visit to Egypt to celebrate completion of the first phase of the Aswan Dam. In 1965 the leaders of the Egyptian communist party, including the economists Fuad Mursi and Ismail Sabry Abdullah, both of whom later wrote extensively for *The Vanguard,* announced their decision to dissolve the party; approximately 1,000 party activists individually joined the official Arab Socialist Union in the same month that *The Vanguard* began publication.

The regime's turn to the left came at a time of economic crisis, when a balance-of-payments crunch and a decline in productivity threatened to halt the momentum gained with the first five-year plan. Addressing these difficulties, the Marxists argued that Egypt in the mid-sixties faced a choice between abandoning the progressive thrust of the July Revolution to an eventual resurgence of capitalism or deepening the socialist project through reliance on a socialist vanguard. The Marxists called for extending the nationalizations to the trade and construction sectors, building a political vanguard within the ASU, and refining and spreading socialist ideology.[55] For a brief time, Nasser showed signs of responding positively on all these fronts. After the major nationalizations of 1961, Cairo periodically buzzed with rumors that the scope of public-sector ownership would be expanded. In conversations with a conservative Free Officer colleague, for example, Nasser suggested that a private capitalist with three trucks who hired three drivers to run them was an exploiter who should be nationalized.[56] By the mid-sixties, Nasser was openly discussing the extension of nationalization to trade and construction.[57]

Nasser's actions in 1964 convinced the Marxists that he agreed on the necessity of "an effective party organization of committed and conscious activists to serve as the cutting edge of the drive to socialism."[58] When leftist militants were released from the jails and camps, they were drawn initially into official information and propaganda work designed to promote the regime's turn to the left. Nasser promised a larger role. In meetings with the governing body of the ASU, held from the late fall of 1964 through the spring of 1965, Nasser publicly called for a body of "tightly organized socialists" within the ASU; he explained that while the workers and the peasants constituted the social forces with the real interest in socialism, socialism was made to work by "a minority that leads."[59] Nasser spoke suggestively of a "coming stage" in which his own efforts might be focused on "completing the structure of the political organization of the working powers of the people allied in the Socialist Union."[60] He seriously considered leaving the presidency in order to devote himself to forging the ASU into an effective political instrument of socialist transformation.

The Marxists concluded that Nasser had adopted their view that the "revolutionary state" could not sustain a process of socialist transformation without an effective political organization; they presented themselves as the core of a potential cadre of militants on whom the revolution could rely. In the charter's definition of the vanguard, the Marxists had no trouble recognizing their own ideal of a political body that "recruits the elements qualified to lead, organizes their efforts, crystalizes the people's revolutionary impulses, and feeds its needs and helps to find the right answers for those needs."[61] The Marxists gave the "chartist" formulation greater class and ideological depth. A key member of the *Vanguard*'s editorial board, Michel Kamel, argued that only a vanguard structure could be "the critical carrier of socialist thought" and could be relied upon to "spread this thought to the working masses, intellectuals, and peasants"; only the vanguard, "with its revolutionary conception of socialism, with its scientific laws that comprehend the problems of material reality in which we live, is capable of drawing the path of revolution, planning and realizing the action of transformation on the path of socialism, and securing its foundation."[62] Nasser's talk of a leading role for a socialist minority appeared to signal acceptance at the highest level of precisely this vanguard idea.

Then, Nasser wavered. In March 1965 he decided against leaving the presidency. Instead of committing himself to building a real political party that could implement the program for deepening socialism, he stood for reelection to an additional six-year term. Later, Nasser's spokesman, Muhammad Hassanein Haikal, explained that the president feared "handing over the levers of command to the elements that had formed the 'centers of power.' "[63] The military, led by Abdul Hakim Amer, constituted the most powerful of those power blocs. Sadat later claimed that he had warned Nasser explicitly that any move out of the presidency would leave "Amer and his assistants . . . in sole control of

Egypt."[64] The president's decision dealt the vanguard idea a severe blow.

Nasser's appointment of Aly Sabry to head the ASU somewhat lightened the blow to the left because Sabry represented the official, non-Marxist left in Nasser's entourage. The new secretary general immediately launched an ambitious program of revitalization. In an interview with Lutfy al-Kholy, Sabry announced bold plans to place public-sector industries, labor unions, and professional associations under the direct supervision of a restructured ASU. The key element of his reform program was the formation of a Central Committee that would function as the "brain" of the party, enabling the ASU to supervise the government. Sabry's radicalization program opened a power struggle that eventually pitted the ASU, as champion of Sabry's version of political radicalization, against the military, as defender of economic and political moderation.

The Marxists felt misgivings about Sabry's program. To them, it indicated an ASU power bid for corporate control of Egypt's key institutions rather than a strategy for deepening socialism. Deprived of Nasser's direct leadership, the direction the ASU took would depend more than ever on the way Sabry formed and defined the vanguard. Optimistically, *The Vanguard* had pronounced 1965 the year of political organization and called for a central role for genuine socialist militants in remaking the ASU. Sabry's selection of the Central Committee suggested that different standards, more responsive to personal power struggles, would in fact be used.[65] In the spring of 1965 Vice-President Kamal Rifa'at announced that the selection process for the vanguard would emphasize "personal acquaintances" and "direct contacts."[66] Sabry pronounced that "we select the suitable elements on the basis of their work experience and their pursuit of the struggle," without ever spelling out precisely what standards these airy formulations implied.[67] If the rhetoric was vague, actions clearly showed that the Marxists would have only a marginal role. Of the key figures charged with responsibility for the vanguard, most came from the security apparatus; none had any real leftist credentials. The *Vanguard's* editors charged the ASU vanguard had been infiltrated by "parasitic and opportunistic elements" who were exploiting it for reactionary and bureaucratic aims.[68]

Having thrown in their lot with the regime, the Marxists had little choice but to respond to the opening that Sabry's brand of leftism still left them. The *Vanguard* writers called upon the left to work for a longer-term strategy of training ideologically motivated activists who might yet remake the amorphous Arab Socialist Union. For the two years from 1965 to 1967, institutions such as the Socialist Youth Organization, the ASU Secretariat for Ideology and Propaganda, directed by Kamal Rifa'at, and the Institute of Socialist Studies under the Marxist economist Ibrahim Sa'ad Eddine provided models of what could be done. The practical work of such bodies, the *Vanguard* writers noted, involved large numbers of young Egyptians; in the mid-sixties the Socialist Youth Organization alone had over 200,000 members. From the Marxist perspective, by directly engaging Egyptian youth in the struggle for socialism, these public bodies were creating the human resources for a socialist future.[69]

Others, notably the military, apparently shared the Marxist judgment of these successes in mobilizing the youth and inculcating it with socialist values; they did not, however, share the enthusiasm for them registered in the pages of *The Vanguard*. In the fall of 1966 these misgivings produced a first strike against the Marxist activists. Military intelligence claimed that a vast network of communist infiltrators, committed to the violent overthrow of the regime, had gained control of the Socialist Youth Organization. In all, some seventy-five activists were arrested; the army used the incident as a pretext for closing the institute. Charges of being in contact with the alleged communist apparatus were lodged against Institute head Ibrahim Sa'ad Eddine and *Vanguard* editor Kholy. After an independent investigation by the minister of the interior the charges were dropped for lack of sufficient evidence, but the affair put the left on notice that socialist successes had prompted a military counteroffensive.[70] This skirmish revealed that so long as Nasser remained in power, the left would retain some freedom of maneuver. The framework for socialist action on the economic plane, in particular, remained sharply limited, until it was destroyed altogether by the Israeli strike in 1967 "aimed at the social revolution in Egypt."[71]

According to the *Vanguard* writers, the most important consequence of Nasser's failure to translate his radical thinking into effective socialist political instruments was not the political infighting that characterized a regime that sought to stay afloat by balancing competing power centers. The Marxists never accepted this reduction of Egypt's political history to a succession of contentless power struggles. They emphasized instead the way in which these unresolved political conflicts allowed a steady increase in the influence of hostile class forces that remained at the heart of the regime. Deprived of a political instrument to discipline these class opponents of socialist transformation, the regime became increasingly susceptible to their power. In the mid-sixties, *The Vanguard* argued that these hostile class forces had effectively prevented Nasser from making "further demands on the richer classes." Only an ideologically steeled political instrument could have withstood these pressures, especially when they found expression through the military "center of power." The ASU, with Nasser at its head and galvanized by an effective vanguard structure, might well have played this historic role. Instead, Nasser ultimately relied on his carefully balanced relationship with the military rather than on a radical political structure. Nasser's more conservative decision allowed him to survive not only the economic crisis of the mid-sixties but also the Israeli defeat in 1967. In the Marxist's eyes, however, he did so at the cost of ultimately allowing reactionary class elements to block further transformation of the regime.[72]

The failure of the revolution to move forward at the critical juncture of the mid-sixties put all its gains at risk. After 1966, *The Vanguard* periodically carried articles with the views of workers and peasants who articulated the threats to the revolution of the new parasitic class forces that increasingly dominated the political field. These commentaries emphasized the ineffectiveness of the political organizations in both the villages and the urban areas, and the masses' resultant sense of vulnerability. The 1967 defeat and Nasser's death vastly increased these dangers.

"Cooperatives must be controlled by the poor peasants," commented one peasant with one-half feddan rented and one-half owned; "the poor know the sufferings of the poor, and those with enough should stay away."[73] In a parallel way, a worker commented on his role in the June 9 demonstrations urging Nasser not to resign after the 1967 defeat. "When I went out for Nasser on the 9th of June, it was because I knew that if reaction succeeds, there will be no factory for me to work in and capitalism will return. The peasant, too, went out to protect his land. We went to the factories barefooted, and we ran because we understood that the departure of Nasser means no socialism."[74] The *Vanguard* writers argued that the "simple worker" understood that "the old elements are still in control." However, deprived of a real political instrument, the left felt impotent: "In spite of the 8th and 9th of June uprising, we are unable to combat the old forces as long as we revolutionists are unable to organize ourselves. None of the true revolutionary elements is in an authority position." When asked to make sacrifices for the war effort, the simple worker responded with commitment but also with a growing suspicion that the upper classes were not doing their share: "We are ready . . . to die and by our death prevent strangers from occupying our land. However, others must be willing to do the same."[75] From the workers and peasants came warnings that the rich and powerful were eating up the gains of the revolution and refusing to carry its burdens.

Vanguard writers used these disgruntled voices of the masses to give resonance to their persistent warnings against the new class danger. According to Adel Ghaneim, for example, new right-wing social forces had developed through the processes of industrialization and rural social change carried out under the Nasserist banner.[76] Michel Kamel argued in a series of detailed empirical studies that a large group of administrative and technical government employees at the top of the bureaucracy had positioned themselves to exploit the resources nationalized by the state. "From this group," he warned, "emerges the 'new class' that seeks to arrest development and exhaust the public sector for its own interests, including participation in speculation and commercial transactions, investing the surplus of its income in real estate and agricultural land."[77] The absence of a vanguard party deprived the regime of an instrument with which to discipline parasitic social forces that had only an exploitative interest in the socialist transformation.[78] The chief reactionary threat came from high-level urban managers in state and public-sector institutions; they tacitly allied themselves with the rural notables who dominated the countryside after land reform broke the power of the old feudal families. Both the urban and the rural new class appropriated for themselves a disproportionate share of the advances the revolution made possible. Rifa'at al-Said, journalist and first secretary general of the NPUP, judged these newly ascendent social forces and the new forms of exploitation they engendered more dangerous than the "old right" with its social base in the old landowning class.[79] The new class distorted economic, institutional, and ideological development; later, the Marxists charged that Sadat used these distortions of socialism to accelerate his move to an economic opening.

According to the Marxists, the economic power wielded by the most influential members of the new class derived from their authority to make public-sector economic decisions from which they could personally profit. They "attempted to plunder and bleed the public sector and to sabotage it from within; for this reason, this period [1961–1967] is considered a period of cancerous growth for the new class."[80] The general characteristics of the new class could be seen with particular clarity in the activities of trade and construction companies. Michel Kamel drew attention to the expansion and growth in the sixties of powerful economic and social forces based in these "fertile and extremely prosperous fields for capital accumulation; these sectors achieved great profits at fantastic rates for the bourgeoisie, especially the parasitic elements within it, which are more closely connected to some corrupt elements in the government and public-sector departments."[81] *The Vanguard* reported that in the years 1961–1965 the private sector had handled 70 percent of all construction activity, which totaled L.E. 700 million, or 47 percent of total investment in the five-year plan, while the public sector had handled only 30 percent.[82] The Marxists considered Osman Ahmed Osman's powerful construction firm, the Arab Contractors, as the prototypical new class economic institution that "achieved excessive profits through the bleeding of public-sector resources." They pointed, in particular, to the way in which the Osman public-sector parent company had channeled enormous profits to the family's private-sector companies through a complex system of subcontracting; in this way, public resources were transformed into private profits. The general assessment of the construction sector stressed that "the backwardness of production relations within this sector has helped and continues to help tie workers and craftsmen to the contractors."[83] Huge profits, connection to high government officials, and feudal loyalties gave the Osman circle enormous economic power.

New class economic activities were not the only drain on public resources. The *Vanguard*'s assessment also noted new forms of bureaucratic deformations caused by "overindulgence in creating public agencies and corporations." The Marxists explained that the unprecedented growth of the state and public-sector bureaucracy in the wake of nationalizations created fertile fields for new parasitic social groups that joined forces with the old reactionaries already ensconced in the bureaucracy. Corrupt officials easily infiltrated the bloated public structures and exploited their positions to amass immense illegal fortunes, often by selling special privileges to the private sector.[84]

These distortions found expression in reactionary ideologies that challenged scientific socialism. These varied ideologies shared a "technocratic, bourgeois general coloration . . . with its utilitarian values and experimental outlook."[85] The less reactionary members of the new class continued to reject capitalism as a road to development and industrialization; however, they blocked the development of socialist political forms: expansion of public ownership was fine as long as it did not entail effective political organization of the masses. As one writer explained bluntly, adherents to this view "believed in public property and defended its continuation [but only] in a manner that would enable them to control it and manage it for their own benefit"[86] Socialism meant no more than a practical solution to the technological problem of industrializing the country; not surprisingly, this ideology derived strong support from technocratic leaders in the public sector. In practice, this orientation justified "bureaucratic state capitalism."[87]

A second line of thinking likewise opposed political radicalization but was even more conservative toward socioeconomic change. Its supporters argued that restrictions on private ownership through nationalization and land reform had gone far enough; the revolution should be arrested or "frozen." Moreover, they sought to revive the private capitalist sector by putting the public sector in its service. Ultimately, this ideology rationalized an evolution to the kind of parasitic capitalism that in fact took shape in the seventies.[88]

The Marxists argued that although the new class elements responsible for these economic, institutional, and intellectual deformations of the revolution emerged during the fifties and sixties, they did not coalesce into a class while Nasser remained in power. As long as the regime at its highest political levels remained either hostile or ambivalent toward them, these social forces were unable to act openly in ways that allowed the development of a unified consciousness and organizational resources. In the words of one writer, "the seeds of this class" did exist, however, and they were "trying to coalesce."[89] Only later, under Sadat, did the new class fully emerge and maneuver to advance its interests.

The Marxists contrasted Nasser's ability to contain these reactionary elements in the mid-sixties with Sadat's unwillingness to do so a decade later. In his assessment of the January uprising, Kholy commented bitterly that not only were the external demands the same in the mid-seventies as they had been in the mid-sixties; even the people making the demands had not changed. Nasser had contained the internal forces that pressed for a return to capitalism; he had also parried the international capitalist pressures that stood behind them.

In 1967 it was external forces that overwhelmed the revolution. Israel struck the decisive blow against Nasser's vulnerable regime, according to the authoritative *Vanguard* editorial, "in an attempt to abort the deepest Third World attempt to challenge imperialism and to overcome socioeconomic backwardness since the historic renaissance of nationalist movements in the fifties."[90] The Marxist analysis of the June War claimed that the American interest in backing the attack centered on containing the perceived threat of an Egyptian-led Arab revolution to U.S. economic and strategic interests; Egypt's involvement in the Yemen civil war, seen as a first step to challenging the American-backed, oil-rich regime in Saudi Arabia, triggered U.S. alarm. The defeat also aimed to deflate the appeal of the Nasserist model of socialism, advanced for the larger Arab nationalist movement. Even partial successes of socialism in the Arab world threatened to liquidate the classes and social forces on which the Western powers in the area depended; the strike aimed to destroy Egypt's capacity to assert its economic independence and to compel the most powerful and populous Arab state to return to the international capitalist system. Once Egypt was forced back into its dependent position, the United States would be able to impose Israel's leadership on the region and create an American peace to which all Middle Eastern states could be compelled to adhere.[91]

Egypt's socialist possibilities did fade rapidly after 1967. Although Nasser survived in power until his death in 1970, the "revolutionary state" lost its dynamism; the process of political radicalization, already made problematic by Nasser's decision not to head the ASU, halted. In addition, funds earmarked for the regime's ambitious agenda of domestic transformation had to be diverted for rebuilding the armed forces to fight Israeli occupation and prepare for "the Arab battle of liberation."[92] The "seeds" of the parasitic new class found fertile soil in an Egypt disoriented by the death of Nasser and "opened up" by the 1967 strike.

Vanguard writers explained that the "opening" to the capitalist world produced a distorted economic formation. Egypt was reintegrated into the world market by having its development tied to foreign monopolies; by the encouragement of formerly illicit activities such as importation of foreign luxuries, currency speculation, and middle-man functions; and by a shift from a productive to a consumerist orientation. The consolidation of the American position in Egypt strengthened this "parasitic capitalism" by legitimating and even directly supporting a whole new array of economic activities centered in the private sector. The Marxists pointed out that the American-sponsored emphasis on the private sector met the consumption appetite of the new class rather than the production needs of a strong national economy. In fact, the American role weakened the productive bourgeoisie. "The return of the foreign banks and commercial agencies diminished national independence," the journal stated. It also "harmed the productive capitalists, causing them to declare bankruptcy, close their shops and small factories, and join the parasitic groups." Of the fate of Egyptians in the Sadat era of economic liberalization, the American connection, and the peace with Israel, the Marxist Fuad Mursi explained: "Under the existing conditions there is no hope of realizing prosperity for anyone other than the

same parasitic class who will add new riches to their fortunes by cooperating with Israel and throwing themselves more and more into the
arms of international capitalism. For the people, there will only be more
of the misery it has tasted itself and seen with its eyes throughout the . . .
years in which the opening policy has been implemented."[93] Indeed,
while the mass of Egyptians suffered under the burdens imposed by the
confrontation with Israel, a small minority prospered as Sadat moved to
implement his economic liberalization strategy.

The Marxists warned that, from a U.S. perspective, the normalization of relations with Israel had two aims: first, securing Egypt's dependency on the international capitalist system, in which Israel plays the role
of the go-between who receives commissions from both sides; second,
establishing an organic relationship between the Israeli and Egyptian
economies that would allow the development of whole areas such as
Sinai, which is being prepared to be the sphere of the future meeting
between Egypt and Israel in areas such as tourism, hunting, solar energy,
irrigation, and agriculture. It also aimed at creating ties of cooperation
with sections of Egyptian workers, craftsmen, and technocrats, eventually creating a "mixed society" to serve as a buffer zone, protecting Israel
within its expanded borders.

To complement the new parasitic economic patterns, the Open
Door policy also promoted "sick" social values and beliefs. All progressive thinkers were attacked in a climate of false religiosity, though the
Vanguard editorials regularly claimed that "true religion is innocent of
such actions."[94] The memory of Gamal Abdul Nasser was expunged
from history, and the Soviet Union and all the socialist camp were
painted as unrelenting enemies of Egypt's interests. According to the
Marxists, this reactionary ideological offensive falsely blamed all of
Egypt's difficulties on its socialist experiment; Sadat used the myth of
failed socialism to discredit the notion of a real socialist possibility in
Egypt's future and to screen his capitulation to capitalist class forces.
Cooperation with the United States and its ally Israel also constituted a
regionwide attack on pan-Arab nationalism. Such a compounded blow
to leftist goals led the *Vanguard* editors to warn that if Sadat succeeded,
"the efforts and sacrifices of about a quarter of a century of struggles will
be wasted."[95]

Lutfy al-Kholy suggested ironically that the left's role in indicating
a broad alternative to capitalism was the only real sense in which the
Marxist left could be blamed for the disturbances in January 1977. In

1977 the government blasted a "communist conspiracy," but its real aim was to eliminate the material traces of the victories Egyptians had won in their battles for socialism and to obliterate the very memory of the socialist values and ends that inspired those struggles. The passing of the revolutionary leadership and the reintegration of Sadat's Egypt into the world capitalist system put all the gains of the Nasser revolution at risk; to work to preserve them, central figures of the *Vanguard* circle joined other leftists in the official National Progressive Unionist Party. Muhammad Sid Ahmed, a political analyst with an international reputation and a member of the *Vanguard* core group, characterized the NPUP as "having two faces, one of agreement between the various currents that comprise it and one of variance and difference between them." Justifying the *Vanguard* circle's decision to join a party within which Marxism would be only one of several currents, Sid Ahmed called the "coalition or unionist" formula a "historical necessity." He stressed that a left coalition, unlike those of the right, could be based on principles and programs rather than on expediency, and called on the left to act to make the party work. "A historical necessity," he explained, "is not realized spontaneously, but is the result of practice and conflict—a conflict within the party for unity and a conflict against the enemies of the left, the party's enemies outside it." Sid Ahmed urged the left to respond to the new opportunities for broad collective action created by the regime's commitment to a multiparty system, "even if it means it to be only a facade."[96]

That decision flowed directly from the *Vanguard* assessment of the meaning of the Nasserist experiment and the role of *Vanguard* activists in it. Fuad Mursi explained the "unionist" dimension of the left party as a "formula that includes all the forces that strive for revolutionary implementation in Egyptian society. These forces comprise, on the social side, workers, farmers, revolutionary intellectuals, professionals, merchants, employees, and the productive sectors of state capitalism. It also comprises, on the political side, Nasserist, Marxist, religious, [Arab] unionists, and democrats." According to Mursi, the formula was the correct one because "the Egyptian revolution is a national, democratic one, with social, progressive contents—that is, not yet totally accomplished. Its enormous and diversified forces are still working for more revolutionary change in our country." Mursi explained that the experience of the Nasser years had created a diverse social reserve for the revolution that could be tapped by the unionist formula. "The Egyptian revolution," he argued, "has reinforced the forces that desired revolutionary change, with new supplies of land reform farmers, public sector workers, and educated persons who are the children of farmers and workers." Mursi concluded that "the experience of political action, under the July revolution and particularly within the framework of the socialist trend, has asserted the unity between the country's forces, despite their differences . . . Consequently, the forces of revolutionary change were in a situation that necessitated collaboration to confront dangers threatening their country."[97] Abou Seif Yusuf summed up the *Vanguard* hopes that the party would "present a realistic and carefully studied alternative to the policy presented by the ruling party." He explained that "the crux of the party's policy is to continue the progressive gains of the July revolution and to double them, overcoming any negative aspects that may have occurred, with the object of protecting the political and economic independence of the country."[98] Reaching the public through their journal and their leadership role in the NPUP, the *Vanguard* circle acted out their claim that the Marxist left was not a "conspiracy" but rather the critical consciousness of the socialist alternative, an historical presence with durable roots in Egypt's revolutionary tradition.

The *Vanguard* circle sought to comprehend and shape society in ways that advanced the socialist alternative, and their analyses aimed to clarify the goals and strategies of practical political struggle. In this spirit, Kholy concluded the *Vanguard*'s assessment of the January 1977 uprising with a strategy for the left. He brought the socialist alternative to life with an action program that called for a productive economy, social justice, Arab solidarity, steadfastness in the face of Israel, and contact with the Soviet Union; in the difficult conditions of the late seventies, he charged Marxists to work within a broad coalition of the left for the realization of these aims.

The *Vanguard* proposals in 1977 indicated how a socialist perspective offered precisely definable goals of practice for both domestic and foreign affairs. Urging the regime to "liquidate parasitic economic activities and protect national capitalism from its dangers," Kholy argued for the drastic overhaul of an economic policy that "allowed capital to flow out of Egypt and luxury goods into the country." In his view, only the reinstatement of central planning would "put an end to luxury consumption and provide for essential consumption at a level that would assure citizens their share of required goods at a reasonable cost." In the interest of social justice, *The Vanguard* called for a "redistribution of income from the rich to the deprived classes, coupled with an example set by the responsible classes of wise spending and savings."

To achieve these domestic aims and also to fulfill its international responsibilities, Egypt must draw strength from its Arab ties. According to the *Vanguard* position, long-term resolution of Egypt's economic ills depended on the economic integration of the Arab world, funded "by the blood of soldiers and the oil of the wealthy." On the global level, the *Vanguard* position sought to correct Sadat's one-sided dependence on the United States. Pointedly, Kholy argued that "our present relations with the United States, which still unreservedly supports Zionism and Israel, should not prevent us from reconsidering friendly relations with the Soviet Union and the socialist world, which have always supported the Arab cause and the Palestinian cause."[99] Kholy's sweeping analysis of the domestic and foreign situation showed how socialism remained a historical possibility genuinely available to Egyptians; a national strategy set within its broad outlines would preserve the gains of the Nasser era and reopen the path to progressive transformation.

The Marxist program explicitly countered official assertions that no viable alternatives existed to Sadat's so-called liberalization policies. Regime propaganda relied heavily on the prestige of its U.S. connection to lend an air of inevitability to the American-style economic liberalization and the American-sponsored accommodation with Israel. For example, the *Vanguard* writers attacked official justifications of the Open Door that appealed to abstract "economic reason" advanced by American experts; they argued that invocations of economic necessities that supposedly dictated this policy course simply masked class interests. To the standard argument heard from International Monetary Fund and American foreign aid specialists that Egypt simply could not afford food subsidies, the left responded that "Egypt imported luxury cars at the price of 475 million pounds, while the removal of subsidies from popular goods would save only 96 million."[100] The economic imperatives advanced by Sadat and backed by the United States strengthened the parasitic middle-class social forces on which the United States relied to preserve its position in Egypt, while sapping the strength of those with an interest in socialism.

The left also warned Egyptians to pay no heed to the official "myth that there is no solution to the Middle East question except the American solution."[101] The pages of *The Vanguard* regularly carried rebuttals to the American claim that while the Soviets could arm the Arabs, only the United States could bring them peace. A representative treatment of the Egyptian-Soviet tie concluded that "the friendship of our country with the Soviet Union is based on solid material achievements such as the High Dam, the iron and steel industries, and the modern weapons with which our soldiers and officers arm themselves."[102] The historical record indicated that "America did not give us one factor that contributed to the building of basic industries required for establishing an independent national economy," wrote one analyst.[103] The left argued that the actual history of Egypt's relationships with the two superpowers scarcely justified Sadat's acquiescence in the American drive to exclude the Soviets from the Middle East.

The *Vanguard* writers also responded to the government's manipulation of Islam to strike at the left. The NPUP charged that the government "raised the banner of religious fanaticism in the face of all progressive social and national trends."[104] According to the Marxists, the only religious issue was the deliberate exploitation of religion by antisocialist ideologies and movements, rather than the atheism or nonatheism of particular individuals or groups. The Marxists argued that the government used charges of atheism to put progressive thought on the defensive, drain its energies in combat, and deplete its moral and political reserves. In response, the NPUP set itself firmly against the growing tide of Islamic fanaticism; as Rifa'at al-Said explained, "It has always been the mission of our party to liquidate or isolate this ideology and its organizational expression among Egyptians whenever possible." Khaled Muhieddin argued that repression of the radical Islamic elements had not worked for the Nasser regime and was unlikely to work now. Muhieddin added that the appropriate response to the misuse of religion was the creation of an "enlightened religious trend" with which discussion and negotiation was possible.[105]

Both the regime-sponsored American presence in Egypt and the manipulated revival of Islam weighed heavily on the left in the seventies. To meet these challenges, the *Vanguard* circle turned to the NPUP as the most effective legal agency fighting for the suppressed socialist alternative. Originating as the left platform of the ASU, the party incorporated a coalition of leftist forces that grouped both Marxist and Nasserist elements.[106] Since its founding congress in 1976, the organization and ideology of the party bore a Marxist imprint. From party leader Khaled Muhieddin on down, Marxists played an important leadership role. Muhieddin, a Marxist member of the Free Officer conspiracy, drew heavily on radical left intellectuals for top party positions;[107] Rifa'at al-Said,

Marxist journalist, served as the party's first general secretary, while Lutfy al-Kholy headed its Arab Affairs Bureau. Both the party secretariat and Executive Committee had a strong representation of Marxists. At middle and lower levels a heavy sprinkling of activists from the Socialist Youth Organization and the Institute of Socialist Studies preserved the party's radical left coloration. With its particularly strong appeal to the working class and lower middle class, the party sometimes had as many as 150,000 official members; its size made it the best-organized legal opposition force. With about 20,000 activist members, the NPUP boasted a national political structure that reached down to the factories, neighborhoods, and villages.[108]

The ideological content of the NPUP platform and party newspapers indicated the Marxist presence even more powerfully than did the heavy Marxist representation in leadership positions. Essential planks in the party's most authoritative statement of purpose read as though lifted unchanged from the pages of *The Vanguard*. Into the left-nationalist consensus that provided the ideological common denominator of the NPUP coalition, the *Vanguard* group threaded a Marxist class analysis, stressing the historical contradictions that drove social change in Egypt:

> Egyptian society now suffers from a basic contradiction that is at heart a class contradiction, occurring on the political and social levels. In this contradiction international imperialism, headed by the United States of America, stands in confrontation with the popular and democratic national forces. These classes and groups come from the working class, poor and midlevel peasants, craftsmen, small manufacturers, small merchants, productive capitalists, and revolutionary intellectuals. The United States, in turn, is backed by its Zionist ally Israel, Arab reactionaries, and old and new local reactionary forces led by parasitic capitalism.[109]

In formulating the party guidelines, the Marxists responded to the clash in Egypt between the social forces that sought to advance the revolution begun in the fifties and sixties and those that sought to destroy it. They also interpreted the exigencies of class conflict in Egypt in relation to the regional and worldwide struggle for socialism.

The party program expressed the "tasks" of the revolution in explicitly class terms, deliberately eschewing abstract language that echoed official slogans.[110] National liberation was not an end, but rather a necessary stage to prepare the way for "the socialist choice of the Egyptian people." In place of vague calls for modernization, the program called on the NPUP to "fight to halt the turning back on the road of socialist transformation" that alone would secure "the social gains for the workers, poor and midlevel peasants, and the working people in the face of traditional and new forms of colonialisms." A revolutionary class content infused all talk of democracy; the program called on the left to "stand firm against any attempts at oppressive dictatorship or the despotism of the bureaucracy" because these evils blocked "popular participation in running the affairs of the country and all sectors of society." The move to socialism required not Western-style political liberalism but rather a leading political role for an "independent political organization of the popular classes, under a socialist leadership, composed basically of the workers, peasants, and revolutionary intellectuals." In a passage that could have been quoted from any number of *Vanguard* issues, the program spelled out the meaning of the idea of democracy:

> True democracy means first and before anything else that political author-ity be in the hands of the socialist forces with the interest in continuing and completing the revolution, in the hands of the alliance of the working people as stipulated in the National Charter and permanent constitution. Affirming the authority of the alliance of the working forces of the people requires a guarantee of the representation on all levels of the masses of workers, peasants, and revolutionary intellectuals, because they are the forces with the heaviest social weight and with the greatest interest in the continuation and forward movement of the revolution.

NPUP commitments to Arab unity and the Palestinian cause were part of what the left took to be an international struggle for socialism, opposed by the United States and its ally Israel. In contrast, the Sadat orientation had its roots in the repudiation of socialism and the turn to capitalism; the program explained that the regime

> adopted the policy of peace through the United States as a natural result of its social choices and economic policy of the opening; these resulted in their own logical conclusion: Sadat's visit to Jerusalem, the Camp David accords, and the Egyptian-Israeli treaty, which in fact meant a partial settlement of the Arab-Israeli conflict and a separate peace between Egyp-tian and Israeli governments, which included abandoning the Palestinian cause in exchange for the return of a demilitarized Sinai with incomplete sovereignty over it.[111]

In setting itself *against* the Sadat peace, the NPUP was acting *for* so-cialism.

With the shutdown of the journal in 1977, the *Vanguard* circle relied on the party press to carry its analysis to guide the left in Sadat's last years. The party's general circulation paper, *The Masses* (*al-Ahaly*), with a circulation of over 100,000, brought the Marxist explanation of the failure of Nasserism and the continuing commitment to a socialist alternative to a wider public. Article after article drove home the central theme that "the NPUP defends the turn toward socialism as the sole solution possible for the problems of backwardness and social injustice, while cleansing it of whatever impurities have become attached to its application."[112] The party press provided Egyptians with a leftist explanation for the failings of the Nasserist project that kept the commitment to the socialist alternative intact. The Marxists popularized the explanation of the shortcomings of the Nasserist project in the class terms worked out by the *Vanguard* writers, explaining the class deformations of the Nasserist experiment and condemning their dire consequences in the Sadat years. Marxists also explained how such key events of the post-Nasser period as the worsening economic crisis, increased government repression of the left, the militancy of political Islam, and the Sadat peace with Israel affected the prospects of socialism.

The pages of the party press brought the concepts of the new class and parasitic capitalism colorfully to life. "There are many reasons behind the Egyptian economic disaster," explained Fuad Mursi, "the most important of which is the new group of parasites who invaded Egypt through the widest door, the economic Open Door policy, which began five years ago; in these five years they accomplished what foreign colonialism could not accomplish in seventy years." Mursi chronicled "the quick hit" approach of the new class, "whose activities are essentially commercial, particularly importing, as well as tourism, transportation, brokering, currency speculation, and real estate." He explained that these groups "use the same techniques as foreign capitalism when it enters a country to colonize it, using all manner of plundering and looting." Writing in 1978, Mursi summarized the devastating results for the national economy: "we have been transformed from a producing to a consuming country. Our consumption is 125 percent of production. In simple terms, we carve out from our 'living flesh' to eat."[113]

Mursi judged that the Egyptian economy, having fallen prey to the new class and its international imperialist supporters, suffered a deindustrialization, collapse of basic services, critical housing shortage, brain drain, and increasing threat of international receivership. The only way out of the crisis, the NPUP party writers argued, was a return to the sixties strategy of centrally planned industrialization. Through an efficiently run public sector, taxation on the rich, and an immediate end to conspicuous consumption, Egypt could find the resources to return to the socialist path.

To present this socialist alternative, the NPUP required as open a political climate as possible. When the party press raised the banner of democracy, it did so to expose the hypocritical authoritarianism that lurked beneath the democratic facade of Sadat's regime. To make this point, party leader Khaled Muhieddin regularly recited a litany of the president's excessive powers and privileges: "He is president of the state, the director of the executive authority, the judge between authorities and constitutional institutions, the supreme commander of the armed forces, the head of the national defense council, the director of the supreme police council, and the presiding officer of the judicial organizations' highest council; he appoints the prime minister, ministers and their deputies and ratifies treaties; in addition, he has the power to declare a state of emergency and the right to dissolve the parliament."[114] In unrelenting detail *The Masses* persistently documented the way the regime used this presidential power to harass and undermine the political left.

The Marxists interpreted support for democracy in class terms; they reminded followers that the battle for socialism included but transcended such liberal ideas as freedom of speech and conscience. "The liberal trend in Egypt," wrote the NPUP's first general secretary, Rifa'at al-Said, "established important traditions of press freedom, liberty of intellect, creed, and party affiliation in the face of harsh difficulties." Yet, the liberal achievements remained in "isolation . . . from the masses of the Egyptian people, [its benefits] restricted to a narrow social circle."[115] In the seventies, the left's obvious interest in democratization as a means to curb the prosecuting zeal of the regime involved no dilution of the notion that democracy, as the *Vanguard* writers put it, "could not mean the same thing to Abboud [a millionaire manufacturer of the old regime] and to a hired worker in his sugar factory in Kom Ombo; also the meaning of democracy could not possibly be identical in the dictionary of Badrawy Ashour and the peasant or tenant farmer on his vast estate in Bahout." The liberal commitment to democracy could not substitute for the left's demand for socialist transformation; in a representative formulation, an editorial explained that democratization as the left understood it was inseparable from the exigencies of the struggle to liberate the occupied territories, to protect national independence, and, above all, to maintain the achievements of the national revolution in economic, social, political, Arab, and international spheres.[116]

The left's call to democratization, while primarily articulated as a struggle against the authoritarianism of the regime, also developed into a warning against the fascist danger represented by political Islam. The left press warned against the Islamic mobilization of the lower middle class around slogans that fetishized power, stimulated intense nationalism, evoked corporatist themes that promised transcendence of the class struggle, and above all prompted an obscurantist reliance on terrorism.[117]

While attacking the fascist overtones of Islamic political militancy, the left recognized no conflict between religion, properly understood, and the socialist alternative. Drawing on the *Vanguard* analysis of Islam in public life, NPUP writers argued that true religious values supported the socialist transformation. Journalists typically argued that "there is a common ground between religion and socialism in the construction of a world of human brotherhood in which man's value as man is emphasized; the point to be agreed upon is that just as Islam was a driving force in the dawn of national revolution, it must also be a driving and supporting force for social liberation in the age of victory of socialism."[118] The party press emphasized that the common drive for "an end to human misery" united the religious and socialist impulses.[119] Periodically, the party's Committee on Religious Affairs and National Unity reported on its efforts to "emphasize the deepening of the proper understanding of religion, stress its rational side, study and publish the common aspects among divine religions, and emphasize the role of religious liberation movements facing social injustice, political dictatorship, and imperialist dominance."[120]

While emphasizing that Egypt's battle with Israel contributed to the larger struggle for world socialism, the *Vanguard* writers also indicated that the conflict in some respects adversely affected the class struggle at home. For the Marxists, strategic questions became entangled with the struggle that pitted the military as an institution and as a center of power against the forces of the left. For this reason, the *Vanguard* writers consistently argued that the battle against Israel should not be the monopoly of the armed forces and a justification for its privileged position. Marxists argued that the conflict with Israel was an Arab national liberation struggle against world imperialism that could be won only by the forces of popular resistance. In his editorials Kholy emphasized a long-term struggle that would require "more cohesion between the armed forces and the popular masses through popular defense armies and the like." He pressed, in particular, for "ending the mechanical distinction between political and military action; this requires walking the road of revolutionary struggle with firm footsteps that depend on organized and conscious mass mobilization."[121]

The Marxists linked the strength of reaction at home to American regional and global preponderance. American hegemony in the Middle East made the potential power of its Israeli surrogate the central issue in the battle for pan-Arab unity. From the *Vanguard* perspective, the United States posed the ultimate threat to Egypt's socialist transformation; Israel, quite apart from its racist Zionist ideology, functioned primarily as an extension of American power into the Middle East for the purpose of securing U.S. domination of the area. Thus, Egypt faced "large and small imperialisms"; the *Vanguard* writers emphasized that "the United States of America is the leader of international imperialism, antagonistic to the Arab liberation movement."[122]

In the long view taken by the *Vanguard* circle, "The final defeat of the Zionist presence in the Arab world will take place over a whole historic phase."[123] The long-term strategic commitment to undermining the Zionist presence was coupled with tactical flexibility and realism. When Sadat, newly in power, was pressured to engage the Israelis in "a year of decision" Lutfy al-Kholy used the *Vanguard* platform to argue against "adventurism," reminding his readers that "the Israeli military capability equals in kind and fighting capability the collective Arab military force in the area."[124] For the same reason, the militancy of the left toward the Zionist state did not prevent the *Vanguard* writers from accepting the idea of a "political" solution in principle, provided that it did not endanger Egypt's national independence and that it honored the principle of "not giving up the legitimate rights of the Palestinian people."[125]

In the wake of Sadat's opening to Israel, the party press attempted to bring this complex reasoning on war and peace to a larger mass public. The NPUP judged that Sadat acted precipitously and from a position of weakness when he made his historic trip to Jerusalem. The left was unmoved by the president's confidence in his American partner to offset Egypt's position of military inferiority. While not ruling out negotiation with Israel, the Marxist left considered it possible only from a position of strength based on unified Arab action, the oil weapon, and a willingness to reopen hostilities. Sadat's break with Arab ranks and unconditional, unilateral gesture of peace left Egypt too vulnerable to negotiate a just settlement. Khaled Muhieddin wrote: "If they tell us peace is coming, we say no . . . because the aims of the Zionist movement have not changed, given [Zionism's] drive for expansion and domination of the Arab area. Whereas, the Egyptian authorities want to stop the conflict and open the doors to Zionist culture and trade, even changing the educational curriculum to avoid mentioning enmity toward Israel." To this policy of official capitulation, the NPUP proposed a model of "comprehensive confrontation" on the Nasserist model: "In these dark days, we remember Abdul Nasser and the July Revolution and we hold on to the policy of comprehensive confrontation, the policy of economic and social liberation, so that Egypt may emerge from this long nightmare and proceed on the path of liberation with the rest of our Arab nation."[126]

Despite evidence of support for Sadat's initiative from the rank and file, the highest party leader sharply attacked the 1977 Jerusalem trip. Lutfy Waked, an important figure in Nasserist circles, explained:

> It was on the premises of our belief in Egypt's Arab identity and the necessity of Arab unity in the face of present and future challenges and of our studies of the nature of the Zionist enemy, that the party's evaluation of President Sadat's visit to Israel was made. Despite the overwhelming support the visit received on its first days, our party had to be honest with itself, its masses, and history, and take a bold stand announcing its opposition to the visit.[127]

The NPUP opposed not peace but a Sadat peace that could neither protect Egypt's interests nor secure justice for the Palestinians:

> When our party opposed the Camp David accords, that did not mean that it opposes efforts for peace. On the contrary, its opposition was, and still is, based on the principle that in order actually to realize peace, it must be comprehensive, just, and capable of lasting. A solution is no peace that refuses to recognize, from a colonial and Zionist outlook, the Palestine Liberation Organization, and offers the Palestinian people not only less than that granted it by international legitimacy, but even less than is offered by the government of South Africa to the people of Transkei, an offer rejected in that case even by the United States.[128]

Initially, the stand against the Sadat peace provoked unrest and even rebellion among war-weary Egyptians in the party rank and file.[129] Before long, however, party leaders could point to developments that vindicated the NPUP's position. Israeli prime minister Begin promptly resumed Israeli colonization of the West Bank. Within Egypt, the isolating impact of the break with the Arab world began to make itself felt, along with the oppressive weight of the enlarged American presence.

To an increasingly receptive party and mass public, Marxist intellectuals argued that both the United States and Israel had had their way with Egypt with little gain, aside from the return of the Sinai, to the nation or to the Palestinians. Israeli settlements on the West Bank were destroying the prospects of a Palestinian homeland in historic Palestine. At the same time, the United States used the so-called process to inject itself as a political and military presence in Egypt.

The Marxists consistently pressed for an alternative to the Camp David formula. Muhammad Sid Ahmed argued that the failure of self-rule negotiations for the West Bank—a symptom of the larger unresolved Palestinian issue—could precipitate a general crisis in the area that, by threatening the West's access to oil and the Arab bourgeoisie's thirst for regional stability, might just produce a new opening. He looked to various European initiatives to find an alternative to Camp David based on the Palestinian right of self-determination. Sid Ahmed noted that in the summer of 1980 "opposition to the Sadat peace was no longer limited to the NPUP, anti-imperialists, or Islamic-based groups." The Egyptian middle class, increasingly disillusioned with the regime on both economic and democratic issues, also saw the dangers of the present regional crisis: "The opposition of the Egyptian bourgeoisie is fostered by the opposition of the European and Arab elements who have an interest in the stability of the Arab oil market and its dealings with the West. [The Egyptian bourgeoisie] also finds itself incapable of protecting its own interests in the face of parasitic elements and in the face of a policy that, evidence now shows, is abandoning the national interest."[130]

Emphasizing these actual outcomes, the left characterized the so-called peace agreement as "an Egyptian-American military alliance that demilitarizes the Sinai and injects American forces into the area. Our party emphasized from the beginning that the Camp David agreement is not a peace treaty, but an Egyptian imperialist military alliance threatening the Arab and African people."[131] The left concluded that Sadat had effectively made Egypt a partner of the small and big imperialisms.

Sadat's separate peace with Israel, along with his unrestricted opening to foreign capital and strategic alignment with the United States, brought the left party into open confrontation with the regime. The NPUP's defense of the people's right to demonstrate in January 1977 and its open attack on the Sadat peace process shortly thereafter exceeded the limits officially set for the opposition. The regime imposed what Khaled Muhieddin called a "siege" on the NPUP that ranged "from stopping our mass congresses to harassing anyone distributing our statements to citizens, from repeated confiscations of *The Masses* to the outright banning of the party paper."[135] Party leaders responded defiantly:

> At dawn on Saturday, April 7, 1979, the state security police broke into the central residence of the NPUP and seized printing equipment and typewriters because they print material that opposed the Egyptian-Israeli agreement ... This is the third time that "dawn visitors" from the security police have broken into the premises of a legitimate party and seized its equipment and tools. Dawn visitors from the security police cannot frighten us. They only reveal to Egyptian, Arab, and world public opinion the truth of the democracy that "will increase after signing the Arab-Israeli treaty." Our party opposed this treaty and will continue to oppose it.[133]

Khaled Muhieddin later described this period as one of the most trying times for the NPUP. He went on to claim, however, that the "government harassment was a good chance for the party to get rid of weak and hesitant elements." Although several thousand NPUP members did abandon the party, more-militant leftists who had remained aloof from a government-sanctioned party replaced some of these losses. Therefore, the party's time of troubles "was also a chance to show the strength of thousands of party members and of leftist and progressive forces who were not members of the party; these forces hastened to join the party after an experience that assured them of its independence."[134] One prominent party leader summarized the steeling effect: "by virtue of the challenges it has faced, the party has acquired immunity against the worst of diseases in political life—that of opportunism."[135]

The left displayed its hold on public opinion when the trials opened for those accused of complicity in the January "conspiracy." The defendants and their lawyers succeeded in turning the proceedings into an indictment of the regime before the informed public, not only for the illegalities of its investigation and prosecution of the case but also for the policies that caused the January events in the first place. The defense built its case on the legal right of the Egyptian people to resist the regime's unconstitutional "coup" by the Open Door policy. According to the defense, the government's economic policies "made the people of Egypt, under the Open Door and as a result of the Open Door, poorer than they ever were before 1952, despite the fact that a minority became richer than any minority that existed since the beginning of the twentieth century."[136] During the trials, press reports hammered away at the illegal harassments endured by defendants exercising their constitutional rights to resist unjust and illegal policies; for perhaps the first time, the public received a full sense of the handicaps under which the left operated, making the political actions and electoral achievements of the NPUP seem all the more impressive.[137]

The "siege" backfired against the government in other ways as well. Defense lawyers skillfully introduced as evidence confiscated issues of *The Masses* and *Progress* (*al-Taqqudum*); detailed discussions of their contents, reported at times even in the national press, gave readers a precise idea of the issues and arguments the government sought to repress.[138] To embarrass the regime, one lawyer for the defense pointed out that evidence used by the prosecutor came from secret police tapes that President Sadat, in a celebrated incident to announce his new era of democracy, claimed he had personally burned.[139] A writer charged with possession of "printed and handwritten stories that carry an opposing line and a Marxist tendency" confessed his guilt of the charges, adding, however, that "my excuse is that I was not previously informed that one of the conditions of writing novels is to have a 'supporting' position."[140]

The publicity of the trials provided opportunities to broaden support for the party, and the NPUP eagerly seized them. Khaled Muhieddin reported, for example, that the party formed "a democratic committee for the defense of liberties, including lawyers who were non-party members, coming together around the principle of providing all the guarantees of legal defense to those imprisoned for their opinions and supporting their families." Reaching out to all dissident elements, Muhieddin commented that "we are proud that our party did not abandon any persons of opinion during these four years, whether or not they agree with party positions. This is considered a great achievement in Egypt, as no one is afraid for the future of his family any longer. This practice has become part of the democratic heritage in Egypt and was adopted by other agencies, especially the Bar Association, which now plays a great role in defending those accused in political cases."[141] When articles in the national press personally attacked Muhieddin, impugning his patriotism because of statements against the Sadat peace, Muhieddin sued; he won the case and was awarded damages of L.E. 20,000, indicating the sympathy of the courts and of public opinion for the left.[142]

In the end, the Egyptian judiciary refused to credit the charges brought against the left. Of the 815 arrested in the government's security campaigns, only 176 were ever brought to trial; the rest were released for lack of sufficient evidence to render the charges made against them credible. Of the nearly 200 arrested after the January riots, only 20 were sentenced to jail. All of those received lenient sentences on minor charges of from one to three years.

Writing in 1966, Lutfy al-Kholy condemned reactionaries who screamed that any progressive thought was communist and conspiratorial: "To talk about communists in our society today is to talk of something that does not exist. There are no more than a few hundred Marxist citizens in our society. After all, Marxism is not an ideology that has ready-made solutions, but just a method for thinking and analysis."[143] Later, Kholy reasoned that in the seventies this Marxist method delivered a compelling indictment of Sadat's American-backed liberalization by evoking the socialist alternative to it. Sadatists often argued that Sadat's internal liberalization and shock diplomacy had created new opportunities for Egypt. In contrast, the Marxists of *The Vanguard* argued that Sadat simply capitulated to forces and arrangements that Nasser had judged unacceptable and resisted successfully, In June 1968 Sa'ad Zahran wrote in *The Vanguard:*

> America wants to sell us Sinai in return for entering Cairo; that is, some reactionary forces say that if we accept America's conditions, we could generate American pressure on Israel. And, of course, the American conditions are those it has been trying to impose throughout the age of the Egyptian revolution, namely the entrance of U.S. and Zionist influence into Cairo economically, culturally, and politically.

A decade later, Lutfy al-Kholy had only to restate these arguments as an indictment of the policies Sadat had pursued.[144]

At the end of the Sadat era, the Marxist left believed that developments had vindicated its assessment of what the January uprising would mean for Egypt, for the left, and for the socialist alternative. In Sadat's last years, domestic repression was billed as political liberalization; humiliating concessions to Israel necessary to win Western support were obscured by a so-called peace process, and Egypt's reintegration into the Western economic and security system was hailed as "development and progress." Sadat's grand foreign policy reorientation, coupled with his tilt toward the rich at home, had driven the left into continuous opposition that provoked ever more severe official reprisals. Acting on the "facts" that a socialist perspective and a socialist practice made real, the *Vanguard* circle had produced an energizing critique of government policies that won a responsive audience for the left in the political and cultural life of Egypt. Abou Seif Yusuf argued that the government and the mainline press aimed to "prevent the people from searching for progressive alternatives and solutions."[145] Through their writings and their practical role in the NPUP, the Marxists of *The Vanguard* aimed to give notable substance to the historical socialist alternative that shadowed the established order in Egypt.[146]

5

Creative Empowerment: The Wissa Wassef School

What I am suggesting is that change is continually occurring but that its consequence is never the absence of the norms, standards, and certainties we desire, because they will be features of any situation we happen to be in. This means that while we can never specify value once and for all—that is, label a sentence ambiguous or unambiguous in itself—we can always specify value within the circumstances informing our perception—that is, perceive sentences as ambiguous or unambiguous in context. This is to say . . . there always is a standard story and as characters who are embedded in it, we are never without a conviction of facts, consequences, responsibilities—of everything that comprises our sense of being in a world

—*Stanley Fish*

The boy made his own small loom out of a few pieces of wood held together with string; on it he somehow succeeded in weaving a very irregular tapestry. Sophie and Ramses Wissa Wassef had told young Aly that they could not take any more children from the village for their new art school. That rule dissolved in the approving laughter evoked by the boy's insistent ingenuity. Aly is now middle-aged and a master weaver. For more than a quarter-century he has been sharing in a way of life, the creation of "tapestries from Egypt."[1] The Wissa Wassef School in the village of Harrania is world famous, and the story of Aly's first loom is a treasured founding myth.

In 1952 two young artists, Sophie, a water colorist, and Ramses, a sculptor and architect, bought land near the small village of Harrania as the site for their art school. The young couple went regularly to their land on the road to Sakkara just outside Cairo, sat at the foot of a tree near an irrigation canal, and waited for the village children to come running, as they still do when an outside face promises some new adventure. A game of ball, laughter, and a respectful exchange of names were the school's first structures; the program and the buildings came later, added room by room in shapes dictated by the children's activities and Ramses' belief that architecture should arise naturally from its setting. The weaving of wool tapestries was the initial focal point; creative work in pottery, batik, cotton tapestries, and stained glass came later.

Ramses and Sophie saw Harrania as a small arena in which to test large ideas. The most important concept was Ramses' belief in the universality of artistic potential, to which Sophie wedded an impatient insistence that the artist's creation of beautiful things should also result in the creation of a better self. Ramses called the school they founded an experiment; for Sophie it has always been a reform. Together they created the Wissa Wassef School as a model of a "reform as experiment."[2]

At Harrania, Sophie and Ramses set out deliberately to test two propositions: every child is born an artist, and as artists children can create their own better lives. The school's founders realized that these theoretical notions were obstinate denials of the realities of village life. Peasant children as artists whose most important creations were more beautiful selves: these were social facts yet to be created. Some considered the national education system to be the natural place to experiment with these ideas, but Ramses and Sophie concluded that this possibility was closed to them. From his father, Ramses had learned disillusionment with an active role in public life. An ardent nationalist of the prerevolutionary era, the elder Wissa Wassef had decided that genuine service to Egypt was impossible in the public sphere. From her father, the educator Habib Gorgy, Sophie knew at first hand the frustrations and profound disappointments of public education. For all its initial promise, both Sophie and Ramses judged that the 1952 Free Officers' revolution did not alter this inheritance.

Initially, Ramses' father had been caught up in the exhilaration of the liberal age. Wissa Wassef's strong nationalist feelings were apparent in his support, unusual for a Copt, for the nationalist leader Mustafa Kamel, whose strong anticolonialism was heavily freighted with Islamic fervor. However, Wissa Wassef was most active politically in the era of Sa'ad Zaghloul's leadership. From Wissa Wassef's perspective, the nationalist leader Sa'ad Zaghloul's defiance of the British united all Egyptians—the pasha and the peasant, the educated and the illiterate, the Muslim and the Copt. When Egypt declared its independence in February 1922 and hastened to enshrine its liberal nationalist faith in the constitution of 1923, Wissa Wassef believed that a new constitutional order anchored in a substantial middle class of professionals, officials, and intellectuals was about to be born. Wissa Wassef was the scion of a prominent Coptic family.[3] Egypt's Orthodox Christian minority responded positively to the inclusive nationalism of the Wafd, and Wissa Wassef became a power in Zaghloul's nationalist party. He had joined the Wafd at its inception and in some ways became a symbol of the Muslim/Christian unity in an Egyptian nationalism that to the present day characterizes the Wafdist stance. Wissa Wassef, for example, was elected to the parliament by an entirely Muslim constituency. His dramatic career ranged from imprisonment with a death sentence to a leadership role in parliament.[4] Yet, in the end the constitutional era gravely disappointed Wissa Wassef. The chaos and corruption of public life in the forties, notably the political maneuvering of the crown, the minority parties, and the British, as well as the generally low level of public morality, proved deeply disillusioning. After a lifetime given to politics, Wissa Wassef concluded that an abdication of intelligence and integrity had become the virtual precondition for success in public life. He urged his children to explore other paths to serve Egypt.[5]

Sophie's father, Habib Gorgy, responded to Taha Hussein, Egypt's greatest educator of the modern era, when he pronounced that education must be as free as air and water. By the late forties, however, Gorgy concluded that these hopes had been consumed by upper-class greed, continued foreign interference, corruption, and violence. Gorgy welcomed the 1952 revolution, with Nasser's call for an end to corruption and the rebirth of a strong and independent Egypt. But he soon concluded that the young officers ruling Egypt saw the role of their people as approving onlookers of a revolution from above, with neither responsibility nor creative involvement in the changes in their lives. Sophie grew to adulthood in an atmosphere colored by these disappointments.

Deeply affected by his father's disillusionment with a life in politics, Ramses turned to the arts, especially sculpture. Persuaded by his father that architecture was the father of all the arts, he became an architect. While teaching in art school, Ramses met Sophie's father, then chief inspector for the arts curriculum in Egypt's primary and secondary schools. Ramses moved immediately into Gorgy's circle of artists and educators. He was initially surprised to find the independent Sophie a respected participant in group discussions; such a role for a young, unmarried woman was unusual. In this company, Ramses was directly exposed to the influence that was most powerful in Sophie's life: her father's conviction that institutional education, when not ignoring the child, actively and systematically killed whatever creative spark existed. A play on his first name gave Habib Gorgy the informal title "Lover of the Child." Gorgy railed against the imposed mediocrity of public education. He cited the practice in art classes of slavishly copying from the masters as symptomatic of the general mindlessness of an education system based on static repetition and memorization. Such training, he argued, taught children to restrain and ultimately despise their own creative impulses. "If you don't like the spontaneous art work of the child," Gorgy would say, "you don't like the child."[6]

For Ramses and Sophie, liking the child meant considering every child much as a gardener views a young tree, as something with an intrinsic nature that requires only the right conditions to flourish. The power of the metaphor lay in the implicit demand for respect of intrinsic creativity; however, the comparison to the realm of nature masked the problem of determining what conditions were required to trigger and sustain the human creative impulse. The only persuasive proof that such a nurturing environment existed was the creative process and the work it generated. To answer inquiries about the success or failure of their experiment, Ramses and Sophie issued invitations to come to the school, meet the artists, and see their creations.

Once realized, the creative impulse always appeared magical. The tapestries from Harrania were typically described with terms such as "flowers of the desert."[7] Yet, the very beauty of the tapestries, pottery, or batiks obscured the conflicts in the social world out of which they came. Only the stories that made sense of particular events in the life of the community could make those human struggles understandable; one such event that occurred during the period when I regularly visited the school involved the pottery atelier.

It was April 28, 1980, and Sophie had just learned that all the young potters had left, presumably for good. Located just inside the main gate, their open-air studio was an introduction to the school. Said Sid Ahmed, the master potter who worked with the children, did not seem to notice. He moved through the potters' spaces with his usual absorption. Seeing him work alone for the first time clarified the way in which his movements structured an atelier out of a simple open court. Said, Sophie explained, could not sit still. He had begun as a weaver some twenty years earlier but had found the work too constraining.

Conversations with Said had always been punctuated by interruptions from the half-dozen or so young boys who were working with him at any one time. The boys at their wheels were themselves a diverting magnet. At first, it was hard to be drawn into Said's fluid calm because of the noisy presence of the young potters. Suzanne, Ramses and Sophie's daughter, was often in the atelier because she gave the pottery section her special attention. On this day, she and Said had been experimenting with a new glaze, and the first samples were just emerging from the kiln under Said's approving watch. The moment was perfect: the ten or so pieces to be inspected anchored Said in the bright sun of the court yard. There was time to talk about more than the disappearance of his students.

Said commented that the glaze was less red than expected; in the same even tone he noted that the boys had left to work in a commercial shop. Said reacted to this disruption of years of intimate involvement by working and by talking about his own life. His reflections that day fixed for me the meaning of the principles and structures that buttress the Wissa Wassef experiment. From Said's account of the loss of the boys emerged a clear image of the problems that he, and other members of the Wissa Wassef community, understood themselves to be confronting in their work.[8]

The extended conversation with Said made it clear that the community at Wissa Wassef derived its essential coherence from a compelling theory of artistic creation. The creative artist was the key symbol of group life; it was a self-representation that aggressively appropriated a title of respect that could be shared by the peasant weavers and potters and the middle-class founders of the school. To be an artist in the sense given to the term at Harrania was understood to entail an active resistance to prevailing social forces that acted against creativity; for this reason, the symbol helped strengthen the bonds of community.

"Ramses gave me the mud and let me work it."[9] In recalling his own artistic relationship to Ramses Wissa Wassef, Said effectively denied even the possibility of failure as a teacher. He could not fail as an instructor, for that was not his proper role. Like Ramses, he had only to provide the means for others to work as artists beside him. Said's certainty rested on a profoundly humanistic conception of creativity as a common human potential; this conception was fundamental to his experience at Harrania. Ramses was very explicit and self-conscious on this point: "The idea, or feeling, that drove me to act was to all appearances a very utopian one, but it very quickly took shape and became part of my life, and that of the group . . . I had this vague conviction that every human being was born an artist."[10]

The reinforcing evidence of Said's own artistry was displayed all around him, not least in Suzanne Wissa Wassef's sudden appearance to review the results of their latest experiment. Her response to the loss of the potters appeared as direct and unthreatened as Said's: "The boys have left to make more money than we can pay them. Perhaps they'll return. If not, others will come." As if to corroborate that faith, Said brought another group of plates from the kiln. In their surprise and delight with the variations of the unexpected new color, I could almost hear the laughter and excited talk of the children who would be drawn from the village to fill the empty spaces at Wissa Wassef School.

"I'm not a worker here. Suzanne, . . . like her father, treats me as a creative artist."[11] Said on some level was aware that he and Suzanne had been acting out publicly their roles as artists. The ease of their "performance" established it as an approved and familiar scenario, valued as a dramatization of the distinctive character of work and work relations at the school. The aesthetic realm in which he and Suzanne acted was one of experimentation in which playful sensibilities imprint themselves on the material environment of shared lives. In the interaction of Said and Suzanne, the reality of that realm was reaffirmed against its momentary denial by the young potters.

For all the initial material advantages of work at Wissa Wassef, Said understood that once he had acquired basic skills as a weaver or potter he could have earned much more at any one of the innumerable commercial craft shops that catered to tourists; in Egypt, there was always a profitable market for folkloric craft items turned out en masse. From the outset, Sophie and Ramses had not ignored the material side of the Wissa Wassef experiment. The principled character of their approach did not make it naive; the children who worked at the school were always paid for their very first tapestries. To complete a piece, whatever its artistic merits, meant the mastery of basic techniques, and payment signaled the end of the very briefest period of the only "apprenticeship" that the artists at Wissa Wassef would ever know. Ramses and Sophie agreed that there could be no training in the properly aesthetic realm because they both believed that true creativity requires a unique combination of technical manipulation of the material world and an intensely personal vision. Payment, therefore, was not a reward for creating art, nor was it an end in itself. Financial reward was rather a practical sign that an important technique had been learned and could be practiced. A salary for even the youngest of the artists offered the promise that they could support themselves as part of a community of artists in which the priority was development of their own creative potential. Finished tapestries were thereafter paid for by a simple method: the weaver received a sum determined by multiplying the area of the rug by a coefficient that depended on a judgment of the "care taken and the attractiveness of the work." The working definition of "attractiveness" was evidence of individual creativity.[12]

Both Sophie and Ramses insisted on the centrality of novel creation to the value structure of the Wissa Wassef community. The primary evidence for its operational significance was the artistic range and variety of the tapestries themselves. Ramses marveled at the fecundity: "The result was a whole new language, an unlimited source of poetry that came to light early and has remained abundant for twenty-five years."[13] Over and over again in hundreds of conversations he reaffirmed that value, demonstrating its power more often than not with references to work in progress. Virtually his only criticisms or self-criticisms of an aesthetic nature touched on this value. Invariably they were whispered, more in disappointment than in censorship: "He is repeating himself," or "She is quick but seems to be copying," or "Why are you so interested in that piece? I've done one like it before."[14]

"Of course the money is important," explained Said. "I built my own house in the village and I have a TV and a fan. The money is important but the main thing is the work, my work."[15] This internalized yet explicit orientation, putting the highest value on the free expression of self in the work process, was one of the most powerful shields protecting the Wissa Wassef community. It was not foolproof: the very young and inexperienced were naturally susceptible to the greater material incentives that purely commercial enterprises offered. Without exception the senior artists were all approached regularly with such opportunities. The experience of those who did leave was always the same: they repeated themselves. Their development was frozen in standardized, accelerated, and profitable production.

Knowledge of this outcome buttressed the Wissa Wassef School. From the outset Sophie and Ramses understood the dangers of pressures from society at large. Ramses spoke of an "army of external influences" that threatened "the children's own rich natures" and from which they must be shielded.[16] Only an effective communal shield would allow the unfolding of the child's innate gifts. Despite this emphasis, however, Ramses always acknowledged the limited role of the school itself in the creative process; the gifts were born to the child, and they could not be taught. Moreover, Ramses and Sophie recognized that the child's own aroused creative impulse was in the end the only positive force powerful enough to counteract diverting social pressures. No sanction or reward could substitute for it. In the event of failure, the only alternative was other children. Said's balanced and calm absorption of the loss of the potters finds its explanation here. The Wissa Wassef community knew that built into the task of creating the conditions of success was the necessity to allow for failure.

The Wissa Wassef experiment, then, taught the wisdom of letting go. Such a recognition that not everyone could live as an artist came, however, only after a struggle. Over the years, demanding and complex strategies emerged to fortify the resolve to live as a free, creative person. External forces that threatened the community, whether economic, political, or social, were actively countered. In addition, within the school great care was taken to protect each child's unique drive to create from the adverse impact of new forms of spontaneously generated authority, however subtle or well intentioned.

Both the costs and the rewards of the level of commitment required were reflected in the lives of all those attached to the school. To "act for" the school at times required unusual social courage. The peasant artists naturally felt the pull of the village from which they came; they were always vulnerable to its powerful, internalized social traditions. An incident in the adult life of Aly, who as a boy had made his own loom, offered a prototypal scenario. The head of a family and the father of five, Aly was intent on enjoying in the village the full status of a successful adult male. That position was compromised by the character of his work. To the villagers, it appeared that Aly did the same work as women at Wissa Wassef; they too were artists, creators of tapestries that commanded the respect of the community. At one point, this burden of daily and public acceptance of the equality of women in the work process threatened to become too heavy to bear. Aly withdrew into constant prayer, isolated himself, and spoke less and less to the other weavers. His work suffered. Sophie has always kept a record of the tapestries of each of the master weavers and periodically reviewed their work with them. The discussion with Sophie of the clear indications of the decline of his artistry prompted Aly to express his discontent. Sophie was unwilling to compromise the equal status of the women weavers but she did manage a face-saving rearrangement of the weavers' space that allowed Aly to regain his balance.

The children, too, experienced the pains of the competing pulls of two worlds, but few as pointedly as teenaged Mahrus. The boy's mother had two sisters at Wissa Wassef, and she saw his work there as a good opportunity. After almost six years, her husband had still not accepted the idea. He needed the boy to work the land he rented. Mahrus, who before coming to the school had worked "for three years in the sun," had lost all the peasant's proverbial attachment to the land. At first he tried to placate his father by farming in the morning and weaving in the afternoon. The quality of both his work and his health suffered. Mahrus chose to defy his father. Matter-of-factly, he observed that "the beatings are less frequent now." His younger brothers were now "on the land." Once the decision in favor of the school was made, Mahrus' tapestries suffered only from his temptation to work too quickly, perhaps to validate his life choice by his earnings. However, Mahrus had made himself a part of the community, and Suzanne, who worked with him, was optimistic that he would yet become a master weaver.[17]

Ramses and Sophie's commitment to the school occupied most of their time and energy, leading their daughter Yoanna to complain that "the school stole my parents."[18] Yoanna, a specialist in French language and literature with a degree from the University of Cairo, spoke in flawless French of her earlier plans for a career in teaching and perhaps writing. As a child, Yoanna recalled, she resented sharing her parents with so many others. "I never thought I would come here," she said quietly. Suzanne, a graduate of the Institute for Social Work, acknowledged the school's dominating presence in her early life with a quite different reaction. "I felt betrayed," she remarked, "because I was sent to schools in Cairo." Suzanne was jealous of the village children and the freedom of their lives at Wissa Wassef. "Why," she wondered, "have my parents given me over to those jailers?"[19]

As adults, both Yoanna and Suzanne succumbed to the powerful attraction of their parents' life work. The reflective Yoanna found her advanced studies too closed and unrelated to her own cultural experience; she found "more life and more human contact" at the school. Suzanne, always susceptible to the pull of the school, concluded that the social work that was unavoidably a part of the Wissa Wassef experiment was "simply more important than anything I can do anywhere else."

Sophie's life, however, was the most convincing proof not only of the validity of the theory of artistic creation that she shared with Ramses but also of the power of her parents' critique of the prevailing social conditions that continue to act against it. Her life showed how a critical experiment such as the Wissa Wassef School could carve out a place for itself against external constraints.

The death of Ramses was inevitably a crisis for the school, perhaps the most severe of the tests faced by his and Sophie's ideas in action. Their shared understanding of the meaning of school had allowed no place for the idea of an indispensable charismatic founder; to succeed in the terms Ramses and Sophie had themselves set, their reform as experiment would have to continue without him.

Sophie acknowledged the hardships of the transition period that followed Ramses' death with characteristic honesty. She reported that the work of the master weavers declined in quality almost immediately, a reaction to the loss of the constant discussion with Ramses of their difficulties and discoveries. Sophie overcame her doubts that the school could continue by an active resolve to spend even more of her own time with the weavers, supporting and encouraging them. At this time of vulnerability, pressures from the outside increased.

Ramses had left no sons. Though both daughters married, their husbands played no role in the school. Sophie had in every sense been a full partner in the Wissa Wassef experiment: without her, its particular character was inconceivable. Most accounts of the Wissa Wassef School miss the centrality of Sophie's role as cofounder and full partner. She is typically cast as "carrying her husband's message."[20]

Without Ramses, it did look for a time as though a school run by three women would not survive. With little subtlety, men from the village offered their "services" to Sophie; without Ramses, they concluded, his widow and daughters would undoubtedly need their protection. Sophie understood that toleration of such an intrusion would have irreparably damaged the shield laboriously built around the school environment. Her firm refusals met with nighttime vandalism at the school. Undaunted, Sophie moved from her home in a Cairo suburb into the main building of the school. From then on she countered noises in the night by firing a rifle into the air. The harassment soon stopped.

Not all nor even the most dangerous of the social assailants of the creative process at Harrania have been so clearly external. The founders early recognized the traditional educational process, as it touched even the village children, as a major threat. Ramses saw the problem of art's social context clearly if somewhat abstractly. "Art," he insisted, "is condemned to be superfluous when it is separated from life."[21] For that reason, he opposed the artificial preservation of craft industries that had lost their traditional raison d'être. The art of Wissa Wassef would be a response to new needs, not to those artificially revived from an earlier age. This point is frequently misunderstood, especially in popular press treatments. *Al-Ahram* of January 17, 1980, for example, treats the tapestries as somehow representing a revival of the weaving arts of ancient Egypt. In fact, there was never any copying of old folkloric designs at

Harrania. Nor were the village children ever placed in the shadow of the great names of art history, as was the usual practice in art schools. In all of this Ramses was quite deliberate:

> I took care not to provide the children with works of art to imitate, and I never took them to visit museums or art galleries. And if I set up my workshop near this village, it was certainly not in the hope of finding vestiges of artistic or craft traditions, but knowing that there were no such traces, and particularly to ensure isolation from the influence of the city and its harmful effects, and above all from "artistic" influences. I wanted to shield my children from the slightest tendency to share in the general plagiarizing that goes on.[22]

Ramses thus insisted that the children's own inventiveness was a sufficient reservoir, while Sophie understood the complex link between personal creativity and social freedom. Sophie brought this insight to her life vocation at the Wissa Wassef School from earlier experiences, first as a student and then as a young art teacher. Sophie had been especially responsive to her father's insistence that the true work of art was the free expression of a unique social being. Herself a watercolorist, she developed an enduring aversion to drawing: it was the "art" taught in schools, taking the form of slavish imitation of the masters. Sophie's own rejection of art understood as plagiarized technique was grounded in her insistence on the importance of an artist's own working environment. For Sophie, to love art was to love the artists and their ability to create a more beautiful world.

As a child in the Coptic school in the Bulaq district of Cairo, Sophie responded to the plea of the ministry of social work for funds to finance a medical campaign against worm infestation of the children in the school. With three pounds saved from pocket money to buy materials, and with the help of her friends in three days of feverish and covert activity, Sophie's talent produced over a hundred original gifts and toys that were sold to earn several hundred pounds for medicine. Sophie took this story to mean that there was nothing otherworldly or untried in art's magical social properties.

As the new young art instructor in the school in Old Cairo, Sophie arrived with definite ideas. She immediately banished the pencils and sketchpads that debased art to imitation and replaced them with piles of colored threads and mounds of clay to be given texture and form. The children reacted with surprise to the notion of "play" in school. The headmaster, too, was surprised; he found the new creations more primitive than original and concluded that the results would not be so embarrassing to the school if the children were given "appropriate" models. To say no to rote imitation required leaving the job; Sophie invited some of her more promising students home with her to continue their work.

Sophie brought these rich experiences to discussions with her father, his reward for the unusual freedom he had given his daughter. At a time when women had few rights, Sophie had enjoyed the kind of social freedom usually reserved for boys, the opportunity for higher education and encouragement and support for her own career. To critics of his childrearing attitudes, Habib Gorgy would explain simply: "She is a person; she should find her own way."[23]

It was only natural, then, that Sophie discussed ideas with the young men, artists and educators, who gathered around her father, Ramses among them. The ideas the two later brought to Harrania were hammered out jointly in such discussions. With time, it became difficult to distinguish their thinking about art and society. Their practices, however, remained distinctive. For all their agreement on abstract ideas, there was a tension in their relationship, a creative stress to which both of their daughters attribute much of the success of the school they founded. To Sophie's insistence that to create always meant to create a better world, Ramses counseled the patience that was to prove so essential to sustaining their project.

Sophie's impatient drive was combined with Ramses' pragmatic restraint to create the balanced, minimal rule structure that governed artistic work at their school. At Harrania the conditions were created to evoke the innate creative impulse of the child, without in the process subjecting it to new forms of authority. Sharp and respectful limits were placed on interference, however well meant, with the child's natural expressiveness. Aside from the intrinsic discipline derived from the physical properties of the medium in which they worked, the young artists at Harrania observed only three rules: no preliminary drawings, no external aesthetic influences, and no criticism from adults.[24] The tapestries, the batiks, the pottery of Harrania all emerged from the inner life of the children, conceived in free choice within this minimal rule structure.

Initially, the protective screen erected by Sophie and Ramses was the indispensable guarantor of such free creation. Gradually, however, as the artists saw what they could do and experienced themselves and through others the power of their work, their own confidence became the most effective shield. It was not that the village was cut off from the world, although its relative isolation was at first deemed a great advantage. As word of the remarkable tapestries spread throughout Egypt and the world, visitors to the workshops (both Egyptian and foreign) increased greatly in number. Exhibitions were held around the world, and some of the young artists traveled with them. Unburdened by a search for identity or dignity, they met the world as self-assured artists.

One exhibition in Cairo drew large numbers of artists and critics, as much interested in the peasants who made them as in the tapestries themselves. "Why do you use so many colors?" Garia Mahmud was asked. "It's quite obvious you live in the city; if you have time, come for a walk in our part of the country, and you'll see even more colors." "Why not design the tapestries first? Aren't you afraid of making mistakes?" "I can't draw, but I can weave. If I feel I am going to make mistakes in my weaving, I don't even sit down in front of the loom. I go and sit in the sun."[25]

For Sophie and Ramses, true art held the promise of liberation rather than enslavement. No matter how splendid the products of a traditional craft such as oriental rugs, they judged that there was something as profoundly depressing as the modern assembly line in the mechanical repetitiveness of the work process that yielded them. Men and women seemed degraded rather than ennobled by artifacts that are often stunningly beautiful in themselves. Wissa Wassef tapestries were art rather than craft; in their work the young people at Harrania understood themselves to be creating not only works of art but themselves as artists. The new needs for self-expression, for freedom, and for community bound the artists of the Wissa Wassef School together in their world apart.

The Europeans from the Cairo suburb of Maadi who brought Said the pictures of the kind of pottery they wanted to "order" could not have known how inappropriate their behavior was. "I don't do that kind of work. Here are all my shapes." Similarly, Sophie never forgot the woman who asked sweetly if she wouldn't mind cutting a piece two feet square from a larger woven panel. "We are not," she told her, "a pastry shop."[26] The art works from Harrania were an extension of the lives of the artists who produced them. They "belonged" to them as the products of a work process that enhanced the self. Their lives were mirrored in them, sometimes in the overt themes and always in the creative process itself. The large tapestry by Karima Aly called "War by Horses" recorded a painful year in her life. When her husband married a second time, her unhappiness and anger were woven into the panel in bleak representations of cactus and the desert, of men killing and dying. Denied effective recourse by the norms of village life, Karima expressed her protest on the loom. When her husband returned to her house and Karima adjusted to his second marriage, the mood of the tapestry lightened. A pool of water was added and a relaxed man on a horse appeared. Throughout her crisis, Karima had continued to weave.

Often the self-expression basic to creativity at Harrania reached beyond the aesthetic realm. For women especially, the work made it more possible to say no to restrictive or repressive social arrangements. Simply to earn one's own way directly through the weaving had a liberating effect. Karima, though unable to prevent a second marriage of which she disapproved, at least could not be abandoned by it in an economic sense. Her house was her own, one of the seven built on the school land for the weavers. Attachment to village life remained for all the weavers a powerful and in many ways a satisfying one. Yet, at the same time, the school was an alternative community, and at times a refuge, that made creative work and greater social freedom possible.

From the beginning Sophie was most aggressive in speaking and acting for such a role. Ramses and Sophie were, after all, both middle class and Christians. Ramses always understood that Sophie's natural rapport with children was indispensable to reaching across to the peasant children of a Muslim village to establish "good friendly relations with this world of little people."[27] As the years passed, Ramses recognized that the art school was bringing about great changes in the life of Harrania; Sophie took the most active part in them.

In theory, Sophie was eager that the social impact of the school be felt slowly and without friction. With the children she concentrated first on sanitation, personal hygiene, and interpersonal relations. Always there were tact and respect: "You look so beautiful when your hair is clean."[28] The marriages of the young girls presented a first severe test. Village custom forbade a married woman to work outside her husband's or mother-in-law's home. The first young women to marry were forced to abandon their weaving. "The next few girls," Sophie explains, learned from that experience, for they "agreed to marry poor fellaheen, making it a condition of marriage that they should go on with their weaving."[29]

Garia Mahmud's experience became a model for Sophie of the way the school could force a progressive redefinition of a woman's role: Garia, one of the strongest personalities in the group, came from a very poor family and became passionately interested in her tapestrymaking. At an age when nearly all the other girls were already married, she would not accept any of the suitors who presented themselves. Apart from her enthusiasm for weaving, she had very determined ideas about possible husbands—not about their financial position, but about their personal qualities. She was not in the least worried about remaining unmarried until someone who suited her turned up. For two years, she refused to marry a prosperous young man whose family demanded that she give up her work. In the end she had her way.[30]

Interaction with the village was not always smooth. Sophie was frank about how the birth of a child to a widowed weaver severely undermined the school's reputation. Painfully, she was forced to send away the child's father, himself a gifted weaver, in order to calm the storm raised by the village notables.

Yoanna, greatly impressed by her mother's largeness of spirit, also came to understand why Ramses worried about the dangers it might confront. When one of the women came repeatedly to the school marked by beatings from her husband, Yoanna agreed with her mother that something had to be done. After going to the police to get help, the woman was afraid to return home and took refuge with Yoanna in her house in Aguza suburb. Yoanna was alone and frightened when four angry men from the village knocked at her door, and she was powerless when they took the woman back with them. The gulf separating village life from her own, Yoanna now feels, was larger than Sophie's embrace was prepared to acknowledge. The school in some situations was no match for the village. Still, Sophie's obstinate and generous courage had opened doors and created new possibilities.

Though not completely achieved, though certainly unable to counter all the forces that beat against it, Sophie's better world did exist in the speech and actions of members of the community. Though not fully realized, it could be partially experienced and fully imagined. To reconstruct the environment at the Wissa Wassef School is to know better the creative artists of Harrania, "to find," as Wittgenstein put it, "one's feet with them."[31] It is also to understand the miracle of the "flowers of the desert" as the product of theoretical intelligence and social courage applied to the problem of determining under what conditions a child's innate creativity will erupt and grow strong enough to defend itself for a lifetime. Wissa Wassef succeeded when the artists recognized as their own the powerful human need to create.

Wissa Wassef is important not as a microcosm of Egypt, but as an exceptional refusal of prevailing social realities. Nor can it be taken as a model for the transformation of Egyptian society. The daunting general conditions that drove Ramses and Sophie to a small village at the margins of their society have kept their school there. Still, from that small place they have made a "startling" statement about the transformative power of the human creative impulse.[32] All Egyptians could discern in the artists' way of life at Wissa Wassef what Rilke called "the *Weltan-schauung* of the ultimate goal." In their constant engagement with the constraining forces of traditional village life the peasant weavers recall Rilke's explanation that art is "always in response to a present time," but that "the times are resistance." In the lives lived and the tapestries woven at Wissa Wassef could be glimpsed a successful resistance that showed "the sensuous possibility of new worlds and times."[33]

6

Thinking in the National Interest:
The Ahram Center for Political
and Strategic Studies

The third way in which the social scientist may attempt to realize the value of reason and its role in human affairs is also well known, and sometimes even practiced. It is to remain independent, to do one's own work, to select one's own problems, but to direct this work *at* kings as well as *to* "publics." Such a conception prompts us to imagine social science as a sort of public intelligence apparatus, concerned with public issues and private troubles and with the structural trends of our time underlying them both—and to imagine individual social scientists as rational members of a self-controlled association, which we call the social sciences.

—*C. Wright Mills*

The *al-Ahram* building rises twelve stories of glass and steel from one of Cairo's poorest neighborhoods; it still dominates the area, despite the elevated extension of the October Bridge that directs traffic rudely in front of it. Editor-in-chief Muhammad Hassanein Haikal, Nasser's powerful spokesman, frequently drew attention to the symbolic importance of the site he chose for the most impressive journalistic complex in the Arab world. In Haikal's vision, the *al-Ahram* complex would be one of the clusters of "islands of excellence," along with the public sector, the Suez Canal Authority, and the High Dam, that would serve as signposts of Egypt's future; the setting would remind journalists of the responsibilities that went with their privileged positions.[1]

Haikal's complex houses journalists who are also critical intellectuals. In the regime's earliest years, Nasserist military authoritarianism alienated intellectuals.[2] Haikal believed that Nasser held intellectuals in contempt; the Nasserist state, he wrote later, "broke with the intellectuals and underestimated their role on the assumption they could contribute only words and more words."[3] In Haikal's view, no society, least of all a poor one with large aspirations, could afford to dispense with the creativity of its most cultured citizens. Haikal believed that the intellectuals felt and expressed the dreams of the nation: "An intellectual, or cultured person, is someone whose sufferings comprise the sufferings of others. A person whose interests go beyond those of his personal interests. Thus, an intellectual feels the feelings of others, expresses them and crystallizes their ambitions and hopes, and alerts them to their historical rights even though they may not yet be as dear to them as they are to him."[4] In the *al-Ahram* building Haikal hoped to create an environment that could heal that break and win the talents of the intellectuals to the revolutionary regime.

Haikal sought to represent the diversity of Egyptian cultural life within the *al-Ahram* complex, approaching his goal on both an individual and institutional level. Therefore, in addition to the professional staff and production plant of the largest Egyptian mass daily, the *al-Ahram* building provided offices for some of the most admired intellectuals in Egypt, ranging from the popular novelist Ihsan Abdul Kudus, to the Marxist journalist Lutfy al-Kholy, to the playwright and social critic Tewfik al-Hakim. Haikal also opened the *al-Ahram* complex to two institutional clusters of intellectuals. He backed the expansion of the *Economic Ahram* (*al-Ahram al-Iqtisadi*), a specialized journal that is the subject of the next chapter; and in 1968 he founded the Center for Political and Strategic Studies (CPSS), the focus of this chapter. Both the *Economic Ahram* and the Center trained and supported members of a new generation of intellectuals who aimed to use their specialized social science knowledge to contribute to the common life of Egyptians.

"What is it I want from this collection of thinkers and intellectuals in *al-Ahram*?" Haikal once asked rhetorically. "They aren't just golden ornaments for *al-Ahram*'s chest. They have a function and a role that is indispensable for Egypt. All their views and attempts, both the right and the wrong, all their ideas penetrate into all sides and corners of our national life, enriching this life endlessly." According to Haikal, through the dialogue or conversation of intellectuals a society comes into contact with all currents and tendencies: "The worst thing that could face a society and a regime was to find itself in a given situation with no choice, with only one way to act, with no alternatives as if governed by the rule of fate." The trauma of the 1967 defeat by Israel stimulated Haikal's project. Intellectuals, with their breadth of vision, "enlarge the circle of available alternatives in any situation."[5] Roughly a decade later, when Egyptians faced the prospects of the Sadat peace with Israel, the *al-Ahram* intellectuals strived in just this way to preserve a reasoned alternative to official definitions of the national interest.

                    *   *   *

"More than five million people welcomed me home" was Sadat's preferred description of his return to Egypt from his momentous visit to Jerusalem in November 1977. The president left for Israel from the military airport at Bani Suweir with the security predictably high. He returned to Cairo International Airport with an escort of Mirage jet fighters gleaming in the sun. After a welcoming band played both the Egyptian and Palestinian national anthems, the "Hero President" disregarded security precautions to make his way through the cheering multitudes assembled all along the flag-draped route from the airport to his house in a Cairo suburb. Not even the heavy-handed government planning that transported truckloads of peasants and workers into the city could dampen the spontaneous joy of the Cairenes who poured into the streets to celebrate. The spectacle of Sadat riding "upright and radiant, in an open limousine through the human colonnade" captivated Western journalists as well. The crowds, already celebrating a Muslim holiday, shouted their willingness to sacrifice blood and spirit for their president, who, so one banner proclaimed, "has carried the truth . . . into the heart of Israel."

Huge headlines in *al-Ahram* dubbed Sadat the "peace-warrior," and a commentator added that the Egyptian president's visit had been "100 percent successful—thirty years of war [were] eliminated in thirty hours." From the dais of the Israeli Knesset, Sadat explained the reasoning that made his trip a triumph for peace. The October 1973 War, he argued, had destroyed one barrier to peace between Israel and the Arabs, namely "Israel's alleged invincibility, the assumed ability, that is, of its long military arm to reach and strike anywhere." Yet, Sadat continued, another obstacle to peace remained, "a psychological barrier between us, a barrier of suspicion that constitutes 70 percent of the problem." Addressing this obstacle, Sadat stated: "Yet today I tell you, and I declare it to the whole world, that we accept to live with you in permanent peace based on justice."[7] In Sadat's view, that declaration, uttered so magnanimously after so many wars, had shattered the psychological barriers that prevented Arabs and Israelis from making peace.

The national press echoed this theme and used it to enhance the jubilant mood of the people. Popular journalism emphasized the sheer drama of the event and stimulated pride in the global attention that Sadat's daring coup won for Egypt. The bureaucracy, the army, the media, and the state institutions all lined up to praise the miraculous crumbling of old walls of hostility. True, none of the authentic political forces, legal and clandestine, supported the initiative, and prominent figures in Sadat's own entourage, such as Foreign Minister Ismail Fahmy, protested the move. Yet, in the face of mass enthusiasms, criticisms from the likes of Khaled Muhieddin, head of the left opposition party, sounded like resentful carping. Similarly, the harsh attacks by Arab leaders only augmented Sadat's status; their condemnations strengthened antiwar sentiment in Egypt with a strong dose of purely Egyptian nationalism that took on an anti-Arab coloration. *Al-Ahram* replied to Sadat's Arab critics that without Egypt there was no Arab world; *October* magazine labeled figures such as as Mu'ammar Kaddafy of Libya and Houari Boumedienne of Algeria "mice and monkeys, dwarfed by Sadat's presence."[8] Only a few months earlier, nationwide disturbances over price increases had rocked Sadat's regime; now he was the "master of decision" whose foreign policy triumph saved Egypt from the horrors of war. The mass press gave few clues that Egyptians had any questions about the nature of the pressures that drove Sadat to Jerusalem or any misgivings about the results that would flow from his action.

Neither the title nor the lead paragraph distinguished the first article in the three-part assessment from the torrent of celebratory coverage that flooded the dailies in the weeks following Sadat's trip to Jerusalem.[9] Called "The Psychological Dimensions of the Arab-Israeli Conflict" and published in *al-Ahram* under the emblem of the Center for Political and Strategic Studies, the article opened with a straightforward statement of the fundamental assumption behind the Jerusalem initiative: "Sadat's initiative was based on the important role played by psychological factors accompanying the Arab-Israeli conflict, which, if solved through direct negotiations, would take the peace process several steps forward." According to the article, the president had claimed first that 70 percent, and later that 90 percent, of the Arab-Israeli conflict was psychological, an idea that the Egyptian and Western media lost no time in publicizing. The article then reviewed the important Western literature supporting Sadat's emphasis on this psychological interpretation, including the work of such American scholars as Fouad Ajami, and concluded that indeed the search for peace in the area could not ignore "the psychological conflict between us and Israel."

The critical turn came only at this point, with the scholarly and analytical tone firmly established: "Though important, the psychological factor is generally a result of the conflict and not a cause of it." This general rule applied with particular force in the Middle East because the conflict centered on the attempt to achieve a specific material goal, namely control over historic Palestine. The misconceptions and sensitivities surrounding the Arab-Israeli conflict "emerged on the Arab side because of the Israeli occupation of Palestine and the continued threat of aggression"; the Arab reaction to these realities was "a form of awareness that we cannot properly describe as faulty or misinterpreted." The psychological factor could not be assuaged without an examination of the economic, military, political, and social dimensions of the conflict that played the primary role in its crystallization. The article concluded with the open-ended proposition that "the real challenge is whether the parties in conflict will be able to achieve harmony of their interests and security for their borders after thirty years of conflict and contradiction."

The second article in the Center treatment, called "The Peace Dialogue on the Knesset Platform," provided a stark assessment of the results achieved in Jerusalem. In his speech to the Knesset Sadat outlined a five-point position that provided for ending Israeli occupation of the territories taken in 1967: recognizing the basic rights of the Palestinian people, including the right to establish their own state; affirming the right of the countries of the region to live in peace with secure borders; committing each country to observance of United Nations principles in the conduct of regional relations; ending the state of war in the area; and convening a comprehensive peace conference, attended by all parties concerned and resulting in a treaty signed in Geneva.

Without editorial comment, the second article reported that Prime Minister Begin and President Peres had not responded positively to Sadat's program: "when Sadat stressed that Arab land was sacred, Begin and Peres said that everything was negotiable," and Begin ignored the Palestinian problem; "his words on that issue could be counted on the fingers of one hand." Instead of responding to Sadat's proposals in a clear and specific manner, Begin and Peres restated the traditional Israelis approach to peace, emphasizing the importance of direct and separate negotiations between each party and giving no new indication of any changes in the aims they hoped to achieve. Although Begin called for forgetting the past, his speech emphasized precisely those dimensions of the past that "aroused hatred and deepened conflict." The article noted that "Begin was keen on referring to the old guilt complex and recalled the German persecution of the Jews and tried to legitimize the Israeli military force that established Israel." Finally, the article emphasized that "while President Sadat mentioned living in peace, Begin . . . interpreted these relations as establishing diplomatic and economic ties."

The article concluded that Sadat's trip raised critical questions that could not yet be answered: "Will Begin actually give up his old ideas that peace does not require relinquishing the territories occupied after 1967, thereby requiring the Arabs to make major concessions with respect to borders? Will Peres give up his idea of prolonging the conflict by offering to give only a part of the occupied land for peace? All these questions will be decided in the near future."

The third Center article, titled "The Political Parties in Israel Discuss the Palestinian Question," assessed the likelihood of a positive Israeli response to these questions with a close review of Israeli domestic politics. Opening with Sadat's statement that "the Palestinian problem is the crux of the entire problem," the Center study reported that "it is worth noting that Begin did not refer to the issue in his speech at all, while Peres spoke only of a 'Palestinian existence that doesn't jeopardize the security of Israel and Jordan.' " The article then reviewed the views of the Israeli Likud and Labor party leaders on the Palestinian problem, noting their coalescence into three trends that agreed in denying Palestinians the right to form an autonomous state, differing only in the degree of limited recognition they were willing to accord them.

Only three small political groups, the Israeli communist party and two left-wing splinter forces, challenged this reigning political consensus with a call for full recognition of Palestinian national rights; all of these groups had "limited weight in Israeli society." Thus, a real change within Israel on the Palestinian question would require not just a shift from one ruling group to another, but a fundamental change in the entire political elite—a change that, in Sadat's words, transcended "all forms of fanaticism, self-deception, and worn-out superiority theories." The article ended with the question: "Will the recent developments open the door for such changes?"

Although it appeared in the government-controlled *al-Ahram* daily, the three-part Center study of the Jerusalem initiative departed from standard accounts in that it neither celebrated Sadat's action nor portrayed it as decisive in ways that advanced Egyptian national objectives. Juxtaposed with the flattering outpourings of a mobilized press, the deliberately cool and rigorously analytical tone carried a contrary message. According to the Center, Sadat's visit to Jerusalem was a gamble that raised dangerous questions rather than a victory that provided safe answers. This alternative assessment rested on the explicit judgment that the Egyptian political leadership overemphasized the psychological aspects of the Arab-Israeli conflict while downplaying the conflict of interests over Palestine that undergirded it. By the Center reading, the trip to Jerusalem signaled a change on the Egyptian side alone; the Israelis had given no indication of either modifying their view of the nature of the conflict or exploring new ways to settle it. The Center interpretation of these realities indicated that Sadat had taken his initiative in the absence of any decisive regional shift in the power relationship in favor of Egypt; the established positions of the dominant political forces in Israel ruled out optimism about any significant shift in Israel's hard-line position on the Palestinian question.

The assessment of Sadat's opening to Israel reflected in both form and content the distinctive identity and purpose of the Center for Political and Strategic Studies under whose collective name it appeared. The Center originated in the judgment that ignorance of Israel explained at least part of Egypt's terrible defeat in June 1967. In the wake of the "disaster," Egyptians across the political spectrum agreed that they could not afford to view Israel through a haze of ideology and wishful thinking. The tendency to ignore Israel or, even worse, to rely on stereotypes of the Jews had left Egyptians unprepared for their historic role in the confrontation with Zionist power. Later, a popular journalist pointed out that an encyclopedia published in Egypt in 1965 contained no entry for or mention of either Israel or the Zionist movement. Hostile stereotypes filled this intellectual void:

> Only now we can be frank to ourselves and admit that the media presented every Jew as a Shalom, a mean, twangy, and lazy fellow who is ready to sell his father and mother for the lowest prices and to give the buyer his wife and children as a bonus . . . This is the Jew "Shalom" whom we fought. Cartoons represented Shalom to us as a man with a hawk nose and a bent back, most often old. But certainly [we have learned that] Jews have other qualities of ability and accurate knowledge of our conditions . . . Jews are people like any other people; it is not their color or their noses but their Zionist threat that must matter to us and that we must be ready for, and neither neglect nor ignore.

Reliance on negative images of the enemy and refusal to acknowledge his strengths produced only "a paralysis of thinking; hatred becomes a kind of passiveness that hides truth from us. To fight the enemy we have to know him."[10]

Haikal looked to experts at the Center, rather than to journalists and ideologues, to provide the reliable knowledge of Israel the national interest demanded.[11] He believed that the intellectual resources of a Center for Zionist and Palestinian Studies (as Nasser called the project in his founding directive of 1968) would strengthen his role as policy adviser and mouthpiece of the president.[12] In fulfilling this role, the Center operated officially as the research unit of the government-controlled *al-Ahram* foundation. Haikal placed it under the overall direction of Butrous Ghali, with the general charge of studying issues of world politics that related to the Middle East and contemporary Egyptian and Arab society; a distinguished academic, Ghali became acting foreign minister and the minister of state for foreign affairs in 1977. Ghali chaired the two governing bodies of the Center, the Council of Advisers and the Council of Experts. High-level government and non-government specialists constituted the first body; they set the Center's general research and publications program, nominated candidates for the staff, and approved the budget. The second group, consisting of senior researchers, met weekly to develop and implement the research programs planned by the Council of Advisers. In recent years Ghali has delegated these governing responsibilities to the current Center director, Sayyid Yassine.

From 1968 until roughly 1974 the Center operated as an official brain trust and enjoyed considerable influence on policy. Hatem Sadek, Nasser's son-in-law and the Center's first director, drew young researchers primarily from the sons and daughters of upper-class influentials. Because Haikal enjoyed the intellectual atmosphere at the Center as a place to brainstorm on the big public policy issues, he made a good deal of classified material available; he also used his considerable influence to protect the Center from heavy-handed government interference. In addition to writing a page or more of international commentary in *al-Ahram,* researchers provided the government with policy recommendations through Haikal. The quality of academic output, however, did not match the policy importance of the Center in this initial period. Center intellectuals did edit several useful documentary collections, such as the proceedings of the 1966-1967 Israeli Knesset and of the twenty-seventh Zionist Congress. However, experienced researchers brought in from the outside produced the few serious studies published in the late sixties and early seventies. In particular, Sayyid Yassine's study *The Arab Personality* set new standards of quality that attracted Egyptian academics such as Aly Eddine Hillal and Sa'ad Ibrahim. These men assumed the leadership of the Center and remade Haikal's showplace in their own image.

The opportunity for redefinition came when Sadat forced Haikal out of his position as editor-in-chief of *al-Ahram* shortly after the October 1973 War. Hatem Sadek immediately resigned as director, and for several years the Center floundered under interim directors who took only marginal interest in its work. The turning point came with Sayyid Yassine's appointment as head of the Center. The voluntary departure of many of the old staff facilitated Yassine's reform efforts. By this time, the Sadat liberalization of the economy had taken hold and created a host of new opportunities for the upper-class researchers who had dominated the Center staff. Their language skills and social connections made them attractive candidates for managerial positions in the new foreign companies and banks.

Yassine came to the Center with seventeen years' experience at the National Institute for Criminological Research and a solid reputation for reliability in official circles. Raising the banner of social science competence and objectivity, Yassine sought to secure the same exemptions from autocratic and bureaucratic interference that the Haikal link had provided; he did so with a different version of the national interest rationale. Writing in *al-Ahram* on August 20, 1982, Yassine argued that "the scientific and national importance of studying Israeli society is now agreed upon in the Arab world"; he noted, however, that "the serious scientific beginning of exploring the main features of this aggressive society, and the developments influencing its trends saw the light in Egypt only with the establishment of the Center for Political and Strategic Studies in *al-Ahram* in 1968." In justifying the Center's special role, Yassine called for a "critical perspective that does not abandon the national obligation, on the one hand, or considerations of scientific objectivity on the other." The passing of Haikal from the active political scene meant that the Center lost its closest link to power and could no longer address itself directly to top-level policy-makers. Yassine responded by identifying the general educated public as the primary audience for the Center's work.

Over the next decade Yassine stabilized the Center as an institution with an important role in Egyptian public life. Under his direction, Haikal's general idea of the importance of intellectuals acquired a distinctive form. Yassine's conception deliberately moved beyond Haikal's representational model, which identified the importance of intellectuals with the anticipation and representation of ideological and political trends. Yassine emphasized instead the social role of critical intelligence in the public life of any society. He justified that role by appealing to the national interest in the cultivation and deployment of new social science intellectual skills that could address the most significant public policy issues on a scientific basis. Yassine believed that the appearance of a new generation of men and women with such training and the consolidation of the social space within which they could use it resulted from the level of socioeconomic development that Egypt had attained; in this sense, he viewed the Center as an embedded social project, responsive to the needs of the society that gave rise to it.

Yassine attached great importance to the inauguration of the Center in the period of acute national self-awareness prompted by the defeat of June 1967. The search for an explanation of the disaster provided the Center with its initial agenda. "We all lived through the post-1967 period," he explained later, "when all Arab thinkers with different political attitudes tried to explain the causes of the defeat." Yassine considered four competing views: an explanation blaming the defeat mainly on the abandonment of religion, a technological theory emphasizing "the civilizational gap between us and Israel," a reactionary one identifying socialism as the cause, and a "national character" explanation attributing defeat to certain presumed flaws in the Egyptian and Arab character. Yassine regarded the last theory as the most misleading and devoted the major part of his critical review to it, in part because Haikal had offered an authoritative treatment of Egypt's military unpreparedness in precisely these terms.[13] Additionally, the adoption of the national character explanation presented by Haikal as the "official" Egyptian explanation reinforced Western use of the argument as a potentially damaging weapon against Egypt and the Arab world. Yassine's critique helped define the Center's intellectual style and set the trajectory of its intellectual project in its formative decade.

In an article titled "The Enemy Knew More than He Should Have Known" in *al-Ahram* on June 28, 1968, Haikal wrote:

> Israeli calculations relied on some behavioral flaws resulting from lack of discipline, namely delay in reporting the truth, if it is negative, to higher levels of authority. This failing gave the enemy ten minutes, which was exactly what he needed for the surprise attack on eleven air bases, on which he concentrated his first blow; there were raids on some advanced airports in Sinai, but the behavioral flaws played their role in the slowness of reporting, and invaluable, priceless minutes were lost. The fact of Israeli reliance on such behavioral flaws was not a deduction but was mentioned directly by the Israeli air force leader . . . when he explained the timing of his plan.

According to Yassine, Haikal's analysis provided confirmation for both Western and Arab researchers that the mistakes made in 1967 resulted from some set of inherited negative characteristics.[14]

Yassine objected strongly to this line of reasoning, emphasizing that many of the traits attributed by Haikal to all Egyptians characterized particular groups and classes, notably the lower middle class, which predominated in the Nasserist ruling groups. More pointedly, he criticized the failure in such studies to distinguish between the situational failings of a particular political elite in "mobilizing the people for the battle or the sudden collapse on the battlefield resulting from the confusion of the military leadership and the innate characteristic of the national character."[15] The Egyptian character, Yassine argued, was not rigid in form; rather, national character at any particular historical moment was a reflection of the prevailing pattern of society, including not only economic relations but also an inherited cultural dimension. The many negative or passive qualities of the Egyptian character reflected the backwardness of production patterns, traces left by the experience of imperialism, and the effects of economic and political exploitation by the elite. Yet there were also positive aspects derived from the "nationalists struggles of generations of Egyptians who fought honorably and selflessly against foreign occupation, refusing, despite the difficulties of their conditions, to give up one small part of Egypt's land, and of class struggles by peasants, workers, and intellectuals who fought against all sorts of exploiters to achieve social justice for the masses."[16]

According to Yassine, national character studies had a particularly pernicious effect in the Arab case because scholars using this approach regularly contrasted the negative, traditional characterizations of Arabs with the positive, modern attributes of Israelis. Often these paired characterizations were used to characterize the battle with Israel as a "civilizational struggle." Yassine denounced such artificial contrasts as "a warmed-over variety of the old racism" that diverted Arabs from the true nature of their conflict with Israel. He cautioned Egyptians against adopting these Western-inspired categories that aimed subtly to deplete the Arab national will by their invidious comparisons of supposedly intrinsic characteristics. Reviewing the relevant literature, Yassine concluded that Western scholars regularly attributed any adverse characteristic of a particular group to Arabs in general and used studies with an extremely limited compass, often of a single village, and a weak and anecdotal methodology to make the broadest generalizations. Yassine stressed that these distorted representations covered up a good deal of contemporary Arab history. While Western and particularly American media and experts emphasized the poverty of the Arab masses, for example, they rarely mentioned the "imperialist (colonial) invasion of the Arab world and the West's continuous conspiracies to destroy it, hinder its progress, and prevent its national, political, and social integration—all for the purpose of plundering its wealth; all of these are factors in the low living standard that Arabs suffer. Of course, the American press doesn't deal with such points.[17]

Yassine noted that negative representations of Arabs figured directly in political struggles against them, often in subtle ways. For example, studies that allegedly demonstrated the civilizational "immaturity" or "irrationality" of Arabs played into psychological theories about international conflicts in ways that hurt the Arab cause. Yassine noted that Western theorists of international relations drew a basic distinction between what they called a "conflict of interests" and "conflicts of understanding." They regarded the first type as resulting from such material factors as scarcity of resources or disputes over territory; the second category derived from misreadings of intentions or an imperfect grasp of the essential nature of the adversary. According to these views, whereas a conflict of interest could be resolved only by mutual and genuine concessions, a conflict of understanding could be resolved by psychological adjustments that left the material conditions unchanged. The theorists of "conflicts of understanding" argued for the "formulation of a joint culture between the conflicting parties and even the creation of organizations in each country that aimed for the reduction of differences."[18]

Yassine warned against this model of conflict resolution, because it implied that the Arab-Israeli conflict could be resolved without dealing with the material question of the Israeli occupation of the West Bank and Gaza.

In making the Center a forum from which Egyptians could address such theories, Yassine relied heavily on Aly Eddine Hillal and Sa'ad Ibrahim, academics who had benefited from the social mobility afforded by the Nasser revolution. Yassine, Hillal, and Ibrahim used their analytical skills, administrative experience, and ties to the Egyptian establishment in ways that afforded the Center protection but did not stifle its new academic style of independent and critical public commentary. Hillal, a professor of political science at Cairo University, responded to students' demands, after the 1967 defeat, that serious courses be offered in the main universities on Israeli foreign and domestic politics. Not only did he initiate courses with a comparative and international perspective on contemporary Israeli politics; he also recruited his most talented students as Center researchers. Ibrahim interpreted the latest social science theories and methods for the young researchers, bringing intellectual excitement to Center discussions and training programs. The practical journalistic and political experience of the well-known journalists Samy Mansur, Khiry Aziz, and Muhammad Salmawy supplemented the solid academic core provided by Yassine, Hillal, and Ibrahim.

It was the third generation of researchers, however, who gave the Center its vitality. For the second-generation academics and journalists, the Center provided refuge from political harassment or a quiet place to read, reflect, and comment, often obliquely, on the political issues of the day. For the young researchers, though, the Center was an extension of their political activism as students, either in the Nasser youth groups or the student movement that erupted in 1968 and again in the early seventies.[19] As pure products of the Nasser era, they had grown up with a national movement on the rise; they felt the despair and frustration of 1967 intensely and personally. By the mid-seventies, when the new Sadat orientation became clear, they found themselves trying to hold fast to issues and views that had fallen into disfavor. The Center provided an environment in which they could reexamine those values to specify what went wrong in the struggle to realize them; they sought to determine how the best of the fifties and sixties might be preserved in the seventies and eighties.

The Center, redefined by its second generation and invigorated by its third, provided an independent forum for critical reflection in the national interest, free from harassment. In their political orientation, Center scholars ranged generally from the center to the left, although every major ideological current found its way into discussions. Membership in the Center, however, hinged on the possession of a political consciousness rather than on adherence to any specific ideology. Center researchers knew something of politics and thirsted to know more; they sought involvement in the public affairs of Egypt and the Arab world.

This political consciousness combined with a sustained commitment to intellectual work, offsetting the researchers' occasional fears that they would lose their social roots in *al-Ahram*'s privileged environment were the opportunity to work with intellectuals of international reputation, including some of the brightest and most socially conscious graduates of Egypt's universities, a constant stream of lectures and forums with visiting intellectuals and political figures, and recognition and tangible support for talent and hard work. Yassine guarded the Center from the patronage corruption that had overwhelmed comparable institutions elsewhere in Egypt. Senior experts expected members to be well read and well informed in seminars as well as in informal exchanges; they made frequent publication the norm by discussing and evaluating each other's findings and encouraging trainees to do the same. In such an environment those few admitted only because they were well connected soon left on their own. For the researchers who stayed, these exclusions reinforced their sense of Center as a place worth protecting.

Membership in the Center also opened up worlds beyond Egypt. Visibility as a member of a distinguished research center meant scholarships and grants for academic projects and study abroad, at the same time, all the researchers could build a publication record in the *al-Ahram* page set aside for the Center and in its quarterly journal *International Politics*. An established reputation in turn led to opportunities to publish in periodicals serving the entire Arab world. By the time the most productive researchers were ready for promotion to the Council of Experts, they were usually supporting their families largely by their writings for a larger Arab audience.

Not all the pressures that solidified the group life of the Center were so positive, however. A natural tension existed in the relationship between the research environment of the Center and the mass press environment of *al-Ahram*. Journalists who wrote for a mass audience were skeptical of the "doctors" of the Center who addressed themselves to the educated public in Egypt and the Arab world. A certain prestige was associated with the Center and its high-quality production; this prestige, along with the academic style of the Center intellectuals, set them apart from members of the mass press. Instead of competing with the journalists in the coverage of day-to-day events, the researchers presented themselves as scholars with advanced training in the social sciences who addressed the large issues of common life in a less immediate way. In doing so, they created a new path, self-consciously different from those of the journalists and of the old-style grand intellectuals who also shared their space at *al-Ahram*. While personally admiring such distinguished figures as Tewfik al-Hakim or Ihsan Abdul Kudus, the young researchers did not take them as models; in fact, they openly deplored the emotional, ideological, and undocumented way in which such figures often presented their views to the public. Origins in a different social world partly explained the break with the established tradition of intellectual discourse. Self-consciously, the Center intellectuals avoided the title of government journalist or the mantle of official mandarins, preferring to see themselves as a patriotic brain trust, endowed with modern critical intellectual skills and committed to the larger national interest.

*   *   *

Yassine had few illusions about the difficulties of realizing his ideal of a genuinely independent role for critical intelligence in Egyptian society. In his view, Egyptian and Arab society in general suffered from a preponderance of intellectuals acting as apologists and spectators, and a virtual lack of intellectuals acting as critics: "Arab intellectuals have struggled bravely to play the role of critic. Yet, obstacles have stood in the way of the effectiveness of this role. The most important obstacle is the relationship between the intellectual and the political authority in Arab society; this is the core of the problem faced by modern Arab society."[20] In Yassine's view, political authorities throughout the Arab world regularly prevented intellectuals from exercising their essential critical faculties, fearing that an intellectual critique would develop into political opposition.

In a series of publications, the Center developed a careful assessment of Nasserism that balanced limitations on critical thinking and democratic expression in general against an appreciation for the social advances achieved in the fifties and sixties.[21] In this respect, Center writings on Nasserism implicitly dissented from the official de-Nasserization campaign of the seventies by portraying the Nasserist experience as a revolution from above that achieved concrete social and economic gains such as free education, medical care, land reform, and the creation of a public sector. Nasserism, in the Center view, gave important new impetus to a process of social mobility already under way in 1952; it also consolidated the Arab character of Egypt's nationalist revolution.[22] Nevertheless, Yassine pointed out that intellectuals in the Nasser era for the most part played the role of apologist or silent spectator to events over which they had no control.

These inherited restrictions on political freedoms, however, did not constitute the only barriers to a full critical role for intellectuals in the seventies. Another was the rise of technocrats who willingly served power without insisting on any critical role and without a common language of intellectual discourse. Finally, Yassine believed that Arab intellectuals suffered from a lack of theoretical consensus that severely hindered communication among them and hampered creation of a common audience for their work.

According to Yassine, Arab thought ranged along a continuum "of conflicting views, marked by Islamic thought on one end and Marxism on the other." Yassine recognized that these ideological and political divisions among the intellectuals constituted a potential advantage to sharpen critical skills and make available a wide range of alternative practices and theories. However, he noted the absence in Egypt of institutionalized forums within which theoretical differences could be argued; as a result, Yassine judged that these deep ideological divisions became destructive:

> The situation is critical not because of the existence of political divisions between Arab intellectuals resulting from differences in the theories and ideologies they adopt, but because of the absence of any real debate among them. Without unity within particular countries and on the national Arab level as well, Arab intellectuals cannot create an audience to listen to them. Consequently, they will not be able to play an effective role in society. By "unity of intellectuals" is meant their organization within institutions based primarily on their creative initiatives for continuous dialogue between all intellectual trends within an environment that permits reaching consensus through disagreement.[23]

Arab intellectuals, Yassine wrote, should work to create institutional forums of this kind.

In his own evaluation of the Islamic current, Marxism, and Nasserism, the major ideological and political trends in Egypt, Yassine attempted to show that dialogue and possibly even synthesis were possible and beneficial to the nation. Yassine argued that both the Islamic and the Marxist prerevolutionary intellectual trends provided the resources for genuinely critical alternatives; however, each did so with a distinctive focus and shortcoming. Drawing on the ideological debates of the seventies, he noted that "if we may use the terms 'the authentic' and 'the modern,' which have become popular in Arabic literature in the last years, we would say that the aim of the Muslim Brotherhood to create an Islamic state constituted a search for authenticity without sufficient attention to modernity. In contrast, the Marxist aim of establishing a socialist state signified a search for the modern without sufficient attention to the authentic.[24]

Despite his critical stance on the Islamic trend, Yassine credited the Muslim Brotherhood with developing "detailed opinions diagnosing the ills of Egyptian society and the means to reform them." He noted that Brotherhood intellectuals called for nationalization, industrialization, and land reform. Yassine also pointed to the movement's success in establishing Islamic economic, educational, and medical institutions as concrete evidence of the validity of their Islamic teachings. However, the Islamic trend as represented by the Brotherhood "neglected to analyze the complicated relationships between the social classes in Egypt," chiefly because it lacked a modern analytical method. Instead, the Brothers relied on a return to the "pure fonts of Islamic law that left them in many cases standing impotent before numerous problems requiring contemporary understanding, analysis, and diagnosis." In direct contrast, the Marxist thinkers presented "a scientific, comprehensive methodology for thought, but" did not take sufficient account of the Islamic heritage.[25]

Having established the Brothers and the Marxists as the dominant poles of prerevolutionary Egyptian thought, Yassine located Nasserism as a progressive trend that crystallized through trial and error; during this process, Nasserism found itself face to face with the Marxist and Brotherhood visions of changing Egyptian society. According to Yassine, Nasserism took a middle position. It borrowed some elements from the Brotherhood's vision, especially the reliance on a spiritual framework for society; at the same time, Nasserist intellectuals also adopted key elements of the Marxist vision, notably reliance on scientific socialism as a means of understanding the laws of conflict and dialectic change in social trends.[26]

Yassine envisaged the Center as a forum in which proponents of all the major intellectual currents could meet and engage in free dialogue. Such a forum would allow for critical reflection on the most important public policy issues facing the nation, while scrupulously maintaining the distinction between serious intellectual criticism and political opposition. In this sense, Yassine operationalized Haikal's founding conception of the Center as a vehicle to "enlarge the circle of available alternatives."[27] Center researchers devised a variety of novel formulas for the presentation of independent views. These strategies included indirect commentary, represented by the work of Samy Mansur, and responses to government commissions that relied on scrupulous academic integrity to tell the regime more than it wanted to know, exemplified in the historical study of democratic socialism prepared by Osama al-Ghazzaly.

While responsive to regime needs, the Center strived to maintain sufficient distance to preserve its credibility as an independent voice in civil society. When the regime on rare occasions did make direct demands for support, the Center complied with a subtle intelligence that preserved its quasi-independent status. Under Yassine, the senior researchers regarded the generation of applause for regime decisions as the task of the mass mobilization press, not of a research institute. They also persuaded the regime that a government that appealed for Western support on the basis of its liberalization policies was better served by an independent intellectual forum where visiting scholars and political dignitaries could experience directly the new atmosphere of freedom. The Center could not play this role if its research output took on the character of official hack work.

Senior researcher Samy Mansur drew on his experience as a fixture of Nasserist journalism to establish himself as a master of oblique commentary. In a series of articles on U.S. relations with Third World regimes, Mansur provided a critical assessment of Sadat's American connection with direct, though unstated, application to Egypt. As part of his Western orientation, Sadat regularly denounced the Soviet threat to the independence of Egypt and other Middle Eastern and African states. The regime used the "threat" to justify a range of new departures, including a heavy American involvement in security and military resupply, containment of Libya (officially described as a Soviet proxy), joint U.S.-Egyptian military maneuvers, and periodic hints of an Egyptian military role as part of the American security system in the Middle East and Africa. Indirectly, Mansur criticized all of these official policies in a way that called attention to their unintended and possibly unwanted consequences.

Mansur used an article dealing with the American-Pakistani relationship to throw his critical assessment of Egypt's American connection into sharp relief. The title, "Not by Arms Alone Are Nations Protected," suggested that Mansur was casting a net wide enough to include Egypt. On the issue of American armaments, Mansur noted that "no country in the Third World got armaments like the Shah's Iran"; yet, not only did this military arsenal fail to protect the regime, it was "one of the causes of the revolution." He went on to warn of the danger of taking American rhetoric of a Soviet threat too seriously. The hunger of the masses and not Soviet invasion was the real threat: "Hunger is one of the biggest sources of revolution in the world, and hunger is not resisted or dealt with by arms but only with food."[28]

Mansur's warnings to political elites that relied too heavily on a militarized American connection took a more direct form when he wrote about the manipulation of law and the media in Third World states. Asking why regime changes so often caught the outside experts unawares, he commented that repressive regimes hid negative developments behind a smokescreen of rhetoric about development, prosperity, and democracy while the conditions of the masses worsened and liberties eroded. With these facts hidden from them, international research institutes were unable to anticipate mass reactions to deteriorating conditions and regime repression. In a commentary ostensibly about conditions in South Korea, Mansur wrote: "Even if we assume it is theoretically possible to measure these reactions, the assessments aren't made, because the ruling regimes hide the truth from the world's surveillance apparatus. They do so either by controlling mass media, publishing misleading information on development and prosperity, or frustrating liberties, as happened in Korea when emergency measures and the curfew continued for many years until the president was murdered."[29] Sadat's assassination in 1981 after a far-reaching crackdown on political opposition made that warning appear prophetic.

Mansur's indirection, achieved through an agile and suggestive style, did not lend itself to routinization. Other Center intellectuals developed different strategies to exercise critical intelligence within sharply circumscribed boundaries. A series of books and articles on Sadat's democratic socialist ideology, produced in response to a request from the regime, provided one such model. Sadat apparently hoped that the reformist formula of democratic socialism would allow a break with Nasserist conceptions of scientific socialism without discarding the socialist label altogether. Democratic socialism also appeared to be a brand of socialism that would be acceptable to Egypt's American ally.[30]

Rather that a potboiler elaboration that served immediate regime ends, the Center intellectuals produced a penetrating historical study of social democracy in Europe and the Third World. Detailed case studies addressed such central concerns of the seventies as social justice, multiparty democracy, and development as understood from the perspective of socialist democracy. Osama al-Ghazzaly Harb used the opening provided by the regime's invitation to lay the groundwork for a challenge to the official wisdom, prevailing since the mid-seventies, that the multiparty system suited Egypt better than a Nasserist-style one-party system. In the first volume of the series, *Historical Origins of Democratic Socialism,* Harb compared the reformist and revolutionary trends within the international socialist movement; he concluded that the social democratic reformers accomplished very little of relevance to Egypt.

Without commenting directly on the actual conditions of democracy in Egypt, Harb observed that democratic socialists "had no mission in countries in which it was not possible to hold elections in a genuine way, other than to protest the measures that kept them out of power." Even in countries that had authentic parliamentary systems, democratic socialists hoped merely for a "gradual transformation among the majority of the people toward socialism and a gradual improvement of economic and social conditions." Under this reformist strategy, the capitalist system continued to operate alongside "certain socialist features that might be added to it." Even less was accomplished in the realm of socialist theory:

> If one wonders about the production of democratic socialism's theoreticians of new and significant thinking, the answer is that what they produced was very little . . . no book on democratic socialism during the postwar period has any special importance. . . . Many democratic socialist writers spent more time attacking communism than they did developing their own thoughts; as a result, a large part of the better writings tackled particular projects of economic reform or nationalizations rather than general problems of the theory of socialism and its general policy.[31]

The unstated conclusion was that despite official rhetoric, Egyptians had little to gain from the practice or the theory of democratic socialism.

This negative conclusion bore most directly on the issue of political freedom invoked frequently by the regime as justification for its break with the Nasserist past. In their book *Freedom and the Multiparty System in the Ideology of Democratic Socialism,* Hala Abou Bakr Sa'udy and Wahid Muhammad Abdul Meguid pointed out that the multiparty political system was linked historically to capitalism, which historically demonstrated certain characteristic drawbacks along with its strengths: "Although the capitalist pattern of development succeeded in making use of the factors of production, raising the living standard, and generating new technologies, it led at the same time to inequality and social injustice; the capitalist pattern favored a small minority at the expense of the majority and led to cycles of inflation and depression and to the prevalence of nonparallel and distorted development expressed in growth of some areas at the expense of others."[32]

According to Sa'udy and Abdul Meguid, a Third World context rendered the democratic socialist formula even more problematic. The Western idea of freedom served particular class interests and might well be harmful to a Third World country. Liberal democracy and its brand of political freedom were not the only types of democracy and freedom on earth; indeed, for all the attractiveness of the democratic ideal, the authors concluded that "democracy is not like an arithmetic operation or scientific experiment that can be transferred exactly the way it is [from one setting to another]; democracy is . . . related to a society's conditions and to the historical experience of its groups, mass psychology, and general ambitions." In an interesting way, Sa'udy and Abdul Meguid's scholarly volume penetrated deeper in its critique than the political opposition, which tended to object only to Sadat's imperfect application of the multiparty system, and seldom addressed the more fundamental issue of the suitability of a multiparty system to Egypt's needs in the seventies and eighties. In their view, powerful developmental reasons favored a single party, rather than the multiparty approach of democratic socialism: "The challenge of overcoming backwardness in Third World countries . . . requires a process of fundamental change in the economic and social relations of the traditional society, which is inevitably accompanied by the collapse of some institutions . . . full mobilization of society's potentialities in human and natural resources . . . cannot be provided except under one party that organizes a mass movement and raises mass awareness by exterminating the symbols and values of the old society." Sa'udy and Abdul Meguid argued that Third World countries often also suffered in varying degrees from the danger of national fragmentation brought on by the pressures of "family, tribe, regional, religious or linguistic fanaticism as a result of the colonial presence." Given these conditions, a multiparty system would reinforce these deep cleavages, weakening the nation in the face of its colonial and neocolonial adversaries. Sa'udy and Abdul Meguid acknowledged the possible dangers of one-party rule such as personalization of power, bureaucratization, and corruption. Yet, on balance, they concluded that the one-party form met more fully the economic, social, and political needs of Third World societies.[33]

The Center brought critical intelligence to bear just as effectively in the sphere of foreign policy, responding directly to Haikal's original charge to enlarge "the circle of available alternatives." The Sadat regime blocked meaningful debate of foreign policy; not even in the official rhetoric did the regime suggest that the liberalization of the seventies would extend to its monopoly over the conduct of foreign affairs. Anwar Sadat pronounced the Egypt of the seventies a "state of institutions" marked by "the rule of law," yet he explicitly deprived the important public bodies of any real power over the conduct of foreign policy and used the law to enforce his monopoly. When the regime first established political platforms, for example, it placed foreign policy questions beyond their consideration. Later security measures endorsed by referenda, expressly forbade public opposition to the treaty with Israel.[34] Thus, critics in Egypt found it extremely difficult to mount a sustained frontal challenge to the massive regional and global realignments of the seventies. There was public discussion of the great issues of war and peace, but circumstances gave them a sharply limited scope and fragmented character. The left opposition press, for example, could brave confiscation by questioning the wisdom of some excessively conciliatory gesture to Israel. The Bar Association might risk government disruption by holding seminars to debate the regime's approach to the question of Palestine, or the resignation of a foreign minister might communicate an inarticulate dissent. Overall, however, the government party orchestrated the treatment of foreign policy issues in parliament, and the national press was subjected to harsh prepublication censorship.

Under these circumstances, the Center developed a sustained critique of foreign policy. Its treatment of the American-backed accommodation with Israel exemplified this role. While the mass press simply echoed official slogans, celebrating the new relationship with Israel and the United States, the Center's articles and books presented a probing assessment of the problems raised at each stage of Egypt's new regional and global alignments. Its assessment of the Sadat initiative crystallized all of these concerns and expressed the shared conclusions of the Center researchers. Sober realism about Israeli power, unsentimental calculation of Egyptian, Palestinian, and Arab national interests, appreciation of the costs as well as the benefits of the American connection, an analytical reliance on a calculus of power rather than on appeals to international law or sentiment characterized the Center's assessment of Sadat's trip to Jerusalem and of Egypt's evolving relationship with Israel and America.

Muhammad al-Said Ibrahim's book, *The American Conception of Israel,* exemplified the mainstream Center style that relied on a dispassionate, analytical approach, viewing events "using the scientific method and in the light of national commitment at the same time." Writing in 1979, Ibrahim remained unmoved by the official talk of an Egyptian partnership with America. To make his central point, Ibrahim quoted Zbigniew Brzezinski: "Arabs must understand that American-Israeli relations cannot be parallel to American-Arab relations, because American-Israeli relations are strong ones based on a historical and spiritual heritage that is continually strengthened through the political activity of American Jews, while American-Arab relations involve none of these elements."[35] In international affairs, Ibrahim insisted that interests and not sentiments counted most.

Despite the Sadat regime's tilt toward America, Ibrahim reminded his readers that the United States in the fifties and sixties opposed Egypt as the carrier of a "radical nationalist current that was more dangerous to American interests than anything else." The July 23 Revolution and

Nasser's leadership set the general Arab trend against submission to American hegemony by providing it with the positive goals of nonalignment and the creation of a single Arab state capable of defending such Arab national resources as oil: "These goals totally contradicted American security interests, which aimed at placing the Middle East area under American influence while combatting any Soviet presence in the area; they also contradicted American economic interests, which aimed at securing American hegemony over the area's wealth; it was thus necessary [for America] to fight this Arab trend and bring down its leadership by any means."[36]

In this atmosphere of antagonism between the Arabs and the United States, Israel presented itself as a military arm to protect American interests. For Ibrahim, the 1967 Israeli attack on Egypt, "planned and supported by the United States," consolidated this role. Through this successful military strike against the most powerful Arab state, Israel "gained absolute American confidence and acquired an important status in the popular American mind; all these factors helped crystallize and form the American view of Israel on which the United States' relation with Israel was founded."[37] Ibrahim's historical account of the U.S.-Israeli relationship made the implicit judgment that no Arab state, least of all one with Egypt's history, could hope to play the same role for the United States that Israel did. Ibrahim's reasoning also made clear the degree to which American hostility was a response to the progressive character of the Arab nationalist movement, rather than solely to disagreement over the Palestinian issue. Suggesting that the United States opposed the general line of the Nasserist revolution both at home and abroad, Ibrahim responded to the Sadat regime's view that Nasser's commitment to the Palestinians came at the expense of Egyptian national interests.

Ibrahim based his interpretation of the American-Israeli connection on Israel's regional role in behalf of U.S. interests; however, he also remained alert to the special influence exerted in Israel's behalf by Jewish Americans. Matter-of-factly, Ibrahim commented on their large and direct financial support of the Jewish state and on the political pressure they exerted to secure backing for Israel. Jewish Americans also concentrated on "cultivating a certain American conception of Israel based on mutual interests between the United States and Israel, and not on sympathy or moral aspects, as some have tried to show." According to Ibrahim, the particular characteristics of the American political and social environment provided the Zionist movement with advantageous conditions in which to advance its aims. Rejecting conspiracy theories, he explained the successes of the Zionist lobby by pointing to such factors in American political culture as "the nature of the electoral system, the party system, the role of pressure groups, and the general attitude toward minorities.[38]

In explaining the peace process, Ibrahim stressed that the key precipitating actions came from the Arab side. He pointed out that the Egyptian regime first indicated its interest in a peaceful settlement chiefly from a desire for "financial aid from Western countries and its general intention to move toward an open-door policy that encouraged the flow of foreign capital into Egypt." Thus, the dramatic shifts in the seventies "did not come from any change favorable to Egypt in the political and economic strategy of the United States in the Middle East, in the American system, or in Zionist influence within that system." By implication, this analysis explained Egypt's weak negotiating position vis-à-vis the Americans and especially the Israelis. Ibrahim concluded that "only if the Arabs could threaten some material interest of the United States and relate that action directly to American one-sided support of Israel could they hope to create new incentives for the pragmatic American citizen to call for changing American policy in the Middle East."[39]

Muhammad al-Said Ibrahim's study of the American-Israeli connection, like the Center itself, distinguished itself by a style that was self-consciously *autonomous* and *analytical,* and a substance at once *Arab* and *progressive.* The intellectuals of the Center for Political and Strategic Studies believed that the Egyptian official rethinking of Arab-Israeli relations in the seventies constituted a step backward for the Arabs in several important ways. The earlier Arab view of the conflict with Israel as a conflict of interests rather than of understanding resulted in a reading of Israeli society that was in many ways more accurate than the naive views encouraged by the psychological approach. In an open letter published in *al-Ahram* commenting on a symposium convened for psychiatrists from the United States, Israel, and Egypt at Alexandria University in 1982, Sayyid Yassine asked why one of the Egyptian history professors who participated in the seminar had asserted that "the conflict was a sickness, and sickness needs to be diagnosed, and diagnosis needs concentrated studies of social, economic, political, and other conditions." Such a description of the Arab-Israeli conflict as a sickness was a "total surrender to the Israeli point of view, making sense of the problem as a psychological one. And was the struggle between British colonizers and the Egyptian people a sickness or a battle between colonial powers and a movement of national liberation? There is a vast difference between making sense of the Arab-Israeli conflict as a sickness needing doctors to diagnose it, and understanding it as a battle needing resistance fighters and politicians to solve it and all other methods of politics and resistance." Yassine argued that what was needed was not a psychological but a political dialogue: "As to the participants, the Palestinian resistance must play an active part in the dialogue. The basic topic must be the right of self-determination of the Palestinian people, and their right to establish an independent nation, in the framework of a complete peace based on the withdrawal of Israel from all occupied Arab lands without exception, to ensure the right of each nation to live within its recognized borders in peace."[40]

Quite apart from his concern with the question of Palestine, Yassine objected to the redefinitions of national purpose flowing from the changed conception of Israel that gained ground in the seventies. The new thinking implied that Israel, as a "modern" state locked in conflict with "traditional" Egypt, could be a model for Egypt's own development; under American aegis and in cooperation with Israel, Egyptians could acquire those characteristics that underlay Israel's superiority in the civilizational sense. In Yassine's view, Israel did not present Egyptians with a civilizational model worth following: "To the contrary, by virtue of its racist policy toward the Palestinians in the West Bank and Gaza, it is still lacking in the truly civilized understanding of peaceful relations with peoples." On the military and technological planes, Yassine added that Israel did not have a monopoly over this type of superiority: "In the October War, we were able to put our hands on the basic keys of modern military development. If Israel is technologically advanced in some areas, this advancement is principally borrowed from American and European technology. If we can go to the origins, in terms of transferring technology, what need have we to loiter in the back streets?"[41]

Yassine argued that Arabs should not waste their creative energies following "the alleged Israeli genius or contemplating the artificial Israeli accomplishments." Instead, he urged Egyptians to address their real problems:

> Have we really reached the point where democratic socialism is the new ideology? And, if that is true, what is the relation between this ideology and governmental policies and programs and the realities of everyday social life? Has science been established as a basic value in our society, or is it still

in the same position, a jewel we wear for decoration when we desire? Have we found a solution to the problem that raises its head every now and then on the place of religion in our society? Are we a religious community that should be governed by God's law or a secular society that should be governed by human laws?[42]

Yassine urged Egyptians not to allow the Israeli diversion to deflect them from consideration of these "vital issues" debated by politicians and intellectuals throughout the previous century. Yassine and his fellow researchers struggled in the seventies to make the Center an intellectual forum within which new generations of Egyptian intellectuals could analyze and debate these large questions of national purpose and a platform from which their considered views could reach the informed public.

7

Anticipating a Free Press:
The *Economic Ahram*

In politics, the belief that certain facts are unalterable or certain trends irresistible commonly reflects a lack of desire or lack of interest to change or resist them.

—*E. H. Carr*

"The economic legacy Nasser left me was in even poorer shape than the political," wrote Anwar Sadat in his autobiography. According to official historians in the seventies, Sadat inherited an economy in ruins in 1970: Nasser's socialism had pauperized the nation with an inefficient public sector and a bloated state bureaucracy; his adventurous Pan-Arabism added the burden of excessive military spending and risked absorption into the Soviet bloc. Sadat's supporters also charged that Nasser's irresponsible involvements abroad antagonized the United States and its conservative Arab allies, the only external powers with resources sufficient to aid Egypt. Sadat claimed that "when I took over power, I realized the bitter truth. I summoned Dr. Hassan Abbas Zaki, then Minister of Finance and Economy, and asked him about the economic situation. He said simply that the treasury was empty and we were 'almost bankrupt.' " Chronic balance-of-payment problems, low rates of investment, and deterioration of the economic infrastructure signaled the bankruptcy of socialism at home, while the continuing Israeli occupation of the Egyptian Sinai after 1967 marked the decline of Egypt's standing in the world. Sadat stated simply that Egypt's "economy had been destroyed by the Yemeni War, the Marxist application of socialism, and the disgraceful 1967 defeat"; he suggested that only fear of repression held the bankrupt Nasserist polity together in its last years.[1]

According to this official view, the brute facts of economic failure dictated a complete reversal of the nation's course; Nasser's successor had little choice but to pursue economic and political liberalization. Economic necessity drove Egypt to an opening to the international market and the advanced technology and capital reserves of the West. According to the government, liberalization also brought the large-scale American assistance necessary to revitalize the national economy. At home, the Open Door strategy released the pent-up energies of the private sector and invigorated the nationalized industries by competition from private-sector firms.

The mass media of the seventies declared all these liberalization efforts a national economic success story. In the middle and late seventies, official press reports interpreted the exceptionally high growth rates of 7, 8, and even 9 percent as vindication of the regime's economic strategy. Egyptians also heard from the new regime that an age of democracy had dispelled the reign of fear, while shock diplomacy had enabled an economically strong and democratic Egypt to regain its occupied territories. Sadat's leadership was moving the nation from a failed experiment in Nasserist socialism to a mixed economic order with a vibrant private sector that was bringing prosperity and returning Egypt to its rightful place in the world.

The *Economic Ahram* (*al-Ahram al-Iqtisadi*) developed the most powerful internal critique of this official history. From the unlikely quarter of this specialized journal of economics issued a sustained challenge to the key aspects of the official definition of the economic realities that Egyptians faced in the seventies and early eighties and their meaning for the nation. On February 15, 1976, Editor-in-Chief Lutfy Abdul 'Azim announced the main themes of the *Economic Ahram*'s dissent: "I am happy with the Open Door, emphatically so; in fact, my happiness is without limit." On the normally staid pages of the journal, the bitter sarcasm of 'Azim's account of "the glitter" of the opening had great effect. 'Azim gave special emphasis to the transformation of Cairo to suit the insatiable taste for pleasure of foreigners. "Cairo," he explained, "which was once shamed by comparison to Western capitals for the depressing character of its nights and its limited opportunities for amusement, now offers unlimited possibilities to guests not only in its public but also in its private amusement places, which virtually no building in the city lacks." 'Azim portrayed an Egypt awash in unnecessary foreign goods that undermined domestic production. "I need only walk into any grocery store," he wrote, "to breathe freely and to thank God that he has compensated us so well for the long period of frustration and deprivation." German and Dutch beers were everywhere, and to go with them "there were no less than twenty types of imported cheeses to tempt anyone who had been forced by circumstances to make do with the old Egyptian white cheeses and water."

'Azim's ironic account announced that the "consumption opening" solved all the pressing problems of the poor in the most ingenious way. 'Azim dismissed the "housing crisis" with the announcement that apartments were now available everywhere. True, prices put them out of reach of the mass of Egyptians. Key money (an illegal prepayment used to circumvent rent control) ranged between 5,000 and 200,000 Egyptian pounds, and condominiums sold from 15,000 to 300,000; however, "the availability of the apartments and the ease of getting one, even by telephone," offset this "slight" rise in prices. In parallel fashion, the "torrent of expensive cars flowing through Cairo" presented an alternative to the terribly overcrowded buses. Food, too, no longer posed a problem, thanks to the Kentucky Fried Chicken and Wimpy hamburger shops that "were appearing everywhere to transform the Egyptian people from making do with beans to eating hamburgers and chicken seasoned with twenty spices." The availability of myriad brands of foreign cigarettes eased disappointment over the virtual disappearance from the market of the inexpensive local brands. Ironic praise for the new pattern of national investment concluded 'Azim's editorial. "How could I fail to be happy with the Opening," he remarked, "with its hundreds of millions of petrodollars and Lebanese bullion, all used for commercial and speculative transactions?" 'Azim offered "thanks to God that they [Arab investors] have stayed away from establishing any new industries that could cause more pollution to the Egyptian environment."

A follow-up commentary elaborated the sober political implications of deteriorating economic conditions by comparing the implementation of the Open Door in Egypt with the "Beirut contract." The "gleaming picture" of Beirut in its heyday had turned Egyptian heads: "the comparison was always between Lebanon the 'open' and Egypt the 'closed'; the squares of Beirut full of everything that one could desire in food, drink, and the latest rage from Western fashion houses." Yet, this kind of opening caused "Lebanon's destruction and wars because it contained within it increasing poverty for the poor and increasing wealth for the rich." 'Azim warned that the pursuit "in the most ignorant blindness" of such a consumption opening would "lead to an increase of class hatred and a convulsion of the social system in Egypt." The editorial appeared on November 15, 1977; exactly two months later, Egypt experienced the disturbances of January 1977. In cities from Cairo to Aswan, Egyptians protested a government decision to reduce subsidies on basic commodities with the most serious display of mass unrest since the forties. The government railed against leftist conspirators. The *Economic Ahram* read the January 1977 disturbances as confirmation of the correctness of its critical assessment of the Opening.

'Azim considered the consequences of the liberalization to be the central social issue confronting Egyptians.[2] He evaluated the Open Door policy not only in terms of its contribution to national productivity but also in terms of the protection it afforded to the interests of ordinary citizens. His vision of a productive national economy that met the basic needs of all Egyptians provided the normative thread of a critique with unavoidable political overtones. From a mosaic of commentary, a pointed and authoritative alternative to the official view took shape. As the *Economic Ahram* saw it, the government in the seventies failed to protect the economic national interest. Egypt's economy enjoyed a surface prosperity because of windfall income from worker remittances, tourism, Sinai oil, and Suez Canal user fees. This *rentier* income, however, did not contribute to the nation's productive capacity. In short, the economy grew in the seventies, but it did not develop. In fact, while the seventies yielded short-term and maldistributed gains, the productive foundations of the national economy in industry and agriculture eroded. The journal pointed to the intolerable burdens the new economic strategy placed on Egypt's poor citizens and signaled the dangers of growing foreign domination that compromised the exercise of free political will. The crystallization of this bundle of themes gave the *Economic Ahram* its program of research and commentary for the remainder of the seventies and into the eighties.

Lutfy Abdul 'Azim set a large agenda for a small institution. A modest three-story sandstone building located next to the *Ahram* tower housed the *Economic Ahram,* with its small editorial "family" of under a dozen persons. The location signaled that the journal, though specialized, operated as part of the national press. The *Ahram* imprimatur saved the journal from the ghettoization of the opposition party papers; though small, the journal's readership belonged to the mainstream of public life. Later, the *Ahram* establishment consciously looked to the *Economic Ahram* to provide a counterweight to the strong Marxist accents in Egyptian journalism. Lutfy Abdul 'Azim welcomed this role. 'Azim saw himself as a man of the center-right; at a time when Sadat functioned as a mainstay of Nasserist socialism, 'Azim identified himself as an open advocate of liberalization.

The original conception of the *Economic Ahram* as a forum for public interchange of responsible citizens gave its editorial voice a distinctively multivocal quality. Founded in 1958, the *Economic Ahram* provided a privileged platform for interchanges among "those who write, those who think, and those who govern"—that is, among journalists, scholars, and government officials. Editorials reached for as large an audience as possible, often using a provocative journalistic layout and style. Yet, the journal never belonged completely to the press; the university and public service also shaped its character. Butrous Ghali, one of the journal's founders and later Sadat's acting foreign minister, claimed that university professors created the *Economic Ahram*. Under Ghali's editorship from 1958 to the mid-sixties, the journal prided itself on being a field for "scientific battles" waged on theoretical issues, with university students a large part of the readership.[3] During those first years, lengthy magazine supplements aired the views of academic specialists on national and international issues of political economy.[4] An academic consciousness remained a prominent part of the journal's self-conception; the articles of the permanent staff remained studded with reports of their "research findings," and the editorial family always considered research to be as important as reporting. The authoritative style of the policy adviser blended on the pages of the journal with those of the journalist and the scholar. Later, Ghali created his own work with the *Economic Ahram* with "directing me to involvement in the political affairs of my country."[5] The journal's founders had left the university halls to address the problems of the nation for a larger audience.

After the 1967 defeat the *Economic Ahram* deepened these public policy commitments and strived to broaden its appeal. Spurred by a 75 percent drop in circulation, closely linked to a mood of national despair, the editorial board responded to the need for public introspection by focusing on the economic problems of the nation in sharp relief. During the seventies the journal established a public identity at once narrowly technical and broadly critical. Many of its pages continued to deal with specialized economic matters. The technical sections provided detailed accounts of the activities of companies, the new inventions, and movements in the money market, while appendixes recorded major economic decrees and laws. At the same time, the editorials invoked a broad social function, describing the journal as one part of the national press that "presents what others do not." However, whenever the journal came under fire for its critical commentary, the staff withdrew behind a screen of technical articles and charts.

Any reconstruction of the *Economic Ahram* view of the Open Door obscures its incremental and piecemeal character. This unavoidable distortion both overstates the cohesiveness of a critique that took shape gradually over the course of a decade and understates the power of an emerging collective judgment that rested on laboriously accumulated and well-documented case studies. Because the editors approved liberalization in principle, their commentary focused on implementation. Four major themes dominated their critique: productive versus nonproductive economic activities, the public sector versus the private sector, economic distribution, and the role of foreigners in the Egyptian economy. Clashes with the authorities resulted as each issue was raised.

The staff of the *Economic Ahram* identified themselves as advocates of economic liberalization. They did not, however, share the regime's view that economic necessity set the course of the policy. "The decision to undertake economic liberalization," 'Azim stated plainly, "was a political decision." To be sure, 'Azim considered the policy initiative a plausible attempt to meet Egypt's economic needs in changed circumstances. Yet, he argued that there could be no direct reading from the new international and domestic situation to a particular policy response. As 'Azim saw it, the political leaders made that translation, and they did so with an exercise of political imagination and will that made them responsible for both the conception and implementation of the policy.[6]

The *Economic Ahram*'s analyses provided strong advocacy of an economy more open to the world, while its editorials objected to the sweepingly negative official judgment on the socialist era from 1956 to 1966 and the years of transition that followed it. The difference reflected the greater weight given to the impact of external factors, particularly the conflict with Israel, on the performance of the economy. From a vantage point that emphasized the need to confront Israeli power, the strength of an economy with its foundations in a public sector of nationalized industries proved more impressive than the official version allowed.

Economic Ahram editorials divided Egypt's recent economic history into three clear periods, demarcated by the country's changing regional role. The first period of economic "encirclement" stretched from 1957 to 1967; during these years, Egypt's socialist experiment met the active hostility of the United States and its regional ally Israel. After the attack on Egypt in 1967 came a period of "steadfastness," extending from 1967 to 1973. During these years Egypt recovered sufficiently from the damage inflicted in 1967 to redress the power balance; the Egyptian army's crossing into the occupied Sinai in the October 1973 War represented a successful reassertion of the national will against Israel. The years since 1973 constituted the period of economic "crossing" and reconstruction along liberal lines, made possible by Egypt's improved performance in the October War.

The journal's editors argued that during the steadfastness period the government overcame economic hardships and created conditions conducive to the later opening. In identifying these hardships, analysts pointed to the damage inflicted by the Israeli occupation of the Sinai, specifying the loss of oil, manganese, phosphate, and Suez Canal revenues, as well as the decline of income from tourism. An important journal study also noted that the beleaguered Egyptians "received no important economic aid from either East or West during these difficult years." The same study cited military spending of L.E. 4,254 million from 1964 to 1973; this drain on resources was made worse by the human and material costs of the war effort. Despite these military burdens, the journal assessment reported the political leadership gave priority to increasing national production. Largely because of "the satisfactory growth rates generated from within the economy, which made available investments for development," the regime was able to prepare the country for a successful war effort by spending L.E. 10,000 million on the military and development.

The journal argued that the figures for the period 1967–1973 as a whole did not confirm the Sadat regime's later bleak portrait of the economy before the Opening; those figures showed that "between 1966 and 1973 total output increased by 40 percent, national income by 40 percent, and personal consumption by 40 percent; investments in this six-year period of 'steadfastness' totaled L.E. 1,846 million." The analysis made the point that the October War effort rested ultimately on the public-sector foundations created in the socialist period. At the same time, the journal credited the early Sadat years with the "clear vision of military goals that were coordinated with the advancement of economic projects." Unlike the official analysis, the article also highlighted the importance of Arab aid.[7]

For the period after the October War, when the confrontation with Israel no longer loomed as large, the *Economic Ahram* used domestic reconstruction, including reintegration of the recovered Sinai, as a measure of economic performance. The post-October War liberalization would result in "more economic growth, liberation, and reconstruction," building on Egypt's existing economic strengths by consolidating basic industries such as cement, fertilizers, and textiles while encouraging new agricultural and industrial projects. The specifically liberalizing *Economic Ahram* platform advocated freeing exchange and external trade from all constraints, reorienting foreign trade to the European Community, streamlining the public sector by liquidating losing projects and encouraging profitable ones, and mechanizing agriculture.[8] The public sector suffered from "the accumulation of twenty years of ignorant planning and waste of resources." 'Azim also condemned the practice of "accepting obsolete Russian factories, which increased our dependence and poverty, as well as furthering horizontal rather than vertical expansion for propaganda purposes, which resulted in a lot of bottlenecks."[9] Yet, for all its criticism of these failings of the public sector, the journal stood firmly against its liquidation, calling instead for rehabilitation and use use of its profits. The new liberalizing orientation must give special priority to meeting the people's pressing needs in such areas as housing.[10]

Given these standards, a note of urgency colored the journal's endorsement of the Open Door. On January 1, 1977, 'Azim warned that Egypt could not fulfill its national responsibilities unless it gave the economic battle its top priority: "With this understanding, the *Economic Ahram* stands at the gates of a new phase and a new year strongly believing that our ability to face the coming challenges depends on the success of the Opening; the only way out of the national crisis is this Opening whose banners we have been raising for months but whose progress the different responsible organizations have been lazy in advancing." 'Azim described the Open Door as "an expression of a hope sustained by the Egyptian people throughout long years of deprivation." He alerted the leadership that outcome of the policy affected the hopes of all Egyptians and therefore the legitimacy of the regime; the policy was "a means and not an end in itself." Precisely because the *Economic Ahram* judged the success of the Opening to be so critical, 'Azim warned that "we do not hesitate to describe any neglect or hesitation in executing it to be less than a national crime against the hopes of progress and development in Egypt; with the new year, we consider advancing and supporting the Open Door policy a basic mission of top priority in all our publication projects."

From the outset, the *Economic Aharm* staked out a position that endorsed the political decision to liberalize but questioned its implementation. In an influential editorial on January 1, 1978, Lutfy Abdul 'Azim carefully distinguished between the "tempo of political action and that of administrative action": "The political leadership in Egypt, especially since the decision to launch the October 1973 War, has been

characterized by an incredible dynamism in the sphere of political maneuvers, whereas the administrative structure has not been able to keep
pace with these developments; the Open Door policy is an example of
this lag." Soberly, 'Azim observed that promulgation of the new policy
had taken the executive structure completely by surprise. The ministries
possessed neither studies on how to make the change from a closed-door
policy to an open-door one nor experience on how to adapt and control
the policy to distribute its benefits justly. According to 'Azim, this lack
of coordination between the political and administrative spheres explained the inconsistencies in legal and administrative guidelines for the
Open Door policy. 'Azim also criticized administrators for having sur-
rendered all initiative to the political leadership. For example, when the
government announced that Egypt would no longer export cotton to
eastern bloc countries, the administrative organs had no contingency
plans. The lag between policymaking and implementation surfaced even
more destructively when the regime announced the necessity for "an
administrative revolution." According to 'Azim, this decision "reflected
the hopes and suffering of the Egyptian people." However, the transformation of this political decision into reality clashed with "the negative
nature of the administrative structure." 'Azim reported that he could
discern no real plans for treating the "hardening of the arteries" of the
administrative organs in Egypt. As a result, the "administrative revolution" became "not much more than a group of slogans uttered by officials; lately, even the slogans have disappeared."

More generally, 'Azim warned that sloganeering of all kinds could
not substitute for the kinds of institutional and legal arrangements that
the Open Door policy would require. Candidly, he remarked that "the
historical and grave circumstances in which Egypt finds itself" require
Egyptians to "act responsibly and cease making exaggerated statements."
'Azim disapproved, for example, of a statement by the minister of industry a few days after Sadat's historic trip to Jerusalem; the minister
announced that "industrial production in Egypt has realized a great
increase in the past few days because of the president's peace initiative
and the resulting high morale among workers." 'Azim remarked that
"these are words we do not believe would please President Sadat at all
in a stage that requires deeds not words."[11]

Insistence on actions not words became the theme of a special
section in virtually every issue devoted to implementation of the Open
Door; the articles exposed bootlenecks in decision making and administrative incompetence and corruption. Consistent opposition to empty

official posturing inevitably brought the *Economic Ahram* into open conflict with the government ministries. One particularly dramatic confrontation occurred in 1981 with the minister of economy. The *Economic
Ahram* published a World Bank document critical of Abdul Meguid and
his policies. Meguid defended his performance by claiming that his
administration had succeeded for the first time in years in balancing the
budget, a claim the *Economic Ahram* promptly denounced as based on
statistical manipulation. Meguid countered by asserting that the World
Bank document that had triggered the controversy was itself a forgery.
The minister invited his critics, including those at the *Economic Ahram,*
"to die of their spite." The editor-in-chief of the *Economic Ahram* responded defiantly:

> Ever since that day, inquiries have been flowing into the *Economic Ahram*
> asking us to comment on the minister's denial. Here we would like to say
> that the soundness of the document is beyond question, and he himself
> knows this, as do all other banking, economic, and financial circles. The
> forging that took place with the figures of the budget in order to end up
> with a surplus for the first time in ages is also well known; anyone with an
> elementary knowledge of finance knows that the surplus is an illusion and
> the deficit is still there. That is something that will not be eliminated by the
> "spite" of the economic group leaders, unless every critic of Dr. Abdul
> Razzaq "dies of spite." In that case, only he will survive in the field of
> economics, and then, perhaps, the transformation of a deficit into a surplus
> would be an easy thing to accomplish.[12]

'Azim explained that he attacked sloganeering because of the political dangers it posed. Behind the issues of implementation lurked the
fundamental question of economic justice. The clearest statement of the
dangers came in a 1980 editorial that opened with a discussion of Sadat's
promise that in the era of peace, Egypt would become a society of
prosperity: "No doubt Sadat meant this promise when he repeated it
several times. But a danger arose when the executive bodies did not
translate Sadat's ideas into realistic policies, turning them instead into
slogans that every official repeated for any reason or no reason; the
examples were numerous, such as the 'administrative or managerial revolution,' the 'green revolution,' or 'food security.' " 'Azim charged that
"every official hides behind these slogans, concealing their lack of scientific planning required to deal with the problems." He warned that
slogans did not deceive the masses and could have dangerous consequences because of the aspirations they stimulated:

The class that hears about the "society of plenty" is the one working in the big cities with continuous contact with the outside world through cinema and TV films and with the superficial prosperity in Cairo of huge buildings, big cars, and expensive consumer goods . . . In the absence of an accurate definition of the concept of "plenty," official promises, combined with signs of parasitic prosperity, feed this class with serious and dangerous class ambitions and widen the gap between reality and aspirations, while creating consumption patterns that hinder development plans.[13]

The *Economic Ahram* had warned the regime of these dangers from the outset. On March 16, 1978, for example, an editorial by 'Essam Rifa'at titled "Consumption Open Door and Production Open Door" sharply criticized the commercial and consumer rather than the productive character of the bulk of the projects undertaken. Rifa'at also warned against the hostile attitude developing toward the public sector and the increasing gap in wages: these shortcomings were creating opposition to an Open Door that "many accused of leading to foreign dependency by the return of privileges for foreigners, the resurgence of family capitalism, and the weakening of Egyptian national culture because of the invasion of foreign cultural influences." Two months earlier, had 'Azim charged that "the Arabs and those Egyptians working with them have transformed Egypt into a first-rate consumer society without any consideration of the requirements of development."[14] In the years from 1977 to 1981, detailed statistical studies of all these trends substantiated the charges. According to Rifa'at, "the door was opened to provide unlimited facilities for any importer and adventurer to operate without constraints; when the state discovered the necessity of consumer protection and tried to interfere to achieve it and to organize the import trade, the voices of merchants [supporting these excessive privileges] became louder."[15]

A pattern emerged of foreign investors in alliance with private-sector elements driven only by the profit motive, stimulating fears that the Open Door was taking a direction that threatened the overall national interest. The Pyramids Plateau project, calling for the Disneyland-style development of the desert area surrounding Egypt's most impressive complex of pharoanic monuments, prompted an even stronger condemnation of the excessive rights accorded to foreign investors. In the wake of the scandal, the *Economic Ahram* judged an insistence on concern with national interest, rather than simply profit, to be the necessary criterion for all projects. "Foreign investments must not affect the cultural, sociological, and economic independence of Egypt." To secure this end, Rifa'at urged formulation of a "moral constitution for investors" that required "respect for the inherited culture over searching for economic profits."[16]

'Azim recommended that regulations be developed to prevent foreign capital from "permeating areas that would harm rather than benefit" the Egyptian people and the economic development of the country: "We must study the question of prohibiting non-Egyptian capital from investing in certain areas, regardless of its nationality. Our thoughts would turn immediately to services, real estate, and trade as areas that should be limited to Egyptian capital. Non-Egyptian capital should be directed to areas of industrial investment coordinated with the five-year industrial plan."[17]

In this context, the *Economic Ahram* reasserted its belief that the public sector had an important role to play in the national economy in Egypt or any other developing society. Editorials focused on the special difficulties faced by the nationalized sector as the country turned to the West. Writers emphasized that a consumption Open Door flooded Egypt with foreign goods that directly competed with national industries; moreover, they did so unfairly, since the public-sector industries operated under a variety of socialist laws and regulations, such as those governing employment, that did not apply to the private sector. The journal attacked with particular vehemence changes in the customs laws that led to "murdering" local industry: "Tariff customs have been converted from a protective and nurturing tool of the nascent industry to an instrument of slaughtering the public sector, that, given its long experience, is now actually *the backbone of the Egyptian economy* [emphasis added]." Any piecemeal liquidation of the public sector diminished Egypt's current economic capabilities and also deprived the country of a long-term alternative should the liberalization fail. With this possibility in mind, the article cited a study in the British *Economist* of November 13, 1976, outlining one such alternative. The *Economist* opined that the solution for Egypt's economic crisis might be "through the industrial public-sector firms all working with their maximum productive capacities and giving them the chance for local and external marketing."[18]

In place of empty slogans, 'Azim called for a clear definition of national purpose, with a productive liberalization as its centerpiece. Prosperity for Egypt involved materially improving the less privileged sectors of society without undermining the status of others. According to 'Azim, this goal could be accomplished by creating a national economic "framework" for the "efficient use" of resources:

> We call on Egyptian economists and officials to formulate a scientific vision of Sadat's ideas of the prosperous society that takes into account Egypt's true present and future capabilities. This comprehensive vision must be the main foundation of our financial and economic policies, as related to the Open Door policy. There must be a carefully thought out timetable to achieve the steps that would lead to a society characterized by true prosperity [for all classes of society] and not the distorted prosperity of the "inverted pyramid" [which gives unearned privileges to a narrow elite.][19]

According to the *Economic Ahram,* consumerism provided the most telling measure of Egypt's distorted liberalization. An article in August 1977 reported that "imports of consumer goods represent one-half of export capacity and are responsible for 40 percent of the deficit in the balance of payments." The article also reported "an increase in the import of consumer durables by 75.5 percent from 1975 to 1976 and those of nondurables by 18.4 percent." From the productive perspective of the *Economic Ahram,* these new economic facts demanded immediate attention: "The structure of foreign trade needs a complete reorganization in the light of the development plan; we now import many products that we use to produce and hence are in need of import substitution; we must support the public sector and we must control the import of consumer goods."[20]

In an editorial addressed to the minister of trade, 'Azim argued against application of laissez-faire thinking to the import sphere. A flood of "provocative" imported consumer goods, he wrote, did not serve the national interest "in a poor, a very poor country where the average annual income of an individual, according to the World Bank, is $260." 'Azim warned against ignoring the "explosive factors inherent in the Egyptian economy under the illusion of 'market dynamics' or 'demand and supply' factors."[21]

'Azim also took exception to the standard regime argument that imported goods would improve local production by competition. He did not accept the official view that local industry would begin by competing with foreign products inside the country so that it could compete with it abroad as the next step: "This is merely a reversal of the truth of matters. *It is clear that we are gradually killing our national industry.* There are many examples of this; the cigarette industry, for example, is deteriorating and is unable to compete with the flood of foreign cigarettes [emphasis added]." 'Azim concluded this assessment with the suggestion that if the minister used less of his own budget for publicity photos of himself and more for market studies "we would not have reached this level of disorientation in production!!"[22]

Recognizing the need for productive economic activity that served the interests of ordinary Egyptians also produced disillusionment with much of the private-sector activity stimulated by the Open Door. The *Economic Ahram* initially welcomed the unshackling of private initiative, frequently quoting, for example, Sadat's speech in parliament in which he contrasted "Nasserist socialism, based on one swollen bureaucratic leg, which is the public sector, to an Arab Egyptian socialism, which is the socialism of prosperity and which derives from national roots and relies on two legs, the public sector and the private sector."[23]

From the outset, however, the *Economic Ahram* also warned against monopolistic and exploitative practices in a variety of areas: "wholesale traders of fruits and vegetables who control the market from the production end to the retailing end; importers who monopolize selling some imports; traders in Port Said who direct the economy of the city to consumption; hidden hands behind the commercial Open Door that want to transform it to their benefit." The same article discussed a law, devised the year before, that sought to limit profits to 30 percent. The merchants opposed it vigorously; the *Economic Ahram* reported that investigating committees found profit rates as high as 150 percent: "This is just one of the many attempts by capital to control the economy to its own advantage."[24]

The *Economic Ahram*'s support for productive agricultural or industrial activity eventually made it critical of the expansion of Egyptian tourism during the seventies. Initially, editorials welcomed the new opportunities in tourism created by the increased foreign confidence as a result of the peace treaty. An early review of the prospects of tourism concluded that Egypt's climate, even more than its antiquities, drew foreigners. After a survey of facilities in Alexandria, 'Azim concluded that hotels were too often "dirty, with poor service, and facilities that don't work." With planning and attention to quality service, however, he concluded that Egypt could look forward to real expansion of revenues from foreign visitors.[25]

Five years of experience, particularly with tourists from the Arab world, convinced 'Azim and his staff of the error of their judgment. In an article titled "Will Tourism Destroy the Egyptian Economy?" 'Azim discussed the "invasion" of Egypt by Arab tourists and the difficulties they created, particularly by renting furnished apartments. Because the hotel infrastructure in Egypt could not support the expansion of tourists, the rental of apartments contributed in an important way to raising housing prices. The rise in rents also benefited wealthy Egyptians who owned such property. In a society in which a university graduate saved for an average of ten years to secure an apartment, the rental of luxury units at inflated fees to Arabs for "recreation" threatened "to shake society's foundation." He also identified the phenomenon as "a primary reason for the horrifying breakdown in Egypt's morals, winning Egypt the unfortunate title of the Bangkok of the Arab world." Moreover, with Arab tourists everywhere, 'Azim argued that when genuine businessmen came to Egypt they could not find a place to stay. With their incredible purchasing power, the Arab tourists simply magnified the gap between the rich and the poor at a time when "the general budget is burdened with ensuring food for the poor Egyptian people, an effort that mostly benefits those with the highest purchasing power." By the mid-seventies 'Azim had also concluded that tourism inevitably fed black-market currency speculation: "this tourism and all the spending that accompanies it take place outside the legal money markets. As a matter of fact, tourism is the primary source for the black market and luxury imports, at a time when the agonized Egyptian still hopes to be able to buy beans and lentils." 'Azim concluded with a call for stricter regulation of tourism. The editorial prompted an immediate response from the minister of tourism, followed by an extended discussion in which the *Economic Ahram* held to its revised, sharply critical position.[26]

The *Economic Ahram* reported that the emerging pattern of consumerist and exploitative economic practices widened gaps in the distribution of income. Housing provided a particularly salient measure of the dilemmas created, and treatment of the housing issue brought the journal into sharp conflict with the regime, apparently precipitating a temporary suspension of 'Azim. 'Azim opened the series in July 1978 with a discussion of key money, which had become standard practice in the seventies, and clearly signaled the class dimension:

> Certain classes in our society no doubt profit from these conditions. On the one hand is the private sector, which builds the new apartment buildings and displays housing units for sale at prices much higher than those of their counterparts in New York, Geneva, and Hong Kong. In addition, there is the class that specializes in renting furnished apartments, mostly consisting of those who have apartments in buildings at old rent rates and then rent

them furnished for thousands of pounds. These elements all fall under the "exploitative private sector."[27]

'Azim's analysis did not stop there, however. He asserted that exploitation in housing extended to the public sector as well: "In fact, the government and public-sector companies are considered the main factor behind the horrifying waves of imbalances in the rental markets. In the last period, since the Open Door began in Egypt, the housing crisis grew more acute. The prices of apartments and the amounts charged for key money grew. But we are sorry to say that the exploitative private sector behaves on the basis that 'if the head of the house beats the drums, the people of the house will all be dancers.' " 'Azim's suggestion that public-sector agencies set the exploitative tone included a discussion of "the strange story" involving Osman Ahmed Osman's company, the Arab Contractors. The article reported on an Arab Contractors housing project that promised apartments at a set price with specific furnishings: when the apartments were ready the price was increased by 100 percent in less than two years and did not include the promised finishing. The company ascribed the increase to rising costs, but 'Azim's treatment of the case clearly implied that this public-sector company had engaged in exploitative behavior.[28]

In an important article 'Essam Rifa'at summed up the *Economic Ahram*'s position on housing. Rifa'at called for protection "of citizens from the greediness" of building speculators and for an official system to determine a fair profit for builders. In this regard, he cited the argument of Housing Minister Osman Ahmed Osman, who had stated that the profit should not exceed 20 percent. Rifa'at also noted, however, that under Osman and all subsequent ministers that guideline was "not observed by private or public companies such as the Arab Contractors."[29]

While these articles on housing appear to have played a key role, the *Economic Ahram* never published the details of 'Azim's suspension during the late seventies. His name simply disappeared from the masthead. An editorial under 'Azim's name on December 1, 1979, signaled the end of the affair:

> It was a crisis, but it ended. Although I will not treat it in detail, I shall take this opportunity to renew an oath you know well as a result of following the clear line of this journal, the line it has adhered to since the late sixties, in spite of all the obstacles it faced.
>
> I'll renew the oath, dear readers, that the magazine will continue to be issued with the help of your direct and indirect participation in order to serve Egypt through defending the economic interests that affect the fate

of millions of Egyptians who are lost in the crowd and who have every right to dream of a brighter and less frustrating future. This may come about one day as a result of productive economic development, well planned in accordance with the real needs of the Egyptian people.

Driven by the logic of this perspective, the *Economic Ahram* pressed relentlessly on the Sadat regime's ban on all criticism of foreign policy. The global and regional reorientation of the seventies directly related to the regime's strategy to improve Egypt's economic prospects. 'Azim's "oath" therefore required an independent assessment of such controversial foreign policy issues as the impact on ordinary Egyptians of the shift from the Soviet to the American sphere, the peace with Israel, and the break with the Arabs. The *Economic Ahram* covered them all.

With very few exceptions, the mass press followed the official lead in denigrating all things Soviet. In contrast, the *Economic Ahram* asked calmly how the earlier Soviet trade and aid connection had affected Egyptian development and contrasted the record of the Russians in the fifties and the sixties with that of the Americans in the seventies. While the dailies trumpeted each announcement of additional millions in U.S. aid with banner headlines and few concrete details, the *Economic Ahram* asked how much aid was actually received and put to use, with what conditions, and for what purposes. Official pundits celebrated the promised peace and the prosperity it would bring. Writers in the *Economic Ahram* questioned what productive role foreign capital played in the economy and eventually concluded that assertions of Israeli power in the post–Camp David period would ultimately threaten Egyptian national interests.

"Development: In Whose Arms?" asked Lutfy Abdul 'Azim in the title of an editorial on October 3, 1983. Summarizing a decade of careful scrutiny of Egypt's relations with powerful external powers, 'Azim responded: "Finally, not in the arms of the Soviet Union, the United States, or the Common Market, nor even in the arms of the petrodollars of our Arab brothers—but only in the arms of Egypt." 'Azim approached his theme with a claim to impartiality based on a record of resistance to any foreign encroachment on Egypt's sovereignty; the *Economic Ahram* first raised the broad question of the appropriateness of a growth pattern fostered by a friendly superpower some fifteen years earlier. At that time the journal had questioned the wisdom of establishing an iron and steel complex with a large export capacity. The Soviet Union backed that project. The *Economic Ahram* made an essentially economic case against an iron and steel project with a yearly capacity of 1.34 million tons, of which 588,000 were targeted for local consumption and 782,000 for export. 'Azim reasoned that only Arab and African countries would buy Egyptian steel. However, the projected Egyptian export capacity would constitute almost 40 percent of total Arab and African demand. Given intense competition from established steel producers with international reputations, the *Economic Ahram* doubted that Egypt could capture so large a share of the market.

In response to the *Economic Ahram*'s critique, responsible government officials claimed that the Soviet Union had agreed to purchase any product surplus. 'Azim opposed this solution even more strenuously. The Soviet Union, he pointed out, exported steel on a large scale and obviously had no need of Egyptian steel on purely economic grounds. Clearly, the Soviets had political ends in mind. 'Azim argued that any agreement that did not serve mutual economic interests "would not last long." In the meanwhile, it would place Egypt in an unfavorable situation. The artificial Soviet absorption of the steel surplus would distance Egypt from its natural market and from the healthy pressures to adjust to its demands. Moreover, since there was no real demand for the surplus steel, unlike the case of cotton, the Egyptians would develop dependency on the Soviets. The Egyptian government planned to invest L.E. 400 million in the project. 'Azim was loath to give any external power such leverage over so costly an investment; he therefore denounced the proposed project as "the most dangerous to our industrial revolution."[30]

Fifteen years later 'Azim returned to the issue of dependency, this time warning against the U.S. role in the Egyptian economy. Detailed technical studies of the American trade and aid relationship appeared regularly in the journal. The statistical record compiled in the *Economic Ahram* found the U.S. aid program to be much smaller than the official figures in the mass press suggested. Journal writers also concluded that the aid went primarily to the nonproductive sectors of the economy. The American program neglected industrial activity, especially the public-sector industrial enterprises. The *Economic Ahram* also criticized the U.S.-Egyptian trade imbalance; imports from the United States were rising sharply while exports stagnated or declined. 'Azim described himself as "shaken" by the realization, based on a study of American reports in 1982, that imports from the United States constituted 31 percent of total Egyptian imports. At the same time exports to the United States were unchanged, at 13 percent of total exports. 'Azim noted further that even the low export figure was misleading because the export of crude oil, over 90 percent of the total in 1982, "does not constitute a stimulus to our national industries."[31]

As the pattern of U.S. Egyptian relations unfolded in the seventies, the *Economic Ahram* declined to share in the official enthusiasm for the American era of prosperity. 'Azim argued to great effect that his basic position in no way reflected an anti-American bias: "What we criticized in the sixties, that is, placing most of our eggs in the Soviet basket, has changed only to the extent that our eggs are now in the American basket."[32] Yet, the very even-handedness of 'Azim's characterization of the role of the two superpowers contrasted with the official version of Egypt's recent history, which credited Sadat with rescuing the country from dependency on the Soviets. 'Azim suggested instead that the regime had simply exchanged one dependency for another.

The editor of the *Economic Ahram* pushed the comparison further to American disadvantage. In a study of the Soviet and American eras from the perspective of their developmental impact, he took his theme from the reflections of a poet "on a time that caused me to weep, but once it was gone I was led to weep for its return." With these words, 'Azim recalled his earlier warnings against the Soviet connection and suggested that the American link constituted "an even greater danger." 'Azim argued that Egypt's industrial capacity grew in the sixties with Soviet help, despite all the problems associated with the Soviet development model. According to 'Azim, the country had something to show for the debts it owned to the Russians. During the sixties, the Soviet Union funded and implemented more than 100 industrial projects, including the High Dam, power stations in Aswan, the steel and aluminum complexes, the cement industry, and pharmaceuticals. In addition, the Soviets provided industrial training for thousands of Egyptians in the Soviet Union and in numerous training centers established in Egypt. Surveying the period 1974–1982, 'Azim asked how the American aid and trade program matched that record. He noted that the Americans concentrated on infrastructure improvement and contributed little or nothing to the expansion of the economy's productive capacity in either industry or agriculture. He reported that during the years of the American connection, "Egypt's debt rose to almost 20 billion dollars, with no significant addition to our industrial base despite this monstrous indebtedness."[33]

For its sharp criticism of the U.S. role in Egypt, the *Economic Ahram* received a medal from the American embassy, or so 'Azim characterized an incident that he saw as an American attack on the journal.

'Azim wrote that U.S. Ambassador Alfred Atherton held a reception to introduce the new press and cultural attaché to the Egyptian press corps. During the reception, one of the political officers at the embassy informed 'Azim that he had been looking forward to seeing him "in order to discuss what's published in the journal about the United States." 'Azim reported that the diplomat characterized those reports as "yellow journalism." 'Azim explained to his readers that "in the West the term denotes the kind of press based on scandals, sex, and distorted news" that aims to excite the passions of the reader:

> Anger was my immediate reaction to this insult, the likes of which I had never heard during my eighteen years at the *Economic Ahram*. But after a while I realized that there was no reason for anger, because if an American diplomat considered the *Economic Ahram* to be "yellow journalism," then this should be considered a medal of which we should be proud. No doubt there is no yellow journalism, from the American viewpoint, in a country such as El Salvador or any other country that Americans try to keep under their feet. Therefore, I offer thanks at this display of American diplomacy.[34]

Two weeks later, the journal published a historical treatment of the "yellow journalism" phenomenon in the United States. The report turned the charge of sensationalist reporting against American press coverage of Egypt in the fifties and sixties, reminding Egyptians that American journalists had regularly denounced Nasser as a "fascist" and still routinely and indiscriminately designated Palestinians as "terrorists," offering these instances as more appropriate examples of yellow journalism than anything published in the *Economic Ahram*.[35]

Given the *Economic Ahram*'s emphasis on the need to expand Egypt's productive capacity, neither the peace with Israel nor a link with the conservative Arab regimes alleviated its dismal picture of the consequences of the American connection. Initially, the *Economic Ahram* welcomed the peace and the economic opportunities it might bring. On January 1, 1978, Lutfy Abdul 'Azim wrote that "throughout nearly a quarter of a century we moved in a vicious circle of war. This circle has been broken by Sadat's visit to Jerusalem."

However, enthusiasm for Sadat's grand initiative was tempered by reservations. Although 'Azim was convinced that Egyptians sought "a just, lasting peace" and "not just any peace," he also feared that "the Israelis might miss this historical chance to achieve peace after thirty years of war." Popular approval of the peace process in Egypt, 'Azim also cautioned, rested on hopes for the economic improvement it would generate: "the people believe that peace will be followed without the slightest delay by a solution to all the problems that crush them with every step they take." The editor questioned the realism of those hopes and the wisdom of the regime in encouraging them.

Egyptians required an administrative blueprint of an economy at peace. 'Azim cited with admiration the Israeli example of planning for peace at a time when the Arab regimes were still "calling for Israel to be thrown in the sea." Egyptians, he wrote, must rethink issues such as the role of the military in a society at peace and a shift of resources from armaments to development. In addition, a peace economy would have to remedy what 'Azim considered the "grave structural problems" that hampered Egyptian development; a series of structural imbalances constituted "the real problems of the Egyptian economy." His analysis emphasized the imbalance between the industrial and agricultural sectors, the contradictions within the industrial sector due to the lack of economic balance between heavy, medium, and light industries, and weak coordination between Egyptian industrial production and the needs of the local market. In 'Azim's view, the regime must remedy these structural problems in order to make the best use of peacetime resources.

'Azim also warned that an Egypt at peace would face the additional problems of the cessation of Arab aid and possible Israeli domination of the economy. Timely planning could cope with both issues. 'Azim pointed out that Arab aid had disadvantages that made its loss somewhat less damaging. In the past Arab donors had made their aid directly dependent on political conditions; because the regime could not control either the volume or the timing of the assistance, these restrictions made long-term economic planning difficult. As for the possibility of Israeli economic domination, effective planning could create an institutional and legal environment that both welcomed foreign participation and controlled its potentially adverse effects: "Either the economy of any state is protected by the regulations necessary to stand between it and the domination of any foreign economic power, or there are no regulations and it is vulnerable to domination by everyone." Egyptians should neither exaggerate nor underestimate the danger of the Israeli economy, but merely "learn from our experience with the Open Door" about effective measures to protect Egyptian interests.[36]

The *Economic Ahram*'s critical assessment of Israel grew harsher in response to Israeli actions in the region, notably the accelerated settlement of the West Bank immediately after the signing of the Camp David accords in 1978, the strike against the Iraqi nuclear reactor in 1981, and the invasion of Lebanon in 1982. 'Azim's editorials responded with rising anger to each of these developments, opening the journal to accusations of anti-Semitism when he collapsed his denunciations of Israelis into attacks on Jews in general.

The shift in rhetoric began after the attack on the Iraqi reactor, which humiliated Egyptians because it came only a few days after a meeting with Sadat and Begin, thereby suggesting possible Egyptian complicity. A June 15 editorial titled "We Are With You, Begin" praised the Israeli leader in a vituperative style as the only "honest" Israeli "who doesn't try to hide his awful terrorist face and his long history of shedding blood with one head while carrying the Torah in the other." Discarding the distinction between individual Israeli leaders and Jews in general, 'Azim argued that Begin only did openly what others masked by "another kind of political shrewdness, which is called Jewish shrewdness based on trickery, deceit, and hidden intentions with a cover of sweet words until they can attack their enemy in a deadly way." Referring to the attack on the Iraqi reactor, 'Azim wrote of the pained impotence of the "injured and the spectators," made worse by Begin's open declaration two days after the raid that "he doesn't care at all about the world's objections!!" 'Azim responded with a warning:

> To this we say that Arab anger and the real Arab revolution are not yet ripe; they require still more Israeli contentiousness and an Israeli leader like Menachem Begin who doesn't use a gun silencer to hide his crimes. For this reason, we ask Israel to repeat its attack on the Arab nation and to declare every day that Jerusalem is the permanent capital of Israel, and that Palestine and the Palestinians do not exist. Then we say: We are with you Begin, only you are capable of waking up the Arab world from its heavy sleep. And remember, Begin, that history has not been merciful to those who have acted like you. Your end won't differ from that of Hitler or Mussolini, who in the beginning also thought that their power and the whole world's surrender to them would allow them to rob a whole continent, until the world woke up; then, the first ended his life by suicide, the second hanging by his feet until death.

Later in the summer of 1981, 'Azim summarized his feelings toward Jews and Israel in an article titled "All Greetings to Meir Kahane." The piece opened with a reference to a statement by Meir Kahane, the right-wing American-Israeli rabbi who openly called for the expulsion of Palestinians from all of historical Israel. In the letter Kahane had predicted a black fate for Jews who had not moved to Israel, because of rising world anti-Semitism. 'Azim agreed that in the very near future the world would again persecute the Jews, "repeating the tragedy of the concentration camps, which is rejected by any civilized person no matter how bitter he feels toward the Jews." Israel's inability to take advantage of two great opportunities constituted the major evidence "that the Masada complex is still dominating the minds of Israeli leaders, who are leading their people to collective suicide." According to 'Azim, the Jews' first opportunity to alter hostile opinions of them had come with the founding of the Israeli state:

> The stereotypic image of the Jew who knows only usury disappeared and was replaced by another of a young "civilized" person who could establish a state in a brief period, bringing disgrace to 100 million Arabs. That universal admiration for the Israelis blinded the world to the various violations of international laws and human rights upon which this state was established. We still remember how Western peoples celebrated the Israeli victory of 1967 . . . That passion was so great that the world paid no heed to the slaughter of thousands of Arabs at the hands of the Israelis.

Unfortunately, 'Azim continued, the Jews used their national state to continue the persecution of the people they had displaced in its making, rather than seeking some accommodation with them. 'Azim blamed this development chiefly on indiscriminate support of Israel by American and European backers, who failed to hold the Jewish state to universally accepted norms of behavior. 'Azim made his point by recounting a vignette from his own direct experience of Europe:

> I also remember when I was taking a train from Brussels to Frankfurt on the day of the Olympic incident [the murder of Israeli athletes], and passengers noticed from my features that I was an Arab. There were some provocations; and when I tried to talk with some of them, they absolutely refused to hear the reasons that drove the Palestinians to do such things, or the long history of Israeli attacks against the Palestinians and how they usurped their land and killed thousands of them. It was obvious that those passengers refused to hear one single word against the world's spoilt child, Israel.

'Azim noted, however, that this indulgent attitude was beginning to change in the wake of the repeated air attacks on civilians in the Palestinian camps in Lebanon and the strike against the Iraqi reactor; Israel, he suggested, might yet be held accountable for its deeds.

According to 'Azim, the second opportunity for Jewish acceptance into the family of nations had come with the peace with Egypt. In his view, Israeli leaders again failed to act responsibly: "Israeli arrogance . . .

made Israel increase its aggressions against Arab peoples and its denial of Palestinian rights. That stupid reaction from Israeli leaders also reduced world admiration of Israel." 'Azim concluded: "I do wish Kahane to be mistaken in his pessimistic vision of the future of Jews in the world. I also wish that Israel's leaders would reconsider and try to deal with the world in a civilized way that reflects international conventions and human rights and does not deny the real owners of the land the right to return and establish a homeland for themselves on part of their usurped land."[37]

In his long stewardship of the journal, 'Azim consistently recognized those moments when opportunities arose to expand the journal's normal capabilities. In the spring of 1981 two sets of conditions converged to create such a moment. First, the accumulated difficulties of the Sadat policies were being felt with increasing force on all fronts, and the regime appeared to be losing control of the mounting dissent. Second, the elements of the *Economic Ahram* evaluation of the negative consequences of the Open Door for national productivity, economic justice, and foreign policy jelled into a powerful indictment. To give this critique expression, 'Azim opened the pages of the journal to distinguished intellectuals from a range of political orientations in a regular column called "Platforms of Thought." Contributions acquired special urgency from a sense widely shared in the spring and summer of 1981 that an impulsive and increasingly irrational Sadat, unnerved by the mounting failures of his policies, was propelling Egypt toward disaster. In these last months of the Sadat era, 'Azim made the journal a platform for national dialogue.

Among those who took advantage of this opportunity was Galal Amin, an academic economist with an international reputation. In four consecutive issues in May and June 1981, Amin offered the most penetrating critique of the Sadat era and Free Officer rule in general that has yet to reach a wide Egyptian public.[38] The world, especially the Western world, saw in Sadat's assassins the personification of the threat of a religious fanaticism that threatened Egypt's future. In sharp contrast, Amin judged the real "danger to the nation" to be the Western technocratic approach that dominated patterns of thought and government during the Sadat years.

Basing his interpretation on certain insights of social theory, Amin criticized Sadat's claim to have provided an economic solution to Egypt's ills in contrast to the political solution of Gamal Abdul Nasser. Amin recognized that every social order rests on unexamined assumptions about the nature of social reality. These assumptions are built into patterns of thought that are accepted without question as part of existing forms of social discourse. Without these assumptions, collective life would be impossible: they legitimate specific institutions, policies, and vested interests. Amin showed that the prevailing definitions of social reality in the Sadat era were derived from the discourse of economic rationality that underlay Western economic theory. By his analysis Amin relativized those definitions and revealed the special interests they served.

Amin acknowledged that the discourse of economic rationality had both theoretical and material power. The technocratic view claimed for itself the truthfulness of a universal social science that was above politics. At the same time, the regime offered the material prosperity of the West as an illustration of what application of these technocratic truths would mean in material terms for Egypt. But Amin rejected the validity of the theoretical claim and the usefulness for Egypt of the material example. He challenged the technocratic alternative by revealing that its character was historical rather than scientific. The economists of nineteenth-century Europe, like their heirs around the globe today, were the social carriers of utilitarian values that were basic to their economic theories. Translated into economic theory, the principle of utility meant maximum output from limited resources. In theory the standard of judgment for the utility of any political or social policy was to be the greatest happiness for the greatest number of people. However, happiness was understood as both material and quantifiable. Amin emphasized the implications of this reduction of the idea of happiness to measurable material well-being. In Amin's view, this narrow conception of the human possibility had triumphed in both neoclassical and Marxist economic thinking. It was, he judged, a fatal flaw of the culture of the West and the source of the "danger" of Western economic thinking to Egypt.

Amin explained that with the adoption of the Western concept of development, social problems in poor countries were defined by such precise economic indicators as decrease in per capita income or increase in population growth against a fixed resource base. Progress was measured by rising growth rates. By such lights the material constraints of population and resources had the status of an ultimate reality to which all else must take second place, at least for "reasonable" men and women.

Amin rejected this discourse of economic rationality. He argued that it had led to a dangerous and unnecessary sacrifice of cultural integrity and infringement on national political will. Amin believed that since the unexamined assumptions of this reasoning were derived from historical choices made in the West and not from some scientific necessity, Egyptians could and should make different choices.

To clarify the pitfalls that he hoped Egyptians would avoid, Amin examined the three fundamental assumptions of the discourse of economic rationality, which Egyptian proponents of the technocratic orientation attempted to place out of the range of debate. The first assumption was the definition of development as a quantitative increase in material goods, the second the judgment that economic welfare was the essence of social welfare. The third was the belief that the Western model of development, in either its liberal or its Marxist variant, was superior to any alternative that any Egyptian, Arab, or Muslim might create.

Amin spared none of these assumptions. He was quick to point out that less of some things, or even none at all, was preferable to unrelenting quest for more that was the hallmark of the development orientation. Egypt was littered with the unnecessary products of the developed West. Why was a country famed for its wholesome natural fruit juices flooded with expensive 7-Up and colas, all of dubious nutritional value? Amin refused to count as contributions to Egyptian well-being a host of unnecessary and often deleterious luxuries, not least of which was the swarm of foreign experts and consultants with their make-work feasibility studies.

The growth fetish of the technocratic view, in Amin's judgment, produced distortions in both the constitution and the distribution of the national product. Amin noted that as a result of the Western emphasis on growth, the value of social justice had a secondary status in overall social strategies; economic justice became an issue only to the degree that severe social imbalance affected production or even threatened to disrupt it completely by leading to social unrest. Social justice, was "not considered as an end that deserved attention in itself."

Amin demonstrated that a strategy for increasing well-being and not simply growth might require radically different production and distribution decisions. From a growth perspective, a large new building in the capital made the same contribution to national product as ten small ones scattered on outlying villages. In his view, an overbuilt and desperately overcrowded Cairo might well be spared yet another construction site, while ten neglected villages might well experience a glimmer of hope from the sight of a new building.

Amin accepted with equanimity the possible adverse effect of such a policy on the growth rate. He laid out the figures, with their radical implications, with the sparest of commentary. "According to some recent calculations," Amin reported, "5 percent of Egyptians receive 20 percent of national income, while 20 percent receive 5 percent." From these facts Amin concluded that policies that lowered the standard of living of the wealthiest 5 percent to half its present level could at the same time raise the standard of living for the poorest 20 percent to three times its present level. Such a policy would require a radical shift, including a geographic shift, of the prevailing patterns of production. Amin did not concede the usual objection made, that such a distribution pattern would mean a drop in production. But even if it did, "we could still be willing to accept the lowering of the growth rate in return for achieving a more rational pattern of production distribution."

Amin went beyond the debate over production and distribution to raise more fundamental questions. He reasoned that there was a more basic problem with the growth notion of development. Human happiness, in his view, was at least as often a result of qualitative as of quantitative factors. The usual calculations of national product regrettably ignored these subjective factors. Moreover, Amin made the point that significant qualitative changes were within grasp. "There are means of increasing prosperity or welfare that may not appear at all in the form of an increased growth rate." He cited the need for improvement in the intellectual content in the public schools and in the cultural content of public radio and television programs. Such progress required neither more school buildings nor more transmitters.

Amin's position on growth implied a theoretical reassessment of the assumed content of the notion of human welfare. He exposed as a debatable value assumption the development assumption that the material component loomed largest in any such calculation. Amin insisted on taking "the values and habits of our society," rather than the experience of the West, as the starting point for an Egyptian notion of progress. Economic welfare was not the same thing as human welfare: the former was material and measurable, while the latter was "happiness whatever its cause." The cause of Egyptian happiness, Amin reasoned, might well be such nonmaterial satisfactions as the pleasure of a national political will exercised with a minimum of external constraints or a vibrant cultural life that remained resistant to the incursions of the West's "universal" modern culture because it expressed inherited traditions.

Amin challenged even the assumed necessity to limit Egypt's population. Children was a source of great joy in Egyptian life, a joy that did not register in the usual welfare calculations. "The superficial plausibility" of the call to birth control stemmed from the arid logical truth "that every increase in income if accompanied by an equal increase in population would leave prosperity at the same level." Amin did not challenge the logic but did question its relationship to human happiness. Amin pointed out that this logic rested on the debatable assumption that prosperity could be measured meaningfully by average income. There were, he argued, better possibilities. The joy of having a child might in fact outweigh the happiness of having greater spending power. Or, more pointedly, the uses to which an additional income was put might well involve the satisfaction of artificially stimulated and corrupted "needs." According to Amin, such needs created dependencies that limited rather than enhanced human freedom.

Amin questioned the wisdom of blind imitation of the Western patterns of population control, assumed to be "the solution closest to wisdom." For Amin, "there is no proof that the small family in the West turned into a happy family because of its small size, except by the measure of its material standard of life." Egyptian advocates of birth control on the Western model "don't consider the disadvantages of the dreadful loneliness of the aged [in the West] and their vulnerable dependence on the state to provide them with a decent life when they can no longer work."

Through his rich historical analysis, Amin achieved the psychological distance from the West necessary for such a critical stance. He considered the traditional values of Egyptians more humane and just than the narrow economic values of the Western technocratic orientation. Amin therefore questioned why Egyptian intellectuals, especially in the seventies, proved so susceptible to the pull of the technocratic ethos and its Western definition of social welfare. Sadat's official backing of the technocratic vision, particularly as embodied in the projects of Osman Ahmed Osman, provided part of the explanation. He added that the technocratic view naturally thrived in a climate of widespread imitation of the West. Amin saw the seventies as "the period in which surrender to the foreigners reached the highest point . . . during the Sadat years, praise of Western technology and the Western way of life in official declarations and cultural life in general along with denigration of Arab countries was widespread."

Amin knew that intellectuals' receptiveness to the Westernizing vision of the Sadat era must be explained by more than just pressure and propagandizing from above. He pointed to a loss of cultural self-assuredness among Egyptians that greatly increased their vulnerability. Amin contrasted this cultural surrender to the West with the psychological autonomy of Egyptian intellectuals in the thirties and forties. In those years the major issue was not economic development on the Western model but rather the attainment of a national renaissance that authentically expressed Egypt's rich cultural legacy. With irony, one of Egypt's most distinguished professional economists noted that in those years the number of Egyptian economists could be counted on one hand. Then, Amin wrote, the best students and those who cared most for their country studied the arts and law. The study of economics was "taught as a minor subject necessary to an understanding of general issues but never exerting a monopoly over them." Amin regretted the loss of this balanced view of economics both as an academic discipline and as a force in social life. He took that loss as a sign of the abandonment of the quest for an original Egyptian response to the broad problem of human happiness under modern conditions. In the thirties and forties, "the Egyptian intellectual . . . had more confidence in himself than he has now, at least in regard to his attitude toward Western civilization." In those years Egyptian nationalists were steeled by a deep-rooted belief in the worth of Egypt's cultural legacy and the possibilities it offered for the future: "There was still hope for the Egyptian, the Arab, or the Muslim to create something new, something that was not a copy of an original in the West."

Amin extended his intellectual challenge to an aggressive criticism not only of Sadat's institutions and public policies but also of the Nasser years. Dissociating himself from the Westernizing development orientation in its socialist and liberal forms, Amin called into question the entire Free Officer political experience. In some respects, he made Nasserism almost as much a target as Sadatism.

Amin saw the post-1952 period as a whole for reasons that extended beyond the authoritarianism of a regime based ultimately on the military and police. Amin considered the crucial continuities to be broadly cultural. Under both Nasser and Sadat, the regime took the proper ends of political life to be economic development. The political elite explained shortcomings, whether of democracy or social equality, as necessary costs for an effective development strategy. Both Nasser and Sadat quite explicitly accepted the international civilization of the West as the highest expression of contemporary human achievement. Each ruler screened that judgment, Nasser with his talk of Arab socialism and Sadat with his commitment to Egyptian "village" values. As Amin saw it, however, neither Nasser nor Sadat generated an independent cultural project for Egypt.

This insistence on Egyptian civilizational alternatives defined Amin's radicalism; it explained why, for all the influence of Marxist economic insights on his work, he remained distanced from the traditional left. Amin believed that traditional forms of colonial exploitation of labor and raw materials, emphasized by the left, had in fact lost much of their importance in the modern period. Amin emphasized exploitation in consumption instead. Dominant global powers now looked to underdeveloped countries such as Egypt as markets for Western goods, particularly consumer goods. Amin argued that Marxism, with its overriding emphasis on the production process rather than on distribution and consumption, had underestimated this shift. Amin contended that the traditional left used categories of economic rationality and, in key respects, shared the growth fetish of the ruling elite.

Amin applied the historical and philosophical power of his critique to experiences that touched people's lives directly. He dissected small and seemingly innocent incidents to reveal the hidden workings of dominant power arrangements. In doing so, he captured the meaning of complex events that might otherwise elude the mass audience.

In early March 1983 a ten-story apartment building collapsed in a Cairo suburb. Building collapses occurred frequently in Cairo, with its terrible overcrowding and deteriorating housing stock. This time, however, the number of deaths, the luxury character of the building, and the reputations of several of the victims attracted the attention of the mass media. A flood of stories from the legal, architectural, economic, and social points of view appeared in the popular press. Amin used that incident and the popular fascination with it to convey the essence of his complex analysis of the transformations that took place during the Sadat years. By the early spring of 1983, however, the *Economic Ahram* was no longer able to accept the bold work of such critics as Amin; thus, the most effective popularization of Amin's theoretical insights was confined to the narrower audience of the opposition press.[39]

Amin's short article, "All Those Falling Buildings," appeared in *The Masses* (*al-Ahaly*) on March 16, 1983. For Amin, the building collapse was a telling example of "what has happened in our society since the implementation of the great 'Open Door' policy." In Amin's view, this particular incident was reported in the press because of its character as an accident or a crime. As such, it escaped "the strict censorship by political authorities to which political statements and news are subject." Political facts, usually suppressed, slipped through the censor's net be-

cause they appeared as part of criminal investigations or even in obitu-
aries. "It is hard," wrote Amin, "for the chief editor to make additions
or deletions to such news of this building or its owner or its residents.
It is also difficult for newspapers to ignore such an awful event." In a
small event, truthfully portrayed, large things have their reflection. "The
reader," Amin writes, "gets an amount of information that throws light
on the nature of the society in which we live today in a way that the most
accurate and comprehensive social and statistical studies might not be
able to do."

The basic facts behind the collapse of the building read like the
terrible underside of the Horatio Alger stories popularized by the example of Osman Ahmed Osman. The owner of the million-dollar building began his career as an unskilled construction worker. The structure,
legally licensed for six floors, was expanded without permit to ten, resulting in an unresolved lawsuit in 1979. Each floor of the building
contained two apartments that sold for L.E. 50,000 each. An inferior
grade of cement used for the walls did not hold when the owner removed
some support pillars to make room for a new store that he planned to
open in the basement, and the structure collapsed.

In the context of death and destruction, Amin had only to raise
pointed questions to facilitate the unlearning of the dominant definitions
of success in the Sadat years: "What kind of society is this whose economic system allows an unskilled laborer to become a millionaire in such
a way? . . . What kind of tax policy allows such wealth to accumulate for
one person in a poor country? . . . What kind of society is this where
greed and haste to make money reach such an extent?" To all these
questions, Amin offered answers to be found in the rubble of an apparently solid and beautiful structure that collapsed without even the warning of a falling ceiling or a cracking wall. "In this way," wrote Amin, "the
affair reminds one of the Open Door society as a whole. It is, likewise,
a paper house, a commodity that fascinates the eye and attracts the heart
but fails to cool one's thirst or fill one's stomach." Amin observed that
an honest construction worker by his own physical and intellectual effort
would have to save his entire wage, neither eating nor drinking from it,
for at least 500 years to own such a building. "The same applies to the
resources that have made the Open Door society possible. They don't
come from the physical or mental effort of the people. Rather, they
derive from selling material and nonmaterial assets, whether this takes
the form of exporting nonrenewable raw materials or serving foreigners
inside the country or abroad."

Even the profile of the occupants of the building who lost their apartments, and in some cases their lives, had a story to tell. Of the twenty apartments, only eight were occupied at the time of the collapse—three by the owner and family members, and five by foreigners, a Hungarian, an Arab from the Emirates, a Sudanese, a Palestinian, and a Saudi. "This distribution of apartments," Amin observed, "is not very different from that of the new distribution of wealth in Egypt; it is the contractors, or rather middle-men in general, and foreigners who benefit from the new wealth." As for the vacant units, "they were waiting for the arrival of a new tourist or the appearance of a new contractor."

Amin concluded with a brief narrative that showed how the best elements of Egyptian society had been victimized by the profiteers of the seventies. In a small villa next to the apartment house lived an undersecretary of state and his wife and family. His limited resources, Amin reported, allowed him neither to add floors to his villa nor to challenge his neighbor in the courts for having done so illegally. Instead, he stayed in his house and educated his two daughters. One became a teacher at the faculty of languages and the other graduated a physician. All three of them were killed when the collapsing building struck their home. From the household only the mother was saved. She lay in the hospital, quoting a Koranic verse referring to the pre-Islamic practice of female infanticide. She wondered what to say, as the verse went, "when a buried daughter asked for what crime she was killed." Amin used this tragic vignette to illustrate the "powerlessness" of honest neighbors "facing the Open Door society."

The closure of the pages of the *Economic Ahram* to Amin's penetrating criticism was precipitated chiefly by the journal's treatment of Egypt's relationship with Israel. When Israel invaded Lebanon in June 1982, the Egyptian regime acted to restrain public outcry and demonstrations. The anger erupted nevertheless in a variety of public forums, including the *Economic Ahram,* which launched a campaign in support of the Lebanese and Palestinian peoples. Its issue of June 14, 1982, carried the Palestinian flag on its cover, and contained an article by 'Azim demanding the boycott of Israel. The Israelis protested to the Ministry of Foreign Affairs and thereafter regularly lodged protests against the journal.[40] The coverage of the Lebanon invasion, later reports indicated, contributed in a major way to the subsequent removal of Lutfy Abdul 'Azim from the editorship.

'Azim lent his voice to the harshest denunciations of Israel to appear in the press. He commented that the *Economic Ahram* from the outset had urged realism and caution on those Egyptians who were "overoptimistic and who believed the Israelis had sincere peace intentions." The Israeli invasion of Lebanon made the intentions of the Jewish state clear for all to see. With heavy irony, 'Azim commented "that Menachem Begin volunteered the largest contribution to our mission; this brazen and criminal act by this Menachem and his band of bloodletters is the biggest service to the Arab cause."[41]

As reports of civilian casualties in Lebanon mounted, 'Azim's rage spilled over in a September editorial, "Arabs and Jews—Who Exterminates Whom?" He argued that Israel's behavior in Lebanon and the overwhelming support it received from Jews around the world removed all doubts about the hostile character and intentions of the Jewish state, indeed of Jews everywhere, toward Arabs. The scope of the Israeli campaign also indicated the threat posed to Egypt; in 'Azim's view, the problem was not a Palestinian cause or a Lebanese cause, but rather "a destructive war launched against the whole Arab world." To meet this danger, Egyptians must cease differentiating between Israelis and Jews and abandon the illusion that Jews wanted peace with Arabs:

> Let us stop this nonsense and call things by their true names. The first thing that needs correction is the alleged necessity to differentiate between Jews and Israelis. I don't know the reasons for this differentiation if the Jews themselves reject it. The Jew is a Jew. He hasn't changed for thousands of years: his meanness, baseness, shrewdness, carelessness of all values, and the ability to suck human blood for very little money. The Jew of the merchant of Venice doesn't differ from the slaughter of Deir Yassin or the Palestinian camps. They are all identical models in human baseness. Let us, then, forget about this differentiation and speak about the Jews. The second thing is the belief of some that the Jews wish to leave peacefully with the Arabs. This is the greatest lie.

'Azim openly expressed the fears of Israeli military power that lay behind this anti-Semitic language: "God only knows what we will be asking in the future. Maybe we will be begging the United States to intervene to force the Israeli forces to end their siege of Mecca during pilgrimage season, so that the weak Muslims can carry out their pilgrimage. Maybe we will be begging for the withdrawal of Israeli forces from Giza governorate and occupation only of Cairo proper, or increasing the number of international observers at the Street of the Pyramids to protect our monuments from destruction."

'Azim justified his emotionalism by the destructive and bloody character of Israeli fighting in Lebanon: "I am not mocking, for this is not the right time to do so. Had somebody written ten years ago that Israel was trying to annex Lebanon, that its tanks would stay in Beirut International Airport, attack al-Hamra Street [an elegant shopping street in downtown Beirut], and enter Palestinian camps to tear their residents to pieces, people would have mocked him and accused him of being crazy."[42]

'Azim suggested that Israel's plan for a complete destructive war against the Arab nation might have been "one of Israel's motives" for signing the peace treaty with Egypt:

> Is there a way of achieving the destruction of the Arabs better than tearing the Arab nation to pieces, starting with Lebanon at a time when the Israeli flag is raised in Cairo? Surely, giving back the Sinai was a cheap price to pay for the success of this aim. . . . I hope that our naiveness will not lead us to consider Egypt exempt from this bloody Israeli plan. The battle is a battle of life or death between two parties: the first party is the Arabs in their various countries, and the other party is the Jews. There is no difference between the destructive gangs ruling Israel and the Jewish lobby in the rest of the world. This is a battle centering on one question: who will kill and who will be killed?

'Azim concluded:

> As for me—and I don't think I am an exception—I prefer to be a killer rather than be killed. It is illogical to ask me to wait till the Israeli dogs attack me and my wife and children. Is this anti-Semitism? Let me say, frankly, that it is. However, I would like to add that I am not an enemy of the Semites more than the Jews themselves are. We, the Arabs, are also Semites like the Jews, and the Jewish plan is the greatest anti-Semitic plan. The fact is that they are enemies of Arab Semites and we are enemies of Jewish Semites.

Aware that his language had exceeded the bounds of acceptable discourse in Egyptian civil society, 'Azim apologized a second time:

> I did my best . . . not to be emotional, but I don't think I succeeded. All I wanted to get at is one thing I believe in very strongly and I want every Arab to believe the same: that is, that the battle between the Arabs and Jews is a bitter, destructive battle. This makes me warn the dreamers who want to build in Sinai. I assure them that the best Israel could wish for is for us to invest our limited resources in constructing Sinai in order to destroy it one day and make us more crippled. I advise the Arabs not to be deceived by the appearance of protests in and outside Israel. This is a play with well-divided roles. The only disagreement among the Jews is whether or not it is better to warn the victim before killing them. Shedding the

blood of all Arabs, and not only the Palestinians, is something agreed upon by all Jews. As for the weak and the humiliated, the most they can hope for from the world is pity, which is a human mask for contempt.

Ahmed Hamroush, a prominent intellectual of the left, responded to 'Azim's editorial in the next issue of the *Economic Ahram*. The article, he wrote, "makes me put up a red light and say, stop, the road you're treading is too thorny and dangerous." Hamroush granted the correctness of 'Azim's assumptions that "the majority of Jews outside Israel help Jews inside it by offering their financial aid and political support." However, the fact of this support did not warrant dropping the distinction between Jews and Israelis: "Otherwise, we would be eliminating a number of important factors. Among them are Jews who prefer to live with the peoples among whom they were raised instead of going to Israel, the Jews who do not believe in expansionist Zionism and do not see in Israel's existence as a racist state a solution of their problems, as well as some Jews outside Israel who oppose the Israeli government's belligerent policies."

On strategic grounds as well, Hamroush reasoned that it was not good politics to see the enemy as one block or entity: "Let us supply this to ourselves; when we talk about Arabs, which Arabs do we mean: the millionaires who squander money, or intellectuals who are torn by the tragedy of the nation, or workers who struggle for a subsistence life— those who are in power or those suffering under regimes and are deprived of human rights?" Hamroush agreed with the denunciation of the U.S.-backed Israeli action, but argued that the conclusions 'Azim reached were wrong because they "bring to ourselves the charge of anti-Semitism, while deep inside we don't feel this way and in our history we've never had a strand of racist discrimination against Jews or any others."[43]

Lutfy Abdul 'Azim's editorial, expressing the anger triggered in Egypt by the invasion of Lebanon, and Ahmed Hamroush's pointed response turned the pages of the *Economic Ahram* into a forum for the vigorous rethinking of Egypt's relationship with Israel. A broad range of opinion found expression. Some writers supported 'Azim's contention that Jews and Arabs were locked in deadly combat, but they emphasized "our Islamic religious beliefs" rather than the national basis of conflict. From their perspective, only an Egypt that reinvigorated the Islamic roots could hope to triumph.[44] Others reasoned that only by a people's war, patterned on the Algerian struggle, could the Arabs hope to defeat a Jewish state that was in essence a Western colonial society rather than a genuine Middle Eastern nation.[45]

These calls for a renewal of confrontation, whether of Islamic or leftist inspiration, drew a sharply critical response from writers who condemned their lack of seriousness. The implications that the Israelis were not a genuine national entity, triggered by 'Azim's suggestion that no distinction be made between Israelis and Jews, drew the sharpest rebuttal. Writers questioned the scientific basis of the allegation that Israel existed as a settler project rather than as a genuine national entity. Taher Abdul Hakim, for example, questioned the soundness of judgments "that do not depend on any scientific study of the social, cultural, and historical components of Jewish communities around the world."[46] After Camp David and the peace treaty with Israel, a people's war was no longer feasible. Instead, Egypt should support a "cold peace" with Israel that resisted a full normalization: "Fighting normalization is the war for which all our potentials should be mobilized in order to protect our [independent national] will and our cultural and historical identity from subjugation by the enemy. This is a popular war, too ... raising idealistic slogans that can't be acted on under present conditions reflects either an inability to identify the urgent tasks that are dictated for us by our reality or an escape from these tasks."

In line with his own definition of the real tasks confronting Egyptians in the wake of the display of Israeli power in Lebanon, Hakim warned against the internal intelligence danger posed by the peace with Israel:

> The enemy, referring to Israel and the United States, has called up its research centers, strategic thinkers, economists, and sociologists to prepare studies and projects for transforming the region to suite Israel's hegemony in all fields. It has sought the help of many researchers to conduct studies on our people, their traditions, customs, aspirations, and problems in order to identify our weak points and attack us from them. Unfortunately, several of our Egyptian researchers have joined in this project under the cover of working for American research centers and institutions. The result is that now we are having surveys done on Egypt in the fields of sociology, anthropology, economics, culture, religion, etc.

To illustrate the negative slant of much of this work, Hakim cited economic studies that called for integration of the Egyptian and Israeli economies, warning that such ideas could create an Egyptian dependency. He also cited a study by an ex-minister of the Israeli Foreign Ministry and distributed by the World Zionist Organization that argued that "dividing Egypt into separate geographic units" should be the aim of Israel on its Western borders in the eighties, specifically including the idea of a Coptic state in Upper Egypt. The author concluded:

> These strategic intentions should alarm all Egyptians at the popular and official levels, whether they be rightists or leftists, religious or secularists, Muslims or Christians. The target here is the integrity of Egypt as a social, political, economic, and cultural entity that has been unified for thousands of years. . . . This should make us realize the dangerous role played by that Israeli Academic Center in Cairo. We should also recognize the dangers of those American and Egyptian researchers who conduct surveys on all aspects of our life. Our interior is wide open for anyone to collect data and information in order to destroy us. Unfortunately, our enemy does not dream, nor does he base his plans on wishes.

The controversy generated by the attacks on the Sadat peace with Israel exceeded the bounds of regime tolerance. Abruptly, the "Platforms of Thought" column disappeared; the national dialogue in the pages of the *Economic Ahram* ceased; 'Azim was removed as editor-in-chief.

The editorial commentary and special features of the *Economic Ahram* presented definitions of the economic and political realities of Egypt that contested every important aspect of the official history, including its major foreign policy reorientations. When the government removed Lutfy Abdul 'Azim, the journal retreated into its technical identity: the *Economic Ahram*'s record in the seventies remained, however, as an authentic Egyptian experience of a free press.

Galal Amin wrote the eulogy of the *Economic Ahram*'s experiment in press freedom under Lutfy Abdul 'Azim, calling the removal of the editor-in-chief and the suppression of the journal's critical voice a "tragedy."[47] His commentary opened with an evocation of the strong feelings of optimism in the early months of Mubarak's presidency: "I do not exaggerate if I claim that the feeling was first and best manifested in the change that appeared in *Economic Ahram* during Mubarak's first months of rule. The journal started for the first time, when it called "platforms of thought," a section in which writers, most of whom were independents [nonparty members], were invited to express their views on Egypt's future in a free way not enjoyed in Egypt for a period of about thirty years."

Amin noted, in particular, that the *Economic Ahram* "expressed the Egyptian people's consciousness in a manner not expressed by any other journal so strongly." Although the Israeli embassy protested the tone of the journal's response, "the Egyptian Ministry of Foreign Affairs, according to what we heard, rejected the protest, feeling that the *Economic Ahram* said nothing at variance with public opinion throughout the world." According to Amin, the journal redeemed the honor of the press by its protests of Israeli actions.

The *Economic Ahram* apparently angered other powerful forces when it raised the issue of scientific research done by Egyptians with foreign financing. Although Amin noted that a variety of points of view were aired on the issue, "It seems that the frankness with which it dealt with the subject annoyed some of these financing agencies; Dr. Lutfy Abdul 'Azim, the editor-in-chief, was subjected to reprimands and threats from some officials in the Higher Press Council, and the series of articles on the issue stopped, although the journal continued to pursue its nationalist line for a few more months." Amin noted the irony that at the very time that the editor-in-chief was being scolded by press officials, the same officials, when faced with a criticism relating to the democratic experiment in Egypt, would say proudly, "Don't you see the freedom enjoyed by the *Economic Ahram?*"

Amin reported that readers of the journal had been shocked by the sudden and complete change in its character and attitude: "It suffered ideological thinness and idiocy of feeling," while presenting views not much different from those in the official press. "Nationalist writers, seeing their articles rejected one after the other, stopped writing for it; some stopped writing completely and had a growing feeling of frustration and wondered about the meaning of this new democracy they were optimistic about two years ago."

Amin concluded his commentary with an appeal to President Mubarak "to intervene personally in the matter and to settle it, in a way that resolves the issue of the freedom of the press in Egypt. Does he want thought to be confined and imprisoned in the opposition papers, to have the papers described as 'national' monopolized by colorless, hack writers, and to have *al-Ahram* devoid of any thought except the column written by Ahmed Bahaeddine? Or does he want all flowers to bloom and political culture in Egypt to witness real flowering during his rule?"

Lutfy Abdul 'Azim did not return to the editorship. The *Economic Ahram* survived as a journal of specialized economic commentary with a history of having been much more.

8

Return to the Future:
The Muslim Brothers

I have always believed that no matter how abstract our theories may sound or
how consistent our arguments appear, there are incidents and stories behind
them which, at least for ourselves, contain as in a nutshell the full meaning of
whatever we have to say. Thought itself . . . arises out of the actuality of
incident, and incidents of living experience must remain its guideposts by
which it takes its bearing if it is not to lose itself . . . The only gains one might
legitimately expect from this most mysterious of human activities are neither
definitions nor theories, but rather the slow, plodding discovery and, perhaps,
the mapping survey of the region which some incident had completely illuminated for a fleeting moment.

—*Hannah Arendt*

When Omar Telmesany arrived, he attempted to sit in the back of the
room crowded with government representatives, the national press, and
Muslim notables. An official approached Telmesany, however, and insisted that he take a place in the front row, facing the president and the
high-level government personnel who accompanied him. The occasion
was a meeting in Ismailia between President Anwar Sadat and the leaders of Islamic organizations. As titular head of the movement, a survivor
of seventeen years in prison, and editor of the Islamic journal *The Call,*
(*al-Da'wa*),[1] Telmesany personified the Muslim Brotherhood, the largest
and most influential Islamic group in Egyptian public life. Singled out
from the other Muslim dignitaries present, Telmesany understood why
Sadat's confidant, Mansur Hassan, had insisted that he attend this meeting: Sadat intended to deliver a personal warning to the Muslim Brothers
before the national press.[2]

In 1979 Sadat held a series of public meetings with the representatives of important corporate bodies, such as the syndicates of the
lawyers, judges, and the press. On each occasion, the president reaffirmed his hope of containing the political energies released by his liberalization within acceptable levels by working out "codes of conduct"

243

between the various powerful public bodies and his regime.[3] Within this scheme of controlled liberalization, the government gave the Muslim Brothers a privileged place. To counter the perceived threat from the left, the official formula allowed exceptional scope to the religious right for a return to active politics in the interstices of these regulated structures. The arrangement worked well for the regime through the mid-seventies. At that point, however, the Islamic current's disillusionment with government policies, above all with the opening to Israel, created strains. After Sadat's trip to Jerusalem in 1977, the Islamic press, under Telmesany's leadership, launched a pointed criticism of what it saw as the dangerous humiliations that the Israeli interpretation of the Camp David peace process had inflicted on Egypt. Stung by this domestic criticism, Sadat in 1979 decided to rein in the Muslim groups.

Speaking directly to Telmesany at the meeting in Ismailia, Sadat warned the Brothers against treason. For months the official media had been accusing the Muslim Brothers of plotting to undermine the regime.[4] The president declared that he would not "tolerate those who try to tamper with the high interests of the state under the guise of religion." Religion "must not be mingled with politics." The president condemned the Brothers for corrupting young people with "misleading articles in *The Call*" that criticized the key aspects of government policy, above all the accommodation with Israel. Pointedly, Sadat reminded Telmesany that his government allowed publication of the journal, even though it did not legally authorize the Muslim Brothers' organization. In Sadat's view, such exceptional privileges carried responsibilities: "Muslim Brothers are now free people in a respectable community. Their behavior should be in line with Egypt's interests."[5]

Telmesany requested permission to respond to the charges. "If anyone else had said what you said I would have come to you to complain," he began, "but I can only raise my complaint against you to God, who is the wisest of rulers."[6] Telmesany briefly stated the Brothers' key strategic goal of establishing an Islamic social order on the basis of Islamic law, arguing that their "mission" for the seventies served all Egyptians: "You hear from *The Call*," said Telmesany, "only demands that are the demands of the whole nation. We have no private interests." In keeping with the Brothers' belief that Egypt must return to Islamic law, Telmesany argued that the solution to Egypt's crisis required that "God's Law must be applied. It is only when you do this that the masses will be with you."[7]

Telmesany answered the specific charge of conspiracy with a story illustrating his caution and loyalty. On June 12, 1979, the British embassy had asked him to meet with a representative of the Foreign Ministry. Telmesany had replied that he would attend only if the meeting was called to discuss press matters: "If you want to ask political questions, go to the president of the republic." Telmesany said that a copy of this response to the British overture was in the files of the Ministry of Interior. He added that he just as scrupulously avoided all invitations from communist and other radical groups to attend their meetings.

Telmesany tempered his rebuttal by thanking Sadat for "opening the jails and releasing prisoners" when he became president. Upon his own release from prison in 1971, Telmesany had gone directly to Abdin Palace to express his gratitude. "My Islamic upbringing and education," concluded the spokesman for the Muslim Brothers, "do not allow me to conspire against you."[8]

Sadat and the titular head of the Brotherhood met on one other very different occasion not long after the Ismailia conference, in Sadat's secluded resthouse just outside Cairo. This private meeting went unreported in the national press. According to Islamic press reports of the meeting, published only after Sadat's assassination, the president offered to broaden his truce with the Brothers. "He received me very hospitably," noted Telmesany, "and flattered me with words my modesty prevents me from repeating." The president offered to correct the anomalous legal status of the Brotherhood by registering the organization with the Ministry of Social Affairs. In addition, Sadat offered to appoint Telmesany as the representative of the Brotherhood to the government Shura Council. In return, he would expect the Brothers to moderate their criticism of his regime.[9]

Once again, Telmesany resisted the president's overtures. Registration with the ministry would accomplish little, in Telmesany's view, because the ministry would "then have the right to dissolve the society at any time, to change its board of directors, and to submit it to administrative, technical, and financial supervision." The Brothers, he indicated, preferred the ambiguity of a semilegal existence to dependence on government sanction. Similarly, Telmesany declined the Shura Council appointment because "when I am an appointed rather than an elected member, I am in debt to the one who appointed me, a situation that makes me obligated not to clash with him."[10]

To his followers, Telmesany explained the meaning of these encounters with the regime by appealing to the Brothers' self-understanding of the history they were making. His interpretation was as important as the meetings themselves for the collective history of the Brothers. Telmesany based his explanation on the Muslim Brothers' self-image as actors in an Islamic movement with roots not only in Egypt but also in the comprehensive story of Islam.[11] Thus, in the Islamic press Telmesany first rationalized his meetings with Sadat by relating them to the specific political situation in Egypt. He then went on to show how these entanglements with power in one Islamic country also advanced Islam's design for human life on the universal plane.

In the first instance, Telmesany made sense of his meetings with Sadat by placing them in the context of the Muslim Brothers' efforts to achieve the Islamic social ideal in Egypt's special circumstances of time, place, and human need.[12] In the seventies, writers for *The Call* advanced the Brotherhood's alternative as a practical strategy to realize the goal of a new Islamic order in Egypt and throughout the world.

Through the Islamic press, the Muslim Brother leadership called on the followers to make maximum use of the peaceful means the liberalization of the Sadat regime made available to them, to work for an Islamic society. The reconciliation of the mainstream Islamic current and the regime continued under Sadat until 1977, when it was strained by Sadat's peace with Israel. Even in the difficult years 1977–1981, however, the Brothers strived to avoid open conflict with the government. During this final period of Sadat's rule radical Islamic groups such as the Jihad, the Takfir W'al Hijra, and Shebab al-Muhammad spearheaded active opposition to the state through radicalized student unions, direct and at times spectacular militant actions, and participation in sectarian strife. The actions of the radicals culminated in the murder of the president and the uprising of Islamic militants in Assiut in 1981. State repression eroded the power of the militants, while the centrist Brothers gathered strength.[13]

The strategic decisions of the Brothers' leadership in the seventies for limited cooperation with the regime laid the intellectual and practical foundations for the legal expansion in the eighties into nearly all aspects of public life. Particularly after Sadat's assassination, the Brothers reaped handsome rewards for their decision to move toward acceptance of democratic rules. They participated in national elections in shifting alliances with major opposition parties, played a leading role in the doctors' and the engineers' syndicates, achieved a substantial presence in parliament, and created an economic base of Islamic companies and banks.[14] Thus, while the eyes of the outside world focused on the Islamic militants and radicals with their violent means, the Muslim Brother centrists achieved the greatest successes for the Islamic current since the forties by accepting the concept of working through government.[15] In the Sadat years they began the tactical elaboration of an approach that transformed the face of civil society in the eighties.[16]

A key element in laying the groundwork for the Brotherhood's early and formative cooperation with the state was the Sadat regime's effort to oppose Nasserism, which the Brothers saw as the strongest political force opposing their own movement, and thus as the greatest obstacle to the attainment of an Islamic society. During this same period, the Brothers also sought to prevent the Islamic radicals from contesting their leadership of the Islamic current and from precipitating a premature confrontation with the regime.[17] To achieve these broader aims, the Brothers supported the regime's campaigns to contain the members of the radical Islamic fringe. Underlying both of these partisan maneuvers was the struggle to live in conformity with the Islamic social ideal in the face of hostile internal and external pressures. In the context of Sadat's Egypt, these pressures took the specific form of the multifaceted threat that Westernization posed to the Islamic heritage of Egypt. By sustained and forceful criticism, they aimed to show the regime's limitations in meeting the civilizational challenge to Islam while taking advantage of any opportunities it afforded to build the strength of their movement.

Telmesany believed that an extended truce with the Sadat regime made the seventies a time of renewal for the Brothers. Sadat released many of the Brothers from prison and rehabilitated them personally and professionally.[18] Although many critics, especially those on the left, charged that the Brothers made an explicit political deal as the price for their freedom,[19] Telmesany argued that throughout the seventies Sadat "never asked for anything *in particular*" in return for releasing the Brothers. Telmesany cited his own experience to demonstrate that no explicit deals had been made; he claimed that he had not met with Sadat or his representatives before his release from prison. As evidence that the Brothers did not have any particular arrangements, Telmesany cited the Ismailia confrontation. "We Brothers were viciously attacked," he commented. "If there had been any contacts between us or cooperation with the Sadat government, we would not have been attacked in this manner."[20]

To appreciate the full meaning of his meetings with Sadat, Telmesany urged his readers to recognize the "threats and temptations of power" that confronted the struggle for Islam.[21] Although he sought to counter charges that the Brothers collaborated with the Sadat regime,

Telmesany did not claim political innocence. In fact, he openly acknowledged the Brothers' growing implication in regime politics because he wanted his supporters to understand the political and moral complexities of the Brotherhood's involvements with the government.[22] Telmesany's contrasting accounts of the two meetings showed that the Sadat policy was a carrot-and-stick operation. The Brothers resisted both. This was neither defiance nor an acceptance of state authority; in both cases, Telmesany's objective and his desired relationship with the state remained the same. According to Telmesany's reading, the two meetings clarified this relationship to power. The first meeting, as Telmesany interpreted it, showed that the regime was not an ally, but that it could not be defied openly; the second meeting showed that the regime needed the Brothers' help, but that the Brotherhood could not become too close to the government. Thus, Telmesany's readings of the two meetings provided a working definition for the Brothers of their complex and uncertain—but ultimately extremely fruitful—relationship with state power.

In the seventies the leaders of the Muslim Brotherhood realized that both the regime and their own organization had distinct but powerful reasons to act in parallel fashion against the Nasserist left. The Brothers believed that as long as Sadat saw the left as the main challenge to his power, he would seek a tactical alliance with them to control that threat. In 1971, Sadat claimed to have defeated a challenge from a procommunist coalition of party and internal security officials inherited from Nasser. The specter of a Nasserist left hostile to Sadat's rule rose again in 1972 and 1973 when demonstrating students and workers shouted Nasserist slogans. The Brothers judged that the regime recognized the value of their support in the face of such challenges. Only their organization, with its strong ties to the urban middle and lower-middle class, could act as a political counterweight to the radical students and workers who had fallen under the influence of the left.[23]

The Muslim Brothers had their own reasons for assisting in the containment of the Nasserist left. In the fifties and the sixties, thousands of Brothers had been brutalized in Nasser's military camps and jails.[24] In the seventies, the Islamic press, led by *The Call,* mounted an unrelenting attack on all aspects of the Nasser legacy, including Arabism, the industrialization drive, and the socialist measures.[25] Nasser's Arabism, the Brothers charged, contravened the universalism of Islam. Despite Egypt's place in the Arab world, they reasoned that the essential basis of community should be the spiritual one of Islam rather than the racial one of an Arab nation. The Brothers argued that the Nasserist era had weakened Islam in Egypt. Some Brothers went so far as to celebrate the loss of the war in 1967 because the defeat by Israel revealed the corruption of an atheistic regime and weakened the power of the official tormentors of true Muslims.[26]

Nasser's industrialization effort had been flawed, the Brothers charged, by indiscriminate nationalizations and sequestrations that were motivated less by economic criteria than by "personal hatred and revenge." The private sector, services, and agriculture were all neglected, while state funds poured into large-scale projects that were often corrupt and badly conceived. Moreover, the public sector proved to be the breeding ground for a "new class whose wealth exceeded that of the pashas."[27] Telmesany summed up the Brothers' indictment of the Nasser years with the charge that "the era of Gamal Abdul Nasser was characterized by evil and wrongdoing." Telmesany argued that "the bad effects of nationalization and sequestration are still suffered by the Egyptian nation to this day. The communist economy brought us to these deadly crises from which everyone is trying to save the country."[28]

The joint attack on the Nasserist legacy proved to be the high point of agreement between the Sadat regime and the Brothers. Differences over foreign policy eventually strained the cooperation. Even before Sadat's 1977 trip to Jerusalem, however, the difficulties of collaboration were becoming apparent. In their attitudes and actions toward the Islamic university student groups, the Brothers clearly revealed their divergence from regime policies. In its first years the Sadat government fostered the Islamic student groups in order to break the hold of the left on university youth.[29] When the government attempted to curb the Islamic student movement, the Brotherhood leadership demonstrated its political realism by openly cooperating in disciplining the religious students. Telmesany, for example, frankly acknowledged assisting Nabawy Ismail, then minister of the interior. "Whenever anything happened," reported Telmesany, "he used to call and take my advice. The minister," Telmesany continued, "used to send me to some university faculties. When I spoke to the students, they responded to me . . . they accepted my arguments against violence, demonstrations, strikes, and sabotage."[30]

Despite their arguments against the more extreme student actions, the Brothers never went as far as the regime in criticizing the university groups. From the Brotherhood perspective, the Islamic groups' strong appeal to youth was potentially a great resource. To the degree that the religious students looked to the Brotherhood leadership, they provided the Muslim Brothers with a popular base in the student masses. The problem of control, however, was serious. Because the Brothers were not organized as a party, they found it difficult to incorporate the students into their society. The leadership also suspected that the regime deliberately encouraged the rise of militant groupings in order to fragment the Islamic trend and weaken the ability of the Muslim Brothers to assert leadership over it. Telmesany charged that "someone deliberately encouraged this ideology [of the radical groups] in order to undermine the Muslim Brotherhood." He alleged that one of the leaders of the Islamic groups received 150 feddans in Liberation Province to establish a community; the same person was also given an apartment in the populous quarter of Sayyida Zeinab from which to spread his ideas.[31] The Brothers responded to these government maneuvers by acting to contain but not crush the student groups. On the one hand, they did assist the regime in keeping the student activism within bounds. On the other, they chided the regime for treating the Islamic elements too harshly while unwisely sparing what they regarded as the much more dangerous activists on the left.[32]

Despite their pragmatic engagement in partisan politics, the Brothers were neither so opportunistic nor so malleable as Sadat judged. They were unable to accept the complete identification with the regime that Sadat asked for in his second meeting with Telmesany. They understood that the failure of Sadat's promise of peace and prosperity drove him to suggest replacement of implicit cooperation with an explicit understanding. The Brothers realized that Sadat was being hemmed in by external forces and that he hoped to save his position by leaning more heavily on them. They were unwilling to provide this degree of support. The role they could play was shaped more by their own distinctive history than by the immediate political opportunities open to them.

The Muslim Brothers' self-image as "sufferers for Islam" set limits that could not be transgressed. On social and national issues the Brothers stood for a practical program of national resistance and social reform.[33] They maintained that the Islamic trend in public life was the most authentic means by which Egyptians had historically sought renaissance and independence.[34] By their reading, the link between Islam and the contemporary movement for national community reached back to the early nineteenth century and the rule of Muhammad Aly, the founder of the last dynasty to rule Egypt. By the end of the nineteenth and the beginning of the twentieth century political Islam was eclipsed by Western secular nationalism. The floundering of the secular nationalists in the twenties and thirties, however, paved the way for the emergence of the Brotherhood as the most effective modern expression of national self-assertion. The Brothers first established themselves as a mass movement in the forties by responding effectively to the needs of large numbers of Egyptians who were affected adversely by the disruptions of the war and the British occupation. During the war years, the established political parties lost touch with the social and economic needs of the people. In contrast, the Muslim Brothers acted vigorously to realize a program of social reforms that addressed the needs of the poor. The Brothers' vision at that time overlapped with that of the left nationalists. They distinguished themselves, however, by their practical readiness to tackle social and national problems with an impressive network of mosques, educational institutions, hospitals, and clinics to meet the needs of the poor and the disaffected.

The Brothers acted with similar vigor against external threats to Egypt. When the government abrogated the Treaty of 1936, the Muslim Brothers took a leading role in the confrontation with the British in the canal zone. They earned even greater nationalist credit for their bold and decisive opposition to the Zionist movement in Palestine. The Brotherhood sounded the alarm about the colonizing thrust of Zionism, and they mobilized public support in Egypt for the Palestinian Arab strike of 1936–1939. When the strike collapsed, Muslim Brother activists collected funds and weapons to support the Arab military resistance.

When the first Arab-Israeli war broke out in 1948, Muslim Brother volunteers fought the Zionist forces even before the regular Arab armies entered Palestine. They also campaigned in Cairo for more volunteers to aid the Arab resistance. The Brothers played an especially heroic role in the celebrated battle of Faluja, where an outnumbered and encircled Egyptian force, in which Gamal Abdul Nasser served as a staff officer, refused to surrender. In that battle, the Brothers braved Israeli fire to run supplies to the trapped Egyptians. By such actions the Brothers earned the respect and the admiration of many Egyptian officers fighting in Palestine.

When the conspiracy of Free Officers erupted into the coup d'état of July 23, 1952, the Brothers actively supported the military uprising. When the army moved, the Brothers rallied support for the coup in the streets. The supportive relationship was signaled by the close personal ties of Sayyid Qutb, the most important ideological leader of the Brothers, with the new military rulers. In the fall of 1952, the Muslim Brothers issued a comprehensive statement of their desired objectives for the new order in Egypt. The document anticipated the most successful elements of the reform program that Egypt's military rulers implemented over the next decade; land reform, industrialization, and welfare measures were all part of the Brothers' program.[35] Initially, the military rulers welcomed this support. After the military seized power in Egypt, the new rulers erected a monument in the Palestine Cemetery listing Muslim Brother martyrs in Palestine.[36]

The Brothers' commitment to their beliefs, their willingness to fight for these beliefs against external enemies, and their ability to organize their supporters were the factors that made the Brothers successful in Palestine, drew the admiration of the Free Officers, and made them welcome supporters of the new regime. The personal ties between the two movements and the common goals of social and economic reform also drew the groups closer together. By the mid-fifties, however, the regime and the Brothers were locked in deadly combat. What turned them into bitter rivals?

From the Brothers' perspective, the answer was the very strength that initially attracted the Free Officers. The Brothers' commitment to Islam made them a threat to the secular, pan-Arab goals that the military rulers announced after taking power; the activist and aggressive nature of the Brothers' commitments posed a real threat to the officers; and the organizational skills of the Brothers provided the resources necessary to back up their threat. Thus, from the Brothers' point of view, the rivalry with the regime, and the subsequent repression, were the product of the government's fears of the Brothers' superior commitment, activism, and organizational strength. Throughout the fifties and sixties, the regime treated the Brotherhood as its most dangerous opponent. Major Muslim Brother thinkers and activists, including Sayyid Qutb, were assassinated or executed. Thousands of followers were held in political detention camps.[37]

Long years of repression undoubtedly weakened the organization of Muslim Brothers, but the spokesmen for an Islamic alternative survived the harsh repression with their social vision intact. Some of the Brothers were radicalized by the prison experience, and many moved to the fringes of the Islamic trend.[38] During the seventies, however, the mainstream Muslim Brotherhood reappeared in public life to reclaim its past, to express what it had learned from its ordeal, and to stake its claim to Egypt's future. The Brothers renewed their call for a new Islamic order. Although many of the old slogans and phrases returned, there was a decidedly different emphasis. From their jailers, the Brothers had learned some essential lessons. They began to understand, for example, that Islam had dangerous internal as well as external enemies. The Brothers realized that the threat from the military rulers had been increased by the new rulers' appropriation of many of the social and economic issues the Brothers regarded as important, without, however, accepting the primary commitment to Islam. The military officers had spoken the language of anti-imperialism, and they had done so in the plebeian accents of their origins. Moreover, the new rulers had acted on their nationalist convictions, most dramatically at Suez in 1956, and on their economic and social concerns, most effectively with the land reform measures. With these successes, the military drew supporters away from the Brothers.

Two decades of interaction between the military regime and the Brothers had clarified the issues on which the two agreed, such as anti-imperialism, land reform, and a commitment to the poor. During that time, it had also become clear that the basis of support for these issues was radically different. The Brothers, for example, had supported moderate land reform, believing that a harmonious community should minimize disruptive social cleavages; the Free Officers had pushed for a more radical reform because it weakened class forces in the countryside that opposed their rule and created new allies for them. The Brothers had opposed Israel as a threat to Islam, whereas the officers had emphasized the Israeli danger to Arab nationalist goals.

The fundamental source for all of the Brothers' objectives was Islam. Its lack of centrality in the project of the officers was enough to preclude any durable alliance. As the Brothers saw it, Egypt in the fifties and sixties had drifted from Islam. The Brothers judged that, for all the movement by the military rulers on concrete social and national issues, the Free Officers had no clear sense of where Egypt and the Egyptians were going. The military rulers, the Brothers argued, were chasing other people's modernity at the price of the Islamic heritage. The Free Officers failed to create a civilizational project that was authentically Egyptian and Islamic.[39]

Egypt's defeat by Israel in 1967 confirmed the Brothers' sense of the inadequacies of the military regime. Initially, they responded guardedly to Sadat's assumption of power, although they soon actively welcomed the new ruler's de-Nasserization campaign and the opportunity he gave them to return to public life. The liberalization enabled the Brothers to outline their vision of a different future. The coherence and power of the

Islamic future for Egypt that they envisioned made the Brothers critical of the status quo. In this sense, the elaborate critique of state policies that they developed in the seventies was part of their social vision. But it is important to stress that it was not the origin of the vision. The Brothers were not simply a disgruntled opposition who defined themselves in reaction to the regime. Rather, they had their own conception of what their society should look like.

In their journal Muslim Brother writers spelled out a penetrating and explicit critique of the grand policy prescriptions of Nasser's successor. The power of the critique was enhanced by the alternative Islamic way of living in society that the Brothers consistently posed. The success of the Brothers in both the theory and the practice of their critical stance made them, alongside the military, the most cohesive social force in Egypt of the seventies and set the stage for their extraordinary legal involvements in public life under Mubarak.

Initially, the tacit alliance with the Sadat regime appeared to require the Brothers to restrict their commentary to concerns of the faith. In exchange the Brothers were to enjoy the first opportunity since the forties to reestablish themselves openly as a presence in public life.[40] The lessons of repression in the fifties and sixties convinced the mainstream Brothers that a nonviolent strategy to achieve their social ends was best. Eschewing force, however, did not mean forgoing criticism. The Brothers judged that the nonviolent path required them to offer "guidance" to the mass of followers and "advice" to the rulers.[41] From 1977 until the journal was shut down in 1981, *The Call* offered Egypt's most vigorous and widely disseminated public criticism of the Sadat orientation. The Brothers declared Sadat's grand reorientation of the seventies a failure, attacking the American global connection, accommodation with Israel, and key aspects of the economic and political liberalization. They judged the combination of these elements a deadly threat to the integrity of Egypt's Islamic civilization.

The Brothers judged that Egypt's Islamic future required its maximum possible independence of external forces, particularly of non-Islamic states. According to the Brothers, the most dangerous global forces blocking the progress of the Islamic world were the United States, the Soviet Union, and Israel. In the global power struggle, they considered Western "crusader states," "atheistic communism," and "expansionist Zionism" as three equally dangerous antagonists of Islam.[42] The most desirable national policy, as the Brothers saw it, would keep all three of these hostile international forces at bay. That aim was not always realizable. Therefore, the Brothers consistently urged that priority be given to the containment of whichever threat loomed largest at any given period. Apparent inconsistencies in Brotherhood policy made sense in these tactical terms. During the sixties and early seventies the Brothers attacked the Soviet Union because they feared that Egypt, exhausted by wars with Israel, was becoming a Russian puppet.[43] When Sadat swung the nation into the American camp, their assessment of the dangers changed.

From the Brothers' perspective, too great a dependency on the Americans had risks of its own, particularly because of the historic closeness of the Israeli-American relationship. As Sadat moved Egypt's foreign policy toward the West and accommodation with Israel, the implicit understanding with the Brothers became harder to maintain. Sadat's trip to Jerusalem in 1977 was a turning point. The initiative drove the Brothers to launch the sharpest attack of the so-called peace process to appear within Egypt. Telmesany judged that the Camp David agreement fulfilled all Israel's demands and should be fought to the end by all Muslims.[44]

The Muslim Brothers' hostility to Israel long predated the Sadat policy of reconciliation with the Jewish state. According to the Brothers, the colonization of Palestine was an aggression against the home of Islam that allowed no real prospect of peaceful coexistence with the colonizers.[45] Telmesany explained that the Brothers' opposition to Israel came "from the religious point of view, which prevented any Muslim from willingly accepting the occupation of any part of his land." The Brothers argued that the Jews in Palestine could live there as "normal citizens having the same rights and responsibilities as the owners of the land. However, even the least humane, noble, or religious human being cannot consent to the Jews living there as rulers trying to 'Zionize' everything around them and trying to destroy all traces of Islam in Palestine."[46] From this perspective, the Brothers had little confidence in what Camp David would mean for the Palestinian Arabs. With each new display of Israeli intentions to colonize and absorb the occupied West Bank, the Brothers sharpened their critical attack on a so-called peace process that they saw as dispossessing the Palestinians and desecrating Islam's rightful claim to that holy land.

Throughout the seventies the Muslim Brothers emphasized that the primary objective of Egyptian foreign policy had to be the defense of Islamic values. To achieve this end, they proposed an Islamic alternative to Sadat's bankrupt foreign policy. The Brothers called for nonalignment with the superpowers, Egyptian leadership of the Islamic bloc, and revival of the Arab option of military struggle against Israel.[47] This basic platform attracted wide support that went beyond the Islamic trend. By the end of the seventies, according to the Brothers, the United States and Israel had become the main adversaries of Islam. The political vision of the Muslim Brotherhood thus became closely intertwined with anti-Israeli and anti-American sentiment. Although the roots of traditional Islamic tolerance of Jews and Christians went deep in Egypt, what the Muslim Brothers characterized as a deadly American-Israeli drive for subjugation of the Muslim world strained the Koranic view of Jews and Christians as "people of the book." At times, the Brothers expressed their anger against Israel and America in sweeping attacks on Jews and Christians. Increasingly, they stated anti-Israeli sentiment in anti-Jewish terms, just as their growing anti-Americanism gave rise to broadly anti-Christian pronouncements.

The Brothers judged that world Jewry backed the Jewish colonization of Palestine with near unanimity. They concluded, therefore, that Jews everywhere bore responsibility for the wrongs committed by the Zionist movement. In this sense the Muslim Brothers took seriously the Israeli claim to speak for the Jews of the world. The Brothers argued that by their support of the Jewish state all Jews had implicated themselves in the crimes committed against the Arabs of Palestine. In their eyes, the hostile actions of the Israelis in Palestine culminated in the conquest and annexation of Jerusalem, the third holiest city of Islam. The Brothers regarded the consensus of world Jewry behind the defiance of international law and Muslim sensibilities as proof of deep-seated Jewish enmity to Islam and Islamic peoples. The Brothers reminded their followers that Jewish communities had rejected Muhammad's message at the dawn of Islam. They pictured Israeli actions against the Arabs as only the latest manifestation of this historic animus to Islam and proof of the danger it posed to Muslim peoples.[48]

Anti-American judgments appeared almost as frequently as anti-Israeli sentiments in the Islamic press. These hostile sentiments came most often in immediate reaction to American Middle East policy, even as they also revived deeply ingrained suspicions that historic Christian hostility to Islam was driving U.S. actions. The Muslim Brothers did not let Egyptians forget that the United States stood firmly behind the Jewish state. In their eyes a partnership with America in search of an acceptable peace was futile, because the tie with Israel would not allow the United States to recognize the rights of Arabs.[49]

When Telmesany looked at "America from an Islamic Point of View," he saw dangers in U.S. support for Israel and in rampant Westernization within Egypt. In terms of America's regional policies, Telmesany questioned the key American demand that the Palestine Liberation Organization must first recognize Israel. Telmesany argued that the American demand overlooked the question of *which* Israel and *in what form*. Telmesany mockingly noted that the Americans preferred to leave untreated these "details" of the extent of Israel's borders and the rights of Arab Palestinians. He condemned as unreasonable the American demand that the PLO "recognize the right of Israeli existence without clarifying these central issues." Muslims could not be expected to accept "all the claims the Jews make, which no custom, logic, law, right, justice, or manhood would approve."[50]

Deeply committed to protecting Egypt's Islamic heritage, Telmesany also warned that closer ties to America opened the door to a flood of Western influences that were corrupting Egypt's youth and undermining her culture. In addition to the growth of materialist and consumerist values, the Brothers regularly pointed to other tangible risks of American domestic intrusions. Muslim Brother commentators, for example, intimated that the United States was encouraging an unreasonable assertiveness among the Egyptian Christian population, the Copts. The Brothers alleged that foreign influences were attempting to make the Copts a fifth column of the West in Egypt; the enemies of Islam, the Brothers hinted, were not above fomenting sectarian strife in order to turn Egypt into another Lebanon.[51]

As part of their definition of a truly Islamic society, the Muslim Brothers declared that freedom of organization and expression would be guaranteed to all groups. These rights would not depend on the character of the regime in power; Islamic law and custom would guarantee them.[52] During the seventies, although the Brothers welcomed the advances in personal security that Sadat's liberalization made possible, they quickly joined with other regime critics in charging that the democratization efforts were half-hearted. As Muslim activists, they objected to the denial of a political role for Islamic societies and the repeated persecution of the various Islamic groupings. The Brothers pronounced Sadat's slogan of "no religion in politics" un-Islamic and manipulative. Muhammad Abdul Kudus, one of the most astute political analysts writing for the Islamic press, pointed out that Islam does not make the sharp distinction between politics and religion that is characteristic of Western Christianity. He also noted that when religion served the regime's purposes, the slogan was not raised: "When the shaikh of al-Azhar issued a statement glorifying the peace treaty, it was published on the front page of *al-Ahram*. No one dares charge that religion was involved in politics."[53]

Kudus argued that refusal to grant full recognition to Islamic groups distorted the political arena; the real political forces in Egypt such as the Nasserists and the Islamic trend were not represented. He viewed the official opposition parties as simply artificial regime creations, with leaders taken from the ranks of former cabinet and ASU members.[54] In a defiant article, Kudus protested the authorities' abusive treatment of the Islamic current and charged that mistreatment of the Islamic elements revealed the hollowness of Sadat's democracy. Kudus concluded that there could be no genuine democracy as long as the regime circumscribed the participation of organized Islamic groups in public life.[55]

To face Egypt's economic crisis, the Brothers urged greater self-reliance, selective nationalization, increased emphasis on production rather than on consumption, and extended welfare protection for the poor.[56] In addition, their economic program decried the general moral corruption that the Sadat era economic policies caused. They also insisted on some purely Islamic economic policies, such as the replacement of interest by profit-sharing arrangements.

In the Brothers' view, the Open Door policy moved Egypt decisively away from the failed socialism of the Nasser years. The Brothers welcomed it as such. Nevertheless, they raised important questions about the adequacy of the new approach in terms of their own economic vision and expressed grave doubts about the way the new policy was implemented. Especially after the riots of January 1977, the Islamic press attacked the inefficiency, corruption, and injustice that marked implementation of the liberal economic strategy. "Couldn't the vast fortunes of the rich have been used to ease the hardships of the needy rather than wasted in ostentatious display?" asked Omar Telmesany. The Koran, he noted, urged that one take from the rich to give to the poor. In Telmesany's view "the Open Door could have helped in solving part of our serious crisis had it been devoted to productive enterprises rather than to luxury items that only make the situation worse."[57]

The Muslim Brothers left their particular stamp most clearly in analyses of the social and cultural impact of the new economic orientation. One of the strengths of the Brothers was their integrated social vision. At the root of the Brothers' conception was an ideal of Islamic community, in contrast to Sadat's concept of a collection of individuals pursuing their self-interest. With a clear notion of what Egyptian society should look like in terms of Islamic values, the Brothers assessed the developments of the seventies. Thus, one Brother pointed out that here was no "purely economic" policy. The impact of economic decisions always affected society as a whole. He pointed out that the new materialist values invaded social spheres such as education, where they had no proper place, according to the standards of a good Islamic society. In the seventies the practice of teachers' offering supplemental "private lessons" to their students for a fee became widespread. Such payments for preferential treatment effectively undermined the social ideal of equality and tarnished the proper role of a teacher. Education became a consumer commodity like cooking oil or soap whose "price is determined by the laws of the market."[58]

Articles in *The Call* charged that the Open Door policy also created "false needs" that damaged the population. The circulation of foreign consumer products entailed "changing people's ideas so that they will aspire to live in the Western style, as they are made more aware of the way of life in the West." One commentator warned that the new economic climate created "a new group of people who know the rules of the game and enter into it on this basis." Increasing numbers of Egyptians were working with foreigners as representatives of Western multinational companies. The large profits they made as intermediaries gave them a material stake in the foreign presence in Egypt and the economic ties that sustained it. Moreover, the high wages these Egyptians earned distorted the essential moral tie between productive effort and material gain. The Brothers charged that their "success" encouraged use of connections and influence peddling rather than hard work as model behavior for the young.[59]

The Islamic trend in public life reserved impressive intellectual and organizational resources for the task of energizing Egyptian society to meet what they saw as the greatest danger: an assault on Islam. In the Brothers' eyes the essential struggle to preserve Islam took precedence over social goals such as development, revolution, or democracy that other Egyptians regarded as essential.[60] The Muslim Brothers concluded that the basic world conflict in the twentieth century was between competing cultures. In the global civilizational battle, each bloc seeks "to dissolve the character of the other—its thought, religion, language, and heritage." The powerful cultures of both the secular West and the atheistic East threatened Egypt's Islamic heritage. The Muslim Brothers believed that both power blocs were waging an ideological battle against

Islamic countries such as Egypt under the banner of modernity. The attack aimed to deprive Muslims of their history, their identity, and ultimately their capacity to resist. The Brothers warned that both East and West sought first to plunder the resources of the Islamic world and then to destroy Islam, the only power able to challenge their present hegemony. The Brothers drew parallels between the role of the Americans and Israelis in the destruction of Lebanon and the ravages of the Soviet Union in Afghanistan.[61]

The Brothers urged Muslims to draw on their faith and their history to strengthen the Islamic alternative. The founder of the Brotherhood, Hassan al-Banna, explained that Muslims must "rebuild our lives on our own foundations and according to our background, without copying from others."[62] Before they could hope to develop their own distinctive future, Egyptians and all Muslim peoples had first to know who they were. Above all, the Brothers insisted that Egyptians learn to distinguish between what they inherited from their own Islamic past and what was imposed on them from the outside.[63] According to the Brothers, Islam was the core of the inheritance and the key to all authentic expressions of Egyptian collective life. The rule of Islam, the Brothers argued, could provide communal identity and systems for organizing all facets of life. The Brothers worked to build a consensus around Islamic faith, history, and culture. "When the people have become true Muslims," wrote one Brother, "an authentically Islamic nation will naturally evolve."[64]

The Brothers recognized that the general character of this call to Islam left persistent ambiguities on political, economic, and constitutional issues. However, they considered these unresolved issues secondary. Muslim Brother analysts judged that a secure spiritual and cultural identity for the community would be more decisive in the global conflict than the final form taken by the economy or the polity. Despite the prompting of critics, the movement never offered an authoritative projection of the character of the political system or the organization of the national economy. The Brothers asserted only that Islam was compatible with a variety of institutional arrangements provided that certain basic requirements were met, such as application of Islamic law and adherence in some form to the larger Islamic community. As the Brothers saw it, the essential purpose of their society was not to compete for the allegiance of the people with detailed policy proposals, to court votes or win popular gratitude by performing social services. The Brothers did not seek, therefore, to advance a political program. They also judged that their movement was more than the sum of its social projects.[65]

The Brothers believed that the principal task was to educate Egyptians to Islam, understanding "education" in the fullest sense of cultural and spiritual formation. In the seventies the Brothers displayed the fruits of their efforts along these distinctively Islamic lines in *The Call*. Their journal reported developments that showed how Islam was to be lived in Egypt in the seventies and eighties. In their personal quest to live the truth of Islam, individual Muslim Brothers strived to create institutions that would allow them to practice these Islamic ideals. These practical efforts concentrated on transforming such basic social institutions as the mosque, the school, and the family into anticipations of the new Islamic society.

The Brothers regarded official Islam, centered in the great Islamic university of al-Azhar and the network of government-controlled mosques, as an impediment. The Nasser regime had drained mosques of their true vocation. The official mosque was an instrument to sanctify a corrupt regime. The best measure of the decline of official Islam, the Brothers argued, was the fate of al-Azhar University in the Nasser years. The Brothers argued that the regime transformed this great center of Islamic faith and learning into a second-rate imitation of the Westernized and secular universities.[66] They deplored the Sadat regime's continued manipulation of al-Azhar to sanctify its policies.

The Brothers responded to official misuse of the mosque in two ways: they organized and worshiped in private mosques outside government control, and shaikhs sympathetic to the Brotherhood established themselves in government mosques and transformed them. Such figures as the blind shaikh Ahmed Kishk of Cairo won a measure of personal autonomy through the enormous popular response they evoked. Shaikh Kishk developed an alternative theoretical and practical conception of the mosque.[67] "The mosque," commented Kishk, "is not for worship only." Kishk's Friday commentaries established a critical distance from government authority.[68] Sharp criticism of official social and political policies was part of virtually every Friday address. The criticism extended beyond the limits set for the national press. For example, Kishk warned bluntly against the American connection and condemned the peace with Israel at a time when the official press tolerated no critical commentary on either issue. At the same time, the mosque under his direction developed extensive educational and welfare functions that bore effective witness to government neglect. The mosque, Shaikh Kishk explained, "performs the task of several ministries." It was a ministry of culture that provided Koranic commentaries on Fridays and after evening prayers. The distribution of clothes and medicines at the mosque made it a ministry of social affairs. Doctors volunteered their services to the needy from the mosque and thereby transformed it into a ministry of health. Finally, the mosque served as a ministry of education when volunteer teachers gave private lessons without charge to needy pupils.[69] Through a network of such mosques, Shaikh Kishk believed that the Brothers were demonstrating what the real Islam could accomplish in contrast to flawed government efforts. They were meeting essential needs at a time when government services were eroding, thus demonstrating in a practical way that touched peoples' lives what a genuine Islamic order would mean for Egyptians.

No subject enlivened the pages of *The Call* more than the imperative to steel the young with a proper Islamic education. The Brothers expressed alarm at the official mishandling of that responsibility. Their platform for educational reform centered on the problem of misrepresentations of Islam as a spiritual and cultural force. The Brothers charged that textbooks in the national schools mistakenly imparted to the faith "a racist and nationalist spirit of which Islam is innocent." The Brothers objected to what they took to be the misuse of Islam for pan-Arab ideological ends. They argued that Islamic history from the time of the right-guided caliphs through the Ummayad and Abbasid periods was "a history of all Muslims, not just Arabs. The makers and heroes of Islamic history include Berbers, Turks, and Persians." The Brothers also criticized a lack of a true Islamic spirit in official textbooks on Islam, which reduced the Prophet to a political or social reformer and the story of Islam to a succession of battles. The birth of Islam, they cautioned, was an intellectual and spiritual event of world historic importance. In their view it should not be analogized to "the empty revolutions the students read about in newspapers and magazines."[70]

Brotherhood intellectuals urged their fellow Muslims to cultivate an Islamic historical imagination with principles and methods distinct from those of the West or the East. Subjects such as history, the Brothers pointed out, were not "neutral subjects like mathematics or chemistry." They were "closely related to man's vision of the universe, his understanding of the laws that govern its operations, and his faith in what lies beyond them."[71] History, as the Brothers understood it, was not simple facts or events but rather the interpretation of these facts and events.[72] The Brothers explained that the interpretation indicated what facts were important and how they related to each other to form a meaningful whole. A clear Islamic spirit, they argued, should pervade all the human sciences in order to give the young a strong sense of identity as members of a Muslim community.

The Brothers explained that the absence of an Islamic framework was confusing to the young and dangerous to the nation. According to the Brothers, Western scholars used modes of historical analysis derived from the Western experience that risked establishing the history of the West as a false standard for the Muslim experience. History texts based on Western canons of scholarship, they argued, were written "as though we are Europeans with no unique thought or cultural heritage." These texts distorted history by viewing it in a Western mirror. The Brothers charged that philosophy texts in Egyptian schools, for example, followed Western scholars in declaring the conflict between reason and revelation as a universal phenomenon. Although reason did clash with revealed faith in the West and the conflict of church and state dominated Western European history, this was "not true of Islam or the history of the Islamic world."[73] The Brothers argued that an education that downplayed and distorted the unique Islamic spirit disarmed Egyptians. They argued that people who did not have a clear sense of their own cultural and spiritual identity were easy prey to aggressive outside forces.

This assessment of the centrality of Islam to the strength of the community produced a distinctive definition of the nature of the threats facing Egyptians. The Brothers, for example, gave exceptional importance to the danger to language. "Arabic," pronounced Omar Telmesany, "is the basis of our culture." In his view Arabic was a target of foreign attack because it was the vehicle of the unique Islamic sensibility. Egyptian political actors usually identified matters such as alternative institutional arrangements, public versus private ownership, class relationships, or global alignments as the most important questions in their debates over strategies to meet Egypt's needs. The Brothers acknowledged the importance of each of these concerns; at the same time, however, they argued that because Muslims had received the message of Islam through the Arabic language, Koranic Arabic was a thread that bound the Muslim world together. Therefore, the Brothers considered the preservation of Arabic to be a fundamental task.[74]

The followers of every ideology, the Brothers argued, "wish that every other nation of the world would abandon its own heritage to come under the influence of their history, thought, and models of development." To this end, foreigners of both East and West exerted every effort "to extol the virtues of their civilization and its high ideals, which they believe can illuminate for all humanity the way to development, freedom, renaissance, and progress." The effort, though sincere, was far from innocent. The Islamic press explained that "these nations, which are developed in all modern areas, know that a nation without a history is a nation with no civilizational future, that is, with no credentials to prove its right to lead the world. Moreover, they know that a sense of the present devoid of a historical identity leaves its members vulnerable to the acceptance of any foreign allegiance."[75]

Articles in *The Call* considered the fate of Arabic from this perspective of competing world cultures. "Language," wrote one author, "is not a luxury. It is one of man's most important necessities. It contains his thought, it translates his feelings. It is the tool through which he understands others and makes himself understood to them. It is man's only link to his past and heritage." The Brothers charged that the British in Egypt had understood the centrality of language to the autonomy of any nation. For that reason, the Brothers argued, "colonialism put the destruction of the Arabic language in Arab and Muslim countries at the top of its objectives. Colonial powers aimed to destroy the will to resist and to continue the occupation indefinitely." The Brothers pointed to North Africa, where the Arabic language had not yet recovered from the French assault. "Algiers, sixteen years after independence, has not yet been able to make Arabic the language of its people." Although the British had been less successful in undermining Arabic in Egypt, the Brothers pointed out that during the occupation the British had in motion educational reforms that placed both the Arabic language and religious instruction at the bottom of educational priorities. As British-inspired reforms succeeded in denigrating Arabic and Islam as subjects of instruction, they also degraded those who taught them socially, occupationally, and financially.[76]

The Brothers charged that Egypt's post-1952 rulers had not corrected this denigration of Arabic. The writers in *The Call* proposed a fundamental rethinking of Arabic language instruction that would make the study of literary texts part of the general cultural formation of young people. In their view, the best Arabic literature was rich in resources to provide a truly Islamic cultural formation. Great literature, the Brothers reasoned, moved young people by its stylistic beauty and by the values and morals that animated it. In the Islamic schools that the Brothers helped found in the seventies, an effort was made to show how this vision of a truly Islamic education might be developed for all of society. The Brothers hoped to show that Egyptians formed in this way would know who they were and what it was they should value and defend.[77]

Education to the truth of Islam, insisted the Muslim Brothers, should begin in the family. Any weakening of the Muslim family, therefore, particularly threatened Islam. The Brothers warned that attacks on the Muslim family were an important weapon in the arsenal of the internal and external enemies of the faith. Often, the Brothers charged, the enemies of Islam masked their attacks by feigned concern for the status of women in Muslim societies. The Brothers rejected Western definitions of the woman question as one of the rights of women versus those of men; according to the Brothers, the real issue was the right of all Muslims to their faith and to their heritage.

For both men and women, this religious right meant the happiness of participating in the struggle to build a society based on God's laws. In the contemporary movement that resurfaced in the seventies, women have been included as members side by side with men. They have shared in the organization program, aims, and goals of the movement.[78] However, the original society of Muslim Brothers, as the name suggested, excluded women as members. A section was founded for Islamic Teaching for Muslim Sisters, most of whom were wives and relatives of members. After 1932, when the Brothers moved from Ismailia to Cairo, the Organization of Muslim Sisters existed as a separate society whose special emphasis was programs of social work for children, women, and family. During the repression of the fifties and sixties the organizational distinction was preserved, although the two cooperated so closely as to be effectively merged, thus preparing the way for the present inclusion of women.

The Brothers considered the stakes in the debate over women's role to be no less than the fate of the Islamic social ideal. The Islamic press rejected what it saw as attempts by Westernized elites and their foreign backers to undermine the Islamic conception of the role of women in family and social life. To the Western-inspired charges that Islam denigrated women, the Brothers responded that "Islamic history reveals that the Muslim woman has always been better off than women in any other society." For this reason, the Muslim woman was "a stronghold that is not easy to tear down, for her faith and convictions are strong."[79]

The Brothers explained that Islam gave men and women roles of equal honor. The Muslim man established a public order that reflected Islamic values and acted in it to secure the needs of his family; the Muslim woman created a family environment conducive to the upbringing of children in Islamic precepts. For her accomplishments, woman was entitled to full dignity and respect. The Brothers pointed out that women at the time of the Prophet enjoyed economic rights as individuals that were not extended to European women until the nineteenth century. Islam, the Muslim Brothers explained, gave to women all the essential rights of humanity. Above all, women had the right to faith, to knowledge, to recognition, and to equal punishments and rewards before God. Women were also entitled to choose their own husbands and to work outside the home, should the need arise.[80]

The writers in *The Call* emphasized that present-day Egypt was far from an ideal Islamic society. They argued that in a fully realized Islamic society, the needs of all citizens would be met without forcing women to abandon their essential responsibilities to their husbands and children. Authors identified with the Brotherhood wrote that in a true Islamic society women would be paid a salary for the work they do in the home.[81] From this perspective, Zeinab al-Ghazaly, the most prominent woman associated with the Brotherhood and a regular contributor to *The Call,* expressed sympathy for women who were experiencing a fraudulent "liberation" that added the additional strain of work outside the home to the burdens of homemaking. In Egypt, as elsewhere, the result of "the new lifestyle of the 'liberated' woman is physical and psychological exhaustion."[82]

The Brothers asserted the general principle that "knowledge is an Islamic virtue equally for men and women."[83] To prepare themselves for the roles of wife and mother, girls should be properly educated. The Brothers argued, however, that Egypt was an imperfect society that did not yet provide the conditions necessary for women to realize fully these rights. Women were enjoined to study subjects such as child psychology and health care that were most directly relevant to family life, but the Brothers cautioned that girls must be trained in a manner consistent with their own future responsibility for the inculcation of Islamic values. They questioned whether proper supervision of the interactions of male and female students was possible in the overcrowded university lecture halls; separation of the sexes was imperative to provide education in the proper Islamic spirit.

Much of the commentary on the problems of women in society pragmatically addressed the special problems of women in difficult circumstances. The arguments in the Islamic press against the women's movement exemplified this practical tone. Zeinab al-Ghazaly chided the feminists for the essential irrelevance of their activities to the mass of Egyptian women; they wasted their time and efforts in "hollow political meetings focused on private matters, while neglecting public concerns properly understood." From the proper Islamic point of view, the key public concern was the protection of the Islamic heritage by resisting imposition of Western conceptions of woman's role. Ghazaly also charged that middle-class Egyptian feminists neglected everyday problems of prices, housing, and transportation that plagued the majority of women. The feminists, she pointed out, played no role in efforts at consumer boycotts to bring the prices of essential goods within reach. For these reasons, "it is unlikely that the feminist organizations will succeed in establishing any links with the mass of Egyptian women."[84]

Brotherhood writers pointed out that the complex question of Islamic dress was deliberately misrepresented in the West because "the enemies of Islam judge Muslim women who wear the true Islamic dress dangerous because they represent a 'revolution' of sorts."[85] In particular, the Brothers judged Western observers' emphasis on "veiling" to be tendentious and misleading. Commentators pointed out that there is neither an Arabic word corresponding to the word *veil* nor an article of clothing corresponding to the meaning the term has for Westerners. A variety of head and body coverings were available to men and women, and there was extensive discussion in Islamic circles of the relative merits of the different Islamic styles. Head and face covers for women, for example, ranged from the most frequently seen flowing head scarves that covered the hair but not the face to the rarely used hoods that left only the eyes uncovered. The most important feature of Islamic dress in all its forms was the notion of appropriate sexual conduct that it expressed. According to the Brothers, men and women were sexual beings, but sexuality was to be enjoyed by both sexes only within the context of marriage. Appropriate sexual interaction therefore dictated a dress code for men and women that provided such loose covering for the body that its contours were not visible. The question of whether a woman's face should or should not be included in those body parts visible only to the marriage partner was sharply debated.[86]

Discussion of Islamic dress in *The Call* emphasized the way in which the Islamic styles resolved many of the pressing practical problems of women. For example, the Islamic press frequently condemned the tendency of the Egyptian university to be "more a fashion show than an educational institution." The lower classes in particular could not afford a Western-style wardrobe for their daughters. "Girls today," wrote one author, "cost their parents more than they can afford in order to maintain an appearance. This is the big issue today between girls and their parents."[87] Islamic dress for women thus not only made an important statement of principles; it also helped hard-pressed parents meet costs. Moreover, the Islamic groups at the universities made a constant effort to provide Islamic dress for women at subsidized costs.

The writers in *The Call* recognized that not all women could exercise what they took to be their full rights as Muslim women; some had to work in order to meet the needs of their families. The Islamic press prescribed how women might best approximate the Islamic ideal of wife and mother in present-day Egypt. When exceptional need or talent impelled women to act in the public realm, an ideal Islamic government would provide appropriate employment and a safe means of transport whereas Egypt's current absurdly overcrowded public transportation system guaranteed the working woman "a daily trip of torture." In the buses and trains she experienced the "harassment of people who have neither morals nor religion." The Brothers called repeatedly for public transportation restricted to women. They also advised women to seek employment close to their homes so that they could avoid the transportation system. Islamic groups, particularly at the universities, even made their own arrangements for transportation reserved to women. The Brothers argued that when safe conditions do not prevail, "the woman who ventures out for education or employment is unfairly put in a situation in which she risks losing more than she gains."[88]

Because she should give priority to her family responsibilities, the Brothers judged that a woman ordinarily would not play a leadership role in the public affairs of an Islamic society. However, the Brothers did recognize that individual women might well be called upon to discharge their responsibilities to Islam as public figures. The Brothers knew that in the history of their own movement, women had played a key role. During the years of harsh repression under Nasser, they pointed out, women had assumed many dangerous responsibilities such as maintaining communications and preserving documents and records in order to keep the Muslim Brothers movement alive.

The Islamic press offered the life of the activist Zeinab al-Ghazaly as an exemplar of these possibilities. Ghazaly herself argued that in its early period Islam allowed a prominent role for women in political life. Under certain conditions, it could even be a duty. An incident in Ghazaly's autobiography made the point with particular force. In 1954 the regime struck against the Muslim Brothers and banned their organization. Zeinab al-Ghazaly joined a covert effort at reorganization. When her husband became aware of her illegal activities, he expressed concern for her safety. The ensuing dialogue, taken from Ghazaly's autobiography, gave an arresting portrait of her marriage and a firm defense of a public role for women:

"My dear husband, do you remember what I said to you when we agreed upon marriage?"

He said: "Yes, you specified certain conditions, but today I fear for you from these tyrants."

Then he was silent, so I said to him: "I remember very well what I said to you that day. I said: 'There is something in my life that you must know because you are to become my husband, and since you have agreed to this marriage, I must inform you of something on condition that you never question me about it again . . . What I believe in and have faith in is the message of the Muslim Brothers . . . I am bound by an oath to Hassan al-Banna to die for the sake of God although I have not yet taken one step to place me inside the circle of this divine honor. But I believe that I will take this step someday, for this is what I hope and dream for. On that day, if your personal welfare or economic enterprises clashes with my Islamic duties and if I find that my married life will be an obstacle in spreading the Message and establishing an Islamic state, then we must go separate ways.' "

I said: "I know that it is your right to order me and that it is my duty to obey you, but God is greater in our souls than ourselves and his Message is more dear to us than ourselves, and we are in a critical stage of movement toward the Message."

He said: "Forgive me. Work with God's blessing. I wish I may live to see the achievement of the goal of the Brothers, and see an established Islamic state. I wish I were in my youth so that I could work with you . . ."

There was a stream of young men into my house night and day, and my believing husband would hear knocks at the door in the middle of the night only to get up and open it, leading the visitors to my office. Then he would wake up the housekeeper and ask her to prepare some food and tea for these visitors. Then he would gently wake me, saying: "Some of our children are in the office. They look tired."

Then I would get dressed and go to them while he returned to his bedroom, saying: "If you pray together at sunrise, then wake me to pray with you if this causes no trouble."

I would answer: "If God wills."[89]

The Muslim Brothers in the seventies were more than a critical voice for a theoretical Islamic alternative. The way they lived their lives in their schools, mosques, and families prefigured the Islamic order for which they struggled. Moreover, demonstrations of the power of Islam to shape lives were not restricted to the pages of the vibrant Islamic press of the Sadat years. They spilled into the streets. The Society of Muslim Brothers gave ordinary Muslims the sense that they could make a statement about the imperfections of Egyptian society and the need to parry the external threats to Egypt. Through participation in the world the Brothers were struggling to bring into being, they could join themselves to a larger Islamic destiny.[90] The Brothers consciously made small acts part of a larger drama. For example, the Islamic press always gave extensive coverage to the thousands of average Egyptians who responded to calls by the Brothers to public prayers in the open squares of Egypt's cities on Islam's holiest days. On these occasions no overt political platforms or social programs were presented, yet the prayers demonstrated that the military was not the only organized force in Egypt. The Islamic press pronounced them "anticipations" of the true Islamic order they were struggling to achieve. Others, such as the president of Assiut University, wondered "if the thousands who were moved for prayer might not be moved for other purposes, too."[91]

On a Saturday in August 1981 one such prayer drew Egyptians to a huge public square in Cairo. Signs appeared from nowhere to blanket Cairo; the outline of a mosque, traced delicately in green on a white background, indicated a call to prayer: *"Brother believers, you are called to prayer on the occasion of the Prayer Holiday in Abdin Square. There is a place set apart for women. Bring your children."*

Respondents to the call came by the thousands, most heavily from the poor quarters of Cairo. Starting at five in the morning, they moved on foot and in small groups toward Abdin Square. They sat themselves apart by moving through the city at the distinctive pace between walking and running that is prescribed for the procession to prayer. Most dressed in the traditional long white robes; many wore embroidered white skullcaps. For an hour, an estimated 250,000 Egyptians prayed in the square; then they quietly dispersed. Their assembly showed the potential of the Islamic trend, best represented by the Muslim Brothers, to fill the public spaces in Egyptian life.

Part II

KNOWING BETTER: GROUP POLITICS IN EGYPT AND THE THIRD WORLD

9

Re-Visioning Third World Politics: Narratives, Power, and Political Action

I want to maintain that the concept of action is logically linked to that of power, if the latter term is interpreted in a broad sense as the capability of achieving outcomes.

—Anthony Giddens

Politics, in one important sense, always centers on the purposeful actions of subjects who have reason to hope that their concerted actions can empower them to create, sustain, and transform the world in which they live. When people interact around issues they consider central to their lives, they "make *polis*." This suggestive phrase, borrowed from C. West Churchman, captures the generative possibilities of human political action.[1] Acting together to achieve a common purpose, people generate power, and that power makes the realization of collective ends conceivable, if not certain. Unlike other communal animals, our genetic programming does not require us to respond in a fixed way to our environment, to repeat endlessly our past. We have the capacity not only to think of new purposes for our lives but also the possibility to create, necessarily within limits, the new means we require to realize them. Unlike spiders forever weaving variations on the same patterns, we have reason to hope that we can be inventive architects of distinctive futures. We can plan new communities in our private dreams, and, by the stories we tell of the futures we envision, we can communicate them to the hearts and imaginations of our fellows as we build them together in the world.

Thus, the human subjects of political lives are at once the doers of actions and the authors of the shared stories that communicate the meaning of those actions. Making *polis* depends on the creative practices of individuals; political actors understand themselves to be acting together to attain some collective end, and they have the capacity to express that understanding in group narratives. These narratives articulate and sustain their distinctive public worlds of common meaning and aspiration; the shared understandings and common hopes are not locked away in their heads or hearts; rather, they occupy the public spaces that they carve out in struggling for specific ends in the face of particular obstacles. Crafted out of their collective imaginations and prompted by their involvements in concrete circumstances, the stories group members tell about their collective life give form to vague notions of how they should live together; typically, the stories cohere around energizing images of some better future—the self-governing nation of laws, the community ordered by the rules of beauty or the insights of human intelligence, the classless society, the right-guided community of the faithful, the Arab nation returned to glory. Political visions define group actions as efforts to become—and not just to be or to have. Group narratives elaborate these transformative trajectories; through the stories they tell about their struggles, political actors communicate with each other, with those historical figures who paved the way, with future generations who will continue after them—and with other human beings, including social scientists and their readers, who seek to understand the values and ends for which they act.[2]

All such group narratives are political not only because they tell of political trials but also because power springs from the human relations their enactment entails. The power so generated can make them real. In enacted stories, as Hannah Arendt explains, actual men and women—not abstract ideas, economic trends, or social forces—appear as "doers and sufferers," creating new ways to live human lives.[3] At once about meaning and power, the stories human communities tell about themselves draw on and reinforce common meanings that guide actions today and visions for tomorrow. Group narratives preserve the common elements of collective life as reference points against which adherents articulate both agreement and disagreement, cleavage and consensus, as they struggle together in the world.[4] By knowingly relating to one another in terms of common meanings forged in the stream of their collective action, members participate in a collective "sharing of the shared" through which they transform themselves from a random collective of individuals into a human community with a history—and a future over which they can argue.[5]

Narrative self-descriptions safeguard collective meanings and record the tactics and strategies of common struggles. They therefore entail more than the working out of ideological systems that individuals carry in their heads, more too than a catalog of the material and social structures that press on them from the outside. Groups do develop explicit political theories, some more, some less coherent; we should be acquainted with these theoretical notions and the basic propositions they generate. In addition, groups do act in situations shaped by cultural, sociological, and economic national and international structures of which we should be aware. Yet, knowledge of these conditioning circumstances should not be confused with understanding the political life of the group. The enacted stories around which human groups cohere always involve more than systematic belief systems and more than any summation of the structural determinants of their collective action.

Knowledge of politics conceived as practices aiming for better public worlds necessarily passes through the stories that human groups tell about themselves. The study of the politics of others takes off from awareness of those acts of speaking and doing that illuminate a group's capacity to struggle for values and ends that they consider important to the future they desire. Of course, not all projects are successful, and not all obstacles to their completion are know. Yet, we can appreciate the unintended consequences of actions only when we have an idea of the human motivations that did in fact drive them. In just the same way, we can grasp the conditions of which people are unaware only when we have some reasonable sense of just how far their consciousness of situational limitations does extend. Moreover, even the fullest appreciation of unintended consequences and the most complete awareness of the unrealized conditions of action cannot give us a sense of the critical facts of human coherency and creativity. We understand why a collection of individuals considers itself a community when we grasp the ways in which its collective actions open the doors to the creative building of a future that expresses its particularity. To reach this understanding, we must have a vivid sense of the trials that actually engage them for the purposes they have set for themselves; seeing others as faceless shadows living in a world of problems that we judge critical and goals that we desire provides little help.[6] We must acquire familiarity with the story men and women see themselves as living, for out of these enacted stories grows their unique sense of their situation, themselves, and the future that awaits them—as well as the power to change that condition, to make new selves, and to create a different future.

Egyptians, as the preceding chapters demonstrate, have produced a rich variety of narrative self-descriptions that do help us appreciate the internal meanings of their collective practices. The living force of Egyptian liberalism, for example, cannot be grasped by abstract knowledge of its commitment to a society of laws governed by a constitution, the link between middle-class interests and liberal philosophy, or the connection between markets and pluralism. Knowledge of Egyptians who understand themselves to be liberals comes rather from the stories they weave into their collective narrative, such as the account of Mustafa Marei's speech to the Bar Association. An old man rose to speak about the law and the constitution in a crowded and dusty hall in the Bar Association in central Cairo; in old-fashioned language and an outmoded style, he challenged the last in a series of repressive government measures. By the usual calculus, his actions had no great effect, for government bullies easily disrupted the meeting and drove Marei from the hall. Yet, in the telling and retelling by liberals, the concrete events surrounding this particular man and his speech revealed the presence and potential of Egyptian liberalism as a historical alternative. At exactly the right moment, Marei spoke the language of liberalism and acted out a liberal drama in a way that exposed the Sadat regime's pretensions to liberalism. Marei, for a brief moment, became liberalism alive in the Egypt of the seventies. We understand the liberal lawyers as political actors when we grasp what makes liberals recognize themselves as Marei, why they see their best collective selves in that frail figure, how Marei's speech impelled them to feel something, to be something, to do something that marks them as liberals.

This conception of politics as conscious human action in the public world is as old as Aristotle, and as new as the latest debate between today's generation of "action theorists" and the system builders or structuralists against whom they periodically rebel. Classical political philosophers such as Aristotle emphasize the generative possibilities of politics. Aristotle considers a human being a political animal by nature, pointing to the fact that humans have always lived in semipermanent and permanent groups larger than the single family. One key function of these groups is to regulate relations among members; however, in calling human beings "political" and not merely social or group animals Aristotle refers to the human capacity for action and speech in the context of collectivities. In the Aristotelian tradition, the public or the common is synonymous with the political.[7] Human beings interact with one another as speaking and acting subjects who, unlike all other animals, have reason and therefore can hope to define the meaning of their collective lives and the nature of the human world in which they live. Because they have reason, human beings can give accounts of their struggles for better ways of living; these accounts can be shared with others in ways that cement community.[8] Politics in the Aristotelian sense is about human communities striving to secure the good life.[9]

This book relies on Aristotle's way of talking about politics. The group narratives of the first eight chapters recount the ways in which Egyptians act politically, that is, act to transform society at some basic level. Even conservatives act to move society toward a more perfect version of the status quo, reactionaries to some better lost moment. To understand political action, then, is to grasp a particular actor's or group's conception of desired transformation and of how best to achieve it. We know others politically when we can relate the sources and effects of their transformative actions to their own notions of who they are and what they are struggling to become.

There are, of course, other important ways of understanding politics and political communities. Currently, mainstream political science, and certainly the study of the politics of the Third World, are steeped in a tradition that heavily emphasizes the determining impact on human action of the various systems and structures within which we live rather than the action itself. The structuralist movement of the sixties, which originated in the anthropological work of Claude Lévi-Strauss, gave new impetus to this approach to studying human behavior. Lévi-Strauss's work tied together the seemingly isolated cultural phenomena of large, disparate areas of the world by a few underlying principles that he hoped would give him a grammar of culture. These underlying principles and the rules of their operation, Lévi-Strauss contended, explained the character of particular myths and rituals; he believed he could explain why people in vastly different civilizations and parts of the world behaved and thought in certain ways. Lévi-Strauss thought he had found the "keys" to unify and systematize human thinking and action by isolating the structures that generated (and constricted) that thinking and action.[10]

It is not necessary to delve into the details of Lévi-Strauss's work to realize that his basic posture has helped reinforce the underlying character of much social scientific theorizing in recent decades, including that inspired by Marx as well as Weber. In Third World studies, for instance, both dependency and development theories, the most common and influential paradigms, exhibit this impulse to unify and systematize by reducing a complex surface to a simplified underlying system: both traditions of inquiry reduce the politics of the Third World to the struggle to overcome underdevelopment. Scholars working with both approaches identify key structures conditioning the background of political action; for both the liberal mainstream and its leftist critics these social and economic systems essentially determine (produce and constrain) the political life of Third World peoples.

When considering Egyptian politics, it is easy enough to see that such background complexes do have a powerful effect on political action. Orthodox work, including important studies of Egypt, illuminates the economic and societal structures (both national and international) that are among the social causes of political outcomes. Eric Davis' pioneering historical study shows how the pressures from the world market system interacted with social structure and consciousness to shape the transformation of Egyptian politics and society in the latter half of the eighteenth and the early twentieth centuries.[11] John Waterbury provides an indispensable overview of the economic difficulties and challenges that face Egypt, as they appear from a mainstream political economy perspective concerned with development.[12] Leonard Binder's close empirical investigations of the character and composition of the families of rural notables provides a potent reminder of the power and influence of neglected sociological factors in the political life of Third World societies.[13]

The problem is that these three works reduce Egyptian politics to the study of an underlying social or economic system; findings generated by all three approaches tell us a great deal about the national and international economic or social structures on which they focus. They tell us much less, however, about the precise ways in which these structural factors shape actual *political* outcomes. In fact, structural accounts hide much of the Egyptian political landscape; they also distort the way we think about politics there and throughout the Third World. When we are interested in actual human responses (even given a set of more or less conditioning structures) rather than the structures themselves, when we want to know what people do with and through systems rather than what systems do to them, determinants of one kind or another fade in significance, and a rich array of unique ways of living and confronting the world appears. Studies of the political creativity of particular people caution against reading too much about human responses from even the most complete analysis of structural factors. Human beings do not choose the conditions under which they make their history; however, their responses, given those conditions and even despite them, are often more varied and importantly complex than our paradigms let us believe.

There is a conflict, then, between a theoretical posture that views politics on "a surface level"—what people do in terms of what it is they believe their actions are accomplishing—and one that looks for "deep" causes or underlying conditions to which all political action, despite myriad variations of form, is ultimately accountable; the conflict is over the significance of difference. For the former, it is the variations in how people conceive of what is good and bad about their society and how existing social arrangements might be changed, that explains why they act differently at all. The political realm is where various stories that people carry with them clash and meld. A feel for the texture of a society, the cracks and crevices where the gestures that betray these myriad stories appear, is essential to understanding that realm. For the latter, difference is subsumed by a set of general conditioning factors of which all political action is in some sense a function.

The contrast between accounts that focus on the conditioning role of structures and analyses that emphasize the possibilities of human action is strongest in the most influential neo-Marxist analyses, notably world system and dependency theories. These theories argue the existence of a capitalist world system that exerts a determining influence on the developmental process, including its political dimension; understanding of the dynamics of the world system, the neo-Marxists reason, provides the most revealing perspective from which to assess the political and economic evolution of any society.

Focused on actual political struggles, studies in group practice contrast sharply with such generalized descriptions of how the world system works its effects; the emphasis instead is on the ways in which actors devise tactics and strategies to achieve their purposes in the face of the pressures and possibilities generated by the world outside. Without awareness of what the world system means to knowledgeable and skillful human actors, the links between the world system and political effects remain too obscure to be helpful to any groups—including the full range from the "reactionaries" who cooperate with world capitalism to the "progressives" whose political battles the neo-Marxist theorists seek to advance.

In Egypt, for example, the Osman circle celebrates the access to advanced technology and international marketing made possible by the economic opening of the seventies; more to the point, the record of their companies reveals the precise mechanisms whereby agents of the multinationals and strategically placed managers and officials of the public sector and the state bureaucracy manage to flourish in the new economic climate. The Marxists in the *Vanguard* circle provide a different notation; their angle of vision brings out the ways in which the government economic strategy of the seventies increased the gap between classes and sparked political discontents that almost destroyed public authority. Intellectuals in the *Economic Ahram (al-Ahram al-Iqtisadi)* challenge the philosophical grounding of world system theory for privileging material over other forms of human well-being, charging that they share this distorting bias with all other major Western theories. What matters in the narrative accounts generated by a group practice approach is the way systems and structures are experienced as enabling or constraining by the particular collectivities whose stories are retold.

Davis' work illustrates the strengths of a structuralist analysis as well as the contrast to a group practice approach. Though not an orthodox Marxist analyst David does draw heavily on Marxist categories; his pathbreaking study of Tala'at Harb and the Bank Misr industrialization effort of 1920–1941 illustrates the general point that conditioning effects must be related to the responses of particular actors. Davis' careful attention to economic rather than simply political issues and institutions makes a major contribution to our understanding of Egypt's history. Davis asks why that industrialization effort failed. His answer is a "structural explanation": "the constraints imposed by the world market, the domestic class structure, and the characteristics of the Egyptian state placed rather sharp limits on Tala'at Harb's scope of action."[14] The answer is interesting primarily for the way it modifies conventional dependency thinking by a more emphatic reliance on traditional Marxism. Davis also uses this answer to explain his skepticism of modernization theory and his reliance instead on Marxist theoretical tools, notably class analysis and the related notion of contradiction. Each of the three variables in this structural explanation, Davis explains, first supported and then undermined the industrialization effort. This model, therefore, emphasizes contradictions that have been overlooked by mainstream analysis. As Davis hoped, his work has certainly made a "contribution to a larger body of theory rooted in political economy."[15]

From a perspective that aims to make sense of actual political behavior, however, Davis' conclusions are less helpful. How much have we really learned when we are told that the world system, the political order, and class forces have all contributed to the failure to industrialize? Davis does not tell us, for example, how we should weigh the three determinants in his explanation of the failure of industrialization. More important, he makes no attempt to suggest what kind of industrialization strategy might have succeeded. What might Egyptians aware of the limitations he flags have done—if anything—to avoid the collapse of their industrialization effort? Davis' approach cannot answer such questions persuasively because there is no room in his framework for a systematic explanation of how Egyptian political actors themselves understood the pressures on them and what latitude they understood themselves to have in their responses to them. Because the analysis does not illuminate what range of political choices Egyptian actors saw themselves as having, it is difficult for us to understand the meaning of their actions. Davis weds a vigorous profile of sociological forces and economic structures to an anemic politics; he tells us too much about the constraints imposed by class formation and the world market, and too little about the possibilities of political action. The mechanisms that link international market, class, and state pressures to the political behavior of Egyptians are insufficiently examined. In short, Davis' framework leads him to conclusions that stress a structural determination of historical process and political action that downgrades real political actors as agents able to make their own history.

The group practice approach shifts the focus of structural analyses such as Davis' from an elaboration of constraints to a consideration of the strategies political actors devise to work within given systems or to evade their influence when possible. Without denying the reality of structural constraints, the group practice approach requires that these conditioning elements be viewed in a different way; it asks which structures, if any, are relevant to a specific political project and how precisely they are conceived by the human actors involved. A shift occurs from action-depressing elaborations of constraints to energizing depictions of actual human efforts to work through or even overcome them.

At this point, it might appear that the difference between these two ways of studying politics is not absolute. One might argue that there are, after all, conditioning factors to which all political action is accountable. Any rational Third World political power, however different it may be from other groups absorbed with other priorities, simply cannot ignore certain things. For some, it is the realities of coercive pressures from the international capitalist system to which the neo-Marxist accounts such as Davis' draw attention; for others it is the economic facts of feeding a population in conditions of scarce resources that a mainstream development theorist would be more likely to emphasize. At the same time, any structural theorist, Davis included, would admit that over and above these controlling factors politics is also about other things—things like creating a world in which individuals can attain freedom, develop a distinctive identity, or live according to God's word. This reasoning would suggest that the contrast between attention to action and agents rather than to systems and structures is only a matter of emphasis.

I would, however, insist that there is more to it than that. The problem is that there really are no extrapersonal structures that condition political action in some truly determinate way. In the Third World politics literature, the claims along these lines that have attracted most support ground themselves in compelling facts that speak for themselves because they point to pressing human needs that cannot be ignored, social or economic causes about which there is general agreement, or global economic structures whose effects cannot be ignored. All such claims about Egypt of which I am aware are ultimately unpersuasive, even in their own terms. In fact, the danger is that claims for universal relevance or objectivity may at times conceal "interested" political stories that often quite unintentionally tell us too much about ourselves and about those Egyptians who share our interests, and too little about other Egyptian political communities, different yet nevertheless valuable for the human values and ends that they represent.

In this regard, there is no reason to suppose that the politics of people who live in a poor society is conditioned by national and international systems or structures any more severely or any more uniformly than our own. Not even modernization is so irresistible an idea or so unalterable a trend that it can dictate political objectives or directly shape political outcomes. The assumption that the conditions of a poor people "wash out" differences among them and even between them and other poor people does not hold. Not even the most difficult circumstances condition absolutely. Facts and trends about population and resources, for example, remain simply phantoms until we know what significance actual groups of men and women give them. In all cases we must learn about, and not just assume we know, the context in which people are acting and the nature of the material and social givens they face.

Consider for a moment the "facts" of population growth and existing resources as elements in Egyptian political life. These facts do not speak for themselves in any unequivocal way. The temptation to rush to assumptions about "overpopulation" and "scarce" resources as obstacles to development should be resisted. When politics is seen as the group struggle to define the purposes and obstacles of collective life, the certainty afforded by the necessity to confront apparently fixed problems evaporates. Problems, after all, are problems only in the context of particular definitions of one's situation in the light of specific ends.

Egyptians have made the idea of development a highly ambiguous and sharply contested one. Since 1952 Egyptian liberals have questioned whether the regime's drive to industrialize could justify its suspension of democratic rights. Others, notably the Marxists, have pressed those in power at every opportunity open to them to redefine their notion of development in the direction of scientific socialism. Meanwhile, the various Islamic groupings, often at great costs, have challenged the very necessity of development as an overall priority over what they take to be the more compelling collective aims of the renewal of faith and protection of Egypt's cultural integrity.

This long-standing and multifaceted controversy surrounding the definition of what constitutes forward movement for the Egyptian nation has continued into the eighties. Egyptians in particularly large numbers respond to the conflicting definitions of progress and how to achieve it advanced by the Nasserists and the Islamic groupings as they compete with each other and with the regime. The different treatment of the population question by the ruling group, the Nasserists, and the Islamic current illustrates concretely their sharp differences. Western experts with near unanimity pronounce Egypt's population growth the major obstacle Egyptians face, and the U.S. government argues regularly that Egypt's economic problems are insoluble without population control. A regime dependent on the American connection can ill afford to ignore this pressure. Yet, the government also faces the unpopularity of birth control campaigns in important quarters.

The Nasserists see educated Egyptian human resources as one powerful basis for Egypt's claim to leadership in the Arab world; they argue that Egypt must become industrialized so that these human resources can be used at home rather than exported to the oil-rich states. For their part, Islamic elements quite correctly identify population control efforts with foreign influence. They go on to reason that the effort to limit population aims ultimately at depleting the one great material strength, superior numbers, with which Islam confronts its global adversaries.

These diverse group perspectives on population suggest that no transhistorical, nonpartisan "rationality" exists to which we can appeal to assess even so pressing an issue as "overpopulation"; they also help clarify why we can never take for granted the character and the meaning of the forces that shape other people's lives. The best mainstream accounts evince a vague uneasiness on just this point, although it necessarily remains submerged in their structuralist frameworks. John Waterbury recognizes that his approach entails this risk of "falling into crude and insensitive determinism." Unfortunately, those risks are real; they result from the assumption (built into the political economy approach Waterbury adopts) that one can anticipate likely political responses from the delineation of a "reasonable" range of solutions to general economic problems. Waterbury writes that "Egypt appears to be the prisoner of two kinds of situations that severely limit the range of policy responses it can reasonably contemplate . . . One emerges from its socio-economic makeup and the other from its dependency upon external sources of finance capital, technology, markets, and arms." Inserted between these two sentences and enclosed in parentheses is Waterbury's comment that "everything hinges, of course, on the definition of reasonable."[16] In Egypt or any other society, the determination of what is a reasonable policy is a contextual matter, often the object of political contest; definitions of "reasonableness" cannot be read in the abstract from raw economic facts, from economic theory, or from parallel economic situations. Only in the margins and asides of his work does Waterbury draw on his rich direct experience of Egypt to hint at what might be reasonable to particular Egyptians in the context of their political struggles.[17]

The impulse to generalize drives the appeal to universal standards. Accounts that focus on the systems and structures that condition political behavior rather than on human action itself often aim for comparative generalizations about Third World politics that rise above "mere description" of the political particulars of any one case. The political group practice approach, riveted on the actions of particular communities, rules out generalizations of this kind. However, it is not necessary to question the possibility of a general comparative politics to note one distorting consequence of adopting this goal.[18] Scholars who work within the development approach can realize their interest in a subject matter about which such generalizations can be made only by accepting the often unstated premise that the diverse histories of the peoples of Asia, Africa, and Latin America can be simplified and thereby made available to general theory by assuming that their public life essentially centers on the politics of development; or, to put the point another way, the essential struggle in Third World societies is the struggle to overcome material backwardness.

Here the point is not that modernization and the struggle for development are irrelevant to either politics or the understanding of politics. For some Egyptians, modernization is clearly a central concern. Waterbury's book speaks to and for those Egyptians in a genuinely helpful way; they are important, and so is what he says about them. However, knowledge about those Egyptians and the obstacles they face, or should face, and the strategies they pursue, or should pursue, is something quite different from a structural key to understanding Egyptian politics. From the vantage point of other Egyptians with different values and aims, the restrictions Waterbury identifies may simply not be operative in the way he imagines, and the reasonable policies to which his work points may well be irrelevant to their notions of where they want to take society.

Waterbury's book has an important relevance to Egyptian politics, but not the one he imagines for it. Many people, perhaps too many, in Egypt and the Third World do see modernization as the primary need of their society. As Maxime Rodinson observed, "the whole of this Third World, as it is called, is obsessed by the desire to draw level as soon as possible, in some respects at least, with the industrialized world."[19] The story these people (who probably make up most of the present government of Egypt) carry with them is the need of their country to develop. A society of industrial and technological power, of wealth and world influence, is the icon around which their notion of the needs and progression of Egyptian society moves. Yet, although theirs is not the only significant political vision in Egypt, it is only their story that Waterbury tells. Those who hear and understand that story alone will find the actions of many other Egyptians inexplicable (or at least unreasonable).

Whereas Waterbury's work preserves a link to the conscious aims and purposes that actual and important (if particular) groups of Egyptians would recognize as their own, other theorists of development ground their claims to generalize on the discovery of some set of conditioning social or material facts whose existence and importance, they believe, can be established independently of historical or ideological frameworks. Leonard Binder, an influential general theorist of development, singles out the rural middle class as the essential feature of Egyptian society for those interested in understanding its mode of change. Binder points out that both mainstream and Marxist paradigms, for all their other differences, agree on the importance of the rural "second stratum." Relying on this common ground, Binder seeks to identify a conditioning empirical reality about which objective things can be known.

While a political practice perspective would see social classes and groups as a kind of sociological clay with which different political group-ing might work in different ways, Binder identifies his sociological fac-tors as the nonpartisan keys to understanding Third World politics.[20] He confidently asserts that, as a "second stratum," the rural middle class plays a crucial role in the socioeconomic development of modernizing countries. Binder believes that the discovery of "the neglected empirical reality" of the rural middle class allows him to reduce the multiple uncertainties of political life to the analysis of a "single complex pro-cess," that is, the changing structure and composition of the second stratum.[21] He argues that attention to the character of the rural middle class is a more important guide to "monitoring" political change than attention to the overt politics of particular movements or groups, in-cluding those who currently have power.

Binder's approach has theoretical problems and limitations that are related to his claim that a nonpartisan, empirical investigation of the second stratum provides a neutral vantage point from which to survey Egyptian politics and say something about its future course. Binder bases his claim to the objectivity of his sociological approach on the argument that both liberal and Marxist development paradigms recognize the cen-trality of the rural middle class, although in his view neither explains it adequately: "The ideological perspectives and the social analyses may be very different, but the rural middle class, like lucky Pierre, always seems to turn up as a beneficiary of the system." It is an error, however, to regard this common ground as a guarantee of objectivity, free from "relativistic and polemical character."[22] Binder has identified an inter-esting area of common agreement between liberal and Marxist inter-preters of the Egyptian experience, but that is all. Agreement between two paradigms, both of which carry Western normative and historical content, may tell us something interesting about what those paradigms judge to be important; however, such a finding does not for that reason tell us anything important at all about what matters to specific Egyptian political actors in their concrete historical circumstances.

Aside from the doubtful basis of this claim of objectivity, Binder's interpretations of his empirical findings raise questions. He directs at-tention to the long-term constraints on Egyptian political life. His study suggests that what happens to the rural middle class somehow sets those constraints. To this end, Binder reviews the consequences of past poli-cies for the rural notables and gives some sense of what effect future policies may have on this stratum. However complete and accurate his analysis might be on this level, it cannot tell him what choices groups of

Egyptians, including those who have power today and those who might seize power tomorrow, are likely to make. He does suggest what he considers to be reasonable policies. He does not, however, give any sense of what would be reasonable to Egyptians. In the conclusion of his book, Binder acknowledges this difficulty when he qualifies his final prescription—what to "watch for" in assessing the future political strategies of the regime—with the comment: "The intuitions of distant academic observers are bound to differ from those immediately engaged."[23] This qualification, unavoidable given his method, should be taken seriously. No matter how much we know about the rural middle-class groups that Binder judges so important, that information cannot tell us what those with power will do either through or in spite of this social force.

The experience of the Nasser years makes it clear that the ruling elite has been quite capable of shaping available social forces, including rural elements, to meet its own needs.[24] Binder starts with the assumption that the members of his loosely defined stratum have a key role, and he is able to find them in the important places in Egypt. He does not tell us, however, why they are important, how they are understood by others, or what they think of their position. The understanding of actual partisan struggles requires answers to a host of such questions that Binder's method leaves untouched. From the Egyptian liberal perspective, for example, it would be crucial to know if the rural middle class as a whole has a consistent collective position on the issues liberals define as important: democracy, civil rights, the rule of law, and the preservation of Egyptian cultural integrity. In contrast, the Muslim Brothers would be most interested in the character of their faith and the ways they defend and assert that faith. For each of these examples, the important issue would be how the rural middle class would fit or could be made to fit into the group's particular set of objectives for Egypt. Binder's determining sociological structures are not really determining unless he can counter the evidence that the power and influence of the rural notables depend on the posture of those in power.

This critique of Waterbury and Binder demonstrates the difficulties of identifying *generalized* conditions or constraints that operate as the social causes of political behavior. Ruling groups, in their quest for development, for example, may well encounter the kinds of limitations that Waterbury signals, and they may have to devise strategies for dealing with the important rural stratum whose development Binder documents. But a group practice perspective concludes that these are not universal conditions or operative constraints on all political action. Because other political actors may not share the goals of the ruling elite, they may be quite unaffected or only marginally influenced by the factors that constrain Egypt's current rulers.

The large leap from the identification of conditions that do affect those with power to the judgment that such conditions affect all political behavior highlights a problem with the way the prevailing paradigms treat the issue of power. For all their other differences, both dependency and development theorists tend to identify power as the capability of a system—the world market for the dependency theorists, and the dominant political system for the development theorists. In both cases power is understood in a functionalist way—the power of the capitalist core to have its way with the periphery, or the power of those with the guns to impose their conception of where the nation should go. If we restrict our notion of power to those employed by the prevailing paradigms, power has an essentially instrumentalist character. But if we understand power to be the human capacity to project and create new worlds through collective action, then what is required is an Aristotelian notion of power tied to human agency rather than to general systems. The group practice approach employs just such a notion of power: power is considered to be a potentiality of all human groups, not only of those that currently have either a monopoly on the instruments of state coercion or the capacity to manipulate world markets in their favor. Those on the margins do have a capacity to outwit and resist those at the center, and they often do so with a measure of success sufficient to give interest to the submerged histories of their efforts.

We can understand structures and systems in some important new ways and avoid some limiting pitfalls when we become aware of them from the perspectives of those who grapple with them. In particular, a political group perspective sensitizes analysts to the normative and political content of their own theories, especially when those theories intrude directly into the political realities of others. In addition, a group action approach alerts scholars in a forceful way to the obvious advantages of decentering political inquiry and of keeping an eye on the future as well as on the past. Official structures take shape in important part as a result of their responses to the historical alternatives that surround them; the state and its potential challengers represent quite different possible futures. Underlying all these issues raised by a focus on practice and human agency is the necessity to rethink the way we understand power in Third World political studies.

Viewing the findings of orthodox scholarship from the vantage point of a practice approach signals the ways in which such generalizing studies, anxious to pass over complicating and diverting "specifics," risk interpreting other societies using the categories of our own. However, this difficulty is not adequately understood as ethnocentrism, as some well-intentions critics have argued.[25] Watertight distinctions between us and them do not hold. Awareness of the multiplicity of political alter-natives in Egypt brings a heightened sensitivity to the ways in which Western theories, however objective in intent and style, intrude on the Egyptian political scene.

Between the lines of development theory is an impressive, even captivating story of the success of Western societies in transforming themselves from a variety of traditional forms into something that the world recognizes vaguely as modern and quite unambiguously as powerful. Some Egyptians, Osman Ahmed Osman included, know this story and eagerly offer themselves to their countrymen as the empowered bearers of its "good news." By the same token, dependency analysis harbors a terrible anger that drives its story of historical injustices that purchased privilege for a limited few by relegating the mass of humanity to "underdevelopment." Other Egyptians, including a good share of the intellectuals clustered in research centers and around journals, have read this text and made it their own. An emphasis on the variety of Egyptian practices helps bring out the point that the metanarratives that inhabit Western theories make them problematic not simply because they are Western, but because they become political in the most commonsensical way: they take sides in direct and indirect ways in the political battles Egyptians are waging.

The perspective on dominant structures that emerges from the experience of those, like the subjects of this book, who seek alternatives to existing arrangements also works against the inclination of mainstream political analysis to equate politics with official politics. By bringing alternative political projects firmly into view, a political action approach does not play into the totalizing impulse of the state as political actor by an analytical strategy that focuses so closely on state functions that everything else on the political landscape is diminished or "disappeared."

Because conventional studies of Third World politics are preoccupied with the state and its handling of the development project, Western scholars rarely make alternative political practices and the different possible futures they imply the subjects of their inquiries.[26] When they consider alternatives at all, scholars usually deal with marginal groups only when they break into the dominant political history in some way. In such truncated representations, agents and events are always interruptions of someone else's history, never coherent wholes in their own right. Islamic groups, for example, posit their own specific telos for the collective life of Egyptian society. Inevitably, political projects such as those of the Muslim Brothers are defined as "unrealistic" because they appear either to be incompatible with the task of overcoming development or to misunderstand the "real" forces that cause backwardness.

This distortion of the histories of alternative groups denies us a range of potentially interesting vantage points from which to apprehend dominant structures, and it limits our understanding of the political potentialities that are actually available to Third World peoples. It may also contribute indirectly to the defeat of alternative projects. Egyptian groups such as the Brothers and the Marxist left that criticize official politics and practices are almost always subjected to official repression through censorship, imprisonment, or other forms of harassment. Conventional social scientific accounts contribute inadvertently to this repression by ignoring or dismissing the objectives and struggles of groups on the margins of official society. The conventional focus on official politics and elite groups reinforces the claim of Third World ruling groups that they are the only rightful participants in political affairs because the only realistic politics is about state management of economic development.

Only when a group suddenly appears as a threat to the regime do systemic theories regard the group as an appropriate subject for focused attention. Conventional interpreters of Egyptian politics then become concerned with understanding the particular members of a group and their immediate and long-term objectives. This was the case with the militant Islamic group that was responsible for the death of President Sadat; the members of this particular faction of Islamic activism suddenly became very important, both in Egypt and throughout the Middle East. Once again, however, these groups were examined solely in terms of their identification as a threat to the established government. This category predetermined the issues and the structures that would guide the interpretation of the members' activities and statements. Inevitably, the accounts of the Islamic groups generated by this interest emphasized violence and represented the groups as a discontinuous interruption in Egypt's history. Analysis on this basis tended to lump all Islamic groups together, underplaying the differences between tactics and strategies of particular groups.

This distortion applies to political actors with moderate as well as radical strategies. In Egypt, there are important actors on the political landscape who are neither functionaries nor radical antagonists of the state; Ne'mat Fuad, the woman whose campaign halted the Pyramids Plateau project despite its backing by Sadat and Osman, comes to mind. The political group practice approach brings such figures and their actions into view and shows us where and how they struggle to have an important effect on the shape of events.

The point is not that alternative strategies and the actors who carry them are totally absent from conventional accounts, but rather that even when they do make an appearance they are treated in terms of preexisting categories that distort our view of the actors themselves and of the projects they represent. Because both development and dependency theorists treat the regime as the primary and often the sole political actor, the rest of the population is then assigned to certain categories whose primary purpose is to define their relationship to the state. These categories, which typically come with a particular identifying phrase and thus a predetermined set of characteristics, then become the subjects of analyses. Since the categories are primarily concerned with the relationship of groups to the regime, and by extension to the outside world, individuals who have been assigned to particular categories are not understood on their own terms. The categories tell the system theorists how these people will act and what they want to achieve; there seems to be no need to understand the subjects' own definitions of their activities and goals. The difference between a systemic approach and a group politics approach, therefore, is that the former attempts to place the group within the system on the basis of the meaning imposed on the category, whether or not the label is acceptable to the collectivity in question; the group theorist continues to delve into the history, the behavior, and the objectives of the group to determine how much of the group's own distinctive project these labels capture.

The Osman circle represents a group with a clear orientation to the world market; it solicits foreign investment, and it favors private enterprise over state socialism. These characteristics and actual forms of behavior make Osman a representative of either the development theorists' category "entrepreneurial bourgeoisie" or the dependency theorists' category "comprador bourgeoisie." The dependency theorists would then have a place for the Osman circle: it would be seen as part of an alliance with the bourgeoisie and the governments of the capitalist core states and would have a stake in the exploitation of the poor of Egypt. The development theorists would also have a predetermined understanding of Osman and his colleagues; they might argue that Osman was a crucial ally of the Westernizing Sadat regime because he was able to provide necessary links to the external world, manpower, organizing skills, and an ideology attuned to the need to win American support for the regime.

Thus, each of these theories would provide a characterization of the Osman circle that placed the group in a predetermined theoretical structure. In contrast, the group politics approach provides an understanding of how group members themselves respond to such categories and the characteristics and strategies they imply. A dependency theorist does not want to know what Osman thinks about his relationships to the capitalist core or to the exploited poor; the theory is concerned only about Osman's place in these relationships. In a similar way, the development theorist is not concerned about Osman's reasons for supporting a campaign for modernization, but rather about Osman's role in that effort. Group theory, in contrast, seeks to understand not only how the history, activities, and ideas of the particular group have led members to a particular situation, but also how group members respond to their changing contexts and objectives. For a group theorist, therefore, the most important issues are not Osman's role in the world capitalist system or in a global pursuit of modernization; the group theorist tries to find out why Osman is pursuing particular relationships both inside and outside Egypt, and why these relationships make sense in the context of his experience, values, and goals. This interpretative approach explains how the Osman group responds imaginatively to the changing conditions in which it finds itself, how the circle embodies certain values in actual social practices that provide durable and attractive ways of living for group members. The systemic characterizations give little sense of this human experience of an actual—and changing—political project.

The Osman example points to a larger conclusion. Passing over the "surface" of human subjectivity in its struggling responses to particular circumstances, both functionalist and Marxist theories favor "deeper" explanations that analyze underlying determining structures. For all its other advantages of generalization and comparability, *this strategy cannot tell us what Egyptian political struggles mean to those Egyptians who are engaged in them.* Scholars working in both the functionalist and Marxist traditions inform the subjects of their studies of the "real" meaning of their actions, that is, how they are understandable in terms of some general pattern by which underlying structures are shown to work their effects, often behind the back of human actors. While some Egyptians may accept these readings of the history they are making, others do not;

the actions of some—including, incidentally, those familiar with the Western scholarship in question—may involve purposeful struggle to counter systemic effects or, on the contrary, may involve a quite different agenda for which these effects are largely unimportant. Conventional mainstream scholars and their leftist critics tend to dismiss as symptoms of either backwardness or false consciousness those experienced meanings that do not coincide with the implicit values and historical content carried by the paradigms. In this sense, general theories break the connection to the level of historical reality and to the meanings of this reality for individual men and women.[27] Once this break occurs, human actions are deprived of the intelligibility that actual political struggles give them. Actions are "understood" only to the degree that they actually coincide or are seen to coincide with putatively universal patterns in response to general conditioning factors; political struggles are emptied of the historical purposes that Egyptians and other Third World peoples hope to give them.

Political analysis that seeks to retrieve the histories of marginalized political collectivities and to explore their relevance for the future forces us to reconsider the ways in which structures and systems affect human action and its agents. In particular, the role of power in the lives of the subjects of politics cannot be understood simply as the singular instrument of ruling groups—or those who would seize power—to use in pursuit of what they define as collective national ends. If developmental and dependency theorists are misleading in isolating only certain officially recognized constraints as the constraints on all political actors in Egypt, it is because for them the only political actors in Egypt are those who hold power (or, in some cases, who immediately threaten that power). Perhaps the most significant division between the study of politics undertaken in the structuralist accounts and the study undertaken here is the notion of power that informs those studies. It is of course possible to think of power as simply residing with those who have the most guns. But the multifaceted Egyptian experience reconstructed in the preceding chapters reminds us that power is the potential of all human groups to transform themselves and their situations.

The instrumental conception of power that prevails in structuralist studies has it origins in the theories of Max Weber. "Power," according to Weber, "means every chance within a social relationship to assert one's will against opposition."[28] Power is the means to secure one's interests in relationships with others. The state, in Weber's widely accepted formulation, is defined by its legitimate monopoly of the use of violence to attain social ends. Talcot Parsons carried Weber's notion of power into his version of systems theory, which profoundly influenced the development literature: "I have defined power as the capacity of a social system to mobilize resources to attain collective goals."[29] For Parsons, power is the attribute of a total system; the amount of power in a given system depends on "the support that can be mobilized by those exercising power, the facilities they have access to (notably the control of the productivity of the economy), and the legitimation that can be accorded to the position of the holders of power." Development theorists have relied on this instrumental conception of power as the general capacity of a social system "to get things done in the interest of collective goals."[30] The notion of power in neo-Marxist theories has a surprisingly similar functionalist character. In dependency theory, for example, power is a "function" of the world economic system.[31]

Instrumental and systemic notions of power draw analysis to the center; they invariably downgrade the history of forms of power that exist at the edges and obscure earlier and richer notions of the creative role of power and politics in human life. "Interest" in human affairs binds people not only to the material world but also to each other. Men and women who are brought together in a world of things and compelled to associate on the basis of material concerns nevertheless create a web of human relationships that becomes an essential part of the meaning of their common life. An extended community, whatever the material interests that impel it, always has a distinctively human quality that is never entirely defined by external needs. From their relationships to others, actors derive knowledge of who they are and understanding of the world in which they act. For this reason, interpretations of human collectivities can never be simply a calculus of objective needs. We must always know the people themselves in order to grasp how they view both the needs that press on them and the ties with others that they must forge in order to meet those needs.[32]

Useful elaborations of the concept of "the good society" come only in the histories of actual groups of men and women. Because such groups have a real historical existence in a particular society and can be understood only in terms of that society, it is an empirical task to identify political projects that advance such normative claims. It is not possible to circumvent this practical research effort by relying on transhistorical and metatheoretical statements of the proper ends of collective life.[33] Statements about the ends of collective life are embedded in the histories of experienced political practices. Because these statements are available for multiple interpretations both by the actors themselves and by those who seek to understand them, the record of struggles for a better future has a flexible meaning. This ambiguity is a source of persuasive power and creative potential. Ambiguity is an invitation to internal argument over the definition of the shared vision of a better future. By participating in group life members carry the vision they create through time and the specific circumstances of their own existence. The shared vision in turn sustains them by giving particular political and moral significance to their lives.[34] Nasserists, for example, debate the forms that Egypt's connection to the Arab world should take in the wake of Camp David. But the very premise of the debate—that Egypt's future is tied to the fate of the Arabs—sets the Nasserists apart from the Muslim Brothers, whose collective sense of identity is built on Islam and an explicit rejection of Arabism as the organizing center of identity.

There is no skirting the fact that understanding how political groups form and cohere requires confronting the unique. Each group experience differs from any that preceded it. None can one be a reliable blueprint for a later effort. Enacted stories, in the retelling, always have the character of particular histories rather than generalized theoretical reconstructions. This does not mean, however, that theory has no role in their representation. History, as it is understood here, is the most theoretical of disciplines; however, the theory required is interpretative theory. The systemic paradigms that have dominated the study of Third World politics can make only a limited contribution to the reconstruction of enacted stories of political groups. Paradigmatic thinking may alert one to factors that are essential to the understanding of group life, but they cannot reveal how individual actors actually react to these factors. In addition, paradigms, including both the development and dependency models, may themselves become a factor in the politics that one is trying to understand, because political actors may act consciously under the influence of a paradigmatic view of reality. Nevertheless, paradigmatic thinking has no capacity to reflect on its own relative impact when it becomes part of a unique pattern of events; without internal understanding, it is impossible to know how the political actors actually responded to the influence of the paradigm.

Our readings of the historical narratives of others thus have the character of interpretative theories. In effect, the narrative of a particular group explains the stories that historical actors are enacting to themselves and to others. The narrative must be recognizable to its subjects and understandable to those who seek to know them. Interpretative theory has the character of a representation or mapping of the social world in which one is interested.[35] It is grounded in the specific historical context.[36] Theory of this kind makes contextual understanding possible by showing how a unique pattern of varied and seemingly disparate elements is part of a subjectively experienced whole.[37] The test of grounded theory is successful interaction by the interpreter with the men and women who live in that world. Interaction requires the ability to explain and to anticipate behavior appropriate to the social world in question. That ability, in turn, depends on knowing how members weigh and relate the key elements of their social world.[38]

A humanistic social science aims to bring out the potentialities in the human condition. Yet, how are scholars to recognize and analyze changes for the better in the absence of the kind of universal norms of progress implicitly carried by the conventional paradigms? This book demonstrates a new point of entry by grounding critical theory in particular Third World historical experiences and according to internal standards of what constitutes a better social world. The previous chapters show how normative issues can be treated on the basis of the consciousness of Third World political actors. The study of politics is based explicitly on the standards of progress that are generated by the efforts of specific groups of Egyptians who are struggling for what they consider a better life for themselves and all Egyptians.

Misplaced confidence in attributing purpose to other people's political lives prevents us from seeing clearly the political visions they create for themselves and from understanding the practical strategies they devise to realize them. Behind the seemingly benign assumption that Third World politics is about the problem of underdevelopment lurks the refusal to accept the premise that while other people may indeed share some of the ends we set for ourselves, they may do so in novel ways, or they may set quite different goals for themselves. Why, when we study other people's politics—especially people whose worldly power is less than ours—do we suddenly forget the frustrations and limitations of our own political life? Perhaps if we could see them and their struggles more clearly—and not just what we take to be their problems, their defects, and their defeats—we might recover our capacity for openness to others and our willingness to learn from their most promising political experiments.

10

Unseen Struggles: Group Politics, Persons, and Possibilities

What men seek in history are the transformations of the acting subject in the dialectical relation Men-World, i.e., transformations of human society. It follows that the object of the historical sciences is human actions at all times and places in the degree to which they have had or now have an importance for or influence on the existence and structure of the present or future human community.

—*Lucien Goldmann*

It is important to see the faces and hear the voices of those whose politics we hope to understand, especially if they live on distant shores. When we do so, the acting and speaking that define their lives, rather than simply our own interests or fears, can more easily provoke and guide the representations we make of them. The narrative self-descriptions of others carry a rich sense of unique personhood, asserted against particular obstacles. Stories of struggle give us a better chance to know the human subjects who act in them and not just the obstacles they face in carrying their projects forward; by paying attention to these narratives, we can hope to balance appreciation for the constraining effects of structures, both national and international, with awareness of the creative power of men and women acting together to make and unmake these same systems.

Like reading a powerful novel, knowing the stories of other political communities brings to life the character and the trials of others as they strive to use power for human purposes; it may also give us an expressive picture of human feelings, principles, and ends that are poorly formulated or absent in our experience. Taken together, the experience of Egyptians in alternative groups reveals the existence of a variety of public worlds in which Egyptians appear as creative political actors.[1] These discontinuous public worlds provide a surrounding human presence that has a critical dimension in the precise sense that the Egyptians who act in it generate concepts, practices, or structures that they understand as

297

new and better forms of social life.[2] By their interactions, the men and women in political groups create social facts whose importance they believe extends to Egyptian society at large. Unlike stultifying official structures, these alternative arrangements create milieux that are experienced as sustaining collective action to create a better future.

Wherever they are located in the body politic, political groups empower their members to struggle consciously to create such a critical environment of expanded possibilities.[3] Some groups are already social forces on behalf of alternative possibilities; they have some capacity to bring about change because of their link to existing social movements, ideological currents, or social strata that strive for transformation. Other groups embody distinctive values that, if generalized in society, would precipitate fundamental social change. Groups of this kind establish transformative values as a potential force in Egyptian public life. They create an active resource for the future, sustained by partially realized social and economic structures. In doing so they too contribute to the generation of new political potentialities. Despite official containment, they are important for the alternative political choices they create and safeguard.

What these diverse groups display in common is the human potential to create new political possibilities within constraints. Some groups, such as the Osman circle, express new potentialities from within an alliance with the existing regime. Others, such as the liberals, the Nasserists, and the Marxists, emerge from the major but submerged opposition currents. Still others constitute themselves at the margins or, more frequently, in the interstices of official institutions, such as the clusters of intellectuals in think tanks (for example, the Ahram Center for Political and Strategic Studies) and journals (for example, the *Economic Ahram* [*al-Ahram al-Iqtisadi*]). Still more peripheral are impressive experiments such as the Wissa Wassef School at Harrania. Finally, there are groups that are not easily conceptualized at all in relation to the established regime. They are "countersocieties" that haunt the established order. Among such groups in Egypt, the Muslim Brothers demonstrate a particularly wide and enduring appeal.

Interpretative theory makes no claim to judge in any authoritative way the respective merits of these groups from some privileged external perspective. Moreover, because these lives are diverse and the groups they form project incompatible political futures, an interpretative study imposes no harmonizing unity. The juxtaposition of conflicting forms of political life itself prompts critical reflection. Brought into view as integral and distinctive wholes, the narratives seem to comment on each other, fluidly indicating from their shifting perspectives both incompatibilities and points of contact.

Awareness of the variety of political groups in Egypt brings a new sense of the various relations of meaning and power within which political actors struggle to live their collective lives. Such knowledge is not generated by questions about why the subjects of politics say or do things, nor by a primary interest in what they should say or do. The political group approach responds instead to our need to know what it is that they actually say and do and what their speech and action mean in their own right. The normative content of the analysis is essentially theirs and not ours; our theories of the meaning of their actions are built explicitly on theirs.

Interpretative inquiry assumes that peoples on distant shores have their own political truths to which we have no easy access. "Respect in the Other," enjoins Vincent Crapanzano, "the same mystery we expect others to respect in ourselves."[4] Western social scientists interested in the politics of the Third World peoples should be willing to loosen the grip on even their most treasured readings of their own social and historical experience; they should do so partly to open themselves to the value of other human experiences of politics, and partly because they recognize that they understand their own experience imperfectly at best. Such openness, for all the disparagement it has suffered by both the political left and right, encourages the reach that is essential if we are to grasp the inherent meanings of political experiences that other human beings create out of the different social and historical resources available to them.[5]

Openness to the experience of other peoples does not require that we lose our distinctive consciousness, purposes, and practices in an unattainable union with postmodernism's abstract "Other"; nor does it mean that we must obliterate their experience by appropriating it to our own. The consciousness of an interpretative social science recognizes that the effort to understand others inevitably takes off from our own experience and is shaped by our own judgment.[6] Our judgments fix the point of departure of inquiry. In this sense, beginnings are arbitrary because they are not given by the subjects of study; they arise from our own interests and needs. What we set out to learn from others is the answer to definite questions, an answer that is given by *their* experience to questions that generally originate in *our* own. At the same time, the research project requires human interaction that creates possibilities beyond the edification of the researcher. Inevitably, the human subjects of research also learn from and are affected by the encounter. If nothing else, our questions about their lives may suggest a different angle of vision from which to view the things they take for granted. Moreover, the human interaction of the researchers and the subjects of their inquiry may itself create or suggest new possibilities for shared projects. In short, on the plane of the human condition, prudential knowledge of this kind broadens conception of the range of political possibilities available to human beings; what we learn from our interaction about how to cope with or alter circumstances in the light of specific human purposes may well suggest ways out of our own dilemmas as well as theirs.

This conception of the research task explains why interpretation must always overcome the barriers that exist between two equally complex human situations, our own situation and the situation of those we hope to understand.[7] Categories of self-description, present in every human context, are an essential resource for the effort to push through the barriers. Interpreters reach from their own context to touch the situation of others. Yet, ultimately the grasp of the rationality of the lives of other people relies on the development of appreciation for the ways in which those people's thought and action accord with the logic of their situation as they experience it.[8] Human meanings always exist for individual subjects in specific situations. The human meaning of political thought and action derives from its place in a particular experienced world.

Interpretations of the political practices of others that build on self-descriptions, such as those in this volume, can be based on evidence with a clear principle of selection. Is the representation of reality adequate to the self-understanding of the actors, as well as understandable to the more general readership for which it is intended? Because political meanings are public and openly displayed rather than private, the steps by which a particular investigator discerns the contextual rationality in overt political performances can be retraced by other investigators who, on the basis of what they can discover in the historical record about those performances and about the actor's own self-description of them, can evaluate the credibility of an interpretation.[9] This means that delineations that claim to use categories deriving from the self-descriptions of historical actors can be independently assessed, argued over, and corrected, not least by the actors themselves.

For this reason, the character of knowledge rooted in particular experience invites extension of the debate about particular interpretations to the human subjects of that knowledge. Human beings invariably have something important to say about what they are up to in their political lives. Scholars, therefore, have in interest that goes beyond civility in the right of Third World peoples to "speak and write back" to their interpreters.[10] At a minimum, Western scholars writing on Egypt, for example, should actively seek out forums in which Egyptians can contend with them over the method and substance of the interpretative process; findings should be made available to Egyptian publics; and Western specialists should write in anticipation of critical review of their work by Egyptian social scientists who are coequal members of the community of interpreters to which they all belong.[11]

The interpretative process does not end, of course, when standards based on credibility to the subjects of study are met. Group theorists long ago warned that raw self-understandings of political actions must always be further interpreted because political agents may either delude outsiders or themselves or be unaware of important consequences of their behavior.[12] An interpretative social science cannot rest content with the self-characterizations of its human subjects, although, given the aim of an internal understanding, it is hard to see how it could begin anywhere else. Some, but certainly not all, of the important patterns observable in the lives of others do result from their purposeful intentions as revealed in their deliberate struggles, while others just as clearly do not. Yet, in both cases, as Charles Taylor argues, it is possible to make those patterns intelligible by establishing their relationship, however simple or complex, direct or indirect, to conscious intentions.[13] Moreover, knowledge that rests on a grasp of the self-understandings of others facilitates communication and not just manipulation, conversation and cooperation and not just domination; it offers the prospect of mutual learning about how communities can use the power they create to realize human values and ends.

This guarded optimism of interpretative social science questions the most disabling doubts recently expressed by postmodernist thinkers about the possibility of reliable knowledge of others: broadly philosophical questions about the possibility of knowing the Other in some abstract sense distracts us from the problems and possibilities of knowledge of recognizable other persons at identifiable times and places. Historical knowledge of this kind, focused on recognizable human subjects of politics and tied to their self-understandings, is as difficult and as fraught with ambiguity as making sense of any human experience but, in the essential matters of interpretation, not more so.[14]

In Europe and the United States, postmodernist thinkers in virtually all fields are questioning the old foundations of knowledge. Across the intellectual landscape, faith in older paradigms that aimed for knowledge of macrosystems and structures is giving way, in some cases to promising new approaches such as *new* new criticism in comparative literature and Critical Legal Studies in law, in others to disabling doubts.[15] In comparative politics, the destructive effects of the critique are particularly strong; "theory" there is identified for the most part with either outmoded behavioralist or overreaching structuralist approaches that are particularly susceptible to discredit as interested and ethnocentric "discourses." In Third World studies, in particular, attacks on vulnerable structuralist knowledge claims are opening the way for abandonment of all social scientific theorizing. The void left there is being filled instead by a turn to atheoretical strategies that simply abandon any systematic theorizing in favor of traditional history, "native" accounts, or casual and premature theoretical eclecticism. Regrettably, these atheoretical approaches are accelerating the trend, already well established by the older structuralist accounts, to diminish the presence of the human subjects of Third World politics and to discount the importance of their actual political practices.

A recent study of Islam and politics, written "from within the Orientalist tradition of European and American scholarship," illustrates the trend toward the abandonment of social scientific theory; Daniel Pipes dismisses the "recent profusion of writings by social scientists and journalists" in favor of the traditional Western authorities on the Orient, supplemented by occasional privileged insider commentaries such as those of the novelist V. S. Naipul.[16] Other scholars have responded to the disarray in the field by piecing together the bits and pieces of shattered paradigms in awkwardly eclectic frameworks. The notion is gaining ground that resolution of the dilemmas of Third World studies resides in the false choice between fragmented paradigms and traditional authorities, ignoring the interpretative possibility. An influential recent review of the field of Third World studies fails to consider interpretative research strategies.[17] Another otherwise erudite summation of recent work in Third World studies collapses interpretative social science into traditional history, ignoring recent advances both in interpretative theory and in their applications to Third World societies.[18]

Interpretative social science has a claim to register against this pessimistic tide. Rejecting the formal knowledge of structures and systems promised by the paradigms, it seeks historical knowledge of persons and practices, redefining "history" in the process. Interpretations of actual group practices built around self-descriptions understand history as "not simply something that happens to people but something they made—within, of course, the very powerful constraints of the system within which they are operating."[19] Interpretative theory does drag us, as Lévi-Strauss warned, into "the swamps of experience" where the uncertainties of context, consciousness, and contingency work against any inflated sense that our interpretative experiments have fully grasped the experience of others.[20] However, facing these theoretical dilemmas squarely, rather than taking refuge in "authorities," allows us the hope that we can learn things from others in a way reliable enough to enhance human solidarity.

The Third World "informant," in particular, is emerging as one possible means of bypassing theory on the route to knowledge of Third World politics. Faced with the complexities of Arab politics, Western publics are responding positively to the possibility of "letting Arabs speak for themselves." On reflection, the prescription is not as innocent as it sounds, because the immediate question is: which Arabs? Clearly, no single Arab voice can represent the range of opinion that exists even within a single Arab country. Moreover, there is a danger that the voices scholars pick up and amplify will be those that echo Western views. The experience of the colonial era showed how easy it is to find "native" assessments that purvey Western views of non-Western peoples with Arab (or African, Asian, or Latin American) names attached.

At present reports from Third World informants such as the novelist V. S. Naipul are providing a powerful model.[21] On the Arab world, the eloquent political commentaries of Fouad Ajami are bringing studies based on personal witness into the mainstream literature, laying the foundations of a "testimonial" social science for Third World studies.[22]

In Ajami's hands, in particular, the "informant" approach offers much to justify the attention it has received. Responsive to the new interest in language and symbol, Ajami's account of *The Arab Predicament* offers affecting evocations of people and places that dramatize the theoretical issues of Arab political thinking in a striking way. Arguments are augmented by the force of the richly drawn personalities who articulate them, not least the talented author himself. In Ajami's work one gets a vivid sense of ideologies as the utterances of flesh-and-blood, even passionate beings—Ajami appears to offer precisely the human element that is missing in the impersonal accounts of the system-builders.

The authorial voice, an Arab voice, is certainly a reminder that other people are more than crises and problems; they are also creativity and intelligence. The singularity of the voice strengthens the account of ideas, events, and persons by the harmony and coherence it brings, along with insight and capacity to move. The insider status of Ajami's work is won by more than name and self-consciously evoked lineage; the text carries clear internal evidence of an ear steeped in the range and subtleties of Arab political discourse. At the same time, the engaged and provocative commentary on that discourse often provides creative and original interpretations.

It detracts nothing from this appreciation for the vividness of the language, the immediacy of the effect, and the obvious intelligence that enlivens the text to caution that these considerable virtues obscure important limitations from a social scientific perspective that must seek more than a personal reading of people and events. Ajami presents himself as an Arab authority on the Arabs; his work purportedly provides Western publics with authoritative access to the consciousness and speech of the Arabs. Studies that base their authority on the insider status of the author often explicitly ask readers to suspend the usual canons of critical scholarly review. Ajami is exemplary in this respect. He notes plainly that "much of what I have written here has personal meaning to me, and there is no use hiding behind academic objectivity."[23] Yet, the real issue is method and not the unavoidable personal significance of any research effort or some unattainable standard of objectivity. Missing in Ajami's elegantly written work are the principles of selection that have guided his choices and the principles of validation that have disciplined his subjectivity.

Principles of selection do make a difference, especially because Ajami forcefully rejects his subjects' broad definitions of their situation. The explanatory concepts, metaphors, and other analytical devices he employs to make sense of Arab politics are unrelated to the constructs that his subjects use in their ordinary lives. In fact, Ajami argues aggressively that the language of his Arab subjects should be ignored. The claim goes beyond the standard warning about lies and false consciousness, which after all implicitly suggests that the subjects have a capacity for "truth" and "consciousness." Instead, Ajami relies on a generalized portrait of the debased Lebanese press where "no one took seriously what . . . magazines said," where " 'principles' were things that men could not afford," to offer a generalized judgment about the "place assigned to the written and spoken word in Arab politics"; such an undisciplined, negative generalization comes unacceptably close to providing an updated version of the old claim of an Arab mind unable to formulate connections between language and any principled collective purpose.[24]

Pointedly ignoring the accounts of his subjects, Ajami relies instead on his insider's intuitions to lift events and participants out of their historical context and to exemplify the essential points of his interpretation of the meaning of Arab politics. Individuals and actions lose their grounding in their own history and consciousness. They are related only by the logic of Ajami's purely personal intuition, and readers consequently have no independent means to assess them. In addition, the intuitions elaborated in *The Arab Predicament* turn out to have important political implications. Ajami's Arabs, whatever their protestations to the contrary, are defined as victims of dilemmas of their own making. *The Arab Predicament*, in the author's words, is a "chronicle of illusions and despair, of politics repeatedly degenerating into bloodletting."[25]

Ajami's intellectual history uses the story of the murder of Salim al-Lawzi, a Lebanese journalist, as a metaphor for the situation of contemporary Arabs: "In the way he lived and the way he died, al-Lawzi told volumes about what I shall continually refer to as the Arab predicament in the modern world." The report describes Salim al-Lawzi as an opportunist who is neither particularly talented nor honest. Ajami takes his theme from a friend's funeral oration for the journalist: "Freedom is a plant alien to our part of the world. Whenever planted it dies . . . We used to blame the colonialists. Then some of us colonized others and the plant of freedom died over and over again."[26]

Ajami moves from the funeral oration of a man he describes as a third-rate journalist to a generalization about the character of the world in which the Arabs live: "The wounds that mattered were self-inflicted wounds. The outside world intruded, but the destruction one saw reflected the logic of Arab history, the quality of its leadership. The divisions of the Arab world were real, not contrived points on a map or a colonial trick of divide and conquer. No outsiders had to oppress and mutilate. The whip was cracked by one's own."[27]

Why such large claims about Arab history for this particular Lebanese event? Readers familiar with recent Arab history could easily advance alternative examples that have an equal claim to represent more than themselves. Why not begin with an account of the death of a Syrian Islamic militant, killed while seeking to formulate an alternative to the repressive regime in Damascus? Or the story of a nationalist-minded Palestinian Arab mayor who, after asserting the right of resistance of an occupied people, loses his legs in a bombing attack by a settlers' terrorist group on the West Bank? The point is not that these are somehow better examples, but rather that readers are given no criteria by which to judge. Moreover, the choice of a Lebanese "opportunist" to represent the Arab predicament—rather than an Arab figure who is a Syrian religious figure or a Palestinian nationalist acting on principles—reveals a lack of consideration of any alternative social or political worlds for which Arabs are struggling. Ajami is content to pile up one negative example after another in a self-consciously unscientific way.[28] Readers are left with the sense that there is no escape from the traps Ajami describes, except perhaps emigration to the West.[29]

Ajami's claims to see the Arab world reflected in a murder in Lebanon reveal a great deal more about the political prejudices and interests of his adopted American society than they reveal about Arab political experiences. Ajami's pessimism carries a message that the Arabs suffer from self-inflicted wounds: everything Arab is severely and irrevocably flawed; renewal from within the Arab world is impossible. In Ajami's work Western elites find not only an exoneration from any indictment of their colonial past but also an invitation for new involvements to save the Arab world from itself. Clearly, there is a burden to be borne in Ajami's Middle East.

Ajami justifies the starting point of *The Arab Predicament*—with its explicit refusal of Arab self-descriptions that point to the adverse impact of such forces as Western imperialism and neoimperialism, the world market, or the Israeli state on the political lives of Arabs—with a nod to the method of the anthropologist Clifford Geertz. Ajami writes that "the world can be read into small events: In Clifford Geertz's imagery winks can be made to speak to epistemology."[30] Ajami invokes Geertz's name and authority as a cultural interpreter but pays scant attention to his interpretative method, which assumes the knowledgeability of its human subjects.[31] Geertz argues that human beings are suspended in webs of meanings of their own making. His approach aims for analysis that draws out specific intrinsic meanings and suggests the ways those meanings (other people's meanings) speak to large issues. In this way, Geertz aims to gain access to the cultural world in which his human subjects live, to give us, as he puts it, "another country heard from" on human concerns that are of universal interest.[32] In contrast, Ajami uses his considerable imaginative and stylistic flair to "read things into" the events and persons he observes; he does so precisely because he judges that his subjects lack the capacity to speak for themselves and to act collectively in principled ways. The large, dismal issues of what Ajami calls "the Arab predicament" are predefined, and the specific details he provides are mere examples.[33] Ajami monopolizes the Arabs. The Arabs cited and depicted are wrenched from their own webs of meaning to illustrate Ajami's themes; in the end the only voice we hear, the only face we see, is his own.

Ajami does offer reassuring and important observations about his personal intentions: "Some of what is stated here is painful to reflect upon and painful to read, but it is stated neither as some kind of massive indictment nor with any sense of moral and political superiority."[34] I see no reason not to grant requests such as Ajami's that readers suspend the usual standards of methodological accountability and credit modesty and good intentions. Yet we must not consider such works to be social science, however much we admire them as literature, confessions, or—as I regard Ajami's essay—powerfully affecting and elegantly written statements of personal witness and conviction.

From a perspective that looks for historical knowledge of people and practices rather than general knowledge of systems and structures, tinkering with the old paradigms is not likely to be any more promising than "testimonial" accounts as a means of remedying the fundamental problems of Third World studies. In the abstract, the idea of salvaging the most promising insights, ideas, and concepts of general theories and combining them in new ways is appealing enough. Indeed, the most impressive example of this approach applied to Egypt, Raymond Hinnebusch's *Egyptian Politics under Sadat,* has much to recommend it.

Hinnebusch's generous and inclusive strategy credits insights across the board. His primary objective is consolidation of the findings of the functionalists, preoccupied with official political structures and culture as they grapple with problems of power maintenance and modernization. However, he recognizes quite clearly the contribution of Marxist analysts, who emphasize the role of class and imperialism in shaping political outcomes. Hinnebusch's eclectic sensibility provokes few exclusions, and the result is a concise, fair, and reliable summation of currently available information about the Egyptian state. Within the spacious confines of his synthetic framework, Hinnebusch also locates areas for important new empirical research, most notably the composition and activities of elites and counterelites; his findings in these areas expand our understanding of important dimensions of the process of state formation in Egypt.

But Hinnebusch's measured and judicious study pays the price of consensus scholarship in a field from which consensus has disappeared and in which questions now go beyond probing the limitations of a particular generalizing framework (which could conceivably be mended by borrowings from its competitors) to the larger issue of the value of structuralist accounts per se and the kind of overly confident paradigmatic thinking that goes with them. In practice, eclecticism of this kind runs the risk of unwarranted and insensitive self-assurance in using external measures to define in an absolute way the significance of other people's political lives. The temptation is also strong to assume that the resulting combination of strategies somehow captures the best of both worlds.

Eclecticism, in short, all too frequently exaggerates its own coherence and capacity, and the dangers are particularly great in a field such as Third World studies. In Hinnebusch a diluted Marxism coexists uncomfortably with a heavy-handed functionalism. Following the Marxist lead, Hinnebusch finds pressures from dominant social classes and the world capitalist system to be the ultimate stimulus of system change but emphasizes the developmental performance of dominant political structures, the political elite, and official public policies.

The best new work of anthropologists and sociologists, alert to the limits of sure knowledge of others, warns: "In research one never totally succeeds . . . One never fully comprehends social phenomena."[35] In contrast, Hinnebusch makes pronouncements: there "is a natural evolution to which initially populist-oriented authoritarian-modernizing regimes seem vulnerable"; political formations come into being as a "function of a specific stage of state formation and societal modernization." Egypt and other such states change in predictable ways because of the "inevitable transitional character of authoritarian-populist regimes."[36] Relying on the old functionalist certainties, Hinnebusch sprinkles his work with discoveries of "the key" to some "inevitable" characteristic of large categories of states.[37] Wielding the global Marxist labels, he obscures a fluid and unformed class situation by writing of the "bourgeoisie and its international partners" and of the Sadat regime as "a fairly clear form of bourgeois class rule."[38]

Hinnebusch believes that his theoretical amalgam delivers such certain knowledge of Egyptian politics because the two theoretical approaches he uses operate on different levels of analysis and can therefore be combined in a particularly powerful way: the Marxist framework on the level of the world capitalist system and domestic class forces; and functionalism at the level of the state and the political elite. He argues that these two perspectives are partial and therefore can be joined to achieve one complete view. Unfortunately, each perspective in fact has a holistic and distinctive conception of Egyptian politics. When the findings of Marxist and functionalist approaches are run together, the result is more confusing than enlightening.

Hinnebusch's treatment of the 1967 war illustrates these problems. His basic conceptualization of the roots of the Israeli-Egyptian conflict is functionalist. Weber's concept of charisma, Hinnebusch tells us, is "the single most convincing key to understanding the regime."[39] In the context of war, charisma requires heroic performance. Hinnebusch argues that Nasser as a charismatic leader was driven to meet the expectations of his followers and to overextend himself: "Nasser's need to sustain his role as Pan-Arab leader helped entangle him in costly and ultimately disastrous interstate conflicts." Thus, the central argument is the functionalist one that the Egyptian regime was drive by its own systemic needs to "stimulate the very environmental forces which generated a system-transforming crisis."[40] Internal determinants outweigh external forces in this explanation of the outbreak of the 1967 war.

Two pages later, however, Hinnebusch undermines this internal, functionalist explanation with a contradictory dependency view: emphasizing "external forces," which intervened "in the form of the 1967 war in which Israel, with American arms and connivance, struck a decisive blow at Nasirism [*sic*]." This event, portrayed as "a delayed reaction by forces associated with the dominant world order against a nationalist challenge to it," certainly fits the Marxist neoimperialist scenario. Given the theoretical strategy he has adopted, Hinnebusch is left with no option but to present these contradictory views one after the other with no possibility of reconciling them.

Eclecticism like Hinnebusch's that derives from the systems and structures paradigms has another unintended consequence; it unknowingly advances the new postmodernist impulse to downgrade the role of human agency and intention in explaining politics and society. Structuralist thinking paved the way for this de-emphasis of purposeful action by emphasizing that making sense of any act required knowledge of a "background language of practices and institutions"; as Charles Taylor explains, "while there will be a particular goal sought in the act, those features of it that pertain to the structural background will not be objects of individual purpose."[42] Structuralism, and especially its eclectic revivals, submerges human collectivities and their purposes in the rush to delineate determining systems and structures.

In arguing for a strong presence of the human subjects of politics in the Third World political realities we seek to know, the group practice approach argues against the pervasive antisubjectivism of the eighties, which theorizes texts without authors, discourses without speakers, and political histories without political subjects. It is not necessary to deny the power of the background structures and systems of all human action and meaning, to insist that inquiry that aims to understand the transformations possible in human history requires the presence of the conscious and knowledgeable authors of collective human creativity.

We do rely on language to communicate our diverse experiences, and particular languages, tied to particular forms of living, constrain and enable our thinking in ways we cannot consciously control and perhaps do not even recognize. A good deal of what we actually say about our experiences therefore has little to do with what we consciously wish to say. Yet, it is also true that any linguistic system can be maintained only through knowing and through skillful acts of writing and speaking. If we are interested in how and why particular systems of thought and action arise, it is hard to see why we should ignore human actors who live within them, both affirming and transforming them by their actions.[43]

By my reading, the antihumanist temper of the eighties, including the recent "celebrations" of the collapse of the human subject of history, are not really celebrations at all but rather ironic attempts to shock us into recognition of the horror of the human loss, to teach us to live somehow "beyond despair." Yet, surely the histories of the colonial wars, the gas chambers, and the gulag provide more potent warnings against a complacent humanism. And when we give human faces to those who misused humanism for inhuman goals, when we think in concrete historical rather than abstract philosophical terms, to what can we appeal to rally against the repetition of those horrors if not to a humanism that is not complacent, if not to human subjects, including those who live in the Third World, with whom we can hope to act?

The distinguishing feature of the human being, Hans-Georg Gadamer has argued, is "superiority over what is actually present, his sense of the future."[44] The political realm is a human necessity, because it gives concrete substance to the unique ability of men and women to offer each other visions of what Kant called a "better future condition of the human race."[45] There are points of connection between the Egyptian political experience and our own that mainstream theorists and their leftist critics have artificially broken by the assumption of our development and their underdevelopment. For us and for Egyptians, politics is about more than the certainties of structural constraints and government efforts to achieve the end of national development. Things are not advanced much when the postmodernists cast Egyptians and other Third World peoples as the unknowable Other; the programmatic refusal to believe that recognizable other people have stories to tell that we just might understand, in part at least, denies us that potential We who can speak and act together for common projects of all kinds that reduce human misery. Egyptians have provided concrete answers to questions about the human potential to struggle for humane values and ends of collective life in the modern world. Both the searching general questions and the specific narrative answers are of interest to us all.

Notes

Except where otherwise noted, works published in Egypt and other Arab countries are in Arabic; I have translated the titles for the reader's convenience. For the few English-language periodicals published in Arab countries, I have noted the original language in parentheses.

Introduction

1. See David Hirst and Irene Beeson, *Sadat* (London: Faber & Faber, 1981), p. 11.

2. *Newsweek*, Oct. 19, 1981; Hirst and Beeson, *Sadat*, p. 13.

3. Michel Foucault draws attention to the repressed histories of marginal groups, calling them "subjugated histories"; *Power/Knowledge: Selected Interview and Other Writings, 1972–1977*, ed. Colin Gordon (New York: Pantheon, 1980), pp. 78–92. However, Foucault's work on these themes suffers, for my purposes at least, from the downplaying of human agency. More useful has been Herbert Marcuse's analysis of what he calls "the historical alternatives which haunt the established society as subversive tendencies and forces"; *One-Dimensional Man: Studies in the Ideology of Advanced Industrial Society* (Boston: Beacon Press, 1964), p. xii. My treatment of Egyptian groups follows the suggestive lead of the Frankfurt School, with an emphasis on liberating "praxis," rather than Foucault, with his focus on multiple "discourses."

4. In my work I draw freely on the group theory tradition in American political science. Although my own definition (elaborated later in this chapter) of what I call a political group differs from the interest group that has been the main object of study of group theorists, I want to acknowledge the influence of Arthur F. Bentley, in particular, on my thinking. In Bentley's important work I have found reassurance for my own sense of the utility of a functional and operational view of politics, alert to the continuous changes in strategies, tactics, and demands of political actors; confidence to begin the effort to define politically important groups in terms of their

313

self-described political preferences and not their fixed social and economic characteristics; a reluctance to ascribe to groups of human beings objective interests said to motivate their behavior but of which they are unaware; confirmation for my idea of a social science that focuses on purposive, goal-directed social action rather than on any number of alleged determinants of such action; support for my own insistence that observable behavior (including speech) and not verbal claims be the primary evidence for the characterization of political actors; emphasis on social context as the source of political meaning; and, above all, belief that the most relevant actors in a political study are recognizable human beings and not grand abstractions or collectivities such as class, race, or nation that are often too general and too vague to be of help in understanding the human experience of politics. All these attributes of Bentley's version of the group approach are apparent in his classic, *The Process of Government* (Cambridge, Mass.: Harvard University Press, 1967).

5. I agree with Roger Owen, among others, that the most sensible way to explain Arab politics is the factional approach, which looks at power struggles within authoritarian structures. See Owen, "Explaining Arab Politics," *Political Studies,* 26, no. 4 (1978), 507–512. Attention to "families, clans and cliques" in those official contests is clearly warranted, as Robert Springborg has so ably shown. See his "Patterns of Association in the Egyptian Political Elite," in *Political Elites in the Middle East,* ed. George Lenczowski (Washington, D.C.: American Enterprise Institute, 1975). However, the study of alternative political groups extends the definition of politics in ways for which these research strategies are not fully adequate.

6. For a lucid statement of this point see F. Allan Hanson, *Meaning in Culture* (London: Routledge & Kegan Paul, 1975), pp. 35–36.

7. The interest in understanding human groups and the transformative ends they have pursued is discussed in Lucien Goldmann, *The Human Sciences and Philosophy,* trans. Richard Nice (London: Jonathan Cape, 1969), pp. 23–35.

8. In developing my notion of group practice I will insist on the relationship of political power to social praxis that includes both language and action. My thinking is influenced by the hermeneutics of Hans-Georg Gadamer, the two versions of symbolic anthropology of Clifford Geertz and Victor Turner, the critical theory of Herbert Marcuse and Albrecht Wellmer, and the practice theory of Anthony Giddens (rather than the version worked out by Pierre Bourdieu). See especially Gadamer, "Man and Language (1966)," in *Philosophical Hermeneutics* (Berkeley: University of California Press, 1976); Geertz, "The Politics of Meaning," in *The Interpretation of Cultures* (New York: Basic Books, 1973); Turner, *The Ritual Process* (Chicago: Aldine, 1969); Marcuse, *One-Dimensional Man;* Wellmer, *Critical Theory of Society* (New York: Herder and Herder, 1971); and Giddens, "Action, Structure, and Power," in *Profiles and Critiques in Social Theory* (Berkeley: University of California Press, 1982). My thinking has also been shaped by post-positivist philosophy of science, particularly the work of Karl Popper. I share with Popper the conviction that the human world of theories and shared meanings is an "objective world, at once autonomous but a human creation." Popper calls this human reality a "third world" of intelligibles or "possible objects of thought" that is distinguished from the first world of material things and the second world of individual mental or psychological states. I. C. Jarvie explains that the human phenomena of Popper's third world are not understandable in terms of the reasons or intentions of individ-

uals; rather, they are unintended consequences of human thought and action that must be understood in their own right. See Karl R. Popper, *Objective Knowledge: An Evolutionary Approach* (Oxford: Clarendon Press, 1972), pp. 152–190; and I. C. Jarvie, *Concepts and Society* (London: Routledge & Kegan Paul, 1972), p. 43. However, Popper tends to elevate truth over meaning. My own sense is that both theories and collective meanings are real phenomena that can be investigated in a systematic way that allows independent verification of what we learn about them. They are in this precise sense "objective," although the word is such a red flag that I prefer to avoid it. An argument that parallels mine is made in F. Allan Hanson, *Meaning in Culture* (London: Routledge & Kegan Paul, 1975), p. 73.

9. Barrington Moore, Jr., has brought this negative formulation of the value issues of the good-society debate into the social science mainstream. In his work Moore also emphasizes the appropriateness of the study of potentiality and the range of alternatives available in particular societies. These methodological guidelines are found throughout Moore's work, but especially in his studies of humanism and social science methods. See Moore, *Political Power and Social Theory: Six Studies* (Cambridge, Mass.: Harvard University Press, 1958). For a recent discussion of the assumptions of a humanistic social science, see Ken Plummer, *Documents of Life: An Introduction to the Problems and Literature of a Humanistic Method* (London: Allen & Unwin, 1983). Plummer draws particular attention to the moral and political role of a humanist social science in "moving towards a social structure in which there is less exploitation, oppression, and injustice and more creativity, diversity, and equality" (p. 5).

10. Sheldon Wolin makes this point in *Politics and Vision* (Boston: Little, Brown, 1960), p. 20.

11. A parallel definition is developed and elaborated in a fascinating way by C. West Churchman in *The Systems Approach and Its Enemies* (New York: Basic Books, 1979), pp. 155–164.

12. The idea of real but only partially realized social collectivities as the subjects of critical social science is found in the critical theory of the Frankfurt School. See especially the able statement of this position by Wellmer, *Critical Theory of Society*, pp. 1–66.

1. How to Build a Better Future

1. Osman Ahmed Isman, *Pages from My Experience* (Cairo: Modern Egyptian Library, 1981), p. 634.

2. *Al-Akhbar,* Jan. 30, 1981.

3. Official exchange rates, based on the International Monetary Fund's *International Financial Statistics,* were as follows for the Egyptian pound for the period 1952–1989: 1952–1955, $2.862; 1956–1961, $2.838; 1962–1972, $2.30; 1973–1978, $2.5556; 1979–1989, $1.4286. However, in September 1973 the Egyptian government established a parallel market in which the exchange rate differed from the official rate. The exchange situation has been further complicated by a free-market exchange, both black and white.

4. *Al-Ahram,* Aug. 14, 1981.

5. See Sheldon Wolin, *Politics and Vision* (Boston: Little, Brown, 1960), p. 20.

6. Mahmud al-Kady, *Face to Face with Osman Ahmed Osman* (Cairo: Dar al-Mawqif al-Arabi, 1981).

7. *Al-Ahram,* May 13, 1981.

8. Osman, *Pages from My Experience,* p. 359. The Arab Contractors publishes a particularly handsome edition of the Koran and perhaps the best book available on the rituals of the pilgrimage to Mecca.

9. Osman's attitudes toward the British are frequently elaborated in the first part of his autobiography. See Osman, *Pages from My Experience,* esp. pp. 1–150.

10. Ibid., pp. 138–140.

11. Raymond William Baker, *Egypt's Uncertain Revolution under Nasser and Sadat* (Cambridge, Mass.: Harvard University Press, 1978).

12. See Osman's account of the incident in *Rose al-Yusuf,* Oct. 1, 1979.

13. Osman, *Pages from My Experience,* p. 579.

14. Osman, interview, *Rose al-Yusuf,* March 26, 1979.

15. Clement Henry Moore, *Images of Development* (Cambridge, Mass.: MIT Press, 1980), p. 124.

16. The opposition press carried such accusations against the Arab Contractors frequently throughout the seventies and into the eighties. On March 22, 1982, for example, *al-Ahrar* reported that the minister of housing had lodged a complaint against the company for holding up construction of new cement plants because "the Arab Contractors owns, among its 36 companies, a private company for the import of cement that sells it for prices several times higher than the official prices of government cement factories." The most complete review of hidden subcontracting is Amr Muhieddin, "The Building and Construction Sector in the Eighties" (Paper presented at the Seventh Annual Scientific Conference of Egyptian Economists, May 6–8, 1982).

17. *Rose al-Yusuf,* Jan. 1, 1979.

18. Moore, *Images of Development,* p. 124. See also John Waterbury, *Egypt: Burdens of the Past, Options for the Future* (Bloomington: Indiana University Press, 1978), p. 244.

19. *Rose al-Yusuf,* Oct. 1, 1979.

20. Osman, *Pages from My Experience,* pp. 396–397.

21. Interview, *al-Ahram,* May 13, 1981.

22. Osman, *Pages from My Experience,* p. 585.

23. A parliamentary committee, formed on April 13, 1981, to investigate charges that Osman had slandered the revolution and Nasser personally in his autobiography, found the charges groundless. This evaluation of the revolution was part of Osman's own testimony before the committee, reported in *al-Ahram,* May 13, 1981.

24. See Osman, *Pages from My Experience,* pp. 420–422.

25. Ibid., pp. 444–445.

26. Ibid., p. 633.

27. Ibid.

28. Ibid., pp. 446–450.

29. Ibid., p. 551.

30. Ibid., p. 414.

31. See Joseph Kraft, "Letter from Egypt," *New Yorker,* May 28, 1979.

32. The positions, according to Osman, were minister of housing and minister for the High Dam; *Pages from My Experience,* p. 460.

33. Osman, interview, *International Management,* June 1983, p. 31.

34. Osman, *Pages from My Experience,* p. 578.

35. See the characterization by Ahmed Ragab in *al-Akhbar,* Oct. 14, 1979.

36. Osman, *Pages from My Experience,* p. 138.

37. According to Osman, the companies and factories seized "fell into the hands either of a group of thieves who took from them rather than developed them or a group of ignorant individuals who mismanaged them. . . . The result was total destruction"; ibid., p. 286.

38. Sadat manipulated the Osman symbol to signal to Egyptians what they were to do with these new opportunities. Sadat spoke of Osman as a general who had led his "soldiers" in the Arab Contractors to great achievements. On one such occasion Sadat declared: "Today I have no right to speak. Let those soldiers who have done the work we see all around us speak. This is the day to honor them. Let them explain to the people what has been achieved and how we were able to find the right beginning"; *al-Akhbar,* Jan. 30, 1981. For a concise discussion of these social changes themselves see *Rose al-Yusuf,* March 26, 1979.

39. *Rose al-Yusuf,* May 22, 1978.

40. *Rose al-Yusuf,* Oct. 8, 1979.

41. *Rose al-Yusuf,* March 7, 1981.

42. *Rose al-Yusuf,* Oct. 10, 1980.

43. *Rose al-Yusuf,* March 7, 1981.

44. *Rose al-Yusuf,* Oct. 1, 1979.

45. Osman, *Pages from My Experience,* p. 551.

46. *al-Akhbar,* Feb. 1980.

47. Osman, *Pages from My Experience,* p. 363.

48. In a March 1981 interview in *Akhbar al-Yaum,* Osman revealed that as soon as he became minister of housing he stopped all supervisory agency reports on chairmen and directors of companies dealing with the ministry: "I . . . asked to start a new leaf and to forget these reports completely. I would hold them responsible only for the work they accomplished"; see also *Rose al-Yusuf,* Oct. 1, 1979, for a similar statement.

49. *Akhbar al-Yaum,* March 7, 1981.

50. For the clearest expression of this attitude, see ibid.

51. Ibid.

52. For a sensitive discussion of the evolution of the pan-Arab idea in Egypt, see Galal Amin, "The Era of Chivalry Has Gone and the Era of Economists Has Come," *Rose al-Yusuf,* May 10, 1982.

53. Osman, *Pages from My Experience,* pp. 200–205.

54. Ibid.

55. Osman, interview, *al-Wady,* May 1982.

56. On the macro level of what he calls "technocratic thinking" Galal Amin discusses this general evolution of thinking about pan-Arabism and Israel in *Economic Ahram* (*al-Ahram al-Iqtisadi*), May 10, 1982. In his autobiography Osman stresses the high price Egypt had already paid for its loyalty to the Palestinian cause in treasure and lives lost; *Pages from My Experience,* p. 206.

57. *Al-Akhbar,* Jan. 30, 1981.

58. Ibid.

59. Osman, *Pages from My Experience,* pp. 467–468.

60. Quoted in ibid. See Adel Hussein, *The Egyptian Economy from Independence to Dependence* (Beirut: Dar al-Kalema lil Nashr/Dar al-Wihda, 1981), pp. 90–93.

61. The United States under Nixon led the way, followed by Kuwait and Saudi Arabia, in encouraging Egypt with financial aid to reopen the Canal and rebuild the Canal Zone cities. For details, see Hussein, *The Egyptian Economy,* pp. 90–93. Some Egyptian economists charged that use of these resources was skewed by regime political propaganda and Israeli demands. See Muhieddin, "The Building and Construction Sector."

62. This performance was not matched in other fields. Particularly alarming was the growing gap between food production and consumption. The average annual rate of growth of agricultural income was 1.9 percent during the period 1974–1979. During the period 1960–1965 it averaged about 3.5 percent. See Muhaya Zeitun, "The Patterns of Economic Growth," in Gouda Abdul Khalek, *The Open Door: Roots, Harvest, and Future* (Cairo: Arab Center of Research and Publishing, 1982), pp. 139–140. Other indicators of the problems in agriculture are the drop in the value of agricultural exports, from 401.2 million Egyptian pounds (L.E.) in 1973 to 364.2 million in 1980. See Ramzy Zaki, *Studies in Egypt's Economic Crisis, with A Proposed Strategy for the Egyptian Economy* (Cairo: Madbouly Bookstore Publications, 1983), p. 291.

63. See Muhieddin, "The Building and Construction Sector."

64. *Al-Akhbar al-Yaum,* March 7, 1981.

65. These figures are from the official Arab Contractors/Osman Ahmed Osman & Company annual reports, published in Cairo in English.

66. A useful breakdown of company activities is found in Arab Contractors/Osman Ahmed Osman & Company, *Annual Report for 1981/82,* pp. 6–7.

67. *Akhbar al-Yaum,* March 7, 1981.

68. Salah Hafez, "An Experiment That Raises an Issue: The Arizona Farmer and the Arab Adventurers," *Rose al-Yusuf,* Dec. 24, 1979.

69. *Al-Ahram,* July 5, 1980. One feddan equals 1.038 acres.

70. *Al-Ahram,* Dec. 16, 1979.

71. *Al-Ahram,* Aug. 14, 1981.

72. *Egyptian Gazette* (in English), Jan. 30, 1980.

73. *Rose al-Yusuf,* Oct. 1, 1979.

74. See Essam Soliman, "The Original Salhia Cries and Complains," *The People* (*al-Sha'ab*), July 28, 1981.

75. For the most sensitive and informed discussion of earlier land reclamation projects in Egypt, see John Waterbury, "The Cairo Workshop on Land Reclamation and Settlement in the Arab World," *American Universities Field Staff Reports: Northeast Africa Series,* 17, no. 1 (1971), 2. See also Doreen Warriner, *Land Reform and Development in the Middle East* (London: Oxford University Press, 1962), p. 49.

76. The chairman of the Arab Contractors' board of directors, Hussein Osman, spelled out these long-term goals during the inaugural ceremonies of the Salhia project in January 1980; *Egyptian Gazette,* Jan. 30, 1980.

77. At the commercial bank interest rate of 12 percent, the reclamation projects had no chance of attracting private capital. Private Egyptian investors were naturally lured instead either to consumption projects such as 7-Up, or to boutiques, or to commercial representation of foreign firms. In such ventures, Medhat Bahr indicated, profits sometimes reached a phenomenal 80 percent in the first year. "So who," Bahr asked rhetorically, "would close up his boutique and come and reclaim the desert?!" *Rose al-Yusuf,* May 14, 1979. On this point Arab Contractors officials have been quite explicit: without subsidized loans there would be no reclamation. Bahr, the director of the Arab Contractors' Agricultural Products Division, estimated that the cultivation of one new feddan required L.E. 1,200. (In fact the costs were much higher.) But the return on that investment would not exceed 8 percent a year after four, five, or even six years. Reclamation would be profitable only if the government made available foreign funds at the 3 percent it was itself required to pay. Here the mixed character of the Osman companies came into play: though controlled by the Osman family, they were legally public-sector companies. This legal status allowed Sadat to defend the advantages he accorded to Osman by arguing that the enterprises were, after all, government owned.

78. *Rose al-Yusuf,* July 28, 1980.

79. The analysis of the financial arrangements for Salhia is drawn primarily from Hafez, "An Experiment That Raises an Issue."

80. Underlying the complex gadgetry, they explained, were two principles that represented important departures from previous reclamation efforts in Egypt. First, the desert land was not leveled before irrigation and plowing. Second, water was piped to the site and sprayed by a rotating pivot from above. With more detail than one could possibly absorb, they argued that they saved considerably by accepting the natural contours of the land. Not only is bulldozing expensive; it also risks loss of fertile soil. In addition, the spray method of irrigation that made it possible to irrigate uneven land has other merits. The engineers claimed that the system used a third less water than conventional methods. It also distributed the water more evenly and thereby reduced the problem of increasing the subterranean water level. Fertilizers and insecticides were also added easily to the sprayed water. Finally, the traditional canal irrigation took about 11 percent of land area for the waterways, and the canals themselves were breeding grounds for various parasitic diseases; *al-Ahrar,* May 3, 1982.

81. The phrase was picked up and used widely in the press. See, e.g., Hussein Osman, interview, *al-Ahram,* Dec. 16, 1979.

82. *Egyptian Gazette,* Jan. 30, 1980.

83. *Al-Jumhuriyyah,* Aug. 28, 1983.

84. Interview with Arizona farmer Harold Ormsby, *Rose al-Yusuf,* May 14, 1979. The Nasser regime had progressively more limited holdings, first to 200, then to 100, and finally to 50 feddans.

85. Osman explained that when his Ismailia agricultural development company was established, it planned to reclaim 20,000 feddans in the Wadi al-Malak project. He expressed regret that because of inexperience with such vast amounts of land the company retrieved only half that amount; *Rose al-Yusuf,* Oct. 1, 1979.

86. Osman Ahmed Osman, interview, *Rose al-Yusuf,* May 22, 1978.

87. *Rose al-Yusuf,* May 14, 1979.

88. "Ever since the 1930s . . . we have been issuing new laws concerning not only the land but also many other aspects. Where does one who wants to reclaim a piece of land go? The Ministry of Land Reclamation sends him to the Ministry of Agriculture, which sends him to the governorate. Every administrative agency chooses the law that suits him best"; *Rose al-Yusuf,* Oct. 1, 1979.

89. Osman, interview, *Rose al-Yusuf,* May 22, 1978.

90. *The People,* July 28, 1981.

91. The opposition leader Ibrahim Shukry raised these key issues on a visit to Salhia reported in *al-Ahram,* Feb. 22, 1982. 'Emad Ghoneim provides an excellent summary of the critical debate in "What Do People Say about Salhia?" *Economic Ahram (al-Ahram al-Iqtisadi),* March 22, 1982.

92. *Al-Ahrar,* May 3, 1982.

93. See Kady, *Face to Face with Osman.*

94. See the summary of Gouda Abdul Khalek's important study of forty projects involving the Osman companies in 1975–1977, *The Masses (al-Ahaly),* May 3, 1978. Abdul Khalek provides detailed analysis of representative companies in each of the three categories. Also, interview with Ismail Osman, Cairo, June 23, 1980. Also *Rose al-Yusuf,* May 22, 1978.

95. Ismail Osman, interview with author, Cairo, June 23, 1980.

96. The priorities concealed in production decisions are discussed by Galal Amin, *The Arab East and the West* (Beirut: Center of Arab Unity Studies, 1979), pp. 141–142.

97. Muhaya Zeitun, "The Economic Open Door and the Housing Problem," in *al-Infitah: Roots, Harvest, and Future,* ed. Gouda Abdul Khalek (Cairo: Center for Research and Publications, 1982), p. 416.

98. See Abdul Khalek, *The Masses,* May 3, 1978.

99. Osman Ahmen Osman, interview, *al-Ahram,* July 7, 1982.

100. *Al-Ahrar,* May 3, 1982.

101. For details on the Rashad Osman case, see, among dozens of articles, *al-Ahram,* June 21, 1981, *al-Musawwar,* April 2, 1982; *al-Ahrar,* April 12, 1982; and *al-Wady,* May 1982.

102. *Al-Musawwar,* April 3, 1981.

103. *Al-Musawwar,* April 2, 1982.

104. *Al-Ahrar,* May 3, 1982.

105. Osman, *Pages from My Experience,* p. 516.

106. Ibid., p. 515; *al-Jumhuriyyah,* Oct. 12, 1979.

107. Osman, *Pages from My Experience,* p. 527.

108. Interview, *Rose al-Yusuf,* Oct. 6, 1980.

109. *Akhbar al-Yaum,* March 7, 1981.

110. Osman, *Pages from My Experience,* p. 526.

111. For descriptions of these syndicate commercial activities, see *al-Jumhuriyyah,* Oct. 12, 1979; *al-Musawwar,* Sept. 17, 1982. The latter contains an elaborate defense of the syndicate companies.

112. Osman, *Pages from My Experience,* p. 526.

113. *The Masses,* Dec. 29, 1982.

114. Osman, interview, *Al-Wady,* May 1982.

115. Rumors to this effect were confirmed, according to *The Masses* on Feb. 16,

1983, when the company finally sent an official letter to the general secretary of the Syndicate of Engineers indicating that the insurance had been terminated in mid-1982.

116. *Rose al-Yusuf*, Dec. 29, 1982. The charge was made by engineer Adel al-Mashad, who cited *Economic Ahram*, as the source for the bonuses and payments information.

117. On other occasions Osman had reported that other associations were imitating the engineers; *Pages from My Experience*, p. 527.

118. Egyptians who once followed Herodotus in commenting that Egypt is the gift of the Nile began to joke that Sadat's Egypt was the gift of the Arab Contractors.

119. Osman, interview, *International Management*, June 1983.

120. For a review of the charges against him and Osman's responses, see especially *al-Wady*, May 1982. See also the revealing Osman interview in *al-Ahrar*, May 3, 1982.

121. Osman, interview, *al-Wady*, May 1982.

122. Just eight months earlier, Hussein Osman reported to Mubarak on progress at the Salhia desert agricultural site, making very similar remarks; *al-Ahram*, Jan. 6, 1983.

123. *Al-Ahram*, Aug. 16, 1983.

124. Osman, interview, *International Management*, June 1983.

125. Osman, interview, *South*, April 1985.

2. Fighting for Freedom and the Rule of Law

1. For a bold defense of the Bar Association as an open forum for independent and critical national opinion, see Waheed Ra'fat, "Liberties and the Tragedy of the Bar Association This Season," *The People (al-Sha'ab)*, March 25, 1980.

2. While a deputy in parliament, Marei conducted an inquiry into the infamous defective arms scandal; profiteering had led to the provision of faulty weapons to the Egyptian forces fighting in Palestine in 1948. The scandal irreparably damaged the authority of the king, who was judged to have squandered Egypt's honor and the lives of its young men. The prominent journalist Ihsan Abdul Kudus, who had close ties to the Free Officers, pronounced Marei's inquiry into the defective arms scandal "a source of glory and pride for Egyptian officers and soldiers" because it exposed how badly armed Egyptian forces fighting in Palestine were. There is an account of the incident in Sayyid Marei, *Political Papers*, pt. 1 (Cairo: al-Maktab al-Masri al-Hadith, 1978), p. 170.

3. Quotations from Marei's speech are taken from notes made during the addresss, supplemented by press accounts. The following description is based on two eyewitness accounts, supplemented by coverage in the opposition press.

4. For the full text of the law see *al-Ahrar*, Feb. 18, 1980.

5. According to the left paper *Progress (al-Taqqadum)*, Feb. 11, 1980, the president first alluded to the idea in a statement on July 22, 1978.

6. The parliament approved the law in principle at the end of April 1980. The minutes include the text of the law, messages from the president, and previous security measures that the law embraces; Minutes of the People's Assembly, April 27, 28, and 29, 1980.

7. For example, articles in the January/February issue of *al-Muhamah,* reflecting the views of the Islamic trend, made the point that "a sound democratic system cannot be established unless the people's freedom of belief, opinion, assembly, association, education and . . . other freedoms are guaranteed."

8. See Mustafa Kamel al-Sayyid, *Society and Politics in Egypt: The Role of Interest Groups in the Egyptian Political System* (Cairo: Dar al-Mustaqbal al-Arabi, 1983).

9. About 2,000 people attended the seminar. Lengthy excerpts from the main speeches were printed in the opposition press; see esp. *The People,* Feb. 5, 1980; *Progress,* Feb. 11, 1980. The first major speaker was Muhammad 'Asfour. The second, Muhammad Helmy Murad, warned that the latest security law would bring "the final destruction of democracy because it will enable the ruling party to use the judiciary at its will." The third, Nabil al-Hilaly, declared the attack on the courts built into the new law a new and more deadly "massacre of the judiciary." The reference was to the notorious incident in 1968 when Nasser removed independent judges from their posts. Sadat's action was worse, Hilaly declared, because whereas "the 1968 massacre affected individuals, his project will affect the institution itself."

10. Nabil Abdul Fatah provides a history of the Bar Association structured around the struggles for these core liberal values; "A Political Crisis in the Bar Association," *Economic Ahram* (*al-Ahram al-Iqtisadi*), June 7, 1982.

11. The legal style and character of liberal resistance in Egypt are best captured in Salah 'Eissa, *The Egyptian Bourgeoisie and the Diplomatic Style* (Cairo: Matbou'at al-Thaqafa al-Watannia, 1980). From a left perspective, 'Eissa argues (p. 67) that "the domination of legal terminology is not merely related to the fact that most bourgeois leaders were law graduates, but this terminology indicates the limitations of the kind of struggle that the bourgeoisie is capable of undertaking."

12. For Marei one bulwark of a genuine liberal order was an independent judiciary. In a series of speeches and interviews Marei hammered at the theme that "the constitution does not permit courts formed of other than specialized judges who cannot be removed. Each court not comprised of them alone is not a court in the true sense"; interview, *The People,* Feb. 12, 1980.

13. Ibid. Article 165 of the 1971 constitution states: "The judiciary is independent," and Article 166 states: "Judges are independent. In the administration of justice, they are subject to no authority save that of the law. No authority whatever has the right to interfere in pending cases or in the affairs of justice."

14. Marei, interview, *The People,* Feb. 12, 1980. For key excerpts from Marei's statement see *al-Ahrar,* Feb. 18, 1980.

15. *Al-Sha'ab,* Feb. 19, 1980.

16. For coverage of relevant draft legislation see *al-Ahrar,* March 24, 1980.

17. The best account of Egyptian constitutionalism, stressing the colonial context, is Abdul Aziz Ramadan, *Revolutionary Thought in Egypt before the July 23 Revolution* (Cairo: Madboudy Bookstore Publications, 1981), esp. pp. 69–88.

18. Waheed Ra'fat, "The Experience of Political Parties after Four Years/I," *al-Ahrar,* Feb. 23, 1981.

19. See 'Eissa, *The Egyptian Bourgeoisie,* p. 88.

20. This interpretation of the character of the political order within which liber-

alism developed is critical for my understanding of the historical content of Egyptian liberalism. I owe the interpretation to Tarek al-Bishry, *Political Movement in Egypt, 1945–1952,* rev. ed. (Cairo: Dar al-Sharouk, 1983), esp. pp. 482–485.

21. My colleague Karen Aboul Kheir of the American University in Cairo insisted, in her critical reading of this chapter, that the abstract idea of Egyptian liberalism be grounded as fully as possible in actual Egyptian political struggles. I have made use not only of this insight but also of her extensive knowledge of pre-1952 political history.

22. Quoted in 'Eissa, *The Egyptian Bourgeoisie,* pp. 72–73.

23. See ibid., esp. pp. 66–67.

24. For a discussion of the constitutional context required for effective action by the Wafd see Mervat Hatem, "Professional Association in a Developing Country: The Case of the Lawyers' and Engineers' Syndicates in Egypt" (M.A. thesis, American University in Cairo, 1974).

25. For an astute discussion of this turning point in the history of the Wafd see Bishry, *The Political Movement in Egypt.*

26. Waheed Ra'fat, "The Experience of Political Parties after Four Years/II," *al-Ahrar,* March 2, 1981.

27. Waheed Ra'fat, "The Experience of Political Parties after Four Years/III," *al-Ahrar,* March 9, 1981.

28. After the 1967 defeat, for example, *al-Muhamah* was full of editorials with titles such as "The Heroic People and Its Leader Will Achieve Victory." It also published cables of support for Nasser, including one asking him to reverse his decision to resign. Yet, by January 1968 the journal had moved from advocacy of socialism to renewed emphasis on traditional liberal concerns of liberty and democracy. Pointedly, the head of the Bar Association called for a "codification of the revolution" that would eliminate the evil of "exceptional measures"; see Ahmed al-Khawaga, "Freedoms and the Codification of the Revolution," *al-Muhamah,* Feb. 1968.

29. For the liberal account of these events see *al-Muhamah,* May/June 1977.

30. In addition to Baradie's speech see also Mustafa al-Baradie, "Should Syndicates Be Eliminated and Have They Proved Useless?" *al-Muhamah,* Nov. 1960; and Gamal Mursi, "What Are Professional Syndicates?" *al-Muhamah,* Feb. 1962.

31. See Aly Sabry, *al-Muhamah,* Dec. 1966.

32. See esp. *al-Muhamah,* Nov.1966.

33. A major source on Baradie's role is the special issue of *al-Muhamah* for November/December 1977 honoring his career, published the year of his death. A crucial document from the earlier period is the 1962 supplement to *al-Muhamah,* which contains his speeches, including the important one at the Preparatory Committee Meeting of National Action.

34. See Ahmed al-Khawaga, "Freedom and Codification of the Revolution," *al-Muhamah,* Feb. 1968.

35. Muhammad Asfour, "The Concept of Freedom in the Light of Socialist Values," *al-Muhamah,* Feb. 1968.

36. Shawkat al-Tuny, "The Constitution," *al-Muhamah,* Jan./Feb. 1977.

37. Ibid.

38. Ibid.

39. Liberals deplored the fact that the government also refused to accept international judgments. Egypt signed both the International Covenant on Economic, Social, and Cultural Rights and the International Covenant on Civil and Political Rights in 1967. However, the government never ratified either agreement. The guarantees of basic human rights codified in these United Nations documents were consistent with the principles in the 1971 constitution. Liberal opinion unsuccessfully urged their adoption. The Sadat regime also declared correspondence with Amnesty International (AI) to be illegal. The left opposition paper regularly brought AI's findings to the attention of readers. See, e.g., *Progress,* Jan. 5, 1980.

40. From Law 34 of 1972 on the Protection of National Unity, the most important of this cluster of laws.

41. The opposition papers, in particular *Progress,* provide the best coverage of the security cases. For one example of the obstacles the lawyers confronted and their ingenuity in meeting them see *Progress,* April 5, 1978.

42. English texts of the most important security provisions are in Federation of Arab Journalists, *Democracy of Chopping* (Paris, 1980). The Bar Association's reactions to the measures, especially after 1977, are contained in the documents section of *al-Muhamah.* A powerful liberal critique of Sadat's style of repression, on which the following discussion draws, is Ra'fat, "Political Parties after Four Years/III."

43. The official statement was published in *al-Ahram* in January 1977.

44. By 1981 the number of Egyptian lawyers had risen to 36,000. *Akhbar al-Yaum,* July 18, 1981, provides a useful statistical survey of the legal profession and discussion of its problems and prospects. For Sadat's views, see Anwar el-Sadat, *In Search of Identity: An Autobiography* (New York: Harper & Row, 1977), p. 73. Sadat's recommendation is interesting because of the frequent press reports of abuses of precisely this role. For example, the same issue of *Akhbar al-Yaum* reported that "some former government officials have opened legal consultation offices for foreign companies. They secure monopolies for these companies in return for huge fees."

45. Evidence on the occupational sources of recruitment for the cabinet is summarized in Mark N. Cooper, *The Transformation of Egypt* (Baltimore: Johns Hopkins University Press, 1982), p. 145.

46. Amnesty International has commented on the "impartiality of the judiciary in Egypt," remarking in a 1983 report that "it has been amply demonstrated during the past ten years, when judges in state security courts, appointed by presidential decree, have ordered a high percentage of acquittals in cases relating to non-violent political activity." The same report, however, also warns against the use of presidential prerogatives to circumvent the judiciary. See Amnesty International, *Egypt: Violations of Human Rights* (London, 1983), p. 27.

47. The most useful works in English on the Wafd are Marius Deeb, *Party Politics in Egypt: The Wafd and Its Rivals, 1919–1939* (London: Ithaca Press, 1979); and P. J. Vatikiotis, *The Modern History of Egypt* (London: Faber and Faber, 1972). On the New Wafd, see Raymond A. Hinnebusch, "The Reemergence of the Wafd Party: Glimpses of the Liberal Opposition in Egypt," *International Journal of Middle East Studies,* 16 (1984), 99–121.

48. This theme is developed in Fuad Serrag Eddine, *Why the New Party?* (Cairo: Dar al-Sharouq, 1977), p. 54.

49. In October 1983 the administrative court overturned the government suppression, and the New Wafd resumed its activities. For a discussion see *al-Ahrar,* Oct. 31, 1983. In its public celebrations and meetings the New Wafd drew enormous, diversified, and enthusiastic crowds. For example, on August 26, 1983, an anniversary celebration of Wafdist leaders Saad Zaghloul and Mustafa al-Nahas drew 10,000 to the Saidiya School near Cairo University. An eyewitness noted that the crowd consisted of "a majority of common faces, lots of young people, old politicians (some even wearing the tarbush), some beards, a few intellectuals, and a lot of secret police." The gathering was probably the only political meeting in more than thirteen years that matched the attendance at Islamic group rallies.

50. Mustafa Marei, interview, *al-Musawwar,* Jan. 7, 1983.

51. See Tuny, "The Constitution."

52. Minutes of the Governing Council of the Bar Association, Feb. 4, 1978.

53. Ra'fat, "Political Parties after Four Years/III."

54. An able summary of the liberal critique is in Waheed Ra'fat, "The Experience of Political Parties after Four Years/IV," *al-Ahrar,* March 16, 1981.

55. *Al-Muhamah,* Sept./Oct. 1977.

56. The complete text of Mustafa al-Baradie's speech is in Serrag Eddine, *Why the New Party?* pp. 10–14.

57. Nasser had declared in his 1961 Charter of National Action that Wafdist founder Zaghloul had exploited the revolutionary wave of 1919 for his own ends. The July 23 Revolution, in contrast, was painted as the realization of mass revolutionary aspirations.

58. Serrag Eddine, *Why the New Party?* p. 21. All the quotations from the speech delivered at the Bar Association on August 23, 1977, are from ibid., pp. 21–35.

59. The quotations in this paragraph are from ibid., pp. 71–80.

60. The failure of the post-1952 regime to create effective political parties is stressed by Raymond William Baker, *Egypt's Uncertain Revolution under Nasser and Sadat* (Cambridge, Mass.: Harvard University Press, 1978), pp. 235–248; and Cooper, *The Transformation of Egypt,* pp. 126–142. In contrast, the New Wafd Party, according to Serrag Eddine, was "present in the conscience of every Egyptian and in the political street."

61. Muhammad Helmy Murad, "The State of Institutions," *al-Muhamah,* May/June 1975.

62. *Al-Muhamah,* Nov./Dec. 1977.

63. Abdul Fatah, "A Political Crisis in the Bar Association."

64. For the lawyers their syndicate was the institutional embodiment of an inclusive idea that had earned them the title "conscience and tongue of the nation"; ibid.

65. There is a particularly good account of the positions of the candidates in *al-Siyassa,* Oct. 22, 1978.

66. On government maneuvering for the vote of the public-sector lawyers see *al-Ahrar,* Sept. 3 and Oct. 22, 1979.

67. E.g., Robert Springborg, "Professional Syndicates in Egyptian Politics, 1952–1970," *International Journal of Middle East Studies,* 9 (1978), 279.

68. The regime's efforts along these lines were chronicled in the opposition press. *Progress,* in particular, gave detailed attention to the election battles within the Bar Association. For a good sense of the scale of participation and the way the lines were

drawn between regime and independent candidates for Governing Council elections see *Progress,* Jan. 5, 1980.

69. In developing this interpretation I was helped greatly by discussions with the Egyptian specialist on the Bar Association, Nabil Abdul Fatah. His brief history of the association in "A Political Crisis in the Bar Association" is the best available brief account in Arabic.

70. Waheed Ra'fat, "Liberties and the Tragedy of the Bar Association This Season," *The People,* March 25, 1980.

71. Gamal Oteify, interview with author, Cairo, July 8, 1980. Oteify was the constitutional expert who assisted Sadat in drafting his constitution. Moreover, when Sadat had the Governing Council of the Bar Association dissolved, Oteify served as acting head until the dissolution was declared unconstitutional.

72. The comment was made as part of a report on one government disruption of association seminars; *Progress,* March 5, 1980.

73. The claim to speak for the nation, the disruptions by the authorities, and the resultant enhancement of the symposia as national "events" are ably discussed in Ra'fat, "Liberties and the Tragedy of the Bar Association."

74. Consistently, the lawyers argued that Sadat's insistence on a monopoly of foreign policy was unconstitutional. See Murad, "The State of Institutions."

75. See Sayyid, *Society and Politics in Egypt.*

76. A four-and-a-half-hour meeting of the Governing Council on January 22, 1980, to review the normalization with Israel was reported in the opposition press. The statement issued confirms the association's intention to boycott normalization. See *Progress,* Jan. 28, 1980; *The People,* Jan. 29, 1980. The Press Association issued a parallel statement calling for a boycott of Israeli union, professional, scientific, and cultural organizations until the Palestinian issue was resolved; *The People,* Feb. 26, 1980.

77. *Al-Ahrar,* March 3, 1980.

78. The National Democratic Party insisted on selecting its own representatives for the Bar Association's delegation. See *al-Muhamah,* Sept./Oct. 1980, for the association's version of the events in Rabat.

79. *Al-Ahrar,* July 27, 1980. See also the detailed account in *The People,* July 15, 1980.

80. *Al-Ahrar,* July 27, 1980. A more tempered but still hostile account is in *al-Musawwar,* July 31, 1981.

81. *Al-Ahram,* July 28, 1980.

82. The statement was printed in *al-Muhamah,* Sept./Oct. 1980.

83. *Al-Ahrar,* June 15, 1981.

84. A representative statement, issued in the wake of the attack on Iraq, that registered these basic arguments was carried in *al-Ahrar,* May 15, 1981. The lawyers called for "abolition of the treaty with Israel and all that the treaty implies concerning normalization of relations with Israel."

85. *A Year after Normalization* (Cairo: al-Mawqif al-Arabi, 1981), pp. 178–179.

86. Ibid., p. 179.

87. The Bar Association's reactions to these developments have been reported in *al-Muhamah* since January 1981.

88. This religious theme was developed more fully by Said Qossa, "Islam and the

Contemporary Political Systems," *al-Muhamah,* Jan./Feb. 1981. "Egypt is the gift of the Nile, and the Nile is the artillery of life. How can we permit intransigent Israel to have access to this artillery? Islam, too, is against this idea." For a pioneering treatment of other women's success in the public arean, see Earl L. Sullivan, *Women in Egyptian Public Life* (Syracuse: Syracuse University Press, 1986).

All quotations on the Nile issue are from notes taken at the Second Seminar of the Bar Association on Transferring Nile Water to Israel, Cairo, Nov. 7, 1980.

89. See *Rose al-Yusuf,* June 5, 1978. For a succinct summary of the economic dealings involved, see John Waterbury, *The Egypt of Nasser and Sadat* (Princeton: Princeton University Press, 1983), p. 151.

90. See, in particular, the important articles in *al-Akhbar* and *al-Ahram,* July 6, 1977.

91. The account of the seminar that follows is based on notes taken during the session and a record of the proceedings (subsequently published as *The Seminar of the Bar Association on the Pyramids Plateau Project,* Cairo, 1978), interviews with principals, and Ne'mat Fuad, *The Pyramids Plateau Project* (Cairo: 'Alam al-Kutub, 1978).

92. Muhammad Fahim Amin, "Opening Word," in *Seminar of the Bar Association,* pp. 1–6.

93. In an interview in Cairo on October 12, 1983, Muhammad Fahim Amin discussed an earlier case in which the Bar Association acted in parallel fashion to block the sale of the Egyptian Cinema Industry to a wealthy Saudi buyer.

94. Ne'mat Fuad, "Land, Heritage, and Value," in *Seminar of the Bar Association,* pp. 6–20.

95. Fatah, "A Political Crisis in the Bar Association."

96. See Galal Amin, "The Real Harvest of the July 1952 Revolution," *Economic Ahram,* March 8, 1983.

97. Statement by Gamal Oteify, *al-Musawwar,* July 31, 1981.

98. For a lengthy report in the mainstream press, see *Mayo,* March 28, 1983. The opposition press also reported the protests in detail. For a representative treatment, see *al-Ahrar,* Jan. 10, 1983.

99. *The People,* April 5, 1983.

100. For a full report on the case see *The Masses,* June 15 and 22, 1983.

3. Restoring Egypt as Engine of the Arab World

1. Anwar el-Sadat, *In Search of Identity: An Autobiography* (New York: Harper & Row, 1977), p. 210.

2. *Al-Ahram,* June 27, 1977.

3. As late as 1984, the National Progressive Unionist Party (NPUP) was denied permission to hold a public meeting celebrating Nasser's birthday; party officials explained the decision as resulting from "the government's fear of reviving the memory of Nasser in the minds of the popular masses"; *The Masses (al-Ahaly),* Feb. 8, 1984.

4. Amin Huweidy, interview with author, Cairo, May 17, 1985.

5. Kamal Ahmed, *al-Mawqif al-Arabi,* Oct. 1983.

6. *The Masses,* Jan. 1, 1984. See also *al-Ahrar,* Oct. 3, 1983.

7. *Al-Ahram,* April 19, 1974. The parliamentary debates are covered in the national press and the Legislative Council, *The Law for Arab and Foreign Investment and Free Zones,* (Cairo, n.d.).

8. *Al-Ahram,* Nov. 21, 1975.

9. Kamal Ahmed, *al-Mawqif al-Arabi,* Oct. 1983.

10. Quoted in *al-Mawqif al-Arabi,* Feb. 1985.

11. Kamal Ahmed, *al-Mawqif al-Arabi,* Oct. 1983.

12. The citation is from one of the rare statements issued by the underground Nasserist organization and cited in Ahram Center for Political and Strategic Studies (cited hereafter as CPSS), *The Arab Strategic Report, 1987* (Cairo, 1988).

13. The daily *al-Akhbar,* for example, charged that "drugs and money united the members of Egypt's revolution"; according to *Akher Sa'a,* "the case is that of a first-class terrorist gang and not a case of principles or political creed." In contrast, the opposition papers, including some voices from political Islam, expressed broad sympathy with the group's nationalist aims; the one exception was the Wafd. The extensive press debate, including the citations above, is summarized and referenced in Mustafa Bekry, *The Son's Revolution: Secrets and Documents concerning the Case of Egypt's Revolution* (Cairo: Dar al-Huriyyah, 1988), esp. pp. 1–17. The best available survey of the various Nasserist formations is CPSS, *Arab Strategic Report,* 1987 and 1988. See esp. the latter, pp. 536–542.

14. *The People* (*al-Sha'ab*), March 1, 1988.

15. Bekry, *The Son's Revolution,* p. 259.

16. For an excellent summation of these Nasserist themes, along with an independent assessment, see Sayyid Yassine, ed., *The Revolution and Social Change, a Quarter Century after July 23, 1952* (Cairo: CPSS, 1977), pp. 58–66.

17. Hatem Sadek, "Introduction," in *The Texts of President Nasser's Speeches and Interviews* (Cairo: CPSS, 1977), pp. 5–9.

18. *Al-Ahrar,* Oct. 3, 1983.

19. *Al-Ahrar,* Aug. 26, 1983; *The People,* Feb. 7, 1984; see, e.g., the discussions of the various Nasserist factions in *al-Ahrar,* Sept. 12 1983, and June 11, 1984.

20. Kamal Ahmed, *al-Ahrar,* Aug. 26, 1983.

21. Muhammad Salmawy, *al-Mawqif al-Arabi,* Sept. 1983.

22. This definition of the key Nasserist generations is from Zia Rashwan in *The Masses,* Jan. 25, 1984.

23. Nasserist activists reported that in the sixties there were 30,000 in the Alexandria branch alone of the youth organization of the Arab Socialist Union (ASU), *al-Ahrar,* Aug. 26, 1983.

24. For a discussion of the songs by the late Abdul Halim Hafez that carried all these themes, see *Sabah al-Kheir,* March 28, 1985.

25. Quoted in David Hirst and Irene Beeson, *Sadat* (London: Faber and Faber, 1981), p. 218.

26. *Al-Mawqif al-Arabi,* Feb. 1985.

27. The owner of a private company for research and mass communications in the seventies, Ahmed was the director of the Socialist Youth Organization from 1965 to 1967. In 1975 he became a member of the ASU Central Committee and in 1976 was elected to parliament; *al-Ahrar,* Aug. 26, 1983.

28. Kamal Ahmed, "Why the Nasserist Party?" *al-Mawqif al-Arabi,* Sept. 1983.

29. The link between specific achievements of the Nasserist regime and the mass support it enjoyed is persuasively argued by Yassin, *The Revolution and Social Change.*

30. One opposition leader, Ibrahim Shukry, explained the continuing hold of Nasserism on Egypt: "Nasser acted to achieve our dreams of the forties"; *The Masses,* Jan. 18, 1984.

31. Muhammad Auda, *Denigration of Nasserism and Ignorance of Marxism* (Cairo: Rose al-Yusuf Publications, 1977), p. 40.

32. Edward R. F. Sheehan, "Introduction," in Mohamed Hassanein Heikal [*sic*], *The Cairo Documents* (Garden City, N.Y.: Doubleday, 1973).

33. Muhammad Hassanein Haikal, "What Occurred in the Stand," *Sabah al-Kheir,* Jan. 21, 1982.

34. Sadek, "Introduction," in *Nasser's Speeches and Interviews.*

35. Auda, *Denigration of Nasserism,* pp. 35–37, 39.

36. Amin Huweidy, interview with author, Cairo, May 17, 1985.

37. See Robert Mabro, *The Egyptian Economy: 1952–1977* (London: Oxford University Press, 1974), pp. 71–74; Samir Radwan, *Agrarian Reform and Rural Poverty: Egypt, 1952–1972* (Geneva: International Labor Organization, 1977), pp. 16–23.

38. See Nazih Ayubi, *Bureaucracy and Politics in Contemporary Egypt* (London: Ithaca Press, 1980), pp. 377–379; Mabro, *The Egyptian Economy,* pp. 223–224.

39. See Galal Amin, "Toward a New Interpretation of the Economic and Social Crisis in Egypt," *al-Yagatha al-Arabiya,* July 5, 1985.

40. Galal Amin, "The Real Harvest of the July 1952 Revolution," *Economic Ahram (al-Ahram al-Iqtisadi),* March 8, 1982.

41. For an account that makes the essential points in a Nasserist reading, see Sa'ad Ibrahim, "Social Mobility and Income Distribution in Egypt," in Gouda Abd al-Khalek and Robert Tignor, eds., *The Political Economy of Income Distribution in Egypt* (New York: Holmes and Meier, 1982).

42. Muhammad Hassanein Haikal, for example, stated in an interview: "This does not mean that I believe in the theory of a 'conspiracy' or that I imagine the presence of a secret agent under every chair. . . . [However,] I know that a very large part of what occurs in this region . . . is planned abroad"; *al-Mustaqbal al-Arabi,* July 1981.

43. *The Masses,* Jan. 18, 1984.

44. The pamphlet issued by the Karim circle, from which this quotation is taken, is discussed in *al-Ahrar,* June 11, 1984.

45. Quoted by Aly Eddine Hillal in *al-Jumhuriyyah,* Feb. 28, 1985, which offers a strong argument on the essential moderation of Nasser's foreign policy and the priority accorded to internal affairs.

46. Egypt's forward policy in the Arab world of the fifties and sixties paralleled in important respects those of Muhammad Aly more than a century earlier. The motivations were identical; both leaders sought to counter a Western attempt to contain their assertion of an independent national policy. Malcolm Kerr offers this interpretation of the roots of Nasser's Arab policy in "Egyptian Foreign Policy and the Revolution," in P. J. Vatikiotis, *Egypt since the Revolution* (New York: Praeger, 1968), pp. 114–134.

47. For an account of the pivotal Gaza raid that accords with the Nasserist reading, see Hillal, *al-Jumhuriyyah*, Feb. 28, 1985.

48. According to Hillel, ibid., Nasser considered the issues of arms a top priority only after the Gaza raid.

49. [Haikal], *The Cairo Documents*, p. 55.

50. Jean Lacouture, *Nasser* (New York: Alfred A. Knopf, 1973), pp. 169–170.

51. Sadek, "Introduction," in *Nasser's Speeches and Interviews*, p. 7.

52. [Haikal], *The Cairo Documents*, p. 62.

53. Quoted by Malcolm Kerr in "Egyptian Foreign Policy and the Revolution," p. 124.

54. Ahmed, "Why the Nasserist Party?"

55. Abdul Halim Kandil, "October Victory and Legitimacy," *al-Mawqif al-Arabi*, Oct. 1983, pp. 89–92.

56. Nasser's speech is summarized in Robert Stephens, *Nasser: A Political Biography* (London: Penguin Press, 1971), p. 518.

57. Mohamed Heikal [*sic*], *The Road to Ramadan* (New York: Quadrangle/New York Times, 1975), pp. 67, 180.

58. *Nasser's interviews with the Foreign Press, 1968–1970* (Cairo, n.d.), p. 71.

59. In an interview, Haikal quotes Winston Churchill's description of the expected Israeli role as "the 'sponge' that will absorb Arab effort and hinder it from development and from unifying its powers." Menachem Begin's Israel, in Haikal's view, realized this aim. He cited the Israeli leader's remarks that "likens Egypt to a bottle, Sinai to its neck, and Israel to the cork that will close this bottle—here Begin is speaking openly about Egypt and not about Palestine"; *al-Dustur*, July 16, 1981.

60. Muhammad Hassanein Haikal, *al-Mussawa*, Dec. 23, 1983.

61. Quoted in Kandil, "October Victory and Legitimacy."

62. Ibid. For interesting accounts of the role of the students that confirm the Nasserist influence, see Sayyid Marei, *Political Papers*, pt. 3 (Cairo: al-Maktab al-Masri al-Hadith, 1979), pp. 660–663. On the student demonstrations of 1972–1973 Marei writes: "President Sadat for his part had announced the famous peace initiative on February 4, 1971, but it produced no results. He then announced that 1971 would be the year of decision, through peace or war, yet the year passed without anything being decided . . . The student groups inside universities and institutes had started to sweep the capital's streets and squares. Some students had sit-in strikes in universities in Cairo, Alexandria, Mansura, Assiut, and other places; education halls became political arenas where all opinions conflicted . . . there was turmoil in labor groups on the horizon . . . I met with student groups with their different opinions, trends, and ideas at continuous conferences . . . forty-eight conferences in less than a month. We had open debates and discussions on the national issues, including the conditions of the war . . . I sought to remove the gap or the crisis of trust between youth and the political leadership that appeared after 1971." Generally, regime spokesmen depicted the students as Marxist-led, but they described them as "bearers of Nasserist slogans . . . now waving the shirt of Abdul Nasser." See Musa Sabry, *Documents of the October War* (Cairo: Kittab al-Yaum, 1978?), pp. 204–217.

63. Haikal, "What Occurred in the Stand . . . ," *Sabah al-Kheir*, Jan. 21, 1982.

64. Kandil, "October Victory and Legitimacy."

65. Ibid.

66. Mahmud al-Sa'dany, "Those Who Crossed and Those Who Distorted," *Rose al-Yusuf,* Oct. 29, 1984.

67. Auda, *Denigration of Nasserism,* pp. 40–41. Economist Galal Amin gives the most developed version of this argument in "An Attempt to Explain the Transformation of the Egyptian Economy from Independence to Dependence, 1965–1985" (Paper presented at the Sixth Annual Conference of Egyptian Economists, Cairo, March 1981), pp. 3–5.

68. See John Waterbury, *The Egypt of Nasser and Sadat: The Political Economy of Two Regimes* (Princeton: Princeton University Press, 1983), pp. 189–190.

69. Ahmed Kamal, interview, *al-Ahrar,* Aug. 26, 1983.

70. Nasser, Speech to the Conference of the General Union of Workers, March 3, 1968, in *Nasser's Speeches and Interviews,* pp. 319–321.

71. Bent Hansen and Karim Nashashibi, *Foreign Trade Regimes and Economic Development: Egypt* (New York: Columbia University Press, 1975), p. 12. The specter of Muhammad Aly's aborted industrialization effort in the nineteenth century loomed before the Nasserists. Then, Egypt was forced by the European intervention to abandon protective tariffs. Nascent industries withered and disappeared with barely a trace. For more than a century Egypt relied almost exclusively on agriculture to survive.

72. In the Western literature Mark Cooper's account of these developments, with its consistent attention to the left opposition to the Sadat regime, is the best attuned to the debate in Egypt. See "The Policy of Economic Liberalization," in *The Transformation of Egypt* (Baltimore: Johns Hopkins University Press, 1982), pp. 91–125.

73. See Heba Handoussa, an independent academic economist, for careful estimates that substantiate these basic elements of the Nasserist assessment; *The Vanguard* (*al-Tali'ah*), March 1985.

74. Heba Handoussa, "Time for Reform: Egypt's Public Sector Industry," in *Studies in Egyptian Political Economy, Cairo Papers in the Social Sciences,* ed. Herbert M. Thompson (Cairo: American University in Cairo Press, 1979).

75. Abdullah al-Sinawi, "Nasserism after Nasser," *al-Mawqif al-Arabi,* Aug. 1983.

76. The Administrative Supervision Bureau, a watchdog agency, commented on the unfavorable impact of the breadth and speed of these changes. See Adel Hussein, *The Egyptian Economy from Independence to Dependency: 1974–1979,* vol. 2 (Beirut: Dar al-Wihda, 1981), pp. 490–491.

77. Muhammad Hassanein Haikal, *Abdul Nasser: The Conversation with Him Continues* (Cairo: CPSS, 1973), pp. 1–3.

78. Nasser, *General Union of Workers,* March 3, 1968, p. 319.

79. Ahmed Bahaeddine, the journalist whose "letters" to Nasser close this chapter, charged that the elections to ASU basic units in conformity with the March Program were in fact rigged to prevent the infusion of new blood; *al-Ahram,* Aug. 31, 1974.

80. Amin Huweidy, interview with author, Cairo, May 17, 1985. In response to a comment on "the fear and dehumanization" during the Nasser period, Kamal Ahmed asked: "Who are the youths who said that? Are they the youths of farmers and works? . . . I think this argument is issued by the tiny minority that benefited from the consumption and Opening of the seventies"; interview, *al-Ahram,* Aug. 26,

1983. For the Nasserists there were abundant indicators that the common people understood and supported these definitions. "The July Revolution was not anti-democratic," explained another spokesman. "Complete mass mobilization occurred on June 9 and 10, 1967, at Nasser's death, and in January 1977 [during the bread riots]. During the latter event, people angered by the raising of prices shouted: "Nasser, Nasser"; Muhammad Sabry Mabdy, *al-Ahrar,* Oct. 3, 1983.

81. Auda, *Denigration of Nasserism,* p. 43.

82. See Nasser, Speech to General Union of Workers, March 3, 1968, pp. 319–321.

83. Muhammad Hassanein Haikal, "On the American-Israeli Strategic Agreement," *al-Musawwar,* Dec. 23, 1983.

84. Mustafa Amin, for example, dramatized the illiberal character of Nasserism by suggesting that any Nasserist party should take the gallows as its symbol. See his classic commentary on the prospects of establishing a Nasserist party, *al-Ahrar,* April 30, 1984.

85. *Economic Ahram,* Jan. 1, 1980.

86. Mahmud Abdul Fadil, *Oil and Arab Unity* (Beirut: Center for Arab Unity Studies, 1979), p. 51.

87. For a concise summary statement that touches on all these themes, see Haikal, interview, *al-Dustur,* July 16, 1981.

88. Raymond Hinnebusch argues that the NPUP was organized by the nationalist left wing of the Nasserite coalition, without any mention of the impediments the regime in fact placed in the way of a Nasserist party. He then writes as though reaction to the NPUP may be taken as a gauge of the strength of the Nasserist current. For example, he notes that peasants' underrepresentation in the party was "indicative of the small extent to which their support for Nasserism was translated into durable activism." In my judgment, the NPUP is not properly designated a Nasserist party. Therefore, no such inferences about the strengths or weaknesses of Nasserism can be made from its experience. See Hinnebusch, *Egyptian Politics under Sadat* (Cambridge: Cambridge University Press, 1985), pp. 186–190.

89. Salmawy, "The Nasserist Organization and Political Life in Egypt," *al-Mawqif al-Arabi,* Sept. 1983.

90. *Al-Ahrar,* Aug. 26, 1983. Kamal Ahmed was criticized for this stance by other Nasserists. Muhammad Sabry Mabdy withdrew from the last attempt to form a party because of disagreement on the relationship with the NPUP. He argued that the NPUP "encompasses a wide sector of the Nasserists." Mabdy charged that Kamal Ahmed, though recognized as a leading Nasserite, took his initiative to form a party without adequate consultation with other Nasserists; *al-Ahrar,* Oct. 3, 1983.

91. Waterbury, *The Egypt of Nasser and Sadat,* p. 366.

92. *Al-Ahram,* Nov. 21, 1975.

93. *Al-Ahram,* March 28, 1976.

94. *Al-Ahram,* Oct. 15, 1976.

95. For the most complete account in English of the general climate in which the elections were conducted, see Cooper, *The Transformation of Egypt,* p. 217.

96. Salmawy, "The Nasserist Organization." Muhammad Abdul Kudus, a prominent Muslim Brother, advanced a parallel argument, explicitly calling for recognition of Nasserism as a powerful, submerged political current; *al-Ahrar,* Oct. 3, 1983.

97. Muhammad Hassanein Haikal, "On the Return of the Wafd Party," *The People,* Feb. 7, 1984.

98. The main points of the program are summarized and contrasted with competing platforms in Cooper, *The Transformation of Egypt,* p. 185.

99. See Salmawy, "The Nasserist Organization." The judgment about Rifa'at's weight in the organization and his ability to bring members to the NPUP was shared by Kamal Ahmed, who described him as a "star" brought in to give the attempt legitimacy; interview, *al-Ahrar,* Aug. 26, 1983.

100. *Al-Ahrar,* Aug. 26, 1983.

101. Excerpts from the court memorandum are in *al-Mawqif al-Arabi,* Feb. 1984. See also *al-Ahrar,* May 14, 1984; *The People,* Feb. 22, 1984.

102. For a discussion of the activities of the Arab Committee for Commemorating the Anniversity of Nasser, for example, see Said Gharib, *al-Ahrar,* Aug. 26, 1983.

103. The Alexandria University Faculty Club, for example, was often critical of regime positions in ways that indicated a strain of Nasserist thinking.

The Bar Association celebrated the concrete achievements of the fifties and sixties and not just the personality of Nasser. One program, for example, highlighted in music and exhibitions the first Egyptian village in which land reform was carried out; *al-Ahrar,* Oct. 4, 1984. Other meetings were more directly political. On January 18, 1984, a celebration of Nasser's birthday attended by 5,000 people marked the first public appearance of Nasserist figures imprisoned by the Sadat regime, such as Aly Sabry. Khaled, Nasser's eldest son, also spoke: "These days have taught us that granting America the right to hold 99 percent of the cards leads to nothing but the enhancement of Israel's arrogance and insults to our dignity"; *The Masses,* Jan. 18, 1984.

The Socialist Labor Party, in particular, has advanced a claim to the Nasserist mantle. At one meeting attended by Nasser's son Khaled, the presiding party official commented: "Nasser's posterity is not three sons and two daughters; he is the father of all the workers whose conditions he improved and the father of the farmers to whom he distributed land. He is the father to millions of students to whom he opened the universities and schools. Yet, Nasser himself is the son of the Young Egypt movement. The Socialist Labor Party is the continuation of the Young Egypt movement. We are the keepers of the revolution, its principles and its achievements"; *The Masses,* Jan. 25, 1984.

104. Despite these restrictions, the Nasserists opposed the Egyptian-Israeli treaty from the moment of its signature; Ahmed, interview, *al-Ahrar,* Aug. 26, 1983.

105. *Economic Ahram,* Aug. 1, 1973.

106. Fuad Serrag Eddine, *Why the New Party?* (Cairo: Dar al-Sharouk, 1977), pp. 58–59.

107. There were indications that factions among the new military rulers had reservations about unrestricted expansion of the student population. In one notable incident the minister of education and instruction was attacked in parliament for a proposal to regulate the universities. He was "ordered to open the doors of the university to every secondary-school graduate who requested admission"; Anouar Abdel-Malek, *Egypt: Military Society* (New York: Vintage Books, 1968), p. 121.

108. Nazih Ayubi, "Implementation Capability and Political Feasibility of the Open Door Policy in Egypt," in *Rich and Poor States in the Middle East: Egypt and*

the New Arab Order, ed. Malcolm H. Kerr and El Sayed Yassin [*sic*] (Boulder, Colo.: Westview Press, 1982), p. 405. Ayubi estimates that a total of 300,000 Egyptians had received advanced degrees before 1970; in the seventies 565,000 became university graduates.

109. Osman Ahmed Osman; interview, *Mayo,* April 8, 1981.

110. The title of an article in *Rose al-Yusuf,* Nov. 26, 1979.

111. "The Possible Impossible—A School Every Three Days," *Sabah al-Kheir,* May 15, 1980.

112. Both the U.S. government and the international banking agencies regularly lobbied for reduction of subsidies; *Economic Ahram,* March 8, 1983.

113. *Al-Ahram,* Sept. 28, 29, and 30, 1984.

4. Making Revolution Real

1. See Mohamed Heikal [*sic*], *Autumn of Fury: The Assassination of Sadat* (New York: Random House, 1983), pp. 90–92.

2. See ibid.

3. *Al-Akhbar,* Jan. 24, 1977.

4. *Al-Akhbar,* Jan. 31, 1977.

5. Quoted in Seif al-Dawla, *In Defense of the People: The Four-Day Summation before the Higher Court of State Security in Cairo* (Beirut: Dar al-Kalema lil Nashr, 1980), pp. 16–17, 23–26.

6. *Al-Akhbar,* Feb. 4, 1977; translated in David Hirst and Irene Beeson, *Sadat* (London: Faber and Faber, 1981), p. 248.

7. Quoted in Hirst and Beeson, *Sadat,* p. 249.

8. *Al-Ahram,* Feb. 11, 1977.

9. *Al-Ahram,* Jan. 26, 1977.

10. From the left perspective, these responses indicated that the United States and the conservative Arab regimes, while uninterested in Egypt's genuine development, could be counted on to pay dearly to rescue a pro-Western regime from the danger of a left-wing upheaval; Raymond William Baker, *Egypt's Uncertain Revolution under Nasser and Sadat* (Cambridge, Mass.: Harvard University Press, 1979), p. 166.

11. See [Haikal], *Autumn of Fury,* pp. 92–94.

12. For an account of these events, see Baker, *Egypt's Uncertain Revolution,* pp. 124–126.

13. Quoted and translated in Hirst and Beeson, *Sadat,* p. 248.

14. Seif al-Dawla documents the official repression in *In Defense of the People,* esp. pp. 73–92.

15. Evidence presented by Seif al-Dawla, the defense attorney for the 176 people eventually tried for instigating the January riots, implicated the state security police in an effort to "exploit these serious events in order to liquidate the nationalist forces that opposed the policies of those in power." At the trial Dawla argued: "While the general prosecutor records on January 19, 1977, that he was unable to conduct investigations because of the breakdown in transportation, hundreds of state security officers and undercover policemen were traveling in their cars to arrest citizens in their homes. The state security police did not stop, and did not care to stop, to break

up a fight, protect a building, put out a fire, aid a wounded person, carry the injured to a doctor, or remove the body of a dead citizen, nor even to arrest one of the demonstrators, ibid., p. 67.

16. *New York Times,* Jan. 30, 1977.

17. "January, a New Birth for the Party," *The Masses (al-Ahaly),* April 12, 1978.

18. See *The Masses,* Aug. 23, 1978, for detailed coverage of this first wave of government repression.

19. *Al-Ahram,* May 15, 1978.

20. Sarcastically, Kholy remarked that if this antagonistic characterization were proved incorrect because of "Marxist bias," he would both accept the guidance of the government party's "straightforward path to economic recovery" and personally repent to Shaikh Abdul Halim Mahmud, the grand shaikh of al-Azhar, for his "blasphemy and the importation of destructive ideologies"; editorial, "The January Masses between the Government and the Left," *The Vanguard (al-Tali'ah),* Feb. 1977, pp. 5–19.

21. The key figures consisted of the small board, personally selected by Kholy, which met once a week to set editorial policy. Memo by Muhammad Mumtaz Nassar in Defense of Ahmed Lutfy al-Kholy, Cairo, 1977.

22. According to Nassar's memo (copies of original supplied to author). Kholy claimed that before it was shut down because of the 1977 editorial, the journal was issued "without any intervention or supervision from *al-Ahram.*" The memo provides several examples of successful resistance of official intrusions during the Nasser years.

23. Kholy, interview with author, Cairo, spring 1980.

24. Richard F. Starr, ed., "U.A.R.," in *Yearbook of International Communist Affairs* (Stanford, Calif.: Hoover Institute Press, 1971).

25. Kholy, editorial, "The January Masses."

26. Abou Seif Yusuf, "Comments on the January Events," *The Vanguard,* Feb. 1977.

27. This reconstruction of the radical Marxist position to which the *Vanguard* circle reacted is based on a series of interviews with Lutfy al-Kholy, Muhammad Sid Ahmed, Khaled Muhieddin, and Khiry Aziz in Cairo in the spring of 1980.

28. Quoted in memo by Nassar on Kholy.

29. Quoted in Sa'ad al-Taheh, *Egypt between Two Ages* (Beirut: Dar al-Nidal, 1982).

30. Hirst and Beeson, *Sadat,* p. 232.

31. *Forty-eight Hours That Shook Egypt: An Eyewitness Account of One Part of the Events of 18, 19 January 1977* (Beirut: Palestine, the Revolution, n.d.).

32. Kholy, editorial, "The January Masses."

33. Ibid.

34. Ibid.

35. For an elaboration of this theme see Rifa'at al-Said, "Democracy in the Third World State," *The Vanguard,* Jan. 1972.

36. For an able discussion of the problems of the "intrusion of parasitic and oppositional elements" into the structures created by the Nasser regime, see "The Year of the Political Organization," *The Vanguard,* Aug. 1965.

37. Lutfy al-Kholy, editorial, *The Vanguard,* Jan. 1966.

38. John Waterbury, *The Egypt of Nasser and Sadat: The Political Economy of Two Regimes* (Princeton: Princeton University Press, 1983), p. 75.

39. Muhammad Abdul Fatah Aboul Fadl, "Popular Supervision in the Face of New Forms of Exploitation," *The Vanguard,* Oct. 1966.

40. Kholy, editorial, *The Vanguard,* Jan. 1966.

41. The Marxists insisted on seeing the Nasser revolution as one phase in Egypt's revolutionary struggle. In making their case, they quoted Nasser's remark that "I don't see a break between the past and the present, and I refuse to think of a break in the stages of development of a people. Great Egypt's history didn't start with the twenty-third of July; the true value of the twenty-third of July is the natural continuity of struggle of the people and its renewing energies and far-reaching hopes"; Muhammad al-Khafif, "Political Organization of Youth: The Guarantee of the Revolution's Continuity," *The Vanguard,* Jan. 1966.

42. Adel Ghaneim, "On the Issue of the New Class in Egypt," *The Vanguard,* Feb. 1968.

43. Lutfy al-Kholy, "The State and Political Organizations in the Egyptian Experiment," *The Vanguard,* July 1965.

44. Ghaneim, "On the Issue of the New Class."

45. From 1959 to 1964, workers with higher technical training increased from 36,133 (or 15 percent of the total) to 82,788 (or 26 percent); ibid.

46. Ibid.

47. Ibid.

48. Kholy, editorial, *The Vanguard,* Jan. 1966.

49. Ghaneim, "On the Issue of the New Class."

50. Kholy, "The State and Political Organizations."

51. Afaf el-Kosheri Mahfouz, *Socialisme et pouvoir en Egypte* (Paris: Libraire Générale de Droit et de Jurisprudence, 1972), p. 318. The charter was adopted in July 1962.

52. Salah Issa, "The Future of Democracy in Egypt," *al-Katib,* 14 (1974), 20–21.

53. Marxists and leftists tortured and murdered in Egyptian jails in these years included Shuhdy 'Attiya, Rushdy Khalil, Muhammad Osman, and Aly al-Dib.

54. Nasser, interview with Eric Rouleau, *Le monde,* June 5, 1963; cited in Waterbury, *The Egypt of Nasser and Sadat,* p. 319.

55. For a comprehensive statement of the program advanced by the *Vanguard* left at this critical juncture, see Ghaneim, "On the Issue of the New Class."

56. Abdul Latif al-Bagdadi, *Memoirs,* pt. 2 (Cairo: Modern Egyptian Library, 1977), pp. 229–230.

57. For example, in 1966 Nasser announced that "in three years the wholesale trade should all belong to the state, and contracting should go 80 percent to the public sector"; quoted in Abdul Mon'eim al-Ghazaly, "The July 23 Revolution and Parasitic Capitalism," *The Vanguard,* July 1973.

58. Al-Kholy, "The State and Political Organizations."

59. Rifa'at al-Said provides an extensive account of these meetings in *The Nasserist Papers* (Cairo: Dar al-Thaqafa al-Gadida, 1975), pp. 39–75.

60. *Address: Nasser* (Cairo: U.A.R. Information Department, Jan. 20, 1965).

61. Quoted in Kholy, "The State and Political Organizations."

62. Michel Kamel, "Mass Organization: The Party and the Revolutionary Cadre," *The Vanguard*, Feb. 1965.

63. Haikal, editorial, *al-Ahram*, April 5, 1968.

64. Anwar el-Sadat [*sic*], *In Search of Identity: An Autobiography* (New York: Harper & Row, 1977), p. 168.

65. Sabry explained his point of view most fully in a series of articles published in *al-Jumhuriyyah* from January to June 1967.

66. *Rose al-Yusuf*, May 3, 1965.

67. For the complete statement of Sabry's views, see a three-part interview in *Rose al-Yusuf*, Sept. 5, 12, 19, 1967.

68. "The Year of the Political Organization," *The Vanguard*, Aug. 1965.

69. In fact, during the Sadat years, graduates of the Institute of Socialist Studies and veterans of the Socialist Youth Organization resurfaced as leaders of the NPUP.

70. Mahfouz, *Socialisme et pouvoir en Egypte*, p. 318.

71. Editorial, "June 5 and the Mobilization Necessary to Achieve Victory," *The Vanguard*, June 1971.

72. Kholy, "The State and Political Organizations."

73. *The Vanguard*, Feb. 1968.

74. Fathy Ismail, *The Vanguard*, June 1968.

75. Ahmed Mustafa, *The Vanguard*, June 1968.

76. Ghaneim, "On the Issue of the New Class."

77. Michel Kamel, "Problems of Social Forces within the National Alliance," *The Vanguard*, May 1969.

78. Helmy Yassin and Abdul Seif al-Nasr, "The Phenomenon of Centers of Power between the July 23 Revolution and the March 30 Statement," *The Vanguard*, May 1968.

79. See Aboul Fadl, "Popular Supervision." For a later and extended discussion, see Rifa'at al-Said, "The Old Right and the New Right," *The Vanguard*, Oct. 1974, which includes a useful catalogue of the attacks on "socialist advances" in the seventies.

80. Ghaneim, "On the Issue of the New Class."

81. Kamel, "Problems of Social Forces."

82. Ghaneim, "On the Issue of the New Class."

83. Fawzy Habashy, "Limiting Parasitic Incomes in the Contracting Sector," *The Vanguard*, July 1973.

84. Ghaneim, "On the Issue of the New Class."

85. Ibid.

86. Aboul Fadl, "Popular Supervision."

87. Ghaneim, "On the Issue of the New Class."

88. Ibid.

89. Fadl, "Popular Supervision."

90. Khairy Aziz, "Attitude of the Socialist Camp on the Middle East Problem," *The Vanguard*, Aug. 1969. See the discussion in Waterbury, *The Egypt of Nasser and Sadat*, pp. 317–322.

91. See the excellent summation of the left view of the June War in Hussein Abdul Raziq, *Egypt on the 18th and 19th of January: A Political and Documentary Study* (Beirut: Dar al-Kalema, 1979), pp. 51–52.

92. Kholy estimated that from June 1967 to October 1973 Egypt's defense burden amounted to more than L.E. 16 billion; editorial, "The January Masses."

93. Fuad Mursi, interview, *Progress,* Dec. 15, 1979.

94. Kholy, editorial, "The January Masses."

95. Ibid.

96. Muhammad Sid Ahmed, "Our Party: A Union," *The Masses,* April 5, 1978.

97. Fuad Mursi, "Our Party: A Pure Egyptian Formula," *The Masses,* March 8, 1978.

98. Abou Seif Yusuf, "Our Party: The Lost Bet," *The Masses,* Feb. 22, 1978.

99. Kholy, editorial, "The January Masses."

100. Government figures reported in *al-Ahram,* Sept. 21, 1979, are cited in Dawla, *In Defense of the People,* pp. 242–243.

101. Raziq, *Egypt on the 18th and 19th of January,* p. 29.

102. *The Vanguard,* Feb. 1971.

103. *The Vanguard,* Nov. 1980.

104. Raziq, *Egypt on the 18th and 19th of January,* p. 30.

105. For an extensive discussion of the left strategy, see the interviews with key NPUP figures in the wake of Sadat's assassination, *al-Musawwar,* Nov. 13, 1981.

106. The regime consistently misrepresented the NPUP. It sought to discredit Nasserism by identifying it with Marxism and then falsely condemning both as "atheistic communism."

107. Khaled Muhieddin, interview with author, Cairo, spring 1980.

108. Ibid. Because of official harassment, elections are not a good measure of the party's real strength and mobilizing potential; in 1978, the party obtained about 8 percent of the popular vote.

109. NPUP Party Program, chap. 2.

110. The most extensive interpretation of the party program now available in English is that by Raymond Hinnebusch; Hinnebusch's reading downplays the Marxist thread in the NPUP platform. See Hinnebusch, "The National Progressive Unionist Party: The Nationalist Left Opposition in Post-Populist Egypt," *Arab Studies Quarterly,* 3 (1981): 325–351; and his more succinct analysis in, *Egyptian Politics under Sadat* (Cambridge: Cambridge University Press, 1985), pp. 190–192.

111. NPUP Party Program, chap. 1.

112. Mahmud al-Mareghy, "Our Party: Egyptian Made," *The Masses,* May 3, 1978.

113. Fuad Mursi, *Progress,* Sept. 13, 1978.

114. Khaled Muhieddin, interview with author, Cairo, spring 1980.

115. Said, "Democracy in the Third World State."

116. Lutfy al-Kholy, "Comments on Intellectual Conflicts in Our Society," *The Vanguard,* Dec. 1966.

117. For a brilliant summation of the fascist thesis, see Muhammad Sayyid al-Said, *The Masses,* Nov. 21, 1984.

118. *The Vanguard,* July 1968.

119. *The Masses,* April 5, 1978.

120. *Progress,* June 21, 1980.

121. Lutfy al-Kholy, editorial, *The Vanguard,* June 1971.

122. Lutfy al-Kholy, "Facing Large and Small Imperialisms," *The Vanguard*, Dec. 1973.

123. Kholy, editorial, *The Vanguard*, June 1971.

124. Lutfy al-Kholy, *The Vanguard*, Nov. 1971.

125. Kholy, editorial, *The Vanguard*, June 1971.

126. *Progress*, July 30, 1979.

127. Lutfy Waked, "Our Party," *The Masses*, March 29, 1978.

128. *Progress*, March 14, 1979.

129. Khaled Muhieddin later acknowledged these difficulties with the rank and file: "We did not, despite the temporary isolation, stop warning of these dangers, uncovering the defects of this policy, and refuting the claims that it is a road to which there is no alternative to solve the nationalist cause"; Address to the NPUP General Congress, April 10, 1980.

130. Muhammad Sid Ahmed, "After the Failure of the Self-Rule Negotiations: The Alternative to Camp David Agreements," *Progress*, June 8, 1980.

131. *Progress*, July 1, 1980.

132. Muhieddin, Address to the NPUP General Congress, April 10, 1980.

133. *Progress*, April 8, 1979.

134. "January, a New Birth for the Party," *The Masses*, April 12, 1978.

135. Waked, "Our Party."

136. Dawla, *In Defense of the People*, p. 243.

137. For a good summary of the actions taken against the NPUP, see Khaled Muhieddin's letter protesting harassment of the party, *Progress*, Sept. 27, 1978.

138. *The Masses*, Aug. 23, 1978.

139. *Progress*, March 21, 1979.

140. *The Masses*, April 5, 1978.

141. Khaled Muhieddin, Address to the NPUP General Congress, April 10, 1980.

142. *Progress*, July 16, 1979.

143. Kholy, "Comments on Intellectual Conflicts."

144. Kholy, "The January Masses."

145. Yusuf, "Comments on the January Events."

146. Lutfy al-Kholy provides a clear statement of this self-understanding of the *Vanguard* writers in "The Algiers Symposium and the Issue of Socialism in the Arab World," *The Vanguard*, Feb. 1967.

5. *Creative Empowerment*

1. The phrase is the title of the first Western book to describe the Wissa Wassef experiment. W. Forman, B. Forman, and Ramses Wissa Wassef, *Tapestries from Egypt*, trans. Jean Layton (Prague: Artia, 1960). The account of the Wissa Wassef School in this chapter is based on regular visits to the village in the period 1980–1982 and sporadic visits since. I first heard about Wissa Wassef in 1980 from a development economist, Gouda Abdul Khalek, who invoked the experience of the village in the context of a discussion of Egypt's "insoluble" economic problems; he was making the point that creativity in improbable circumstances is part of Egypt's story.

I conducted formal interviews only in 1980, and quotations in this chapter are restricted to notes from those interviews in which the artists at Harrania explicitly agreed to discuss their lives with a Western scholar who intended to write about them.

2. The phrase is taken from Donald C. Campbell, "Reforms as Experiments," *American Psychologist,* 24 (April 1969), 409–429.

3. From the extensive literature on the Copts, see esp. Tarek al-Bishry, *Muslims and Copts in the Framework of the National Community* (Cairo: Egyptian Public Organization for Books, 1980); Nadia Ramses Farah, *Religious Strife in Egypt* (New York: Gordon and Breach Science Publishers, 1986).

4. The fullest discussion of Wissa Wassef's career is in Milad Hanna, *Yes We Are Copts . . . but We Are Also Egyptians* (Cairo: Madbouly Bookstore, 1980), pp. 70–83.

5. Yoanna Wissa Wassef, interview with author, Harrania, Feb. 11, 1980.

6. Sophie Habib Gorgy, interview with author, Harrania, Feb. 5, 1980.

7. The term is used by the Forman brothers in the epigraph of *Tapestries from Egypt.*

8. For a full discussion of the methodology of the reconstruction of such life situations, see Karl R. Popper, *Objective Knowledge: An Evolutionary Approach* (Oxford: Clarendon Press, 1972), pp. 153–190.

9. Said, interview with author, Harrania, April 28, 1980.

10. Wissa Wassef, *Woven by Hand* (London: Hamlyn, 1972), p. 5.

11. Said, interview with author, Harrania, April 28, 1980.

12. Wissa Wassef, *Woven by Hand,* p. 15.

13. Ibid., p. 14.

14. The recognition of the creative artist as a key symbol involves all five criteria described by Sherry Ortner: respondents regularly underscore its importance, they are aroused and interested by discussions of it, it comes up for consideration in a wide variety of contexts, it is a greatly elaborated concept, and its violation brings immediate communal disapproval and sanctions. See Sherry Ortner, "On Key Symbols," *American Anthropologist,* 75 (1973), 1338–46.

15. Said, interview with author, Harrania, April 28, 1980.

16. Wissa Wassef, *Woven by Hand,* p. 14.

17. Sophie Habib Gorgy and Mahrus, interview with author, Harrania, April 28, 1980.

18. Yoanna Wissa Wassef, interview with author, Harrania, Feb. 11, 1980.

19. Suzanne Wissa Wassef, interview with author, Harrania, Feb. 22, 1980.

20. *Al-Ahram,* April 30, 1980.

21. Wissa Wassef, *Woven by Hand,* p. 10.

22. Ibid., p. 13.

23. Sophie Habib Gorgy, interview with author, Harrania, Feb. 5, 1980.

24. Wissa Wassef, *Woven by Hand,* p. 13.

25. Quoted in ibid., p. 35.

26. Sophie Habib Gorgy, interview with author, Harrania, Feb. 5, 1980.

27. Forman, Forman, and Wissa Wassef, *Tapestries from Egypt,* p. 25.

28. Yoanna Wissa Wassef, interview with author, Harrania, Feb. 11, 1980.

29. Wissa Wassef, *Woven by Hand,* p. 34.

30. Ibid.

31. Quoted in Clifford Geertz, *The Interpretation of Cultures* (New York: Basic Books, 1973), p. 13.

32. Afaf Lutfy al-Sayyid discusses the impact on his thinking of the Wissa Wassef experiment in al-Sayyid, *Egypt's Liberal Experience, 1922–1936* (Cairo: al-Markaz al-Araby lil Basth wal Nashr, 1981), pp. 38–39.

33. Quoted in Norman O. Brown, *Life against Death* (Middletown, Conn.: Wesleyan University Press, 1959), p. 66.

6. Thinking in the National Interest

1. Muhammad Salmawy, the Nasserist journalist, explained Haikal's notion of "islands of excellence" to me in an interview, Cairo, Dec. 2, 1979.

2. The crisis of the intellectuals is a major theme in Anouar Abdel-Malek, *Egypt: Military Society* (New York: Vintage Books, 1968).

3. *Al-Ahram,* Nov. 15, 1968.

4. Muhammad Hassanein Haikal, *The Impossible Peace and the Absent Democracy* (Beirut: Publications Company for Publishing and Distribution, 1982), p. 284.

5. Ibid., pp. 315–316.

6. David Hirst and Irene Beeson, *Sadat* (London: Faber and Faber, 1981), pp. 275–276. My description of Sadat's return is paraphrased from this account.

7. Quoted in Hirst and Beeson, *Sadat,* p. 269.

8. Quoted in Raphael Israeli, *Man of Defiance: A Political Biography of Anwar Sadat* (Totowa, N.J.: Barnes & Noble, 1985), p. 236.

9. All three articles appeared on November 25, 1977, under the Center's logo and without signatures.

10. Anis Mansur, *The Wall and the Tears* (Beirut and Cairo: Dar al-Sharouk, 1982), pp. 53, 56.

11. This need was reiterated constantly as the Egyptian-Israeli relationship developed; for a summary of Egyptian concerns in the late Sadat period, see the report on a seminar in the Faculty of Commerce, Alexandria University, on economic relations between Israel and Egypt: "Israel makes detailed and integrated studies to know what's going on in the Arab world at the social, economic, and cultural levels and follows any Arabic thing, even accents, languages, markets, and cultures; it even teaches Arabic in different Israeli schools; the share of those who know Arabic in Israel is 40 percent"; *Economic Ahram* (*al-Ahram al-Iqtisadi*), April 1, 1980.

12. Muhammad Salmawy, interview with author, Cairo, Dec. 2, 1979.

13. Sayyid Yassine, *al-Ahram,* April 4, 1979.

14. Sayyid Yassine, *al-Ahram,* Aug. 20, 1982.

15. Ibid.

16. Yassine, *al-Ahram,* April 4, 1979.

17. Yassine, *al-Ahram,* Aug. 20, 1982.

18. Ibid.

19. This conclusion is based on discussions with virtually all the young CPSS researchers from 1980 to 1985.

20. See "Which Comes First, the Politician or the Intellectual?" *Rose al-Yusuf,* Dec. 24, 1979.

21. See, in particular, Sayyid Yassine, ed., *The Revolution and Social Change* (Cairo: CPSS, 1977).

22. See, in particular, Sa'ad Ibrahim, ed., *The Arabism of Egypt: The Dialogue of the Seventies* (Cairo: CPSS, 1978).

23. Sayyid Yassine, "The Arab Intellectual: Critic, Apologist, Spectator," *Arab Cause,* February 1980.

24. Ibid.

25. Ibid.

26. Ibid.

27. Haikal, *The Impossible Peace and the Absent Democracy,* pp. 315–316.

28. Samy Mansur, *al-Ahram,* May 1, 1980.

29. Samy Mansur, *al-Ahram,* Feb. 15, 1980.

30. The regime apparently made such direct requests rarely; the public record suggests two other such instances. The first was a report on the so-called Black Book documenting the corruption of the Wafd Party in the pre-1952 period, to discredit the liberal opposition. Raising the banner of liberalization as Sadat did invited comparison with the greatest of Egypt's prerevolutionary-era parties, the Wafd. To counter the positive response to a revived Wafd, the official press harped on the reports of corruption that tainted the Wafd's final years. The Center's meticulous, objective account of the Black Book incident, prepared by Yunan Labib Rizk, proved to be a double-edged sword: by the new standards of corruption set in the seventies, the misdeeds of the earlier age appeared almost benign. The Center of course, did not make this point explicitly. See Yunan Labib Rizk, *The Wafd and the Black Book* (Cairo: CPSS, 1978). The Center also published a documentary record of Sadat's trip to Jerusalem in 1978, *The Peace Initiative: The Trip of the Century* (Cairo, 1978).

31. Osama al-Ghazzaly Harb, *Historical Origins of Democratic Socialism* (Cairo: al-Haya al-Masriyya al-Ama lil Kitab, 1978), pp. 145–147.

32. Hala Abu Bakr Sa'udy and Wahid Muhammad Abdul al-Meguid, *Freedom and the Multiparty System in the Ideology of Democratic Socialism* (Cairo: al-Haya al-Masriyya al-Ama lil Kitab, 1978), pp. 88–93.

33. Ibid., pp. 94–122.

34. The relevant measures are Law 40 of 1977 on Political Parties and Law 33 of 1978 on Protection of the Internal Front and Social Peace.

35. Zbigniew Brzezinski, quoted in Muhammad al-Said Ibrahim, *The American Conception of Israel* (Cairo: CPSS, 1979), p. 16.

36. Ibid., p. 83.

37. Ibid.

38. Ibid., pp. 90, 100.

39. Ibid., pp. 180–181, 186.

40. Sayyid Yassine, letter, *al-Ahram,* June 8, 1982.

41. Sayyid Yassine, "The Arabs and the Battle of Civilizational Challenge with Israel," *al-Ahram,* Aug. 20, 1982.

42. Sayyid Yassine, "Cultural Confrontation with Israel: Why?" *al-Ahram,* July 3, 1979.

7. Anticipating a Free Press

1. See Anwar el-Sadat [*sic*], *In Search of Identity: An Autobiography* (New York: Harper & Row, 1977), pp. 213–214.

2. Lutfy Abdul 'Azim, "Economically, Is Egypt Ready for Peace?" *Economic Ahram (al-Ahram al-Iqtisadi)*, Jan. 1, 1978.

3. Butrous Ghali, "Goodby to the Last Page," *Economic Ahram*, Nov. 15, 1977.

4. In the issue of Jan. 1, 1965, launching the journal's seventh year, the editorial described its role as "a journal of leading thought . . . and a meeting place of the greatest economic and political scholars."

5. Ghali, "Goodby to the Last Page."

6. 'Azim, "Economically, Is Egypt Ready for Peace?"

7. 'Essam Rifa'at, "Peacetime Economics: A New Period of Challenge," *Economic Ahram*, Oct. 1, 1975.

8. Ibid.

9. Lutfy Abdul 'Azim, "The Myth of Increasing Exports of Goods," *Economic Ahram*, Sept. 1, 1976.

10. Rifa'at, "Peacetime Economics."

11. 'Azim, "Economically, Is Egypt Ready for Peace?"

12. Lutfy Abdul 'Azim, "Dying out of Anger Isn't a Solution to Economic Problems," *Economic Ahram*, Dec. 28, 1981.

13. Lutfy Abdul 'Azim, "The Concept of Prosperity," *Economic Ahram*, April 1, 1980.

14. 'Azim, "Economically, Is Egypt Ready for Peace?"

15. 'Essam Rifa'at, "Consumption Open Door and Production Open Door," *Economic Ahram*, March 15, 1978.

16. 'Essam Rifa'at, "The Lessons of the Pyramid Plateau Project," *Economic Ahram*, June 15, 1978.

17. 'Azim, "Economically, Is Egypt Ready for Peace?"

18. 'Essam Rifa'at, "The Public Sector Face to Face with the Open Door Policy," *Economic Ahram*, April 1, 1978.

19. 'Azim, "The Concept of Prosperity."

20. 'Essam Rifa'at, "Danger Signals in Egyptian Imports," *Economic Ahram*, Aug. 1, 1977.

21. Lutfy Abdul 'Azim, "An Answer to the Minister of Trade," *Economic Ahram*, Oct. 1, 1977.

22. Ibid.

23. Quoted in 'Essam Rifa'at, "Hands Off the Private Sector," *Economic Ahram*, Aug. 1, 1977.

24. 'Essam Rifa'at, "Hidden Hands That Control the Egyptian Market," *Economic Ahram*, Oct. 1, 1977.

25. Lutfy Abdul 'Azim, "The Power of Attraction and Repulsion in the Tourism Field," *Economic Ahram*, May 1, 1971.

26. For key articles in the debate, see "The Minister of Tourism Answers," *Economic Ahram*, Feb. 15, 1976; and Essam Rifa'at, "The Real Face of Tourism," *Economic Ahram*, Nov. 1, 1977, which develops many of the points made originally by 'Azim.

27. Lutfy Abdul 'Azim, "Schizophrenia in Housing Policy," *Economic Ahram,* July 1, 1978.

28. Ibid.

29. 'Essam Rifa'at, "Those Responsible for Housing," *Economic Ahram,* Feb. 1, 1979.

30. Lutfy Abdul 'Azim, "Iron and Steel Refinery between the Press and the Responsibles," *Economic Ahram,* Nov. 1, 1968; see also discussion in *Economic Ahram,* July 1, July 15, and Aug. 1, 1968.

31. Lutfy Abdul 'Azim, "Development: In Whose Arms?" *Economic Ahram,* Oct. 3, 1983.

32. Ibid.

33. Ibid.

34. Lutfy Abdul 'Azim, "An American Medal for Economic Ahram," *Economic Ahram,* April 4, 1983.

35. Sa'ad al-Tayeh, "A Lesson for the American Diplomat: What Is Yellow Journalism?" *Economic Ahram,* April 18, 1983.

36. Azim, "Economically, Is Egypt Ready for Peace?"

37. Lutfy Abdul 'Azim, "All Greetings to Meir Kahane," *Economic Ahram,* Aug. 24, 1981.

38. Galal Amin's series appeared on May 10, 24, 31, and June 7, 1981. In the following quotations these four articles are treated as a single unit.

39. See Amin's own account of the censorship in "The Tragedy of *Economic Ahram,*" *The Masses (al-Ahaly),* March 28, 1984.

40. "The Editor-in-Chief of *Economic Ahram* Loses His Position," *The Masses,* April 25, 1984.

41. Lutfy Abdul 'Azim, "Arabs and Jews—Who Exterminates Whom?" *Economic Ahram,* Sept. 27, 1982.

42. Subsequent investigations, reported in Egypt, revealed that Lebanese Christian militia, allied with Israel, did the killing in the refugee camps at Sabra and Shatilla, while Israeli troops lit the area with flares and stood guard outside.

43. Ahmed Hamroush, "Stop, the Road You're Treading On Is Too Thorny and Dangerous," *Economic Ahram,* Oct. 11, 1982.

44. See, e.g., Abdul Fattah Muhammad Hussein, *Economic Ahram,* Dec. 6, 1982.

45. See S. Hagras, "The Nature of the Arab-Israeli Conflict," *Economic Ahram,* Jan. 10, 1983; idem, "The Good Israeli, the Evil Israeli," *Economic Ahram,* April 11, 1983.

46. Taher Abdul Hakim, "How Do We Think of Our Enemy and How Does He Think of Us?" *Economic Ahram,* Aug. 15, 1983.

47. Amin, "The Tragedy of *Economic Ahram.*"

8. Return to the Future

1. *The Call (al-Da'wa)* was published from 1976 to 1981 as the official organ of the Muslim Brothers. The journal bore the emblem of the Brothers and frequently carried announcements by branches of the movement in other Arab countries. Its circulation was reported by the Brothers as 80,000 a month (*The Call,* June 1978). A second Islamic periodical, *Perseverance (al-I'tisam),* initially restricted to theolog-

ical issues, began after the mid-seventies to follow the Muslim Brother's lead on issues of current policy. Many of its writers were regular columnists in *The Call*. The journal, published by the Holy Law Society, had a circulation roughly equal to *The Call*'s until it too was closed in 1981. These two journals were the heart of the Islamic press in the seventies.

2. Telmesany explained that in the absence of a "guide" or leader for whatever reason, "the eldest member of the group was to take up his duties. I am not the leader of the Society," he continued, "but I am its representative"; interview, *The Masses* (*al-Ahaly*), Sept. 29, 1982. Telmesany represented the Brothers during the Sadat years. He died in 1986. Important recent works on the Brotherhood in Arabic include Salah Issa, "The Muslim Brotherhood: Tragedy of the Past and Problem of the Future," an introduction to the Arabic translation of Richard Mitchell's *The Society of Muslim Brothers*, titled *The Muslim Brothers* (Cairo: Madbouly Bookstore Publications, 1977); Rifa'at al-Said, *Hassan al-Banna* (Cairo: Madbouly Bookstore Publications, 1978); Muhammad Shawky Zaki, *The Muslim Brotherhood and Egyptian Society* (Cairo: Dar al-Ansar, 1980).

3. See *al-Ahram*, July 31, 1978.

4. Sadat charged that the communists and the Muslim Brothers were simply "the right and the left of the same political school" that sought to overturn his government; *al-Akhbar*, Feb. 28, 1979. For Sadat's accusations, see also *Progrès égyptien*, March 1 and April 16, 1979.

5. *Al-Ahram*, Aug. 22, 1979.

6. Ibid.

7. A second account of the meeting, from which this quotation is taken, appeared in *Perseverance*, Sept. 1979.

8. *Al-Ahram*, Aug. 22, 1979; Omar Telmesany, interview, *al-Musawwar*, Jan. 22, 1982.

9. The Society of Muslim Brothers was outlawed in 1954. Without lifting that ban, the Sadat regime allowed the Brothers to publish *The Call* after 1976.

10. Telmesany, interview, *The Masses*, Sept. 29, 1982.

11. The Muslim Brothers gave regular attention in *The Call* to a reconstruction of their history. They considered the task essential because of the repression of the Nasser years. Articles stressed the continuity in the Brothers' vision of an Islamic alternative for Egypt and the trials they endured to preserve it. These historical accounts were directed in particular to Egyptian youth. They asked questions such as "Why do all Arab governments attack the Muslim Brothers?" and offered judgments such as "Seeking to correct an unjust system is not a crime." See *The Call*, March 1978, esp. pp. 16–17. Telmesany defended this attention to the history of the movement in the Islamic press by arguing that the "Brothers had the right to respond to the lies that were told about them in recent years"; interview, *Rose al-Yusuf*, July 7, 1980.

12. The distinguished thinker Sayyid Qutb explained authoritatively the theoretical assumption underlying this view. See the excerpts from his "The Interpretation of History," in Yvonne Yazbeck Haddad, *Contemporary Islam and the Challenge of History* (Albany: State University of New York Press, 1982), pp. 164–165.

13. Full treatment of the militant groups is beyond the scope of this chapter. A concise summary of what is reliably known about the militants can be found in

Ahram Center for Political and Strategic Studies, *The Arab Strategic Report, 1987* (Cairo, 1988). The political economist Nadia Ramsis Farah has written an invaluable account of the roots and course of the sectarian conflict in the seventies; *Religious Strife in Egypt* (New York: Gordon and Breach Science Publishers, 1986).

14. For a detailed treatment of gains in these various spheres, see CPSS, *Arab Strategic Report, 1987*.

15. Muhammad Abdul Kudus summarizes the achievements of the eighties from the Brothers' point of view; he focuses on the alliance with the Labor Party in the third parliamentary elections of Mubarak's presidency, in the spring of 1987. He also includes a brief, lucid statement of the aspirations of the trend. See *Liwa al-Islam,* May 17, 1987.

16. These extensive developments are the subject of a book on centrist Islam in the eighties on which I am currently collaborating with Karen Aboul Kheir of the American University in Cairo.

17. Telmesany appealed to the regime to legalize the Brotherhood because "it would be better and *more controllable* to have one legal organization of the Muslim Brothers"; emphasis added; "The Muslim Brothers: Past and Present Eras," *The Call,* Oct. 1977.

18. Sadat speech, reported in *al-Ahram,* Sept. 6, 1981.

19. For a review of these accusations and a forceful rebuttal, see *The Call,* May 1981.

20. Telmesany, interview, *The Masses,* Sept. 29, 1982.

21. Omar Telmesany, editorial, *The Call,* Aug. 1979. Here Telmesany addressed the issue of censorship in the context of a general discussion of the Muslim Brothers' relationship to the regime.

22. Telmesany reviewed these involvements in a wide-ranging interview in *The Masses,* Sept. 29, 1982.

23. See Issa, "The Muslim Brotherhood."

24. In 1968 Nasser estimated that 18,000 had been arrested in the fifties crackdown. The second wave of repression, in the mid-sixties, was even more sweeping. One estimate put the number arrested in a single twenty-four-hour period at 27,000; *Akhbar al-Yom,* March 29, 1975.

25. An excellent summary of the Brotherhood's evaluation of the Nasser years is Muhammad Abdul Kudus, "Ten Years after the Death of Egypt's Tyrant," *The Call,* Sept. 1980. Also important is Omar al-Telmesany, *What the People, Not I, Said of Nasser's Rule* (Cairo: Dar al-Ansar, 1980).

26. See K. al-Faramawi, *Military Prison Diary* (Cairo, 1976), pp. 170–174.

27. Kudus, "Ten Years."

28. Telmesany, interview, *Rose al-Yusuf,* July 7, 1980.

29. Sadat worked through two figures to encourage and even finance the student groups. They were Hussein al-Shafei, one of the original Free Officers, and Muhammad Osman Ismail, who subsequently was made governor of Assiut. For one detailed treatment of the government support for the groups, see *Sabah al-Kheir,* Nov. 19, 1981. The Muslim Brothers openly acknowledged their antileft role: "Youth of Islamic groups believe that faith and atheism never meet. That is why Islamic groups have always had a prominent role in clearing the universities of communist and Nasserist thought"; *The Call,* July 1979.

30. Telmesany, interview, *al-Musawwar,* Jan. 22, 1982.

31. Omar Telmesany, "Message to Youth," *al-Musawwar,* Feb. 19, 1982.

32. Omar Telmesany, interview, *The Call,* Oct. 1977. When the government cracked down on the university societies, Telmesany publicly dissented: "I think the Muslim groups that have been established in universities should continue"; interview, *Rose al-Yusuf,* July 7, 1980.

33. From the platform of *The Call* the Brothers argued for the centrality of their role in Egypt's drive for political community. Virtually every issue of the journal carried reports of their part in Egypt's national struggles.

34. For a judicious evaluation of this claim see the new introduction to Tarek al-Bishry's *The Political Movement in Egypt, 1945–1952,* rev. ed. (Cairo: Dar al-Sharouk, 1983). This paragraph draws on Bishry's arguments.

35. The text of the program is in *al-Ahram,* Aug. 12, 1952.

36. The most carefully documented treatment of the Brothers' role in Palestine is Richard Mitchell, *The Society of Muslim Brothers* (London: Oxford University Press, 1969), esp. pp. 16–17, 31, 36, 55–58, 60, 64, 75–76, 90, 99, 173–174, 267–269. In contrast, Gilles Kepel, *Muslim Extremism in Egypt: The Prophet and the Pharaoh* (Berkeley: University of California Press, 1985), discusses the "Islamicist mind" and "the Jew" with scarcely a mention of concrete military and political struggles (pp. 23, 110–121).

37. The most sustained indictment of the Nasser years is Telmesany's *What the People Said.*

38. There is an extensive memoir literature on the Muslim Brothers' prison experience and its impact on the movement. See, e.g., Abdul Halim Khafagy, *When the Sun Disappeared: Memoir of Prisons and Detention Camps* (Mansura: Dar al-Nazir, 1979).

39. A persistent theme in *The Call* was the failure of both Nasser's Arab socialism and the systems of Western thought on which Sadat relied. After these failures, asked one commentator, why not "turn to the Koran as a way of life"? *The Call,* Nov. 1979.

40. The most persuasive assessment of this arrangement is Issa, "The Muslim Brotherhood."

41. For a particularly clear statement of this position see Telmesany, "Message to Youth."

42. *Perseverance,* April/May 1981.

43. Omar Telmesany consistently argued that of the two superpowers, the Soviet Union was "the fiercer in its hatred of Islam"; see *What the People Said,* pp. 28–29.

44. Omar Telmesany summarizes the Muslim Brothers' assessment of the opening to Israel in *The Call,* Oct. 1978.

45. *The Call,* Oct. 1976.

46. Omar Telmesany, interview with a Canadian journalist, republished in *The Call,* June 1978.

47. See a series of four articles on Palestine in *The Call,* Feb. through May 1981.

48. See, e.g., "Muslims of the World, Liberate the Captive [al-Aqsa] Mosque" and "Israel Destroyed 388 Palestinian Villages since 1948," *The Call,* May 1981.

49. For an exceptionally clear statement on the illusory character of Sadat's full partnership with America, see "War Is the Only Solution and the Sole Means to Liberate Palestine," *The Call,* May 1981.

50. Omar Telmesany, "America from an Islamic Point of View," *The Call*, Dec. 1979.

51. The Brothers were deeply suspicious of the role of the wealthy Coptic community living in the United States. They argued that the regime used the communal strife of 1981 as a pretext to strike at the Islamic current. The fullest discussion of the Coptic issue is in *The Call*, July and Aug. 1981.

52. See *Perseverance*, Dec. 1980.

53. Muhammad Abdul Kudus, "Question Marks on Separating Religion from Politics," *The Call*, Nov. 1979.

54. Ibid.

55. Muhammad Abdul Kudus, "The Corrective Revolution Needs Correction," *The Call*, May 1981.

56. For concise statements of Brotherhood economic views see the numerous articles by Yusuf Kamal, such as *The Call*, Jan. 1978 and May 1981.

57. Omar Telmesany, *The Call*, Feb. 1977.

58. Abdul Hamid Abdul Latif, "The Consumer Open Door Policy and Morals," *The Call*, July 1978.

59. Ibid.

60. In the introduction to his brother's commentary on the Koran, Muhammad Qutb emphasizes the pragmatic character of the martyr Sayyid Qutb's legacy: "The author's vigorous struggle, for which he was imprisoned, then killed, was, at the practical level, an attempt to achieve the implementation of Islam in the shape of a community which practises Islam in its life and preaches the need for its realization until it becomes the actual code of practice for the society as a whole." "Introduction," in Sayyid Qutb, *In the Shade of the Quor'an* (London: MWH, 1979), p. xi.

61. *The Call*, June 1978.

62. Hassan al-Banna, *The Collected Works of Hassan al-Banna* (Beirut: al-Moassa al-Islamiyya, n.d.), p. 60.

63. I take this formulation from the distinguished Egyptian historian Tarek al-Bishry, *The Political Movement in Egypt, 1945–1952*, p. 43.

64. Al-Sayyid Aboul Hassan al-Nadowy, *Islam and Rulership* (Cairo, [1952]), p. 3.

65. In a celebrated passage Hassan al-Banna remarks: "Brethren, you are not a benevolent organization, nor a political party, nor a local association with strictly limited aims. Rather you are a new spirit making its way into the heart of this nation and revivifying it through the Qur'an; a new light dawning and scattering the darkness of materialism through the knowledge of God; a resounding voice rising and echoing the message of the Apostle (May God bless and save him!) . . . If some should say to you: This is politics!, say: This is Islam and we do not recognize such divisions"; *Five Tracts of Hassan al-Banna* (*1906–1949*), trans. Charles Wendell (Berkeley: University of California Press, 1978), p. 36. The passage is quoted in *The Call*, July 1977.

66. Omar Telmesany was interviewed as part of a public debate on the crisis of religious thought in Egypt, published in *Rose al-Yusuf* in the summer of 1980. For the Brothers' view of Islam in the Nasser years and critical reactions to those views, see *Rose al-Yusuf*, July 7, 1980. For a detailed criticism of the role of al-Azhar, see *Perseverance*, Feb. 1979.

67. Shaikh Ahmed Kishk, interview with author, Cairo, May 12, 1980.

68. Kishk's Friday addresses were taped and widely circulated in Egypt and the Arab world.

69. Shaikh Kishk discusses his conception of the mosque and his own experience in the seventies in "The Message of the Mosque in Islam," *al-Liwa al-Islam*, Feb. 25, 1982.

70. Abdul Halim Eweiss and Abdou Zayed, "Islamic History in Schools: A War on Islam," *The Call*, June 1978.

71. "The Philosophy Textbook in Schools Adopts the Western Vision and Is Full of Contradictions," *The Call*, Nov. 1978.

72. See, in particular, Sayyid Qutb's writings on historical method, *In History* (Beirut, 1974). There are excerpts in Haddad, *Contemporary Islam*, pp. 162–168.

73. "The Philosophy Textbook," *The Call*, Nov. 1978.

74. Telmesany, "Message to Youth."

75. Eweiss and Zayed, "Islamic History in Schools."

76. Abdul Halim Eweiss and Abdou Zayed, "The Tragedy of Literary Studies in School Curricula," *The Call*, Sept. 1978.

77. Ibid.

78. See the discussion of the role of women in the Islamic movements in Fadwa al-Guindi, "Veiling Infitah with Muslim Ethic," *Social Problems*, 28 (1981), 465–485.

79. See "The Muslim Woman Removes the Dress of the Dark Ages and Dons the Islamic Dress," *The Call*, Feb. 1979.

80. "And to Woman, Her Rights," *The Call*, March 1977. See esp. Zeinab al-Ghazaly, "Women in Islam," *The Call*, Jan. 1979.

81. See "Woman's Position in Islam," *The Call*, Aug. 1977.

82. Zeinab al-Ghazaly, "Women and Work," *The Call*, Jan. 1979.

83. Abdul Fattah Ahmed, "Toward a Muslim Home: Woman's Work and Education," *The Call*, Sept. 1980.

84. Zeinab al-Ghazaly, "Feminist Organizations Are a Fraud," *The Call*, Feb. 1978.

85. "The Muslim Woman Removes," *The Call*, Feb. 1979.

86. See Guindi, "Veiling Infitah."

87. Ahmed Muhammad Aly Ibrahim, "Educating Women in the Desired Islamic Society," *The Call*, June 1977.

88. Ibid.

89. Zeinab al-Ghazaly, *Days of My Life* (Cairo: Dar al-Sharouk, 1979), p. 28.

90. The Islamic social ideal was not, as Sayyid Qutb put it, an "unrepeated miracle." The Arabs of Medina lived under God's guidance as Muhammad had received it, and that social goal was realizable. "Truly this period is not the product of an unrepeated miracle; it was the product of the human effort exerted by early Muslims. It is attainable again when a similar effort is put forth"; quoted in Haddad, *Contemporary Islam*, p. 92.

91. See his misgivings about the Islamic student groups at Assiut University in *Sabah al-Kheir*, Nov. 19, 1981.

9. Re-Visioning Third World Politics

1. This notion is developed in C. West Churchman, *The Systems Approach and Its Enemies* (New York: Basic Books, 1979).

2. See Lucien Goldmann, *The Human Sciences and Philosophy*, trans. Richard Nice (London: Jonathan Cape, 1969), pp. 23–34.

3. See Arendt's chapter "Action," in *The Human Condition* (Chicago: University of Chicago Press, 1958), pp. 175–247.

4. This section relies on the notion of common meanings explained by Charles Taylor in "Interpretation and the Science of Man," *Review of Metaphysics*, 25 (Sept. 1971), 29–32.

5. The important notion of "sharing of the shared" in defining community is taken from the work of Charles Taylor. In addition to the article cited above, see especially "Foucault on Freedom and Truth," *Political Theory*, 12 (Feb. 1984), 152–183. The emphasis on "argument" and its role in community life comes from moral philosopher Alisdair MacIntyre, *After Virtue* (Notre Dame: University of Notre Dame Press, 1981), especially pp. 190–209. Although MacIntyre's formulation gives too intellectualist a tone to a social process of interaction that goes beyond the intellectual, it remains a useful way to discuss the forces that sustain collective life.

6. My view of the centrality of the "problem situation" derives from Karl R. Popper, who argues persuasively that both science and the humanities strive for understanding and that a grasp of what he calls the "meta-problem of understanding a problem" is essential in both domains. To understand a scientific theory it is important to have a sense of the problem with which the scientist was grappling. In parallel fashion, to understand a life situation it is important to grasp the key elements in the problem situation that human actors understand themselves to confront. Karl R. Popper, *Objective Knowledge: An Evolutionary Approach* (Oxford: Clarendon Press, 1972), pp. 180–190.

7. This standard interpretation of Aristotle's meaning is offered by Edward Hallett Carr, *The Twenty Years' Crisis, 1919–1939* (New York: Harper & Row, 1964), p. 95.

8. Alan White, "The Insignificant Other" (Faculty seminar paper, Williams College, 1989).

9. The Greek origins of these ideas about politics and their continuity in the classical political tradition are discussed by Sheldon Wolin, *Politics and Vision* (Boston: Little, Brown, 1960), pp. 8–11.

10. Lévi-Strauss believed that a grammar of culture would identify the units of cultural discourse generated by the principle of binary opposition and spell out the rules of their combination to produce actual cultural outcomes, such as myths and social arrangements; for a concise summary of his main propositions and their relation to the development of theory in anthropology, see Sherry Ortner, "Theory in Anthropology since the Sixties," *Comparative Studies in Society and History*, 26 (Jan. 1984), 126–166. It is my judgment that the influence Ortner observes clearly extends to political science as well.

11. Eric Davis, *Challenging Colonialism: Bank Misr and Egyptian Industrialization, 1920–1941* (Princeton: Princeton University Press, 1983).

12. John Waterbury, *The Egypt of Nasser and Sadat: The Political Economy of Two Regimes* (Princeton: Princeton University Press, 1983).

13. Leonard Binder, *In a Moment of Enthusiasm: Political Power and the Second Stratum in Egypt* (Chicago: University of Chicago Press, 1978).

14. Davis, *Challenging Colonialism*, p. 221.

15. Ibid., p. 11. Davis' work is particularly successful in reintroducing internal notions of class and contradiction into an analysis that stresses the influence of the external environment.

16. Waterbury, *The Egypt of Nasser and Sadat*, p. 4.

17. Faced with an "impossible" economic situation, one can decide to live with it, to change it by some radical action, or even to define it as desirable in some previously unthought-of way. In a given political context any of these responses might be the reasonable outcome of a particular political project.

18. For a fascinating inquiry into the possibility of a general comparative politics, see Alisdair MacIntyre, "How Is a Comparative Science of Politics Possible?" in *Against the Self-Images of the Age* (Notre Dame: University of Notre Dame Press, 1971); Charles Taylor also addresses this issue in "Interpretation and the Science of Man."

19. Maxime Rodinson, *Islam and Capitalism* (New York: Pantheon Books, 1973), p. 1.

20. Binder argues that as a result of social scientists' lack of attention to the role of the rural middle class "some errors have been made regarding the nature of the present regime." He adds that "there is even greater confusion regarding the range of possible developments in the foreseeable future"; *In a Moment of Enthusiasm*, p. 1.

21. Ibid., p. 398. Binder states his general claim most clearly when he evaluates what he sees as the three major "ideological configurations" relevant to Egypt's political future. He concludes his analysis of these alternatives with the comment: "Empirical realities, and especially the empirical reality of the structure of the second stratum, are likely to intrude into and disrupt political change processes which are oriented to one or another of these ideological configurations. From this perspective, concentration upon the political potentiality of the second stratum reunites the branching alternatives into a single complex process which can be monitored, though not easily, by means of empirical investigation into key areas of acknowledged political significance," (p. 401).

22. Ibid., pp. 7, 11.

23. Ibid., p. 406.

24. See Waterbury, *The Egypt of Nasser and Sadat*, especially pp. 272–304; and Raymond William Baker, *Egypt's Uncertain Revolution under Nasser and Sadat* (Cambridge, Mass.: Harvard University Press, 1978), pp. 17–88.

25. See, for example, Howard J. Wiarda, "Toward a Nonethnocentric Theory of Development," in *New Directions in Comparative Politics*, ed. Wiarda (Boulder, Colo.: Westview Press, 1985).

26. See Richard Bendix, *Embattled Reason* (Oxford: Oxford University Press, 1970), pp. 294–295.

27. Such insight depends on gaining access to the coherence between the actions of the agents and the meaning their situations have for them. This formulation of the

object of an interpretative political science is taken from Taylor, "Interpretation and the Sciences of Man," p. 13.

28. Max Weber, *Wirtschaft und Gesellschaft,* 2 vols. (Tubingen: J. C. B. Mohr, 1925), 1:16, 2:1; quoted in Jurgen Habermas, "Hannah Arendt's Communications Concept of Power," *Social Research,* 44 (1977), 4.

29. Talcott Parsons, "Voting and Equilibrium of the American Political System," in *Sociological Theory and Modern Society* (New York: Free Press, 1967), p. 193; quoted in Habermas, "Hannah Arendt's Communications Concept of Power," p. 5.

30. Talcott Parsons, "Authority, Legitimation, and Political Action," in *Structure and Process in Modern Societies* (Glencoe, Ill.: Free Press, 1960), p. 181; quoted in Habermas, "Hannah Arendt's Communications Concept of Power," p. 5.

31. Kenneth Waltz, *Theory of International Politics* (Reading, Mass.: Addison-Wesley, 1979), pp. 39–59.

32. It is exactly this ability to project meanings that then inform their action which sets human beings off as objects of study. Richard Rorty, in his influential essay "Method, Social Science, Social Hope," seems to misunderstand this point that interpretative social science is trying to make. Rorty sees no difference between human beings and fossils as objects of study. He is of course right when he says that fossils are understood no less relationally than human beings. The point is, however, that human beings project a web of meaning that conditions their action; therefore, we cannot understand that action without understanding the conceptual world that informs it. How we relate them to the world is beside the point; what we ought to be after is how they relate themselves to that world. If Rorty realized the distinction that interpretative social scientists are trying to call attention to, he might agree that they offer a better vocabulary with which to come to understand other human beings and their actions. See Richard Rorty, *Consequences of Pragmatism* (Minnesota: University of Minnesota Press, 1982), pp. 191–210.

33. Even statements that coincide with the humanistic value assumptions with which this study begins are too abstract to guide an empirical research effort such as this. An example is Jurgen Habermas' effort to specify a general emancipatory interest and to elaborate a notion of an "ideal speech community" as a model of a political community without domination; "Towards a Theory of Communicative Competence," *Inquiry,* no. 13 (1970), 360–375.

34. See Wolin, *Politics as Vision,* p. 20.

35. This characterization of theory is presented by Ludwig Boltzman, "Theories as Representations," in *The Philosophy of Science* (Cleveland: Meridian Books, 1966), pp. 245–252.

36. Grounded theory, as a strategy for qualitative research, is explicitly spelled out and compared with other approaches in Barney G. Glaser and Anselm L. Strauss, *The Discovery of Grounded Theory* (Chicago: Aldine, 1967). From Glaser and Strauss I take my notion of substantive theory. But I am not in agreement with their view that once a grounded theory is developed, the necessary next stage is its application in a formal and comparative way to as many different areas as possible. Instead, I think, with Barrington Moore, Jr., that in many cases explanation of the unique may exhaust the role of theory. Moore points out that "in many other areas of life men orient themselves to reality by learning its unique features. The navigator, for instance, depends on charts that show the location of individual reefs and shoals";

"Strategy in Social Science," in *Political Power and Social Theory: Six Studies* (Cambridge, Mass.: Harvard University Press, 1958), p. 148.

37. This idea of the logical structure of understanding is derived in part from the work of Wolfgang Pauli. See the discussion of Pauli in Werner Heisenberg, *Physics and Beyond* (New York: Harper & Row, 1971), p. 33.

38. The subjective dimension of the concept of understanding employed here draws on the view of social science that what distinguishes the study of human affairs from natural phenomena is the assumption of inherent meaningfulness. The reasearch implications are spelled out in Peter L. Berger and Hansfried Kellner, *Sociology Reinterpreted: An Essay on Method and Vocation* (Garden City, N.Y.: Anchor Books, 1981).

10. Unseen Struggles

1. The absence of a civil society is assumed in most political histories of Egypt and indeed of the Muslim world in general. Henry Clement Moore, for example, argues that "Egypt typifies the 'unincorporated society,' that is, one in which organized groups are and have always been relatively weak and unimportant"; "Authoritarian Politics in Unincorporated Society," *Comparative Politics,* 6 (Jan. 1974), 195. Bryan S. Turner sees the roots of such ideas in the Western orientalist tradition; "Orientalism and the Problem of Civil Society in Islam," in *Orientalism, Islam, and Islamists,* eds. Asaf Hussain, Robert Olson, and Jamil Qureshi (Brattleboro, Vt.: Amana Books, 1984), pp. 23–42.

2. There is an intentional parallel between my notion of group practice in critical environments and Donald Campbell's idea of "reform as experiment." See Campbell, "Reforms as Experiments," *American Psychologist,* 24 (April 1969), 409–429. The most recent realist versions of science have a similar core notion of a "transformative model" of social activity. See Roy Bashkar, *A Realist Theory of Science* (Leeds: Leeds Books, 1975).

3. I appreciate the cautionary advice of those who have pointed to the ethnocentric tendency to view the political life of non-Western peoples in terms of group structures such as unions and parties that have played so large a part in Western politics. See, for example, Howard J. Wiarda, "Toward a Nonethnocentric Theory of Development," in *New Directions in Comparative Politics,* ed. Wiarda (Boulder, Colo.: Westview Press, 1985), p. 132. However, I would like to register three cautions of my own. First, at times the judgment of the absence of independent group life in the Arab world rests on questionable assumptions about some mystical collective Arab mentality. Samuel Huntington, for example, has brought such dubious notions into mainstream development theory. In a representative passage Huntington quotes with approval one "acute observer" who explains sweepingly that "mistrust among the Arabs is internalized early within the value system of the child. . . . Organization, solidarity, and cohesion are lacking. . . . Their public-mindedness is not developed and their social consciousness is weak"; *Political Order in Changing Societies* (New Haven: Yale University Press, 1968), pp. 28–29. For a critical review of the literature on the "Arab mind" that Huntington's citation exemplifies, see Fouad M. Moughrabi, "The Arab Basic Personality: A Critical Survey of the Literature," *International Journal of Middle East Studies,* 9 (1978), 99–112. Second, there

is a problem of what constitutes a group worthy of attention. Here the salience of Western models of group life distorts the capacity to recognize associations in the Egyptian context. Henry Clement Moore, for example, can write of Egypt as an "unincorporated society" only because, in my opinion, he overlooks a multiplicity of Muslim associations linked to the Muslim Brotherhood that have for decades shown a stunning ability to organize on a basis of trust in the most trying circumstances. See Moore, "Authoritarian Politics in Unincorporated Society," pp. 193–218. Third, I hope to show in this volume that there are also groups not based in religion, such as professional associations, think tanks, and parties, that do play a relatively autonomous and significant role in Egyptian public life, although the history of that role has been repressed.

4. Vincent Crapanzano, *Tuhami: Portrait of a Moroccan* (Chicago: University of Chicago Press, 1980), p. 152.

5. For a review of the political attacks on this position and an able restatement and defense of what such openness means to empirical social science research, see Barry Barnes and David Bloor, "Relativism, Rationalism, and the Sociology of Knowledge," in *Rationality and Relativism,* ed. Martin Hollis and Stephen Lukes (Cambridge, Mass.: MIT Press, 1982), pp. 21–47.

6. For a discussion of the kinds of judgments and interpretations that are involved in historical interpretations, see Ernst Cassirer, *An Essay on Man* (New Haven: Yale University Press, 1944), pp. 171–206.

7. For the clearest statements of the situational character of historical understanding, see Karl Popper's extended discussions of what he calls the method of situational logic or situational analysis: *The Open Society and Its Enemies,* vol. 2 (Princeton: Princeton University Press, 1962), especially pp. 96–99; *The Poverty of Historicism* (New York: Harper & Row, 1957), pp. 147–152; and *Objective Knowledge: An Evolutionary Approach* (London: Oxford University Press, 1972), pp. 153–190. I am also indebted to Edward W. Said's discussion of the interpretative process as the breaking down of barriers between two situations, in *Covering Islam: How the Media and the Experts Determine How We See the Rest of the World* (New York: Pantheon Books, 1981), pp. 154–164.

8. See Charles Taylor, "Interpretation and the Science of Man," *Review of Metaphysics,* 25 (Sept. 1971), 3–51.

9. Of course, there remains the issue of which actor's self-description any given interpretation is supposed to represent. Certainly within any society but even within any, even homogenous, political movement, different actors often have widely varying views of their own and their compatriots' actions. As a group, however, actors within a political community are tied to each other by certain common ideas and beliefs; otherwise they would not identify as a group. It is this common thread that the narrative chapters in this book try to sketch; thus the importance and prominence of collective symbols. Generalization is always precarious, though, and especially so within a methodology that labels particular characteristics as *the* characteristics of a collective made up of individual minds and viewpoints.

10. For a discussion of specific examples of this process, see James Clifford's review of Edward W. Said's *Orientalism,* in *History and Theory,* 19 (1980), 204–205.

11. Of social scientists, the "dialogic" anthropologists are closest to my own notion of the most adequate mode of interaction with the subjects of study in the

human sciences. Edward Said has also discussed the issue of "non-coercive contact" as a subjective experience of the interpreter, without however specifying the concrete forms it might take; see Said, *Covering Islam,* p. 55. But aside from an effort to extend the community of interpreters to include the subjects of knowledge themselves, it is difficult to ground these calls for dialogue in anything very concrete.

12. I take seriously here the Marxist critique of ideology. I recognize that verbal formulations of group members may very well obscure rather than explain because of the delusions that Marxists label "false consciousness." Karl Mannheim provided the clearest statement of the dilemma: "There is implicit in the word 'ideology' the insight that in certain situations the collective unconscious of certain groups obscures the real condition of society both to itself and to others and thereby stabilizes it"; *Ideology and Utopia* (New York: Harcourt, Brace, 1954), p. 40. However, I do not resolve this dilemma by accepting some objective interest perspective. Instead, following Arthur F. Bentley's lead, I try to tread a middle course between acceptance of group subjectivism and the imputation of an objective group interest of which group members are unaware. In this book I stress neither what the participants claim to be seeking nor the conditions of whatever sort that dictate what they should seek. Rather, I emphasize *what they do seek as revealed by their past and present speech and action.* See Bentley, *The Process of Government* (Cambridge, Mass.: Harvard University Press, 1967), pp. 178, 184, 214, 227, 243.

13. Charles Taylor, "Foucault on Freedom and Truth," *Political Theory,* 12 (Feb. 1984), 169–170.

14. See Alan White, "The Insignificant Other" (Faculty seminar paper, Williams College, 1989).

15. For a brief survey from the vantage point of anthropology, see George Marcus and Michael M. J. Fischer, *Anthropology as Social Critique: An Experimental Moment in the Human Sciences* (Chicago: University of Chicago Press, 1986).

16. Daniel Pipes, *In the Path of God: Islam and Political Power* (New York: Basic Books, 1983), p. 24.

17. Wiarda, *New Directions in Comparative Politics.*

18. See Tony Smith, "Requiem or New Agenda?" *World Politics,* 37 (July 1985), 532–561.

19. Sherry Ortner, "Theory in Anthropology since the Sixties," *Comparative Studies in Society and History,* 26 (Jan. 1984), 159.

20. See Marcus and Fischer, *Anthropology as Cultural Critique,* pp. 7–16.

21. See especially V. S. Naipul, *Among the Believers* (New York: Vintage Books, 1982).

22. Most important is Ajami's first book, *The Arab Predicament: Arab Political Thought and Action since 1967* (Cambridge: Cambridge University Press, 1981).

23. Ibid., p. x.

24. Ibid., p. 3.

25. Ibid., p. 4.

26. Ibid., p. 3.

27. Ibid.

28. At one point Ajami remarks, "Social scientists removed from the scene may be able to play with indexes and measurements of power and to determine the ebb and flow in national resources and capabilities, but nations persist in their memo-

ries"; ibid., p. 104. Readers are not told, however, how reliable access to those memories is secured.

29. This has been the personal choice of the most celebrated Third World informants.

30. Ajami, *The Arab Predicament,* p. 2.

31. For a succinct discussion of this method of internal analysis, see Clifford Geertz, "On the Nature of Anthropological Understanding," *American Scientist,* 63 (1985), 47–53.

32. Clifford Geertz, *Interpretation of Cultures* (New York: Basic Books, 1973), p. 23.

33. See Ken Plummer, *Documents of Life: An Introduction to the Problems and Literature of a Humanistic Method* (London: Allen & Unwin, 1983), pp. 113–114.

34. Ajami, *The Arab Predicament,* p. x.

35. See Marcene Marcoux for a sound and sensitive treatment of these limits; *Cursillo: Anatomy of a Movement* (New York: Lambeth Press, 1982), pp. 250 and 250–269 passim.

36. Hinnebusch, *Egyptian Politics under Sadat* (Cambridge: Cambridge University Press, 1985), pp. 1, 2.

37. Ibid., p. 290.

38. Ibid., pp. 1, 2, 290.

39. Ibid., p. 299. The evidence does not warrant such conclusions. The class situation in Egypt is highly fluid and unformed. Clearly, Sadat's policies have favored the haves over the have-nots. But John Waterbury is right to argue that "there is not yet a new dominant class in Egypt. Some amalgam of munfatihun [beneficiaries of the Open Door], private manufacturers, commercial farmers, and former state capitalists may one day constitute such a class, at which point the state may become its creature. But too much else could intervene before such a class took shape"; *The Egypt of Nasser and Sadat: The Political Economy of Two Regimes* (Princeton: Princeton University Press, 1983), p. 432.

40. Hinnebusch, *Egyptian Politics under Sadat,* p. 289.

41. Ibid., p. 291.

42. Taylor, "Foucault on Freedom and Truth," p. 171.

43. Ibid.

44. Hans-Georg Gadamer, *Philosophical Hermeneutics* (Berkeley: University of California Press, 1976), p. 59.

45. Immanuel Kant, "Vorlesungen uber Padagogik," in *Werke,* ed. Ernst Cassirer, vol. 8 (Berlin: Bruno Cassirer, 1922), p. 464.

Index